D0746942

PH   CS
MO   NG
FOR GA   AMMERS

DAVID CONGER

SERIES EDITOR

, XTREME GAMES LLC

INCLUDES CD-ROM

Physics Modeling for Game Programmers

David Conger

THOMSON
————————— ™
COURSE TECHNOLOGY

Professional ■ Trade ■ Reference

ISBN: 1-59200-093-2

Library of Congress Catalog Card Number: 2004108007

Printed in the United States of America

04 05 06 07 08 BH 10 9 8 7 6 5 4 3 2 1

Professional ■ Trade ■ Reference

Course PTR, a division of Course Technology
25 Thomson Place
Boston, MA 02210
http://www.courseptr.com

SVP, Thomson Course Technology PTR
Andy Shafran

Publisher
Stacy L. Hiquet

Senior Marketing Manager
Sarah O'Donnell

Marketing Manager
Heather Hurley

Manager of Editorial Services
Heather Talbot

Acquisitions Editor
Mitzi Koontz

Senior Editor
Mark Garvey

Associate Marketing Managers
Kristin Eisenzopf and Sarah Dubois

Project/Copy Editor
Karen A. Gill

Series Editor
André LaMothe

Technical Reviewer
David Jenner

Thomson Course Technology PTR Market Coordinator
Amanda Weaver

Interior Layout Tech
Sue Honeywell

Cover Designer
Mike Tanamachi

CD-ROM Producer
Brandon Penticuff

Indexer
Kevin Broccoli

Proofreader
Gene Redding

For my children, who make the daily grind worthwhile.

ACKNOWLEDGMENTS

I would like to acknowledge the many talented individuals who helped make this book possible.

First, I would like to thank Professor Russ Higley, master physicist, for his help and moral support. Also, I want to thank astronomer, physicist, writer, and technical reviewer extraordinaire David Jenner. I greatly value my long associations with these two brilliant men.

Thanks also goes to the great support people who helped me along the way. In particular, thanks to Mitzi Koontz and Karen Gill.

Finally, thanks to my wife and children who put up with the long hours I disappear into my office to write my books.

ABOUT THE AUTHOR

David Conger has been programming professionally for more than 20 years. That's 350 years in Internet time. After writing entirely too many programs (graphics display controller firmware for military aircraft, DOS games, multiplayer Internet games, and many, many custom business applications), he decided to become a writer. Despite the protests of his students, he also managed to spend four years as a college professor teaching computer science and business computer programming.

For about seven years, he wrote documentation for Microsoft Corporation. The projects he wrote for included the Xbox Development Kit (XDK), DirectDraw and Direct3D (versions 5 and 6), OpenGL, Extensible Scene Graph (XSG), Image Color Management (ICM), Still Image (STI), Windows Image Acquisition (WIA), Remote Procedure Calls (RPC), the Microsoft Interface Definition Language Compiler (MIDL), and the Mobile Internet Toolkit (MIT).

His first book, published in 1987, was a collection of folktales from India and the Far East. Since then, he's written programming books about C, C++, C#, and .NET Remoting, as well as an introductory textbook on microcomputers.

Currently, David resides in the wilds of western Washington state. There, he continues to nurture dreams of once again traveling the Orient as he walks the back roads with Biggles, his giant dog (or small and hairy horse, whichever you prefer). In addition to Biggles, David is fortunate to find himself blessed with a plethora of fantastic children and a wife of great distinction.

ABOUT THE SERIES EDITOR

André LaMothe, CEO, Xtreme Games LLC and the creator of the XGameStation, has been involved in the computing industry for more than 27 years. He wrote his first game for the TRS-80 and has been hooked ever since! His experience includes 2D/3D graphics, AI research at NASA, compiler design, robotics, virtual reality, and telecommunications. His books are top sellers in the game programming genre, and his experience is echoed in the Thomson Course Technology PTR *Game Development* books. He can be contacted at ceo@nurve.net and www.xgamestation.com.

Letter from the Series Editor

This book is the first in the *Game Development* series to cover physics modeling. As always, I don't want to put a book out that only covers one aspect of game development; rather, I want a book that defines or innovates in that area and creates the target for others to follow. In general, most physics books on game development focus on the physics modeling you would use in games, but then fall short of the actual implementation and practical application of the physics to games.

This book starts slowly with the framework of physics modeling and then moves on to specific physics modeling techniques that are applicable to games, such as point modeling, rigid body dynamics, collision response, and related topics. After you are armed with tools to model basic physics, the book increases the complexity and deals with trajectory problems, gravity, springs, and water dynamics.

From there, the book moves into application programming and applies all these techniques so that you can create physics for land vehicles and air vehicles. This is really the "reward" in the book as far as I am concerned. The ability to use physics modeling to create a racing game, a Jet Ski game, or even a flight simulator is all within your grasp.

There are several books on the market about game physics, but none of them focuses on the detailed use of physics for actual game programming applications like this one does. That is the strength of this text and why it's a must for anyone who wants to become an expert at physics modeling for games. I highly recommend *Physics Modeling for Game Programmers* whether you are in charge of physics modeling, AI, or even general gameplay. This text will get you up to speed. In short order, you will have multiple spring models bouncing off each other, mesmerizing your friends and family.

Sincerely,

André LaMothe
Series Editor, Premier *Game Development* Series

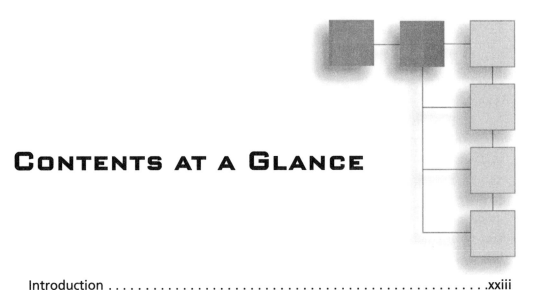

Contents at a Glance

CONTENTS

Part Two: 3-D Objects, Movement, and Collisions

PART THREE: HANDS-ON 3-D SIMULATION   365

INTRODUCTION

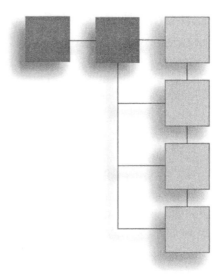

Welcome to *Physics Modeling for Game Programmers*!

Physics modeling is exploding in the game development industry. It's a powerful tool for producing great-looking games, and it's really the only tool for making the action in games look realistic. Companies that employ game programmers are increasingly seeking programmers whose physics skills are strong. These skills can turn someone who has a little programming knowledge and a passion for games into a professional who is in high demand.

Physics modeling is also a lot of fun. A simple model can create effects that the programmer never dreamed possible. A nice physical model of a fire will work and look beautiful, even if you wave it around or put a leg of mutton over it.

Modern computer games are about creating a virtual world. The virtual world can behave in any way that the programmer decides. However, if we game programmers want players to understand and engage with our games, our virtual worlds must mostly model the physical world. The rules about how the real world behaves are what physics is all about.

It isn't just familiarity that makes it a good idea to use real-world physics. The truth is that the world is an amazing place; nobody's virtual worlds are as intricate, rich, and beautiful as the universe around us.

The Book
The book is divided into three parts.

Part One: Physics, Math, and Game Programming

This part covers the basic math required for physics modeling. It also introduces Euclidean geometry. This type of geometry is intimately related to DirectX Graphics, which is also presented in this part. DirectX Graphics is mostly just an accelerated platform for depicting Euclidean geometry in Windows.

Part Two: 3-D Objects, Movement, and Collisions

Part Two introduces particle and rigid body dynamics. Simply put, dynamics is the study of objects in motion. This part of the book presents the principles and equations of dynamics that you can use to make nearly anything in a game move in a realistic way. It also discusses how to crash objects, which seems to be one of the main activities in computer games.

Physics in computer games doesn't have to be limited to dynamics. In this part, you'll also learn about gravitation, masses and springs, and fluids. These topics are often used in computer games for highlights to make the scene more realistic, but as machines become faster, they'll take on a more central role in game development.

Part Three: Hands-On 3-D Simulation

It's not possible to describe everything completely. Computational power is limited, especially for a computer game that has to be calculated and updated no less than 30 times per second. Even if you had all the speed you needed, you would still eventually run into something that wasn't understood. At some point, approximations have to be made. This is the essence of simulation. This part discusses the most common types of simulations used in games.

The CD

The CD is full of good stuff to turn you into a physics modeling genius. Of course, you'll find all the source code to save you that burdensome typing. All the source code is in the Source folder.

In the Tools folder, you'll find goodies that you can use to write killer games. The Tools folder contains a folder called Microsoft DirectX SDK. In it, you'll find a copy of Microsoft's entire toolset that is offered to programmers who are developing games with DirectX. If you plan to follow along with the code samples in this book, you'll need to install the Microsoft DirectX SDK.

The Tools folder also contains a folder called MilkShape3D. In it, you'll find a fantastic little program that enables you to create your own 3-D meshes and models in a simple and straightforward way. The version of MilkShape3D found on the CD is shareware. If you want the full version, you can get it for $20 (U.S.) from chUmbaLum sOft at http://www.swissquake.ch/chumbalum-soft/.

In addition, the Tools folder has a folder called Torque Game Engine that contains a demo of a full-featured commercial game engine called Torque. The Torque game engine is produced by Garage Games. You can find Garage Games on the web at www.garagegames.com.

If your budget doesn't allow you to spend the money for a commercial engine like Torque, you might want to try the CrystalSpace 3D engine. The CrystalSpace 3D engine is a robust open source project. I've included it on the CD in the Tools\CrystalSpace3D folder. The nice thing about this engine is that you can download its source code and customize it any way you want. The project is hosted on SourceForge at https://sourceforge.net/projects/crystal.

What You Need

To get the most out of this book, you need a computer that is running Windows 98 or later with a C++ development environment. This book assumes that you have Microsoft Visual C++ 6.0 or later, but you can use something else if you want. You also need a graphics card that supports 32-bit alpha at 640×480.

I assume that you can program a little in C or C++. I'll be using a sane subset of C++. Many concepts in physics and game programming beg for objects, so why kill ourselves trying to make them into C structures? If you're a straight C coder or your C++ is a little rusty, check out Appendix B, "A Brief Overview of C++."

You don't need to know anything about Windows development or DirectX to read this book. Part One gets you up to speed on writing Windows programs that use DirectX. It might be a bit harrowing, but muddle through it, and you'll be a Windows programmer in no time. To make things easier, I've also provided an introduction to Windows programming in Appendix C, "The Basics of Windows Programming."

This book is about both physics and game programming, so you can bet there's a lot of math. Many people are intimidated by math. However, if you hang in there, you'll see that it isn't too difficult. In case you're still burdened by the ghosts of old math teachers, I should tell you that people like to make this stuff sound harder than it is. All you really need to understand most of this stuff is a mind that's open to some new ideas. With that, you're ready to jump in to Chapter 1, "Physics in Games."

PART ONE

PHYSICS, MATH, AND GAME PROGRAMMING

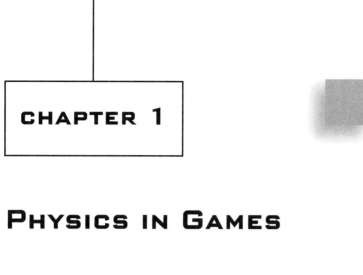

CHAPTER 1

PHYSICS IN GAMES

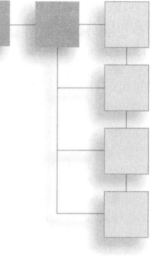

What makes a compelling game experience?

People who write games spend large amounts of time trying to answer this question. The answer they come up with depends largely on what aspects of the game they're involved with. Writers, marketers, producers, and level designers would answer this question differently. However, the vast majority of games involve simulating movement. As you play games, the characters, objects, and scenery move. If you want the player to immerse himself in the game's world, everything has to move convincingly. That's a fundamental fact of games. Making objects or characters move convincingly on the player's screen is another way of saying that you have to model or simulate real-world physics. These days, games are usually in 3-D.

So how do you model the physical world in 3-D?

Answering that question is what this book is about. It means learning the essentials of physics, math, and 3-D programming.

The typical reaction to such statements is panic. People are often fearful of tackling the subjects of physics and math. It's true that physics and math can be involved subjects. However, there's one important fact that game programmers need to remember when modeling physics in software: If it looks right, it is right.

This statement provides us as programmers with an easy out. We don't have to model every aspect of physics to make games look right. And if something looks right on the screen, that's good enough. That relieves us programmers from having to face most of the really complex topics in physics and math. If we know some basic things about physics and we have some reasonable math skills, that's all that's necessary for 90 percent of game programming.

How Much Physics Do I Need to Know to Write Games?

Think about the games you've played. What happens in those games? Does your character run around shooting things? Does he climb, swim, jump, and so forth? Does he throw things? What about explosions? These days, you can't seem to have a game without decent explosions.

Incorporating physics into games means modeling a few basic things:

- 3-D objects
- 3-D scenes
- Movement
- Rigid objects
- Rotation
- Friction
- Air and water resistance
- Gravity
- Collisions and explosions
- Springy things
- Waves

3-D Objects

Creating a software model of a 3-D object is not an easy task. In fact, it took decades for a large group of bright people to figure out how to do it. However, now that those people have done the trailblazing, you and I don't have to. We can use the tools and techniques that are commonly available today to simulate 3-D objects. This vastly simplifies our jobs.

For example, most computers today come with video cards that provide a huge amount of built-in support for 3-D simulations. This both simplifies the job of writing simulations and speeds them up tremendously.

Graphics libraries, such as DirectX and Open Graphics Library (OpenGL), extend the hardware support for simulating 3-D objects. They add an additional layer that handles even more of the work for us. Chapter 2, "Simulating 3-D with DirectX," introduces DirectX, so if you don't know how to use it, don't worry. You'll see that there's an easy way to get up and running with DirectX quickly.

3-D Scenes

Modeling an entire scene in 3-D is just an extension of the techniques used to model 3-D objects. You'll start to model 3-D scenes in Chapter 8, "Collisions of Point Particles."

Movement

Games have a lot of movement. Parts of characters move as characters walk, jump, run, or pick up objects. Characters move through scenes, as do various objects. Making movement happen in a way that looks realistic is a topic that almost every chapter of this book touches on.

Rigid Objects

Imagine that you're writing a game in which the main character is climbing along the outside of a ring-shaped space station that is spinning. As the character moves from the center of the station to the outer ring, the forces exerted on him increase. As he moves outward, he's more likely to slip and go flying off into space. Game over.

A spinning space station is an example of a rigid object in motion. Rigid objects seem deceptively simple. In reality, there's much more to them than meets the eye. Chapters 9, "Rigid Body Dynamics," and 10, "Collisions of Rigid Bodies," introduce the physics of rigid bodies.

Rotation

3-D objects can move forward or backward, left or right, and up or down. However, they can also rotate as they move. Modeling rotation increases the number of forces that your game has to apply to the object. Rotation can stabilize or destabilize an object as it moves.

For example, when a quarterback in a football game (I'm speaking of American football) throws a pass, he deliberately throws the ball in such as way as to make it spin as it flies through the air. The spinning stabilizes the ball, making it easier to catch. If you're writing a game that models people playing football, rotation is an important factor in your game.

Friction

In the real world, most objects eventually come to a stop due to friction. Modeling friction is a common task in games. I've played many games where the character encounters icy or slippery surfaces. The player's challenge is to negotiate the character across these low-friction surfaces, usually while being attacked on all sides.

I've seen programmers waste a lot of time trying to model friction. They tried to overuse the "If it looks right, it is right" rule. They programmed the game and checked it to see if the character moved across the ice or slippery surface in a way that looked right. If it didn't look right, they tweaked the software and checked it again. Because they didn't rely on actual physics, they ended up tweaking and checking over and over and over. They could have saved themselves a lot of time if they had just used the equations of physics to create their software.

Air and Water Resistance

Many game developers ignore air resistance completely. However, no one notices. Games have managed to make things look right without modeling air resistance. Expect this to change. As games become increasingly realistic in their appearance, air resistance is getting to be an important factor in games.

Game developers cannot ignore water resistance, though. Any game that lets characters or objects move through water must model water resistance in a realistic way.

Modeling water resistance involves more than just slowing movement down. Water can also move. The resulting currents increase resistance when a character or object moves in the opposite direction. Currents push things downstream.

Some games model movement through water effectively. An example is the *Legend of Zelda* series. The main character often moves through water. The way the character moves depends on the accessories he has. If the character has a magical mask that changes him into a water creature, he moves quickly. Otherwise, he moves rather slowly. Currents increase or decrease the resistance as the character swims.

If your game involves moving through water, you have to handle this at least as well as the *Zelda* series does.

Gravity

Gravity affects everything. You can't get away from it, even in space. Whether your character is throwing a grenade or piloting a spaceship to Mars, gravity influences the outcome. Your game must model the effects of gravity in all situations. Therefore, I've devoted an entire chapter to it. Chapter 11, "Gravity and Projectiles," teaches you all you need to know to simulate gravity in virtually all situations.

note

About the only situation involving gravity that I don't discuss is inside black holes. The physics required for modeling that case is too involved for this book. If the character in your game goes inside a black hole, my recommendation is to cheat shamelessly. Just make up whatever you want it to look like. The player has never been inside a black hole, so he will probably accept whatever you present.

Collisions and Explosions

What's a game without explosions? Even sedate games like *The Sims* have explosions. I don't know why, but we enjoy crashing things together and exploding them. That's why you see so many car crashes on TV. I often say that Hollywood keeps Detroit in business.

It's impossible to simulate all aspects of a collision and explosion. The physics are far too complex. Fortunately, it doesn't matter. If we can model the physics of the larger forces and interactions of objects in collisions and explosions, we can make it look right. And if it looks right, it *is* right.

Springy Things

Although we don't normally notice it, there are lots of springy things in our lives. When I say "springy things," you probably think of pogo sticks and such. In physics, "springy things" includes such nonrigid items as hair and cloth. Have you ever thought about what it takes to model the movement of a young girl's ponytail? It bounces and sways as she walks. The same can be true of clothing.

For a long time, modeling cloth, ponytails, and other springy things was too difficult to handle in most games. In fact, it was so hard that developers avoided it in computer graphics and animation. The 3-D modeling of the time was good enough to do almost everything but hair and cloth. As a result, we had a spate of animated 3-D movies about bugs. No hair and no clothes.

Recent advances, however, enable us to program springy things like hair and cloth into our games. We can make their movements realistic.

Waves

Dealing with water is more than just resistance and currents. It also involves waves. Old games simulated waves by moving the character or the point of view up and down slowly. That doesn't cut it in today's 3-D games. You need to be much more realistic.

For example, suppose that you're writing a powerboat racing game, such as *Hydro Thunder* (an arcade game). If a wave hits a powerboat head-on as the boat rockets along the top of the water, the boat could be thrown upward. It might even be flipped completely. If the wave hits the boat broadside, it will probably capsize the boat. Both situations depend on the size of the wave, the angle of collision, the weight and shape of the boat, and so forth. You must be able to model these factors correctly in your game.

How Much Math Do I Need to Know to Write Games?

Physics requires math. If you're not a math guru, don't worry. I'll present all the math you need to know for the topics covered in this book. Specifically, you'll learn the following:

- The essential geometry of triangles
- Vectors
- Matrices
- Derivatives

The Essential Geometry of Triangles

3-D computer graphics is based in triangles. If you're going to model 3-D scenes and objects, you must know the basic properties of triangles. For example, given the length of two sides of a triangle, you should be able to find the length of the third side.

Vectors

Physics deals with the interaction of forces with objects. An easy way to represent those forces is with vectors. Vectors provide a handy method of analyzing combining forces and determining which ones affect an object.

Matrices

Programmers who simulate 3-D physics generally convert the force vectors to matrices. Matrices provide an elegant shorthand that simplifies the expression of problems. They make many tasks in 3-D graphics easier to understand and modularize.

For example, suppose that you want to model how a crate acts if your character pushes it at the top as opposed to pushing it at the middle. If you push on one side right near the top of the crate, it should fall over. If you push it in the middle, it should slide across the floor.

To get the physics of the crate correct, you start by analyzing the forces using vectors. Next, you convert the vectors to matrices and use a matrix multiplication to apply the force to all the vertices that make up the crate. This gives you the proper movement.

The technique this example presents is common. Being able to do matrix math is essential for game programmers.

Derivatives

Derivatives are a topic from calculus. Yes, calculus is rather advanced math, which intimidates many people. However, you can simplify the process of using derivatives. If you haven't had a calculus class, I think you'll be surprised at how easy derivatives can be.

How Much Programming Do I Need to Know?

The simple answer to this question is "Not that much." If you can write a Windows program in C++, you're ready for this book. Put another way, if you've had a C++ programming class in high school or college, you'll be able to handle anything we do here.

Alternatively, if you learned to program on your own, and you've been writing Windows programs in C++ for about a year, you should be okay, too.

We'll be using Microsoft's DirectX libraries for our graphics programming. Entire books have been written just on DirectX. It's not necessary for you to have a background with it. This book presents all the DirectX knowledge that you need to do the 3-D physics modeling it covers. However, if you do want to acquire a stronger background in DirectX, you might consider reading *Beginning DirectX 9* by Wendy Jones (published by Premier Press).

If you're a fan of OpenGL or some other graphics library, fear not. Although my programming examples use DirectX, the actual physics modeling is done in code that is portable to pretty much any graphics library. You should be able to use my code with OpenGL or anything else without too many changes.

Summary

To make a realistic game, we as 3-D programmers need to model the physical forces we experience in nature. This requires knowledge of physics, math, and 3-D graphics programming. You'll get all of that in this book. You'll need to begin with the essentials of 3-D programming with DirectX, which is the subject of the next chapter.

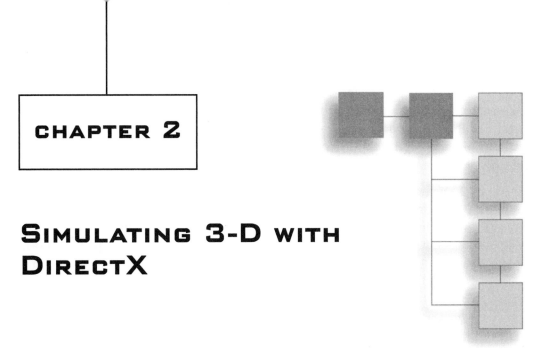

CHAPTER 2

SIMULATING 3-D WITH DIRECTX

In this chapter, you'll get a look at DirectX, which is produced by Microsoft. DirectX is the primary tool that game and graphics programmers use for simulating 3-D. If you're already familiar with DirectX, you might want to move on to Chapter 3, "Mathematical Tools for Physics and 3-D Programming," and begin learning a bit of math. If this is your first time with DirectX, you should read this chapter. It provides you with the following:

- An overview of what DirectX is and what it does
- An introduction to the components of DirectX
- A step-by-step guide that demonstrates how to get DirectX up and running
- A look at the cleanup that your programs need to perform when they close down DirectX

What Is DirectX?

DirectX is an Application Programming Interface (API) that enables game and graphics application developers to perform multimedia tasks in a way that is independent of the hardware involved. This saves you and me from having to worry about what type of sound and video cards users have installed in their computers. DirectX also provides high-level functions for performing a lot of the tasks associated with 3-D simulation. This makes it easy for us to concentrate on our actual games, rather than on tasks such as graphics and sound generation.

Do we really need DirectX? In a word, yes. To understand why, think about how most programs work.

Most applications spend a majority of their time communicating with Windows through an event handler. For example, Windows tells an application when the Close box has been pressed or that the user has clicked somewhere in the program's window. The application then responds appropriately. Alternatively, the application might ask Windows to create a window or draw a line. Windows then fulfills the request.

There are some advantages to this approach. This approach uses an API called the Graphics Display Interface (GDI) to enable programmers to use graphics without worrying about what kind of graphics card is on users' PCs. It also forces applications to play nice with each other. In addition, it allows the user to seamlessly cut and paste between applications. But for games, the GDI is way too slow. The GDI was developed for doing business graphics (such as pie charts) that don't change much over time. You can't possibly use it for real-time 3-D simulations.

Alternatives to DirectX

DirectX is not the only game API in town. DirectX has some serious competitors for its different parts. For example, the Open Graphics Library (OpenGL) is a good alternative to Direct3D, the Open Audio Library (OpenAL) competes with DirectSound, and Berkeley Sockets can implement many of the same features as DirectPlay. The major advantage that these and some other APIs have over DirectX is cross-platform portability. You can use OpenGL on a Windows machine, a Mac, or a Linux box, but DirectX works only on a PC that is running Windows. The advantages of DirectX are those of universal empire; DirectX runs well on most of the PCs out there because most of them run Windows, and a lot of money and time are put into keeping DirectX current.

Although this book focuses on using DirectX to model the world in 3-D, the physics and the physics code are the same no matter which API you use. Don't hesitate to use what you like.

Two Views of DirectX

Microsoft divides the DirectX interface into two primary sets of APIs. One set is low level and accesses the hardware directly. If the hardware needed is not present, this low-level API simulates the hardware. DirectX also contains a set of high-level APIs that are accessible through a group of software objects provided in the DirectX libraries.

The Low-Level View: The HAL and the HEL

DirectX lets programmers access the hardware more directly while keeping the device independence of standard Windows multimedia. No matter what kind of graphics or sound card the player has, you can use DirectX to program it. DirectX commands are translated directly into commands that are appropriate for your users' hardware. Figure 2.1 shows something of how this is accomplished. As you can see, there are two layers between the high-level DirectX APIs and the hardware: the Hardware Abstraction Layer (HAL) and the Hardware Emulation Layer (HEL).

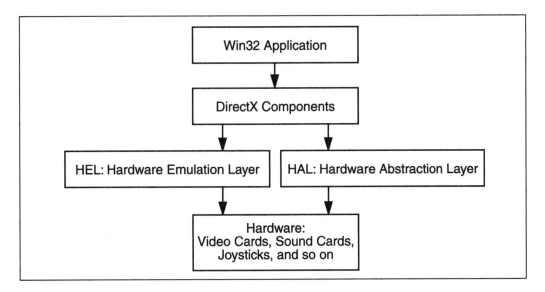

Figure 2.1
The architecture of DirectX.

The HAL translates DirectX instructions into hardware instructions. To make games as fast as possible, DirectX tries to run all its tasks through the hardware. To do that, it uses the HAL whenever possible.

What happens if the hardware doesn't support some feature that DirectX calls for? DirectX just pretends the hardware is there. No, really. It uses its other low-level API, the HEL. The HEL emulates capabilities that might be missing from the user's hardware. This keeps games from crashing when DirectX needs more than the existing hardware provides, but at a price. The HEL is *extremely* slow.

The High-Level View: DirectX Components

In the high-level view, DirectX is divided into several components, most of which you'll use as you learn physics modeling:

- **Direct3D.** This component does graphics, both 2-D and 3-D. Once upon a time, 2-D was done with DirectDraw, but Microsoft incorporated it into Direct3D and made its official name DirectX Graphics. However, nearly everyone calls it Direct3D. Direct3D lets you do 2-D using all the nifty hardware acceleration you find on 3-D graphics cards. We'll be doing both 2-D and 3-D graphics in this book.

- **DirectInput.** This component gives a consistent interface for mice, keyboards, joysticks, trackballs, and, well, any other input device. Microsoft tells an input device manufacturer, "If you want it to work under Windows, you had best write a

DirectInput driver for it." The DirectInput interface is so abstract that it's actually possible for the manufacturers to comply, whether they make trackballs or virtual reality suits.

- **DirectPlay.** This component supports multiplayer networked games. When you use DirectPlay, it doesn't matter whether the network is over modems, the Internet, LAN, or whatever else might come along; all the hardware issues are taken care of. This book doesn't cover DirectPlay, but after you've become a physics genius, pick up DirectPlay to make your own massive multiplayer physics simulation!

- **DirectSound.** This component takes care of all the digital sound. It allows you to access the sound card directly without knowing what kind of soundcard it is, automatically taking advantage of the card's acceleration and special features. There's also support for 3-D sounds and effects.

- **DirectMusic.** This component obviously plays music, but there's so much more. The music can be located in a 3-D environment and can have effects applied dynamically. DirectMusic can even compose music at runtime, based on elements you give it.

- **DirectShow.** This component supports capture and playback of multimedia streams, such as MPEGs, AVIs, and MP3s.

COM Objects

DirectX is nominally based on objects created with Microsoft's Component Object Model (COM). COM is an abstraction that was invented to simplify big programming projects. Whether it actually succeeded or not is a matter of opinion. The idea is that each COM object is a black box that represents some piece of software or hardware. To make a program, you fit a bunch of these objects together like a massive plumbing project. The COM objects are accessed through interfaces. An *interface* is a collection of functions called *methods*.

Much of this should sound familiar to programmers of object-oriented languages such as C++ or Java. In fact, COM objects are binary compatible with C++ objects; within C++, COM objects can be used as if they are objects.

COM objects are dynamically linked at runtime. This means that, ideally, COM objects can be traded in and out of a piece of software without recompiling. That's pretty useful if you want to upgrade a large system or a widely distributed piece of software.

COM objects have all kinds of requirements to make this work:

- Each COM object and interface has a unique 128-bit identification number, called a Globally Unique Identifier (GUID). A program written by Microsoft, GUIDEN.EXE, generates this number, and it's truly unique; the odds are that no COM object or interface created by anybody, anywhere, anytime, will have the same number.

- Upgrades of COM objects must support the interfaces of every previous version. That way, programs that use a COM object will still work, without recompiling, even if the object has been completely rewritten.

- COM objects keep a counter that tracks the number of active references to themselves. When the count hits 0, any resources that the object has are deallocated, and the object is destroyed.

COM is now the basis for ActiveX, OLE, and, most importantly for us, DirectX.

COM, DirectX, and .NET

DirectX did not start out as a COM-based API. Microsoft added COM to DirectX after it purchased the API from Reality Labs, the company that created it. As a result, DirectX has only a nodding acquaintance with COM. Yes, you have to use COM to allocate and free the basic DirectX components. But other than that, you really don't have to deal with it. Becoming a COM expert in the intricacies of COM is not necessary for DirectX programmers.

Undoubtedly, you've heard of Microsoft's big .NET initiative. Everything Microsoft does is being brought under the .NET umbrella. This includes DirectX. Already, Microsoft provides access to DirectX from .NET-based programs. The .NET interface is easier to use than the COM interface. However, the .NET interface adds a bit of overhead to your program. You'll pay a speed penalty of 2–5% when you use .NET. It can also make your program larger. You must decide if the speed and size penalties are worth the added ease of development.

Using DirectX

There are three ways you can get DirectX running and access its functionality. The first is the hard way. That is, you can set up a group of initialization variables and pass their information to a collection of initialization functions. After DirectX is up and running, you can access its functionality through its APIs.

The second approach is to let Visual Studio do a lot of the work for you. When you install the DirectX Software Development Kit (SDK), it automatically adds the DirectX AppWizard to Visual Studio. The AppWizard creates empty DirectX applications for you. All you have to do is add your game or graphics program functionality.

The third way is the easiest. Let me do the work for you. For a variety of reasons, the DirectX AppWizard has some limitations. There are also some drawbacks to using it. Therefore, I've provided a code framework that gets DirectX up and running for you.

The AppWizard and my framework are nice to use, but there are things they just can't do. For that reason, it's important to understand the underlying DirectX APIs. Therefore, we'll take a brief look at how to initialize part of DirectX—specifically Direct3D—the hard way. This enables us to get a glimpse of how DirectX really works. After that, I'll introduce the AppWizard and the framework.

Initializing DirectX the Hard Way

The DirectX components are COM objects. COM objects are realized during runtime as Dynamic Link Libraries (DLLs). When you play a DirectX game, DirectX loads these DLLs, and the game then requests some interfaces. It uses the methods in the interfaces to do all of its drawing, sound, and input.

Writing your own COM objects is possible and probably instructional, but all that most game programmers really need to be able to do is use the COM objects that are associated with DirectX. In fact, we won't even deal directly with DirectX's COM objects most of the time. Microsoft knew it would have to keep the COM stuff to a minimum if it wanted game programmers to adopt DirectX, so it hid most of the interaction with COM in a bunch of DirectX functions contained in import libraries. This is convenient because it lets you get all the functionality you can out of DirectX without the tedium of direct COM programming.

A Few Words About Coding Style

The code in this section follows the Microsoft style of writing code. And in the next section, we'll generate code using the DirectX AppWizard. The AppWizard also writes code in the standard Microsoft style.

My own style of coding is quite different from the Microsoft style for some important reasons. However, I won't bother to climb up on my soapbox about it. I'll just say that for the rest of this book, I'll use the Microsoft style for code that performs the initialization and cleanup of DirectX. Everything else will be done in my own coding style. This will help differentiate application-specific code from the generic code that all games use for startup and cleanup.

Four steps are involved in using a DirectX COM object:

1. Declare a variable to hold the pointer to the object interface. Set it initially to NULL:

```
LPDIRECT3D9          g_pD3D = NULL;
```

2. Call a function to create the object. The function returns a pointer to the object's interface that you can store in the variable created in step 1. If the function fails to create the object, it returns NULL:

```
g_pD3D = Direct3DCreate9( D3D_SDK_VERSION )
```

3. Now that you have a pointer to the interface, you can use it to call methods. For example,

```
g_pD3D->GetAdapterDisplayMode( D3DADAPTER_DEFAULT, &currentdisplay )
```

4. When you're done with your COM interfaces, release them in the reverse order that you created them. Failing to do so causes resource leaks, system slowdowns, and militant gamers bent on destroying your dreams and livelihood:

```
g_pD3D->Release();
g_pD3D = NULL;
```

note

The code shown here is written for initializing Direct3D. Code for the other components of DirectX is similar.

That's everything you need to know about COM to get started initializing Direct3D. Let's try it.

Initializing Direct3D

Direct3D handles 2-D and 3-D graphics. That makes it the most important component of DirectX for us because the primary way that most game environments are experienced is through the monitor. As the physics models become more advanced, we'll add corresponding sophistication to our use of Direct3D. For now, let's just get initialized and set up a display.

Every time you create a project that uses DirectX, you must add the DirectX library files you need. If you're using Visual Studio 6, select Project from the main menu, and then Settings. Visual Studio displays the Project Settings dialog box. Click the Link tab. Look for the Object Library Modules text box. In this box, enter the name of the library files you need. For most Direct3D applications, you'll just need to enter the following:

```
dxguid.lib d3d9.lib d3dx9.lib winmm.lib
```

note

If you're using Visual Studio .NET, right-click the name of the project. Select Properties from the menu that appears. Click the Linker folder, and then click Input. Type the list of libraries shown earlier into the Additional Dependencies box.

Your program must include the header file for DirectX 9.

```
#include <d3d9.h>      // DirectX Version 9.0
```

Now create a variable to hold the interface pointer. Most game developers create global variables for this.

```
LPDIRECT3D9        g_pD3D = NULL; // Pointer to the Direct3D object
```

I'll put the actual initialization in a new function called `Direct3DInit()`. This function will be called from the `GameInit()` function.

You can create the Direct3D object using the function `Direct3DCreate9()`. I'll call the pointer that the function returns by its official name—`IDirect3D9`—where the *I* means *interface*:

```
// Get a pointer to IDirect3D9
if( NULL == ( g_pD3D = Direct3DCreate9( D3D_SDK_VERSION ) ) )
    return E_FAIL;
```

The parameter to `Direct3DCreate9()` should always be `D3D_SDK_VERSION`. There are no other valid parameters. `D3D_SDK_VERSION` is updated when you update DirectX. Passing this parameter lets your program know whether it's dealing with a current enough version of DirectX.

This function returns `NULL` if it fails to create the Direct3D object. If it does that, have `GameInit()` return `E_FAIL`.

When you do COM programming, you'll see `S_OK` and `E_FAIL` quite a bit. All COM methods return a 32-bit integer of type `HRESULT` that tells how the method fared. The standard codes are `S_OK` and `E_FAIL`, but sometimes a method might return something like `E_INVALDARG` if it failed because of an invalid argument, so be careful. The convention is for success codes to start with *S* and for fail codes to start with *E*. If you just want to know whether a method succeeded or failed, use these macros:

- **SUCCEEDED.** Returns `TRUE` for a success code and `FALSE` for a fail code.
- **FAILED.** Returns `TRUE` for a fail code and `FALSE` for a success code.

Because you're returning `S_OK` or `E_FAIL` to `GameInit()`, you can check on a method's success within `WinMain()` by using these macros:

```
// Game console initialization
if( FAILED( GameInit() ) )
    return(0);
```

If `GameInit()` returns a fail code, `WinMain()` bails on us.

Display Modes

Now that you have an interface to the object, you can use its methods. First, let's find out what the current display mode is:

```
// Structure to hold information about the current display mode
D3DDISPLAYMODE currentDisplay;
// Get the current settings for the default display adapter
if ( FAILED( g_pD3D->
   GetAdapterDisplayMode( D3DADAPTER_DEFAULT, &currentdisplay ) ) )
{
    return E_FAIL;
}
```

tip

You can refer to a method in an interface by writing the name of the interface, followed by double colons (::), followed by the name of the method. Therefore, if I write `IDirect3D9::GetAdapterDisplayMode()`, I'm referring to the `IDirect3D9` method `GetAdapterDisplayMode()`.

The `IDirect3D9::GetAdapterDisplayMode()` method takes two parameters. The first is the adapter. `D3DADAPTER_DEFAULT` gives the primary adapter.

The second parameter is a pointer to the structure created to hold information about the display mode. Let's look at the structure's definition:

```
typedef struct _D3DDISPLAYMODE {
    UINT Width;
    UINT Height;
    UINT RefreshRate;
    D3DFORMAT Format;
} D3DDISPLAYMODE;
```

The first three parameters are pretty straightforward. They give the resolution and refresh rate as integers, such as 800×600 at 75 Hz.

The last parameter is the surface format. It specifies how information for each of the pixels is treated. There are numerous format types. Only a few of them are valid for displays and back buffers. (We'll talk about back buffers shortly.) Table 2.1 lists these types.

Table 2.1 D3DFORMAT Types

Flag	Meaning
D3DFMT_A2R10G10B10	32-bit pixel format using 10 bits for each color and 2 bits for alpha
D3DFMT_A8R8G8B8	32-bit ARGB pixel format with alpha, using 8 bits per channel
D3DFMT_X8R8G8B8	32-bit RGB pixel format, where 8 bits are reserved for each color
D3DFMT_A1R5G5B5	16-bit pixel format, where 5 bits are reserved for each color and 1 bit is reserved for alpha
D3DFMT_X1R5G5B5	16-bit pixel format, where 5 bits are reserved for each color
D3DFMT_R5G6B5	16-bit RGB pixel format, where 5 bits are reserved for red, 6 bits are reserved for green, and 5 bits are reserved for blue

If `IDirect3D9::GetAdapterDisplayMode()` worked the way it was supposed to, you now have all this information about the current display mode in the `currentDisplay` structure.

A Digression on Displays

Whatever shows up on the screen is copied directly from a region of memory called the *front buffer*. This memory can be in the computer's main memory but is usually on the graphics card. When a program (or Windows) wants to show something different on the screen, it changes the buffer, and the graphics card sends the buffer to the monitor. The size of this piece of memory depends on the resolution and the bit depth.

Windows, the monitor, and the graphics card limit the resolutions that your computer can support. If you want a particular resolution, then all three have to support it. If you've played computer games or even just messed with the display modes in the Windows Control Panel, you're probably familiar with typical resolutions such as 640×480, 800×600, 1024×768, 1280×1024, and 1600×1200.

The resolution of a display mode also includes a bit depth. The bit depth is the amount of memory that is associated with each pixel in the display. Most of this memory stores colors. For example, if you have a 16-bit display, each pixel can have 2^{16}, or 65,536, colors. A 24-bit display has 2^{24} colors. That's more than 16.7 million colors—better than the color resolution of your eyes!

The screen of a monitor is covered with millions of triads of light emitters. Each triad is composed of a device that shines red, one that shines green, and one that shines blue. By combining different intensities of these three colors, you can generate any color. This system is called RGB for Red-Green-Blue.

note

In most televisions and bulky CRT monitors, these triads are made of phosphors, which shine when an electron gun hits them. These have been the standard since they were invented for color television in the 1930s, but a slew of new technologies are now replacing them. These technologies work in different ways, but they're all still essentially RGB.

Often, the bits that are available to a display are divided among these three emitters. For example, the R5G6B5 format is a 16-bit format with 5 bits specifying the red intensity, 6 bits specifying the green intensity, and the last 5 bits for the blue intensity.

If people can't pick out more than 16.7 million colors, why should you bother with higher bit depths? The answer is that you can use this extra information for other things. The most common use is alpha blending, which allows transparency effects.

Surfaces and Page Flipping

In Direct3D, regions of memory that are the size of the screen are called *surfaces*. When you draw to Direct3D, you're actually drawing to a surface called the *back buffer* while the monitor displays the contents of the front buffer. The back buffer is not displayed; it's just a region of memory that has the same size and organization as the front buffer. When your program needs to make changes to what's on the screen, it writes to the back buffer. When all the drawing is done, you swap pointers so that the surface that was the back buffer becomes the front buffer, and the surface that was the front buffer becomes the back buffer. This process is called *page flipping* (see Figure 2.2).

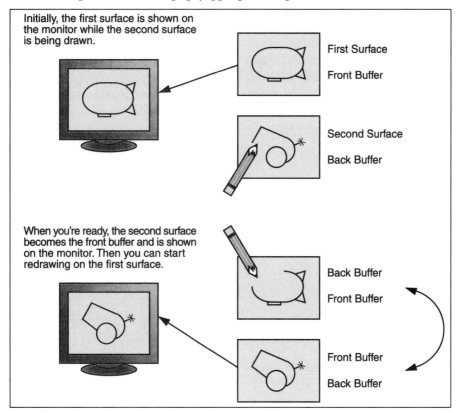

Figure 2.2
A description of page flipping.

Page flipping solves a couple of problems. First, drawing directly to the front buffer can cause a problem called *tearing*. Tearing happens when the front buffer changes while the monitor is still updating the screen, so the monitor ends up showing part of the original buffer and part of the updated buffer at the same time. With page flipping, no tearing is visible because the changes don't go into the front buffer until the program has finished drawing.

Page flipping also allows you to overwrite the buffer without displaying it. Why would you want to do that? An example would be depth buffering in a fake 3-D isometric game such as *Diablo*. Isometric games look like they're 3-D, but from a fixed angle, usually of about 45°. When you render the player and the nefarious critters that are out to destroy the player, you have to make sure that far objects are occluded by near ones. This isn't too hard to accomplish. Render those characters that are farther away first, and then render the closer characters on top. This works fine if you're rendering to the back buffer and then flip the page when you're done, but if you're rendering to the front buffer, sometimes your far-away characters will pop in front of foreground objects.

Creating a Device

Now you're ready to use the IDirect3D9 interface to create another object called the *device*. The Direct3D object was pretty abstract, but the device is much more concrete. It represents a piece of hardware: the graphics card. Any drawing you want to do with that graphics card, you'll do through this interface. If you were to use a second graphics card (not many games do), you would need another device.

To create the device, you'll follow the same procedure that you would for creating any object. First, make a pointer for the IDirect3DDevice9 interface. DirectX programmers often make this pointer global so that they can access it from anywhere in the program, particularly in the GameLoop() function where the rendering will be done:

```
LPDIRECT3DDEVICE9    g_pDevice = NULL;    // Our rendering device
```

Create the device through the IDirect3D9::CreateDevice() method. This method requires quite a few parameters, so let's look at the prototype:

```
HRESULT CreateDevice(
    UINT Adapter,
    D3DDEVTYPE DeviceType,
    HWND hFocusWindow,
    DWORD BehaviorFlags,
    D3DPRESENT_PARAMETERS *pPresentationParameters,
    IDirect3DDevice9** ppReturnedDeviceInterface
);
```

The first parameter to this function, called Adapter, specifies the adapter to which the device corresponds. Most of the time, you can just set this to D3DADAPTER_DEFAULT.

The DeviceType parameter specifies whether to use hardware or software for rasterization and lighting. The three options for device types are listed in Table 2.2. *Rasterization* is the conversion of geometric objects such as lines or surfaces into pixels that can be drawn on the screen.

Table 2.2 DeviceType Options

Value	Meaning
D3DDEVTYPE_HAL	Use hardware rasterization. All the shading and lighting is done with hardware if possible. This is the standard.
D3DDEVTYPE_REF	Everything is implemented in software. This is just HEL. It's slow, but it's sometimes useful for debugging.
D3DDEVTYPE_SW	This is a pluggable software device. Use it when you want to write your own rendering device. It's pretty nifty.

The hFocusWindow parameter of the CreateDevice() function selects the window you want to draw on.

The next parameter is BehaviorFlags, which contains some general flags describing how you want the device to act. One of these flags must specify whether the vertices will be processed in hardware or software. Table 2.3 shows the most common flags.

Table 2.3 Behavior Flags for Devices

Flag	Meaning
D3DCREATE_HARDWARE_VERTEXPROCESSING	The hardware processes the vertices.
D3DCREATE_SOFTWARE_VERTEXPROCESSING	The software processes the vertices.
D3DCREATE_MIXED_VERTEXPROCESSING	Vertex processing is mixed; sometimes DirectX uses hardware, and sometimes it uses software.
D3DCREATE_DISABLE_DRIVER_MANAGEMENT	Direct3D manages resources instead of the driver.
D3DCREATE_MANAGED	Resources are swapped between the system memory and the accelerator as needed. This frees the application from having to handle memory management.
D3DCREATE_MULTITHREADED	This forces the device to be multithread safe, which degrades performance.

The CreateDevice() function's pPresentationParameters parameter is a pointer to the (rather complex) structure that says how you would like things presented. For example, this structure gives the format of the back buffer and whether your program is drawing windowed or full screen.

The final parameter to CreateDevice() is ppReturnedDeviceInterface. This contains the address of a pointer. The pointer points to the new interface you're creating with IDirect3D9::CreateDevice().

Before you can create the device, you're going to have to fill out that pesky pPresentationParameters structure. Here is its declaration:

```
// Structure to hold information about the rendering method
D3DPRESENT_PARAMETERS d3dpp;
```

You can check out all the members of the structure in Table 2.4, but most of these will be set to 0 using the ZeroMemory() macro:

```
// Initialize d3dpp to 0.
ZeroMemory( &d3dpp, sizeof( D3DPRESENT_PARAMETERS ) );
```

Table 2.4 The D3DPRESENT_PARAMETERS Structure

Member	Description
BackBufferWidth, BackBufferHeight	The width and height of the back buffer. If you're running in full screen mode, these must correspond to a valid display format. In windowed mode, it can be anything you want up to the limit that your graphics card can handle.
BackBufferFormat	The back buffer format. This is of the same D3DFORMAT type that you received from IDirect3D9::GetAdapterDisplayMode(). It's listed in Table 2.1. In full screen, BackBufferFormat sets the display mode. In a window, you should set it to match the current display mode. Microsoft says it doesn't have to match, but why make life difficult for yourself?
BackBufferCount	The number of back buffers. The valid numbers are 0, 1, 2, and 3. Usually, you'll just want one back buffer, but the others are there if you need them. If you specify 0 back buffers, DirectX still creates one.
MultiSampleType, MultiSampleQuality	Multisampling is a technique for antialiasing, simulating motion blur, and other effects.
SwapEffect	These flags detail how page flipping is going to occur. Most games use D3DSWAPEFFECT_DISCARD. This tells Direct3D that it doesn't have to preserve the back buffer when it's presented to the screen. Letting Direct3D be a little sloppy with the back buffers can increase the performance.

Member	Description
hDeviceWindow	The handle to the window where the device renders. When this is set to NULL, rendering takes place in the focus window specified in IDirect3D9::CreateDevice().
Windowed	This is TRUE if the application is in a window, and FALSE if the application is full screen.
EnableAutoDepthStencil	Setting this to TRUE tells Direct3D to manage your depth buffers for you.
AutoDepthStencilFormat	The kind of depth buffer you want, if you've set EnableAutoDepthStencil to TRUE. This member is ignored if EnableAutoDepthStencil is set to FALSE.
Flags	Flags that didn't fit anywhere else. These are only occasionally useful.
FullScreen_RefreshRateInHz	The refresh rate in Hertz. The rate varies, but a typical monitor might refresh the screen 75 times per second (75 Hz). Setting this to 0 or D3DPRESENT_RATE_DEFAULT gives the default refresh rate. The default refresh rate is required in windowed mode, but you can set it to any valid rate in full screen mode.
Presentation Interval	Sets how quickly Direct3D presents the back buffer. Normally, you'll set this to D3DPRESENT_INTERVAL_DEFAULT. This is required in windowed mode.

That's basically all you need to get Direct3D working. Your program's call to IDirect3D9::CreateDevice() will probably resemble the following:

```
// Create the device.
if( FAILED( g_pD3D->
    CreateDevice( D3DADAPTER_DEFAULT, D3DDEVTYPE_HAL,
              g_hMainWindow, D3DCREATE_HARDWARE_VERTEXPROCESSING,
                &d3dpp, &g_pDevice ) ) )
{
    return E_FAIL;
}
```

This call creates a device using the default adapter, hardware processing for rasterization, the main window for output, hardware vertex processing, and the d3dpp structure we just examined. The IDirect3D9::CreateDevice() function stores a pointer to the device in the g_pDevice parameter.

tip

Hardware vertex processing is much faster than software vertex processing, but some of the really old graphics cards don't support it. If you're having trouble with this, just change the flag to D3DCREATE_SOFTWARE_VERTEXPROCESSING.

Set Them Free

That's it! Direct3D is officially initialized! At this point, you're ready to start modeling and rendering. It's important to remember that just before your program terminates, you need to release your interfaces in the reverse order that you acquired them. You acquired two: first, IDirect3D9 in the pointer g_pD3D, and then IDirect3DDevice9 in the pointer g_pDevice. You'll release them in the opposite order using the Release() method:

```
int Shutdown(void)
{
    // Release the pointer to IDirect3DDevice9.
    if( g_pDevice )
    {
        g_pDevice->Release();
        g_pDevice = 0;
    }

    // Release the pointer to IDirect3D9.
    if( g_pD3D )
    {
        g_pD3D->Release();
        g_pD3D = 0;
    }

    return S_OK;
}
```

Notice that the code here sets the device pointers to 0 rather than NULL. Either value works.

Initializing Direct3D with the DirectX AppWizard

The DirectX AppWizard vastly simplifies the task of getting Direct3D up and running. In fact, it does more than just initialize Direct3D. It also initializes all the other components of DirectX.

The operation of the DirectX AppWizard varies a bit, depending on which version of Visual Studio you're using. To help you get started, I've provided instructions for using both version 6 and version 7.

Using the DirectX AppWizard with Visual Studio 6

Here's how to use the DirectX AppWizard if you own version 6 of Visual Studio:

1. From the File menu, select New. Visual Studio displays the New dialog box. If the Projects tab is not currently selected, click it with your mouse.

2. The New Projects page shows a list of projects that Visual Studio can create. Click DirectX 9 AppWizard.

3. In the Project Name edit box, type the name for your project. For now, let's just use the name InitDX. Click the OK button.

4. The AppWizard displays a series of dialog boxes that ask you for information about your DirectX project. The first dialog box asks you general information about your application. At the top of the dialog box, the AppWizard asks what type of application you want to create. All the applications we'll write for this book will use a single document window. Therefore, make sure that is what's selected before going on.

5. You will not need DirectMusic, DirectSound, or DirectPlay for any of the programs in this book. When you create a project, always make sure that these check boxes are cleared.

6. For now, do not add extras. Make sure that the check boxes for adding a menu and registry access are cleared. Then click Next.

7. In the next dialog box, the AppWizard asks you what you would like to begin with. Select Blank. Then click the Finish button.

At this point, Visual Studio generates a whole host of files for your project. We'll see later how to tinker with those files.

Using the DirectX AppWizard with Visual Studio 7

The DirectX AppWizard for Visual Studio 7 has a little bit different interface, but it works basically the same as the AppWizard for Visual Studio 6.

1. From the File menu, select New, and then click Project. Visual Studio displays the New Projects dialog box, which shows a list of languages that Visual Studio supports. For each language, Visual Studio also shows the types of projects it can create. Click Visual C++ Projects, and then choose DirectX 9 Visual C++ Wizard.

2. Type the name of your project, and then click OK.

3. The dialog box that appears has a rather funky interface that might seem odd at first. Down the left side is a list of what are essentially tabs. On the right is a space for the pages that are associated with the tabs. Click Project Settings.

4. At the top of the page, the AppWizard asks what type of application you want to create. All the applications we'll write for this book will use a single document window. Therefore, make sure that is what's selected before moving on.

5. You will not need DirectMusic, DirectSound, or DirectPlay for any of the programs in this book. When you create a project, always make sure that these check boxes are cleared.

6. For now, do not add extras. Make sure that the check boxes for adding a menu and registry access are cleared.

7. Click Direct3D Options, which is in the list along the left side of the dialog box. The AppWizard displays a page that asks you what you would like to begin with. Select Blank.

8. Click the Finish button, and you're done.

If you run the application you've just created, you'll see that it displays a window with a blue background. There is also some text giving information about the application's performance.

Although the DirectX AppWizard is helpful in many ways, there are a few problems with the code it generates. First, the code that the AppWizard generates is rather complex. If you're unfamiliar with DirectX, it can be a real pain to figure out what the code does. Unfortunately, this is something you have to do. There are several areas within the generated code that you need to modify for your use. It takes a while to figure out where those areas are and what modifications you need to make.

The second problem with the code that the AppWizard generates is closely related to the first. You need to modify several areas in the generated code to build a game. They are spread throughout the generated code. It would be nice if you could easily separate your code from the code that the AppWizard generates.

Another problem is code bloat. The AppWizard is oriented toward generating code for the samples that come with the DirectX SDK. It's just not made for use as a game framework. As a result, the AppWizard inserts capabilities that no game needs. For example, it adds a dialog box that enables you to configure DirectX. You could delete the extra code. However, because the code is rather complex, it's often hard to know what you can throw away and what you can't.

In addition, the code that the AppWizard generates is not particularly fast. Chances are, you could write faster code yourself. If you're a DirectX guru, optimizing the AppWizard's code isn't a big deal. If you're less familiar with DirectX, the task can be excruciating.

Finally, the AppWizard's code isn't intended as a teaching tool, even though it's pretty well commented. For the purposes of this book, it's easier to demonstrate how things are done if the code I use is brief and to the point.

Initializing Direct3D with the Physics Modeling Framework

To get around the problems with the code generated by the AppWizard, I've written a lean framework that gets Direct3D up and running for you. It isolates its own code from yours. To call into your code, the framework requires that you provide a set of standard functions in your game. These functions give you the opportunity to do anything you need.

note

All the functions in the physics modeling framework are in a namespace called pmframework. Therefore, you'll need to put the statement

```
using namespace pmframework;
```

at the beginning of each of your game's .cpp files.

You'll find all the source code for the framework on the CD-ROM that comes with this book. It's in the Source\Chapter02\PMFramework folder.

The Direct3D Application Class

The physics modeling framework does most of its work through the d3d_app class. This class contains all the information you need to initialize a Windows program and a DirectX program.

Currently, the d3d_app class does only the basics. Specifically, it gets your game up and running under Direct3D in a window. In later chapters, you'll see how to modify this class to get your game running in full screen mode.

Also, if you want to use other DirectX components, such as DirectSound and DirectMusic, you'll need to extend the d3d_app class. First, you'll need to add member data that contains the initialization for the DirectX component you're using. Then you'll have to write functions to set and get the new member data. Finally, you'll have to modify some of the framework's underlying functions to use the member data. Listing 2.1 gives the definition of the d3d_app class.

Listing 2.1
The d3d_add Class

```
1      class d3d_app
2      {
3      private:
4          // App properties
5          bool appInitialized;
6
7          // Window properties
8          std::string windowTitle;
```

```
 9
10          // D3D properties
11          LPDIRECT3D9             direct3D; // Used to create the D3DDevice
12          LPDIRECT3DDEVICE9       d3dDevice; // Our rendering device
13          LPDIRECT3DVERTEXBUFFER9 vertexBuffer; // Buffer to hold vertices
14
15    public:
16          d3d_app();
17          bool InitApp(
18              std::string initialWindowTitle);
19
20          LPDIRECT3DDEVICE9 D3DRenderingDevice(void);
21
22          LPDIRECT3DVERTEXBUFFER9 D3DVertexBuffer(void);
23          void D3DVertexBuffer(
24              LPDIRECT3DVERTEXBUFFER9 vertexBufferPointer);
25
26          friend INT WINAPI AppMain(
27              HINSTANCE hInst,
28              HINSTANCE,
29              LPSTR,
30              INT);
31          friend HRESULT InitD3D(
32              HWND hWnd);
33          friend VOID CleanupD3D();
34    };
```

The d3d_app class contains private member data for the application program, the window, and Direct3D. For instance, line 5 of Listing 2.1 shows the definition of the appInitialized member. This member keeps track of whether the d3d_app class's InitApp() function has been called. That task is specific to the application. Line 8 contains the definition of windowTitle, which is specific to the application's window. Lines 11–13 show definitions for member data that are required by DirectX.

Listing 2.1 also provides the prototypes for the d3d_app class's public member functions, beginning on line 16. The d3d_app class constructor sets all the class's member data to a known state, which is vital for proper functioning of the d3d_app object. The InitApp() function passes initial values for the member data from the game to the d3d_app object.

On line 20, the d3d_app class defines the D3DRenderingDevice() function. This function gets the d3d_app class's pointer to the Direct3D rendering device. Games need this pointer so that they can access the functionality of Direct3D. Most games also use a vertex buffer. The d3d_app class provides a place to store the vertex buffer pointer, so it also provides functions for getting and setting the pointer. The prototypes appear on lines 22–24.

On lines 26–33, the d3d_app class declares that the functions AppMain(), InitD3D(), and CleanupD3D() are friends of the d3d_app class. When I was teaching college-level C++ programming courses, I would strongly recommend that my students not use friend functions. Friend functions tend to undermine the encapsulation of objects. However, in this case, friend functions are necessary to provide an interface between the physics modeling framework and the functions that Windows requires for a program to operate.

You do not have to declare a variable of type d3d_app in your program. The framework does that for you by creating a variable called theApp. This variable is accessible in any of your .cpp files that include PMD3DApp.h.

A Look at WinMain() and AppMain()

Every Windows program must have a function called WinMain(). To save you from writing this function, the framework provides it. However, WinMain() is in the global namespace. It has trouble being friends with the d3d_app class, which is in the pmframework namespace. The framework requires that its main function is a friend. To resolve this problem, the WinMain() function does almost nothing. All the functionality that would normally be in WinMain() is moved into a function called AppMain(). WinMain() calls AppMain(), and AppMain() does the work. Listing 2.2 gives the code for the WinMain() function.

Listing 2.2
The Framework's WinMain() Function

```
1     INT WINAPI WinMain(
2         HINSTANCE hInstance,
3         HINSTANCE hPrevInstance,
4         LPSTR lpCmdLine,
5         INT nCmdShow)
6     {
7         return (pmframework::AppMain(
8             hInstance,hPrevInstance,lpCmdLine,nCmdShow));
9     }
```

As you can see, WinMain() simply calls AppMain(). WinMain() returns whatever value that AppMain() returns. Listing 2.3 shows the AppMain() function.

Listing 2.3
The AppMain() Function

```
1     INT WINAPI AppMain(
2         HINSTANCE hInstance,
3         HINSTANCE hPrevInstance,
4         LPSTR lpCmdLine,
5         INT nCmdShow)
6     {
```

```
7          bool noError=true;
8          WNDCLASSEX wc;
9          HWND hWnd;
10
11         noError=OnAppLoad();
12         assert(theApp.appInitialized==true);
13
14         if (noError)
15         {
16             WNDCLASSEX tempWC =
17             {
18                 sizeof(WNDCLASSEX),CS_CLASSDC,MsgProc,0L,0L,
19                 GetModuleHandle(NULL),NULL,NULL,NULL,NULL,
20                 D3DAPP_WINDOW_CLASS_NAME,NULL
21             };
22
23             wc=tempWC;
24             if (RegisterClassEx(&wc)==0)
25             {
26                 return (0);
27             }
28         }
29
30         if (noError)
31         {
32             hWnd = CreateWindow(
33                 D3DAPP_WINDOW_CLASS_NAME,
34                 (LPCSTR)theApp.windowTitle.c_str(),
35                 WS_OVERLAPPEDWINDOW,
36                 100,100,256,256,
37                 GetDesktopWindow(),
38                 NULL,wc.hInstance,NULL);
39         }
40
41         if ((noError) && (hWnd!=NULL))
42         {
43             if (!PreD3DInitialization())
44             {
45                 noError=false;;
46             }
47         }
48
```

```
49        if ((noError) && (SUCCEEDED(InitD3D(hWnd))))
50        {
51            noError=PostD3DInitialization();
52        }
53
54        if (noError)
55        {
56            noError=GameInitialization();
57        }
58
59        if (noError)
60        {
61            ShowWindow(hWnd,SW_SHOWDEFAULT);
62            UpdateWindow(hWnd);
63
64            MSG msg;
65            ZeroMemory(&msg,sizeof(msg));
66            while(msg.message!=WM_QUIT)
67            {
68                if(PeekMessage(&msg,NULL,OU,OU,PM_REMOVE))
69                {
70                    TranslateMessage(&msg);
71                    DispatchMessage(&msg);
72                }
73                else
74                {
75                    UpdateFrame();
76                    Render();
77                }
78            }
79        }
80
81        UnregisterClass(D3DAPP_WINDOW_CLASS_NAME,wc.hInstance);
82        return 0;
83    }
```

The AppMain() function begins by declaring the variables it needs. Before it does anything else, it calls the OnAppLoad() function. The prototype for OnAppLoad() appears in the PMD3DApp.h file. However, this function does not exist in the framework. Your game must provide it, or the game will not compile. Here's a bare-bones version of the OnAppLoad() function.

```
bool OnAppLoad()
{
    // This call must appear in this function.
    theApp.InitApp("test");

    return (true);
}
```

As you can see, the OnAppLoad() function absolutely *must* call the d3d_app class's InitApp() function. The AppMain() function in Listing 2.3 contains an assertion on line 12. If OnAppLoad() does not call InitApp(), the assertion on line 12 causes the program to crash.

If the OnAppLoad() function is able to perform its initialization, it returns true.

After validating that the application was properly initialized, the AppMain() function creates and registers the program's window class on lines 16–27 of Listing 2.3. This is required for every Windows program. It uses the window class to create the window on lines 32–38.

If Windows successfully creates the program's window, the AppMain() function calls a function named PreD3DInitialization(). The PreD3DInitialization() function is another function that is required by the framework but provided in your game. If your game does not contain a function called PreD3DInitialization(), the game won't compile. The PreD3DInitialization() function provides your game with the opportunity to do any processing you need it to before Direct3D is initialized. This function returns TRUE if it was successful at its task or FALSE if it was not. If you don't need processing done, then PreD3DInitialization() should just return TRUE.

The AppMain() function next initializes Direct3D by calling the framework's InitD3D function. The InitD3D function is presented in the next section. If InitD3D can initialize Direct3D, it returns S_OK, which is a standard Windows status code. If it fails for some reason, the InitD3D function returns E_FAIL, which is a Windows error code.

After initializing Direct3D, the AppMain() function calls PostD3DInitialization(). This is also a function that your game must provide. You can do any processing you want in PostD3DInitialization().

On lines 61–72, the AppMain() function performs the standard tasks of all Windows programs. It shows the program's window and then enters the message-processing loop. If there are no messages to process, AppMain() calls UpdateFrame() on line 75. Your game must provide the UpdateFrame() function. This is where your game does all the processing needed to update and animate the scene. The scene is actually drawn by the call to the Render() function on line 76 of Listing 2.3. The Render() function calls a function named RenderFrame(). Your game provides the RenderFrame() function.

Direct3D Initialization

The initialization of Direct3D is accomplished when the framework calls the InitD3D() function. Listing 2.4 shows its code.

Listing 2.4
The InitD3D() Function

```
1       HRESULT InitD3D(HWND hWnd)
2       {
3           HRESULT hr = S_OK;
4           D3DPRESENT_PARAMETERS d3dpp;
5
6           if((theApp.direct3D = Direct3DCreate9(D3D_SDK_VERSION))==NULL)
7           {
8               hr = E_FAIL;
9           }
10          else
11          {
12              ZeroMemory(&d3dpp,sizeof(d3dpp));
13              d3dpp.Windowed = TRUE;
14              d3dpp.SwapEffect = D3DSWAPEFFECT_DISCARD;
15              d3dpp.BackBufferFormat = D3DFMT_UNKNOWN;
16          }
17
18          if ((hr==S_OK) &&
19              (FAILED(theApp.direct3D->CreateDevice(
20                  D3DADAPTER_DEFAULT,D3DDEVTYPE_HAL,hWnd,
21                  D3DCREATE_HARDWARE_VERTEXPROCESSING,
22                  &d3dpp,&theApp.d3dDevice))))
23          {
24              if(FAILED(theApp.direct3D->CreateDevice(
25                  D3DADAPTER_DEFAULT,
26                  D3DDEVTYPE_REF,
27                  hWnd,
28                  D3DCREATE_HARDWARE_VERTEXPROCESSING,
29                  &d3dpp,
30                  &theApp.d3dDevice)))
31              {
32                  hr = E_FAIL;
33              }
34          }
35
36          if (hr==S_OK)
```

```
37          {
38              theApp.d3dDevice->SetRenderState(
39                  D3DRS_CULLMODE,
40                  D3DCULL_NONE);
41
42              theApp.d3dDevice->SetRenderState(D3DRS_LIGHTING,FALSE);
43          }
44
45          return hr;
46      }
```

After declaring the variables it needs, the InitD3D() function creates a Direct3D object. If the function is successful, it sets the screen parameters on lines 12–15 of Listing 2.4. If you want more control over these parameters, you can add private data members to the d3d_app class. Add parameters to the class's InitApp() function that enable you to set the new data members when your game calls InitApp(). Next, rewrite the code shown on lines 12–15 so that they get the values of the data members you added and use those values to specify the screen parameters.

The InitD3D() function continues by attempting to create the Direct3D device. It first tries to use the HAL on lines 19–22. If it can't, it tries again using software emulation on lines 24–29. If that doesn't work, it gives up.

It's important that the framework make more than one attempt before giving up. Direct3D supports hardware vertex processing. If your user has a video card that is more than a year or two old, that card probably doesn't have hardware vertex processing built in. If the framework made only one attempt and then gave up, most users wouldn't be able to play your game.

After creating the Direct3D device, the InitD3D() function turns off back-face culling. Back-face culling means that Direct3D ignores polygons whose normal vector points away from the point of view. Although back-face culling speeds up the game, it doesn't always give the desired appearance. This is another item that you might want to add additional configuration capabilities to. You use the same procedure as with the screen parameters mentioned previously. That is, you add some private data members to d3d_app, initialize them through the InitApp() function, and access the data members in the code shown on lines 38–40.

On line 42, the InitD3D() function turns off Direct3D's lighting capabilities. This is because the sample programs in the next few chapters don't use it. In later chapters, I'll demonstrate the process for adding configuration capabilities by making it possible to enable or disable lighting when your game calls the InitApp() function.

Game Initialization

If you look back to Listing 2.3 in the AppMain() function, you'll see that after AppMain() calls the InitD3D() function, it gives your game a chance to do some additional initialization. The name of the function it calls is PostD3DInitialization(). Your game must provide PostD3DInitialization().

The PostD3DInitialization() function is for anything you want. For example, you can have your game display a *splash screen*. A splash screen usually displays the name of the game and the company logo of the publisher. This function can also be a good place to show the game's main menu, enabling the player to start a new game or load a saved game.

When PostD3DInitialization() is done, it should return TRUE if it's successful or FALSE if not. If you don't want the PostD3DInitialization() function to do anything, simply have it return TRUE.

After AppMain() calls PostD3DInitialization(), it calls the GameInitialization() function. You must provide the GameInitialization() function because the framework requires it. For most of this book, we'll use the GameInitialization() function to define the objects and scenes displayed by the sample programs.

Handling Messages and User Input

All Windows programs receive messages in a message-processing procedure. Messages include everything from user input to notifications that it's time to redraw the screen. The framework provides a simple message-processing procedure called MsgProc(). Listing 2.5 provides its code.

Listing 2.5
The MsgProc() Function

```
1      LRESULT WINAPI MsgProc(
2          HWND hWnd,
3          UINT msg,
4          WPARAM wParam,
5          LPARAM lParam)
6      {
7          if (!HandleMessage(hWnd,msg,wParam,lParam))
8          {
9              switch(msg)
10             {
11                 case WM_DESTROY:
12                     // Perform game cleanup.
13                     GameCleanup();
14                     // Clean up D3D.
15                     CleanupD3D();
16                     PostQuitMessage(0);
```

```
17                        return 0;
18                }
19          }
20          return DefWindowProc(hWnd,msg,wParam,lParam);
21    }
```

This is a bare-bones message processing function. It begins by calling the HandleMessage() function on line 7 of Listing 2.5. This is another function that your game must provide. If your game handles the message, the HandleMessage() function should return TRUE. If it doesn't, the function should return FALSE. In that case, the MsgProc() function handles the message.

tip

For more information on Windows messages, see the "Window Messages" topic in the Windows Platform SDK documentation.

Currently, the only message that MsgProc() processes is WM_DESTROY. If MsgProc() receives a WM_DESTROY message, it calls the GameCleanup() function on line 13. Your game must provide the GameCleanup() function. The MsgProc() function then calls the framework's CleanupD3D() function, which closes down Direct3D.

All other messages are passed along on line 20 to be handled by Windows.

Updating and Rendering a Frame

To actually get stuff on the screen, your game must provide two functions. The first function is called UpdateFrame(). In UpdateFrame(), your game uses Direct3D to do all the processing it needs to do before drawing the next frame of animation. This is also the area where you'll use all the nifty physics we'll be covering.

Another function your game needs to provide is RenderFrame(). The RenderFrame() function is where you actually draw the frame.

note

Your game does not need to call Direct3D's BeginScene() and EndScene() functions. The framework does that for you. All you need to do is draw your geometry. Usually, that just means drawing the contents of the vertex buffer.

Cleaning Up

As previously mentioned, the framework calls the GameCleanup() function when it receives a WM_DESTROY message. Your game provides the GameCleanup() function. After GameCleanup() completes, the framework calls CleanupD3D(), which is shown in Listing 2.6.

Listing 2.6
The CleanupD3D() Function

```
1      VOID CleanupD3D()
2      {
3          if(theApp.vertexBuffer != NULL)
4              theApp.vertexBuffer->Release();
5
6          if(theApp.D3DRenderingDevice() != NULL)
7              theApp.D3DRenderingDevice()->Release();
8
9          if(theApp.direct3D != NULL)
10             theApp.direct3D->Release();
11     }
```

The CleanupD3D() function releases the DirectX objects that the framework creates. As discussed previously, these are released in the opposite order in which they were created.

note

I've provided a file for you that contains the functions that the framework requires. The functions are empty, so they don't do anything. The name of the file is FrameFns.cpp. It's in the Source\Chapter02 folder. You can use FrameFns.cpp to compile the framework and step through the program to see it in action.

Summary

DirectX is a powerful tool for writing games and 3-D simulations. With the DirectX AppWizard or the physics modeling framework, you can avoid most of the complexity normally encountered in getting a DirectX program initialized or cleaned up. However, to use DirectX well, it's necessary to understand its basic architecture and the use of its important components.

Now that you have a reasonable familiarity with DirectX, the primary tool we'll use for games and 3-D simulations, we can move on to the basic tools we'll use for physics. These tools are introduced in Chapter 3.

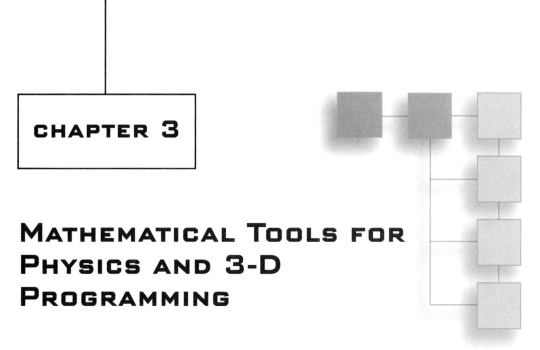

CHAPTER 3

MATHEMATICAL TOOLS FOR PHYSICS AND 3-D PROGRAMMING

In this chapter, we'll look at the basic mathematical tools needed for physics and 3-D programming. Specifically, simulating physics in 3-D programs requires the use of some Euclidean geometry, which isn't as formidable as it sounds. We can do most of what we want if we know some basic things about how to use triangles. And that really isn't tough at all.

3-D programmers also need a familiarity with Cartesian coordinate systems. Along with this, they need to understand how to use vectors. This chapter ends by discussing matrices, which are essential for tasks such as adding perspective to scenes and animating 3-D objects.

The Geometry of Triangles

For 3-D programmers, triangles are one of the most useful tools available. This might seem rather surprising, but it's true. For example, one way to tell if a surface is flat is to draw triangles on it. When you draw a triangle on a plane, the sum of the interior angles is 180°. The sum of the interior angles of a triangle drawn on a sphere always equals more than 180°. This is illustrated in Figure 3.1.

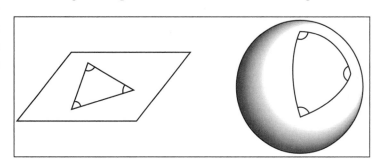

Figure 3.1
A triangle on a plane and one on a sphere.

Triangles, of course, are formed by three intersecting lines. The angles in a triangle are measured in degrees or radians. If we're using degrees, the sum of the angles in a triangle must total 180°.

If one of the angles in a triangle is 90°, the triangle is referred to as a *right triangle*. Right triangles have a handy property that is defined by the Pythagorean theorem. Suppose you have a right triangle whose sides are labeled as shown in Figure 3.2. Using this triangle, we can write the Pythagorean theorem as

$$a^2 = b^2 + c^2$$

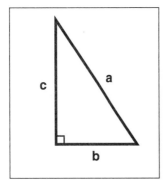

Figure 3.2
A right triangle.

What this formula means is that the length of the triangle's longest side (which is called the *hypotenuse*) squared is the sum of the square of each of the other two sides. Therefore, if you want to find the length of the hypotenuse, you just change the Pythagorean theorem to this:

$$a = \sqrt{b^2 + c^2}$$

Let's see how this works with an actual example. Suppose that you want to find the length of the hypotenuse of the right triangle. Imagine that the other two sides have lengths of 3 and 4. The length of the hypotenuse of this triangle would be as follows:

$$a = \sqrt{3^2 + 4^2}$$
$$a = \sqrt{9 + 16}$$
$$a = \sqrt{25}$$
$$a = 5$$

Therefore, the length of the hypotenuse of this triangle is 5. As you'll see shortly, you can use this technique to find the distance between two points in 2-D or 3-D space.

2-D Coordinate Systems

The geometry of the world exists entirely without coordinates. Rulers aren't built into the universe. Any line, point, vector, or matrix has an existence that is entirely independent of coordinates. Physical laws work the same regardless of what coordinates you use.

You use coordinates when you want to talk about particular things quantitatively. In other words, coordinates enable you to measure things—to put numbers to them. Some examples of coordinate usage include finding the distance to a rock or the height of a skyscraper.

Say that I want to talk about locations in Kansas City, Missouri. I could specify the location of the Nelson-Atkins Museum by saying that you can find it at 4525 Oak Street, or I could tell you to set your Global Positioning System (GPS) to 39.045° north and 94.581° west. Either way, the museum is in the same place, but I still need some set of coordinates to tell you how to find it.

A plane, or some surface locally like a plane (such as the surface of a sphere), needs two coordinates to describe locations on the surface. Again, there are several sets of coordinates you could use that would work. In Figure 3.3, you can see the most common types of coordinates on a plane.

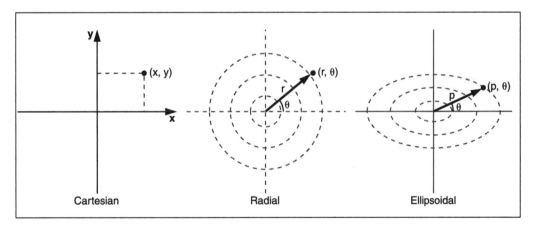

Figure 3.3
Several common 2-D coordinate systems.

Cartesian coordinates are the most commonly used in video games. In two dimensions, you have an x axis and a y axis that are perpendicular to each other. A point is specified giving a value on the x axis and a value on the y axis.

You can write the point with an ordered pair of numbers (x,y). For example, you can find the point (3,2) in the Cartesian coordinate system by counting over three on the x axis and up two from there on the y axis, as shown in Figure 3.4.

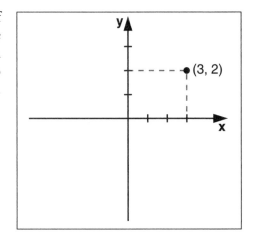

Figure 3.4
The Cartesian coordinate system.

3-D and 4-D Coordinate Systems

Some spaces are bigger than planes. A good example is the universe around you. It has at least three spatial dimensions. Any spatial dimensions beyond three are, at the very least, hard to notice, and time is more or less distinguishable from space.

In that case, you can point out locations in your space with 3-D Cartesian coordinates, as shown in Figure 3.5. You can write any point in space with three numbers (x, y, z).

The concept seems straightforward, but watch out. There's an ambiguity in 3-D Cartesian coordinates. Which way does the positive z axis point? If the y axis is vertical and the x axis is horizontal, do larger values of z mean points closer (coming out of the page) or points farther away (into the page)?

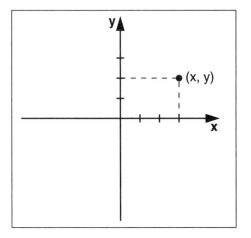

Figure 3.5
Right-handed 3-D Cartesian coordinate system.

The answer is that it's arbitrary. Physicists, mathematicians, and engineers made the standard a right-handed coordinate system more than 100 years ago. That's the one in Figure 3.5. Any book you pick up on physics uses the right-handed coordinate system. Because of this standard, I'll be using the right-handed coordinate system for all the physics and math in this book.

> You might be wondering why the coordinate systems are called right and left handed. Try poking your hand in the direction of the x axis, and then curl your fingers toward the y axis. Stick out your thumb. If it's your right hand, your thumb will be pointing toward you. So a right-handed coordinate system has the positive z axis pointing toward you (out of the page). If you're using your left hand, your thumb points away from you. That makes the positive z axis in a left-handed coordinate system point away from you (into the page).

If right-handed coordinate systems have been the standard for a century, which coordinate system do you think Direct3D uses? That's right! Direct3D uses a *left-handed* coordinate system. To see the difference, check out Figure 3.6.

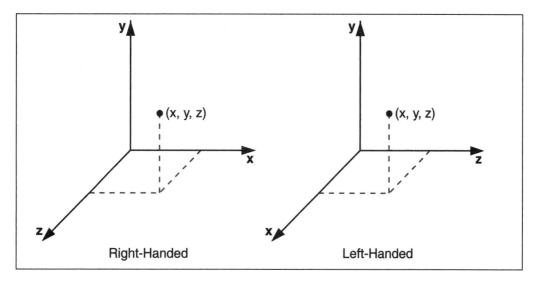

Figure 3.6
Right-handed and left-handed coordinate systems.

> Because of this confusion, many computer programming authors switch coordinate systems without noticing they've done it. Be careful!

This point bears repeating. The physics and math books generally use a right-handed coordinate system in three dimensions. For reasons that have to do with the hardware, most computer-based graphics systems use a left-handed coordinate system.

I should also mention that there's nothing sacred about the y axis being vertical. I could just as well pick up that right-handed coordinate system and turn it around so that the z axis is up, as in Figure 3.7. In fact, this orientation of the axes is probably more common in physics and math books.

What about that fourth dimension? Well, it's a little hard to draw. (Heck, 3-D is a little hard to draw on a flat piece of paper.) Mathematically, though, it's really easy to add more dimensions; just start naming your points with more numbers. In 4-D, you need four numbers. The last dimension is usually called w, so your points have coordinates (x,y,z,w).

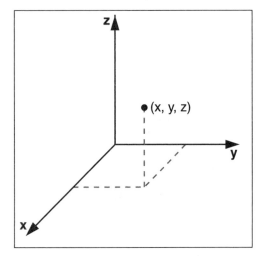

Figure 3.7
A right-handed coordinate system with the z axis pointing vertically.

Units

The numbers that specify a point have units. The spaces we'll deal with are mostly the regular kinds of space that we live in and are comfortable with, so the units will be units of distance, such as meters or kilometers.

I'll mostly use *metric* units in this book. Although it doesn't matter which units you use in a computer game, nearly all physics books (and nearly everybody outside the United States) use metric units, so it will be helpful to think in these units when designing your own physical models. Metric units are also often called Système International (SI) units. Table 3.1 lists the basic metric units, and Table 3.2 provides some comparisons between English and metric units.

Table 3.1 Basic Metric Units

Quantity	Base Unit	Derived Units
Distance	meter (m)	1 kilometer (km) = 1000 m
		1 m = 100 centimeters (cm)
Mass	kilogram (kg)	1 kg = 1000 grams (g)
		1 g = 1000 milligrams (mg)
Time	second (s)	
Temperature	kelvin (K)	

Using these units as the basis is called the *mks system,* for the base units: meter, kilogram, and second.

Table 3.2 Some English/Metric Conversions

Quantity	Conversion
Length	1 kilometer = .6214 miles
	1 mile = 1.6 kilometers
	1 meter = 1.1 yard = 3.28 feet
	1 foot = 12 inches = 30.48 centimeters
Mass	1 kilogram = 0.06852 slugs
Force	1 newton = .225 pounds
	1 pound = 4.45 newtons
Pressure	1 atm* = 101 Kilopascals = 101,000 N / m² = 14.7 lb / in²
Temperature	273 K = 0° C = −32° Fahrenheit
	373 K = 100° C = 212° Fahrenheit

* 1 atm is standard atmospheric pressure at sea level.

Physicists use the metric system because the English system sometimes seems as if it were invented by a mutant on drugs. 12 inches to a foot; 5,280 feet to a mile; 16 ounces to a pound; and so on? A test I was given in college required me to answer in furlongs. After the test, we asked the professor how long a furlong was, and he told us it was 10 times the length of a cricket pitch (the field on which the game of cricket is played).

The metric system is much more reasonable. 1,000 meters to a kilometer; 1,000 millimeters to a meter; 1,000 grams in a kilogram; 1,000 milligrams in a gram—very easy.

How did the English system get to be such a mess? It's a system that evolved for historical reasons. For instance, a foot was set as the length of the king's foot. So there really was a time when the English used their ruler (king) as a ruler (measuring stick).

On the other hand, the metric system, or SI, was designed rather than evolved. It is specifically made to be easy to use. Conversions in the SI are designed to be easy and involve less math than the English system. Because the conversions involve less math, it's advisable to use the SI in games. Doing so places less of a burden on the CPU.

The prefixes on the units in the SI have definite meaning. For example, kilo always means 1,000. So the word kilometer means 1,000 meters, and the word kilogram means 1,000 grams. Table 3.3 lists the prefixes that appear on units in the SI.

Table 3.3 Unit Prefixes in the Metric System

Prefix	Numeric Equivalent
tera (T)	10^{12}
giga (G)	10^9
mega (M)	10^6
kilo (k)	10^3
centi (c)	10^2
milli (m)	10^{-3}
micro (μ)	10^{-6}
nano (n)	10^{-9}
pico (p)	10^{-12}

All derived units and constants in this book are based on the mks system, where the base units are meters, kilograms, and seconds. Table 3.4 lists some derived units in the mks system. When you're plugging in quantities, use these base and derived units. Because the constants will be written in mks, the equations require that you plug in mks units, such as meters, kilograms, seconds, newtons, joules, watts, and pascals.

Table 3.4 Derived Units in the mks System

Quantity	Unit	Conversion
Force	newton (N)	$1\ N = 1\ kg \bullet m/s^2$
Energy	joule (J)	$1\ J = 1\ N \bullet m$
Power	watt (W)	$1\ W = 1\ J/s$
Frequency	hertz (Hz)	$1\ Hz = 1\ cycle/s$
Pressure	pascal (Pa)	$1\ Pa = 1\ N/m^2$

Units are helpful—use them! One of the most common mistakes people make doing physics or engineering is to plug in the wrong units. If a result seems suspicious (say, your massive death robot is scurrying along at 500,000 m/s), check the units for consistency.

Also note that you can multiply and cancel units just like any other algebraic variables. For example, the distance traveled (d) is given by a constant velocity (v) multiplied by time (t).

You can check for consistency by plugging in units on both sides. See how the seconds from the time variable cancel out the seconds from the velocity?

$$d = v \bullet t$$

This technique is called *dimensional analysis*. Checking the units in your equations can go a long way toward ensuring that your answers are right.

$$(m) = (m/s) \bullet (s)$$

Vectors

Physics has physical quantities that are just a magnitude: the mass of an alien, the temperature of a flame, or the elapsed time. These quantities don't depend on the coordinate system you use. They're called *scalars*, and they're just numbers. Scalars are usually written as non-bold, lowercase letters.

Other quantities have both a magnitude and a direction. These quantities are called *vectors*. All vectors have a magnitude and a direction. You can think of a vector as an arrow with a length, as shown in Figure 3.8.

Vectors are written in books as bold, lowercase letters, like this: **v**. To write a vector on paper, put a little arrow over the letter: $\vec{v}$. Although a vector exists independently of any coordinate system, in any particular 2-D coordinate system,

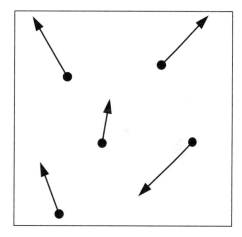

Figure 3.8
Some random vectors.

the vector can be represented by two numbers, which are the *components* of that vector. You can write the components for a 2-D vector **v** in some coordinate system as (v_x, v_y).

If you think of the vector as an arrow extending from the origin (0,0) to the point given by the two numbers of the vector, you have an accurate picture of the length and direction of the vector. If you're having trouble visualizing, check out Figure 3.9. When you imagine a vector this way, remember that a vector has only a length and a direction, not a location. You can drag a vector around anywhere it's convenient.

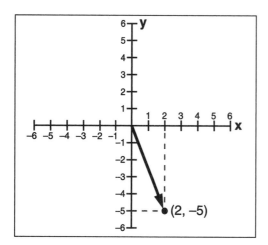

Figure 3.9
The vector (2,–5).

You might justifiably ask why we need vectors to do physics. You can understand the answer from a simple example. Think of a cylindrical probe hanging in space. Imagine that it's just hanging there, not moving. The only way that the probe can start moving is if a force pushes on it. The force has a specific magnitude and direction. The easiest way to represent the force is with a vector.

To use vectors both for 3-D graphics and physics, you must be familiar with vector operations in dimensions one through four. The real trick with vectors is that, as long as you write everything as vectors, rather than as components, everything will work out regardless of how many dimensions you're working in and what coordinate system you use.

There is one exception to the rule that everything works, regardless of the dimension. The cross product exists only in three dimensions. We'll look at this in more detail shortly.

One-dimentional vectors are just scalars. We've already looked at 2-D vectors. You can write the components of a 3-D vector $\mathbf{v}$ as (v_x, v_y, v_z) and the components of a 4-D vector $\mathbf{v}$ as (v_x, v_y, v_z, v_w). If you visualize a 3-D vector as an arrow extending from $(0,0,0)$ to the point given by the components of the vector, that's the length and direction of the vector. Visualizing 4-D vectors is not a trivial exercise.

note

You might be wondering why you need to be able to handle 4-D vectors if you're not doing relativity. As it turns out, 4-D vectors are incredibly important for 3-D graphics.

The *length*, or *magnitude*, of a vector is a scalar that is also called the *norm*. The norm of a vector is often written as the vector surrounded by vertical bars, like this: |v|. Physicists usually write the norm simply as a scalar with the same letter designation, so that the norm of the vector **v** is v.

Note that some people use double sets of vertical bars to indicate their norms, ||v||, to avoid confusion with the *absolute value* of a number, which is also written with vertical bars. This is probably overkill. Because vectors are written in bold, you can tell the difference. |**a**| is the norm of a vector; |a| is the absolute value of a number.

note

The terms *norm*, *magnitude*, and *length* are equivalent when you're talking about vectors.

A nice example of a vector is the position (or displacement) vector. This vector points from one position in space to another. In a coordinate system in which one of those positions is at the origin, the components of the vector are the same as the components of the point in space that the vector refers to, as shown in Figure 3.10.

Figure 3.10
A displacement vector.

The norm of a displacement vector is the distance between the points.

Implementing Vectors in Code: The Physics Modeling Math Library

Modeling physics in 3-D games and graphics programs is mostly a matter of doing math. Therefore, before going any further, we'll begin coding a math library that is specifically for physics. At this point, about the only things we can put in the math library are the definitions for 2-D and 3-D vectors.

Listing 3.1 shows the definition of a class that implements 2-D vectors.

Listing 3.1
The vector_2d Class

```
1     class vector_2d
2     {
3     private:
4         scalar x,y;
5
6     public:
7         vector_2d(void);
8         vector_2d(scalar xComponent,scalar yComponent);
```

```
9          vector_2d(const vector_2d &rightOperand);
10
11         void X(scalar xComponent);
12         scalar X(void);
13
14         void Y(scalar yComponent);
15         scalar Y(void);
16
17         void SetXY(scalar xComponent,scalar yComponent);
18         void GetXY(scalar &xComponent,scalar &yComponent);
19
20         vector_2d &operator =(const vector_2d &rightOperand);
21    };
```

note

You'll undoubtedly notice that I number the lines in all of my code listings in this book. Of course, the actual source code does not contain line numbers. I number each line of code in the listings to make the explanation of the code clearer.

This code listing shows an extremely simple 2-D vector class. It contains two private data members: x and y. These members hold the x and y values of the vector's components.

Currently, the vector_2d class has only nine functions. That will change soon. The current list of public functions begins with two constructors. Next is a function that sets the value of the x component of the vector. That's followed by a function that gets the value of the x component. There is a similar pair of functions for setting and retrieving the value of the y component of the vector. In addition, the class contains functions for setting both components and for getting both components. The class definition ends with an overloaded assignment operator that enables programs to assign a vector_2d object to another vector_2d object.

Because the member functions are fairly straightforward, I won't show them here. If you want to see them, you can find them on the CD-ROM in the Chapter 3 directory in a file called PMMathLibV1.h.

Listing 3.2 extends the vector class into three dimensions.

Listing 3.2
The vector_3d Class

```
1     class vector_3d
2     {
3     private:
4          scalar x,y,z;
```

```
5
6      public:
7          vector_3d(void);
8          vector_3d(scalar xComponent,scalar yComponent,scalar zComponent);
9          vector_3d(const vector_3d &rightOperand);
10
11         void X(scalar xComponent);
12         scalar X(void);
13
14         void Y(scalar yComponent);
15         scalar Y(void);
16
17         void Z(scalar yComponent);
18         scalar Z(void);
19
20         void SetXYZ(scalar xComponent,scalar yComponent,scalar zComponent);
21         void GetXYZ(scalar &xComponent,scalar &yComponent,scalar &zComponent);
22
23         vector_3d &operator =(const vector_3d &rightOperand);
24     };
```

Like the vector_2d class, the vector_3d class has private data members for storing the components of the vector. The vector_3d class defines nearly the same public member functions as the vector_2d class. The difference is that they all accommodate the added z component. Also, there is a pair of new functions called Z(). The first Z() function sets the z component, and the second Z() function gets the value of the z component.

In real-world programming, you would probably not develop your vector classes this way. Generally, you would use either templates or inheritance (or both) to develop more efficient vector classes. For the sake of simplicity and clarity, I'll avoid such techniques for now.

These vector classes are rather basic. They do, however, provide good starting points. In the next few sections, we'll discuss the most common vector operations. As we do, we'll add each one to the vector classes.

Vector Addition and Subtraction

Vectors can be added to form new vectors. This is written **a** + **b**.

If arrows represent the vectors, you can show vector addition by putting the tail of vector **b** on the head of vector **a**, as shown in Figure 3.11. **a** + **b** is the vector represented by the arrow whose tail is on the tail of **a** and whose head is on the head of **b**.

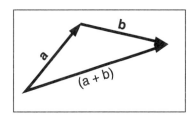

Figure 3.11
Vector addition.

It doesn't matter whether you add **a** + **b** or **b** + **a**. Check out Figure 3.12 to see both produce the same vector. This property is called *commutativity*; vectors are commutative under addition.

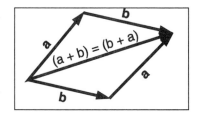

In Cartesian components, you can add 2-D vectors by adding the x components to get the new x component. Adding the y components gives the new y component. Therefore, if the components of **a** are (a_x, a_y) and the components of **b** are (b_x, b_y) in some coordinate system, **a** + **b** has components $(a_x + b_x, a_y + b_y)$.

Figure 3.12
Commutation of vectors under addition.

Extending this to 3-D and 4-D vectors is easy. Just add the z and w components the same way so that in 3-D, **a** + **b** has components $(a_x + b_x, a_y + b_y, a_z + b_z)$, and in 4-D, **a** + **b** has components $(a_x + b_x, a_y + b_y, a_z + b_z, a_w + b_w)$.

What about vector subtraction? Well, subtraction had better be the reverse of addition. That is, you want this:

$$(\mathbf{a} - \mathbf{b}) + \mathbf{b} = \mathbf{a}$$

What's cool about that equation is that it's a connection between addition and subtraction. You can use the same diagram to represent subtraction as addition because the equation *is* an addition! Compare this equation with the equation represented by Figure 3.13:

$$\mathbf{a} + \mathbf{b} = (\mathbf{a} + \mathbf{b})$$

On the diagram, by comparison between the two equations, replace **a** with (**a** − **b**), **b** with **b**, and (**a** + **b**) with **a**, as in Figure 3.13.

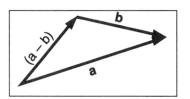

You can see from the figure that vector subtraction gives a vector extending from the tip of the subtracted vector to the tip of the first vector.

Figure 3.13
Vector subtraction.

In components, vector subtraction is exactly what you would expect. If **a** and **b** have components (a_x, a_y) and (b_x, b_y), then **a** − **b** has components $(a_x - b_x, a_y - b_y)$. Vector subtraction is *not* commutative. **a** − **b** points in the opposite direction of **b** − **a**.

It's fairly straightforward to enhance the vector classes so that they can do vector addition and subtraction. The first step is to insert prototypes for the addition and subtraction functions into the class definition. Listing 3.3 gives the prototypes that should be inserted into the vector_2d and vector_3d classes.

Listing 3.3
The Prototypes for the Addition and Subtraction Functions

```
1    // To be inserted into the vector_2d class
2    vector_2d operator +(vector_2d &rightOperand);
3    vector_2d operator -(vector_2d &rightOperand);
4
5    // To be inserted into the vector_3d class
6    vector_3d operator +(vector_3d &rightOperand);
7    vector_3d operator -(vector_3d &rightOperand);
```

The formulas given earlier for vector addition and subtraction showed that you perform these operations by adding and subtracting, respectively, the vector components. Listing 3.4 shows that this is exactly how the functions for these operations work.

Listing 3.4
The Member Functions for Vector Addition and Subtraction

```
1    // To be inserted into the vector_2d class
2
3    inline vector_2d vector_2d::operator +(vector_2d &rightOperand)
4    {
5        return(vector_2d(x+rightOperand.x,y+rightOperand.y));
6    }
7
8    inline vector_2d vector_2d::operator -(vector_2d &rightOperand)
9    {
10       return(vector_2d(x-rightOperand.x,y-rightOperand.y));
11   }
12
13
14   // To be inserted into the vector_3d class
15   inline vector_3d vector_3d::operator +(vector_3d &rightOperand)
16   {
17       return(vector_3d(x+rightOperand.x,y+rightOperand.y,z+rightOperand.z));
18   }
19
20   inline vector_3d vector_3d::operator -(vector_3d &rightOperand)
21   {
22       return(vector_3d(x-rightOperand.x,y-rightOperand.y,z-rightOperand.z));
23   }
```

All four of these functions operate in essentially the same way. They create a nameless temporary variable by calling the constructor for their particular classes. The functions perform their additions or subtractions in the parameter lists of the constructor calls. This is efficient. One reason is that most C++ compilers, including Visual C++, optimize the nameless temporary variables right out of existence. They just return the values that are in the parameter lists of the constructors, which eliminates a call to the constructor.

Another reason these functions are efficient is that they are inline functions. Personally, I don't like class definitions cluttered up with the code for the member functions. I just put in the member data and function prototypes. However, I don't like to lose the efficiency of inline functions, so I tend to use the `inline` keyword whenever I can.

With Visual C++, it's not strictly necessary to use the `inline` keyword. Visual C++ automatically inlines all of the member functions it can. It has its own algorithm for determining which functions to inline. When you compile a release version of a program, Visual C++ applies its inlining algorithm automatically. If you compile a debug build, none of the functions is inlined. This enables you to step through them line by line.

To see the versions of the `vector_2d` and `vector_3d` classes that contain the addition and subtraction operators, look in the file `PMMathLibV2.h`. You'll find this in the `Chapter 3` directory on the CD-ROM that accompanies this book.

As long as we're making addition and subtraction operators for the vector class, we might as well create += and -= operators as well.

note

In C++, u += v is equivalent to u = u + v. u −= v is equivalent to u = u − v.

Listing 3.5 gives the code for the += and -= operators for the vector classes. The file `PMMathLibV3.h` in the `Chapter 3` folder on the CD-ROM has the version of the vector classes with the += and -= operators.

Listing 3.5
The += and -= Operators

```
1      // To be inserted in the vector_2d class
2      inline vector_2d vector_2d::operator +=(vector_2d &rightOperand)
3      {
4           x+=rightOperand.x;
5           y+=rightOperand.y;
6           return(*this);
7      }
8
9      inline vector_2d vector_2d::operator -=(vector_2d &rightOperand)
10     {
11          x-=rightOperand.x;
12          y-=rightOperand.y;
```

```
13          return(*this);
14    }
15
16
17    // To be inserted in the vector_3d class
18    inline vector_3d vector_3d::operator +=(vector_3d &rightOperand)
19    {
20        x+=rightOperand.x;
21        y+=rightOperand.y;
22        z+=rightOperand.z;
23        return(*this);
24    }
25
26
27    inline vector_3d vector_3d::operator -=(vector_3d &rightOperand)
28    {
29        x-=rightOperand.x;
30        y-=rightOperand.y;
31        z-=rightOperand.z;
32        return(*this);
33    }
```

Because these four functions change the contents of their left-hand operators, they cannot return a nameless temporary variable, such as the + and − operators.

Multiplication and Division of a Vector by a Scalar

You can perform multiplication on vectors in three ways. The first is to multiply vectors by scalars (numbers). Multiplying a vector by a scalar changes the magnitude of the vector without changing its direction, as shown in Figure 3.14. This is why a regular number is called a scalar; it lets you scale the size of vectors. The product of a scalar (a) and a vector (**v**) is written a**v**. Scalar multiplication is commutative, so that a**v** = **v**a.

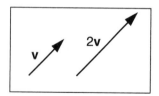

Figure 3.14
Scaling a vector.

In 2-D and 3-D Cartesian coordinate systems, you specify vectors using x,y or x,y,z components. If you do, you can scale a vector by just multiplying each of the components by the scalar. If the components of **v** are (v_x, v_y, v_z), the components of a**v** are (av_x, av_y, av_z).

Finally, you can divide a vector by a scalar. That's equivalent to multiplying by the inverse of the scalar, so that dividing a vector by 2 halves the length of the vector.

Listing 3.6 gives the code for multiplication and division for both of the vector classes.

Listing 3.6
Multiplication and Division Operators for the Vector Classes

```
1      inline vector_2d vector_2d::operator *(scalar rightOperand)
2      {
3          return(vector_2d(x*rightOperand,y*rightOperand));
4      }
5
6      inline vector_2d operator *(scalar leftOperand,vector_2d &rightOperand)
7      {
8          return(
9              vector_2d(leftOperand*rightOperand.x,leftOperand*rightOperand.y));
10      }
11
12     inline vector_2d vector_2d::operator *=(scalar rightOperand)
13     {
14         x*=rightOperand;
15         y*=rightOperand;
16         return(*this);
17     }
18
19     inline vector_2d vector_2d::operator /(scalar rightOperand)
20     {
21         return(vector_2d(x/rightOperand,y/rightOperand));
22     }
23
24     inline vector_2d vector_2d::operator /=(scalar rightOperand)
25     {
26         x/=rightOperand;
27         y/=rightOperand;
28         return(*this);
29     }
30
31
32     inline vector_3d vector_3d::operator *(scalar rightOperand)
33     {
34         return(vector_3d(x*rightOperand,y*rightOperand,z*rightOperand));
35     }
36
37     inline vector_3d operator *(scalar leftOperand,vector_3d &rightOperand)
38     {
39         return(vector_3d(leftOperand*rightOperand.x,
40                          leftOperand*rightOperand.y,
```

```
41                        leftOperand*rightOperand.z));
42     }
43
44     inline vector_3d vector_3d::operator *=(scalar rightOperand)
45     {
46         x*=rightOperand;
47         y*=rightOperand;
48         z*=rightOperand;
49         return(*this);
50     }
51
52     inline vector_3d vector_3d::operator /(scalar rightOperand)
53     {
54         return(vector_3d(x/rightOperand,y/rightOperand,z/rightOperand));
55     }
56
57     inline vector_3d vector_3d::operator /=(scalar rightOperand)
58     {
59         x/=rightOperand;
60         y/=rightOperand;
61         z/=rightOperand;
62         return(*this);
63     }
```

Because scalar multiplication is commutative, there are two versions of the multiplication function in each of the classes. The first uses a vector as the left-hand operator and a scalar as the right-hand operator. The second uses a scalar as the left-hand operator and a vector as the right-hand operator. With C++ binary operators, it's always the left-hand operator that invokes the operator function. If a vector variable is the left-hand operator, it can invoke the multiplication function without a problem. However, if a scalar is the left-hand operator, it can't invoke any of the member functions in a vector class. So the multiplication functions that use a scalar as the left-hand operator can't be members of a vector class. Instead, they must be friend functions. The prototypes for the two friend functions are defined in the vector_2d and vector_3d classes like this:

```
// Goes in the vector_2d class definition
friend vector_2d operator *(scalar leftOperand,vector_2d &rightOperand);

// Goes in the vector_3d class definition
friend vector_3d operator *(scalar leftOperand,vector_3d &rightOperand);
```

Lines 6 through 9 of Listing 3.6 show the friend multiplication function for the vector_2d class. Notice that the keyword friend is not needed on the first line of the function. It appears on the prototype only in the class definition.

Listing 3.6 also gives the $*=$ operator functions for each of the vector classes. In addition, it contains the code for the / and /= operators.

The Dot Product

In addition to multiplying vectors by scalars, you can multiply two vectors. As it turns out, you can do this in multiple ways. One of them gives what is called the *dot product*.

note

The result of a multiplication can't depend on the coordinate system you use. This is the main constraint on the types of multiplication. The dot product follows this rule; regardless of the set of coordinates you define, the result of a dot product will be the same number.

The dot product is sometimes called the *inner product* or (confusingly) the *scalar product*. However, calculating the dot product is not the same as multiplying a vector by a scalar. When you calculate a dot product, you are multiplying two vectors to get a scalar. It's written with a dot between the vectors, like this:

$$\mathbf{a} \bullet \mathbf{b}$$

The dot product can be defined with components:

$$\mathbf{a} \bullet \mathbf{b} = a_x b_x + a_y b_y \qquad \text{in 2-D}$$
$$\mathbf{a} \bullet \mathbf{b} = a_x b_x + a_y b_y + a_z b_z \qquad \text{in 3-D}$$
$$\mathbf{a} \bullet \mathbf{b} = a_x b_x + a_y b_y + a_z b_z + a_w b_w \qquad \text{in 4-D}$$

You can compute the dot product without knowing the components. If you know the magnitude of each vector and the angle between them (θ), as seen in Figure 3.15, the dot product is given by the equation:

$$\mathbf{a} \bullet \mathbf{b} = ab\cos(\theta)$$

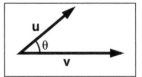

Figure 3.15
The dot product.

Note that, in this equation, the letter a (not in bold text) is the magnitude of the vector **a**. The letter b (also not in bold text) is the magnitude of the vector **b**.

The dot product is commutative, so $\mathbf{a} \bullet \mathbf{b} = \mathbf{b} \bullet \mathbf{a}$. You can show this using either of the two previous equations. The dot product is also *distributive*, which just means that $\mathbf{a} \bullet (\mathbf{b}+\mathbf{c}) = \mathbf{a} \bullet \mathbf{b} + \mathbf{a} \bullet \mathbf{c}$.

Listing 3.7 is the source code for the dot product function for the vector_2d and vector_3d classes.

Listing 3.7
The Dot Product Functions

```
1      // To be inserted in the vector_2d class
2      inline scalar vector_2d::Dot(const vector_2d &v1)
3      {
4          return(x*v1.x + y*v1.y);
5      }
6
7
8      // To be inserted in the vector_3d class
9      inline scalar vector_3d::Dot(const vector_3d &v1)
10     {
11         return(x*v1.x + y*v1.y + z*v1.z);
12     }
```

I mentioned previously that the magnitude of the vector is also called its *norm*. The dot product gives a way to calculate the norm of a vector. If you dot a vector with itself, you get the square of the norm, as shown in the following equation:

$$\mathbf{a} \bullet \mathbf{a} = aa\cos(0) = a^2$$
$$a = |a| = \sqrt{\mathbf{a} \bullet \mathbf{a}}$$
$$a = \sqrt{a_x a_x + a_y a_y}$$

Of course, when you dot a vector with itself, the angle is 0. Because the cosine of 0 is 1, that term drops out entirely. The result is an equation that should look familiar from our discussion of triangles. It's the Pythagorean theorem. It's déjà vu all over again.

The equation for calculating the norm was given in 2-D, but it also works in 3-D. The formula for 3-D would be this:

$$a = \sqrt{a_x a_x + a_y a_y + a_z a_z}$$

The next step is to implement this in code. However, before doing that, it's important to note that if you can get away with using the *square* of the norm in your program, do it. Square roots are incredibly slow to calculate. That's why the physics modeling math library provides two methods for computing norms: one that calculates the norm, and one that calculates the norm squared. These are shown in Listing 3.8.

Listing 3.8
Calculating the Norm

```
1      // To be added to the vector_2d class
2      inline scalar vector_2d::Norm(void)
3      {
```

```
4            return(sqrt(x*x + y*y));
5      }
6
7      inline scalar vector_2d::NormSquared(void)
8      {
9            return(x*x + y*y);
10     }
11
12
13
14     // To be added to the vector_3d class
15     inline scalar vector_3d::Norm(void)
16     {
17           return(sqrt(x*x + y*y + z*z));
18     }
19
20     inline scalar vector_3d::NormSquared(void)
21     {
22           return(x*x + y*y + z*z);
23     }
```

Before ending this discussion of the dot product, we should note that we can also use the dot product to check whether two vectors are perpendicular, or *orthogonal*. Orthogonal and perpendicular both mean that the angle between two vectors is 90°. The dot product of orthogonal vectors is 0. Therefore, if the functions in Listing 3.8 return 0, you know that the two vectors are orthogonal.

The Cross Product

In the dot product, multiplying two vectors together gives a scalar. In the cross product, multiplying two vectors gives another vector. The cross product is written like this:

$$\mathbf{a} \times \mathbf{b}$$

Unlike the dot product or any of the other vector manipulations in this section, the cross product is valid only in three dimensions.

For any two vectors, you can find a plane that is parallel to those vectors, as shown in Figure 3.16. The vector produced in a cross product of two vectors is perpendicular to the plane that is defined by those vectors. That vector is called the *normal vector*. Finding the normal vector is the reason for the cross product's existence.

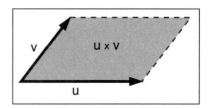

Figure 3.16
Two vectors and their parallel plane.

Suppose that you have two vectors that define a horizontal plane. Which way does the normal point from the plane—up or down? To answer this question, we use a technique called the *right-hand rule*. To find the direction of the normal vector, stick your right hand in the direction of the first vector. Now curl your fingers around toward the second vector and stick your thumb out, as shown in Figure 3.17. The resulting vector points in the direction your thumb is pointing. That's the right-hand rule.

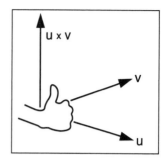

Figure 3.17
The right-hand rule for cross products.

The formula for calculating the cross product of two vectors, which we'll call **u** and **v**, is as follows.

$$\mathbf{u} \times \mathbf{v} = (u_y v_z - u_z v_y)\mathbf{i} + (u_z v_x - u_x v_z)\mathbf{j} + (u_x v_y - u_y v_x)\mathbf{k}$$

In this equation, **i**, **j**, and **k** are unit vectors, which are discussed shortly. For now, we can modify the cross product formula to something a bit easier to write C++ code from:

$$\mathbf{r} = \mathbf{u} \times \mathbf{v}$$

$$r_x = u_y v_z - u_z v_y$$

$$r_y = u_z v_x - u_x v_z$$

$$r_z = u_x v_y - u_y v_x$$

These equations show that crossing vectors **u** and **v** gives a vector we'll call **r**. The x, y, and z components of **r** are calculated as shown earlier. The cross product function shown in Listing 3.9 uses these formulas.

Listing 3.9
The Cross Product Function

```
1      inline vector_3d vector_3d::Cross(const vector_3d &rightOperand)
2      {
3          return(
4              vector_3d(
5                  y*rightOperand.z - z*rightOperand.y,
6                  z*rightOperand.x - x*rightOperand.z,
7                  x*rightOperand.y - y*rightOperand.x));
8      }
```

Unit Vectors

There's another way to write out a vector in terms of components that is sometimes very useful. You can define a 2-D Cartesian coordinate system by two little vectors, each of length 1, pointing along the x and y axes, as in Figure 3.15. Call these vectors $\hat{x}$ and $\hat{y}$. (Read: *x-hat* and *y-hat*.) The hat (^) is a reminder that these are *unit vectors,* or vectors whose norm is 1. In their own coordinate system, the components of $\hat{x}$ are (1,0), and the components of $\hat{y}$ are (0,1).

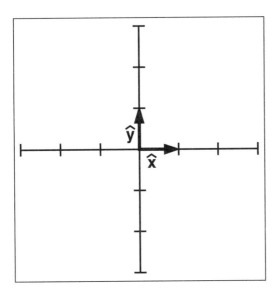

Figure 3.18
Unit vectors in two dimensions.

Instead of $\hat{x}$ and $\hat{y}$, some people prefer $\hat{i}$ and $\hat{j}$ for the same vectors. In either case, they still refer to unit vectors pointing along the x and y axes.

You can write any vector in the Cartesian space by multiplying each of the unit vectors by scalars and adding them together. In other words, for any vector

$$\mathbf{v} = a\hat{\mathbf{x}} + b\hat{\mathbf{y}}$$

for some a and b. a and b are the coordinates of the vector in the coordinate system defined by $\hat{x}$ and $\hat{y}$. Therefore, if a is 2 and b is 3, the vector's coordinates are (1,2) and the vector can be written as $2\hat{\mathbf{x}} + 3\hat{\mathbf{y}}$, or $2\hat{\mathbf{i}} + 3\hat{\mathbf{j}}.$

Unit vectors for the third and fourth dimensions are generally specified as $\hat{z}$ and $\hat{w}$ or $\hat{k}$ and $\hat{m}$. Their components are (0,0,1) and (0,0,0,1), respectively.

note

The $\hat{w}$ (or $\hat{m}$) is not something you see too often in physics or math; it's really more something that 3-D graphics programmers use.

Sometimes you want a unit vector that points in the same direction as another vector. This process is called *normalization*, and it's pretty easy to do. If you divide a vector by its length, you turn it into a unit vector. Write the unit vector with the same letter as the original vector but with a hat:

$$\hat{v} = \frac{v}{v}$$

$$= \frac{v}{\sqrt{v \bullet v}}$$

Listing 3.10 gives the code for the normalization functions for the vector_2d and vector_3d classes.

Listing 3.10
The Normalize Functions

```
1      inline vector_2d vector_2d::Normalize(scalar tolerance)
2      {
3          vector_2d result;
4
5          scalar length = Norm();
6          if (length>=tolerance)
7          {
8              result.x = x/length;
9              result.y = y/length;
10         }
11         return(result);
12     }
13
14
15
16     inline vector_3d vector_3d::Normalize(scalar tolerance)
17     {
18         vector_3d result;
19
```

```
20        scalar length = Norm();
21        if (length>=tolerance)
22        {
23            result.x = x/length;
24            result.y = y/length;
25            result.z = z/length;
26        }
27        return(result);
28    }
```

You might notice that these functions use an input parameter called `tolerance` to check that the norm of the vector is greater than or equal to a tolerance factor. This ensures that the norm isn't so small that the functions would be dividing by 0 (which could send everything crashing to a halt). In this case, the function just gives up and returns a vector of length 0.

Projection

Dotting a vector with a unit vector is called *projection*. A projection picks out the component of the vector that's in the same direction as the unit vector, as shown in Figure 3.19. For example, if you dot a vector $\mathbf{v}$ with the unit vector $\hat{\mathbf{x}}$, you get the x component of that vector, v_x:

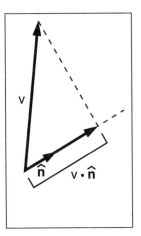

$$
\begin{aligned}
\mathbf{v} \bullet \hat{\mathbf{x}} &= \left(v_x \hat{\mathbf{x}} + v_y \hat{\mathbf{y}} + v_z \hat{\mathbf{z}} \right) \bullet \hat{\mathbf{x}} \\
&= v_x \hat{\mathbf{x}} \bullet \hat{\mathbf{x}} + v_y \hat{\mathbf{y}} \bullet \hat{\mathbf{x}} + v_z \hat{\mathbf{z}} \bullet \hat{\mathbf{x}} \\
&= v_x
\end{aligned}
$$

Example: Bouncing Off a Wall

Projections are often useful when talking about how things behave at some boundary. Take the example of a ball bouncing off a wall. This problem is often called *vector reflection*. The first computer game, *Pong*, was a table tennis simulation that used vector reflection in 2-D.

Figure 3.19
The projection of $\mathbf{v}$ in the $\hat{\mathbf{n}}$ direction.

To make this simulation work, you need a vector to describe the ball and another for the wall. Define a unit vector that points perpendicular to (straight out of) the wall, as in Figure 3.20. This vector is written $\hat{\mathbf{n}}$, and it defines the unit normal vector to the wall. The vector $\mathbf{v}$ is the incoming velocity (speed and direction) of the ball. Another vector, $\mathbf{v'}$ (pronounced *v-prime*), is the velocity of the ball after hitting the wall.

Here's the problem: Given the incoming velocity and the unit normal to the wall, find the final velocity of the ball. Note that there aren't coordinate axes on the diagram; we're going to do this problem without coordinates so that it's completely general.

When something bounces off a wall elastically, the component of the velocity normal to the wall is reversed, whereas the other component, which is parallel to the wall, stays the same.

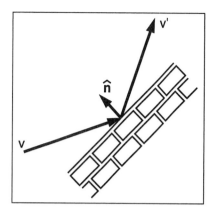

Figure 3.20
Bouncing off a wall.

note

When I say the bounce is elastic, I just mean that the wall is hard and the ball is something like a tennis ball that will actually bounce off the wall, rather than a blob of clay or a snowball. We'll talk more about this kind of thing when we get to collisions.

Because this problem simulates an elastic bounce, we only need to find the component of $\mathbf{v'}$ that is normal to the wall, which is the component of $\mathbf{v}$ in the $\hat{\mathbf{n}}$ direction. You can just copy the component of $\mathbf{v'}$ that is parallel to the wall from the same component of $\mathbf{v}$.

To find the component of $\mathbf{v}$ in the $\hat{\mathbf{n}}$ direction using a projection, take the dot product of $\mathbf{v}$ and $\hat{\mathbf{n}}$ and normalize it, like this.

$$(\mathbf{v} \bullet \hat{\mathbf{n}})\hat{\mathbf{n}}$$

It will be convenient to name the other component of $\mathbf{v}$ (the component parallel to the wall), even though we'll never need to find it. I'll call this component $\mathbf{p}$ because it's parallel to the wall. All this information is added to the diagram in Figure 3.21.

You now can write $\mathbf{v}$ as the sum of these components:

$$\mathbf{v} = \mathbf{p} + (\mathbf{v} \bullet \hat{\mathbf{n}})\hat{\mathbf{n}}$$

The important thing about $\mathbf{p}$ is that it's the same for both $\mathbf{v}$ and $\mathbf{v'}$. The $\hat{\mathbf{n}}$ component is reversed. Therefore, $\mathbf{v'}$ becomes this:

$$\mathbf{v} = \mathbf{p} - (\mathbf{v} \bullet \hat{\mathbf{n}})\hat{\mathbf{n}}$$

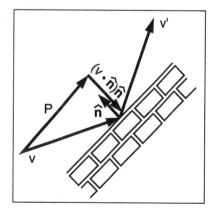

Figure 3.21
Draw everything you know on your diagrams!

Here we solve for p in the first equation and substitute the result in the second equation to get rid of **p**:

$$\mathbf{v'} = \mathbf{v} - (\mathbf{v} \bullet \hat{\mathbf{n}})\hat{\mathbf{n}} - (\mathbf{v} \bullet \hat{\mathbf{n}})\hat{\mathbf{n}}$$

$$= \mathbf{v} - 2(\mathbf{v} \bullet \hat{\mathbf{n}})\hat{\mathbf{n}}$$

Because we derived this without coordinates, the result is valid for any coordinates and in any number of dimensions. Nifty.

Reprise to Bouncing Off a Wall: Plug n' Chug

To apply this in an actual physical situation, you can now do what most physicists call "Plug n' Chug." Essentially, you just plug in the numbers and calculate everything to see what happens.

Say that the player has no aim, so he keeps missing the blood-sucking space fiends and ricocheting bullets off the wall. The bullets are coming in with velocity vector of (–3 m/s, 4 m/s). The wall is facing the $\hat{\mathbf{x}}$ direction.

The speed of the bullet is the magnitude of its velocity vector. Therefore, the first step is to take the norm of the velocity vector (**v**):

$$v = \sqrt{\mathbf{v} \bullet \mathbf{v}}$$

$$= \sqrt{(-3 \text{ m/s}, \ 4 \text{ m/s}) \bullet (-3 \text{ m/s}, \ 4 \text{ m/s})}$$

$$= \sqrt{(-3 \text{ m/s})(-3 \text{ m/s}) \ + \ (4 \text{ m/s})(4 \text{ m/s})}$$

$$= \sqrt{9 \text{ m}^2/\text{s}^2 + \ 16 \text{ m}^2/\text{s}^2}$$

$$= \sqrt{25 \text{ m}^2/\text{s}^2}$$

$$= 5 \text{ m/s}$$

5 m/s is pretty slow for a bullet. No wonder the player can't hit the space fiends!

To find the velocity of the bullet after it hits the wall, first find the projection of **v** in the $\hat{\mathbf{x}}$ direction. Then you can plug **v** and $\hat{\mathbf{x}}$ into the equation just derived:

$$\mathbf{v} \bullet \hat{\mathbf{x}} = (\ (-3 \text{ m/s}) \ \hat{\mathbf{x}} \ + \ (4 \text{ m/s} \ ) \ \hat{\mathbf{y}}) \ \bullet \hat{\mathbf{x}}$$

$$= -3 \text{ m/s}$$

$$\mathbf{v'} = \mathbf{v} - 2(\mathbf{v} \bullet \hat{\mathbf{x}})\hat{\mathbf{x}}$$

$$= (-3 \text{ m/s} \ ) \ \hat{\mathbf{x}} \ + \ (4 \text{ m/s} \ ) \ \hat{\mathbf{y}}) \ - \ 2(-3 \text{ m/s}) \ \hat{\mathbf{x}}$$

$$= (3 \text{ m/s}) \ \hat{\mathbf{x}} \ + \ (4 \text{ m/s}) \ \hat{\mathbf{y}}$$

The y component (parallel to the wall) is unchanged, but the x component has been reversed.

Vectors in Direct3D

Because vectors are so important to 3-D programming, the D3DX utility library for Direct3D includes a bunch of structures and functions for dealing with vectors in two, three, and four dimensions. Although the math and physics modeling library has everything necessary to do dot products and such, it's nice to know these functions are there. We won't shy from using the D3DX functions when doing 3-D graphics, but we'll stick entirely to our modeling library for the physics calculations. Using the modeling library gives us game logic that is highly portable. So if you prefer to write games with something besides DirectX, you'll be able to use most of the code in this book.

The structures for the vectors are D3DXVECTOR2, D3DXVECTOR3, and D3DXVECTOR4 for two, three, and four dimensions, respectively. The structures take one float for each dimension. Using the structures with the modeling library requires the ability to convert between the DirectX with vector structures and the modeling library's vector classes. The modeling library already has functions to handle the conversions from the D3DXVECTOR2 and D3DXVECTOR3 structures to the vector_2d and vector_3d classes. They are the classes' constructors. To convert vector_2d and vector_3d from the classes to the D3DXVECTOR2 and D3DXVECTOR3 structures, we'll have to implement typecast operators for the vector_2d and vector_3d classes. Listing 3.11 contains the source code for the typecast functions.

Listing 3.11
The Typecast Functions

```
1     vector_2d::operator D3DXVECTOR2()
2     {
3         return (D3DXVECTOR2(x,y));
4     }
5
6
7     vector_3d::operator D3DXVECTOR3()
8     {
9         return (D3DXVECTOR3(x,y,z));
10    }
```

To perform the conversion, these two functions create nameless temporary D3DXVECTOR2 and D3DXVECTOR3 variables, store the vector components in the structure variables, and then return the structure variables.

Matrices

A matrix is just an array of numbers with some rules about how you add and multiply them. You're probably familiar with arrays from computer programming, if you haven't seen them elsewhere. In physics and math, they're written as capital letters, such as M. The elements of a matrix are usually written as a lowercase letter with two indices, so that you can write a matrix like this:

$$M = \begin{bmatrix} m_{11} & m_{12} & m_{13} & m_{14} \\ m_{21} & m_{22} & m_{23} & m_{24} \\ m_{31} & m_{32} & m_{33} & m_{34} \\ m_{41} & m_{42} & m_{43} & m_{44} \end{bmatrix}$$

In math and physics, the row and column numbers of matrices usually begin with 1. However, because computer programs use two-dimensional arrays for matrices, and arrays in C++ begin their indexing with 0, many computer programming books number the rows and columns of matrices starting with 0. I'll follow that convention from now on in this book.

The matrix, M, is called a 4×4 matrix because it has four rows and four columns. Usually, graphics programmers deal with square matrices, which are matrices with the same number of rows as columns. The same is true for the kind of physics that we'll be coding. Nearly all the matrices will be square. The modeling library implements 2×2, 3×3, and 4×4 matrices in classes called matrix2×2 and matrix3×3.

In many ways, matrices are simpler than vectors. They aren't coordinate-independent entities as vectors are. They're more akin to the components of a vector in some coordinate system. In fact, the *components* of an n-dimensional vector behave a lot like a 1×n matrix.

With this similarity between matrices and vectors in mind, it probably won't surprise you when I say that matrices have pretty much the same operations available to them as vectors: addition, multiplication by a scalar, and an inner product. Keep sharp, though: Matrices have a few other tricks.

---

note

It's not difficult to make a class that handles matrices of any size. Take a look at *Numerical Recipes for C++* by William Press and Company for an example. However, this is game programming. You're going to need only a few sizes of matrices. Generality can be sacrificed for speed. By implementing only those matrices that you need, you can simplify the code and speed things up a bit.

Listing 3.12 has the class definition for the matrices.

Listing 3.12
The matrix2×2 and matrix3×3 Classes

```
1    class matrix2x2
2    {
3    private:
4        scalar elements[2][2];
5
6    public:
7        matrix2x2(void);
8        matrix2x2(scalar initializationArray[2][2]);
9        matrix2x2(scalar m00,scalar m01,scalar m10,scalar m11);
10
11       void Element(int row,int col,scalar elementValue);
12       scalar Element(int row,int col);
13
14       matrix2x2 &operator =(scalar initializationArray[2][2]);
15
16   };
17
18
19   class matrix3x3
20   {
21   private:
22       scalar elements[3][3];
23
24   public:
25       matrix3x3(void);
26       matrix3x3(scalar initializationArray[3][3]);
27       matrix3x3(scalar m00,scalar m01,scalar m02,
28                 scalar m10,scalar m11,scalar m12,
29                 scalar m20,scalar m21,scalar m22);
30
31       void Element(int row,int col,scalar elementValue);
32       scalar Element(int row,int col);
33
34       matrix3x3 &operator =(scalar initializationArray[3][3]);
35
36   };
```

These matrix classes, like the first version of the vector classes, define operators for getting and setting matrix elements. In the next few sections, I'll present the techniques for performing operations on matrices. However, by now it should be pretty straightforward to implement many of these operations in code. Therefore, I won't bother to show the code unless there's a compelling reason for doing so. The CD-ROM that comes with this book contains a version of the math and physics modeling library with all the matrix functions implemented. You'll find this in the Vectors and Matrices folder, which is in the Chapter 3 folder. The file is named PMMathLibv10.h.

The Identity Matrix

One of the most basic operations on a matrix is to initialize it to the *identity matrix*. The identity matrix is a matrix that is all 0s except for the elements along the diagonal from the upper-left corner to the lower-right corner, which is set to 1s. It's actually easier to show you than to explain it. So here is the identity matrix for a 2×2 matrix:

$$I = \begin{bmatrix} 1 & 0 \\ 0 & 1 \end{bmatrix}$$

For a 3×3 matrix, the identity matrix is as follows:

$$I = \begin{bmatrix} 1 & 0 & 0 \\ 0 & 1 & 0 \\ 0 & 0 & 1 \end{bmatrix}$$

As you can see, there is a line of 1s that goes from the upper-left corner to the lower-right corner. The rest of the matrix is 0s. You'll find the code for the Identity() functions for the matrix classes on the CD-ROM in the file PMMathLibv10.h.

note

The identity matrix is also called the *unit matrix.*

Multiplying by the unit matrix has the same effect as multiplying by the scalar 1. In other words, it doesn't do anything:

$$AI = IA = A$$

Addition and Subtraction

Matrix addition is just what you would think; all you have to do is add each of the components. Given two matrices, A and B,

$$A = \begin{bmatrix} a_{00} & a_{01} & a_{02} \\ a_{10} & a_{11} & a_{12} \\ a_{20} & a_{21} & a_{22} \end{bmatrix}$$

$$B = \begin{bmatrix} b_{00} & b_{01} & b_{02} \\ b_{10} & b_{11} & b_{12} \\ b_{20} & b_{21} & b_{22} \end{bmatrix}$$

$$A + B = \begin{bmatrix} a_{00} + b_{00} & a_{01} + b_{01} & a_{02} + b_{02} \\ a_{10} + b_{10} & a_{11} + b_{11} & a_{12} + b_{12} \\ a_{20} + b_{20} & a_{21} + b_{21} & a_{22} + b_{22} \end{bmatrix}$$

Subtraction proceeds the same way:

$$A - B = \begin{bmatrix} a_{00} - b_{00} & a_{01} - b_{01} & a_{02} - b_{02} \\ a_{10} - b_{10} & a_{11} - b_{11} & a_{12} - b_{12} \\ a_{20} - b_{20} & a_{21} - b_{21} & a_{22} - b_{22} \end{bmatrix}$$

The matrix2×2 and matrix3×3 classes implement +, +=, -, and -= operators. In the matrix2×2 class, I've listed the matrix elements right in the code because there are only four of them. However, in the matrix3×3 class, I used a pair of loops to iterate through the matrix and perform the additions. Although this is slightly less efficient, it keeps the code uncluttered.

Multiplication and Division by a Scalar

This is cake. Multiply each element by the scalar. You can write it just by writing the scalar next to the matrix.

Take a matrix A and the scalar w:

$$A = \begin{bmatrix} a_{00} & a_{01} \\ a_{10} & a_{11} \end{bmatrix}$$

$$wA = \begin{bmatrix} wa_{00} & wa_{01} \\ wa_{10} & wa_{11} \end{bmatrix}$$

In the `matrix2×2` and `matrix3×3` classes, I've included two functions in each class for multiplying matrices by scalars. One function is for doing the multiplication with the matrix on the left. The other is a `friend` function that enables you to do the multiplication with the scalar on the left. You can write code that does this:

```
matrix2x2 m1, m2(1,2,3,4);
scalar s=5;
m1=m2*s;
```

Or, if you prefer, you can write it like this:

```
matrix2x2 m1, m2(1,2,3,4);
scalar s=5;
m1=s*m2;
```

Either way works. I've also added `*=` operators for both classes that enable you to multiply a matrix by a scalar and store the result in the same matrix.

Division by a scalar works like multiplication. To divide a matrix by a scalar, divide the scalar into each matrix element, as shown here.

$$A = \begin{bmatrix} a_{00} & a_{01} \\ a_{10} & a_{11} \end{bmatrix}$$

$$A/w = \begin{bmatrix} a_{00}/w & a_{01}/w \\ a_{10}/w & a_{11}/w \end{bmatrix}$$

Unlike multiplication, division is not commutative, so the `matrix2×2` and `matrix3×3` classes each implement just one / operator apiece. However, there are /= operators for both classes.

Matrix Multiplication

In addition to multiplying matrices by scalars, you can multiply matrices with each other to get another matrix. However, there's a restriction on the size of matrices you're allowed to multiply. You can multiply two matrices only if the number of columns of the first matrix matches the number of rows of the second matrix. That is, you can multiply a p×n matrix with an n×q, but you can't multiply that p×n with a q×n. If you multiply a p×n matrix with an n×q matrix, the resulting matrix is a p×q with p rows and q columns.

note

Some computer programmers like to call matrix multiplication *matrix concatenation*.

Here are a couple more examples of allowed multiplications. Multiplying a 2×3 by a 3×7 yields a 2×7. Likewise, multiplying a 2×3 by a 3×5 gives a 2×5 matrix. Multiplying a 2×3 by a 5×3 is not allowed.

The method for doing this might seem convoluted at first, but you get kind of used to it after a while. You can think about matrix multiplication in several ways. I'll explain a couple, and you can use whatever you're the most comfortable with.

One approach is to think of matrix multiplication as a series of vector dot products. Take the first row of the first matrix. It looks like the components of a vector, doesn't it? Now look at the first column of the second matrix. It also looks like the components of a vector. Now you can "dot" the two together to get a scalar. That scalar is the top-left element of the product matrix.

Here's an example of how this works. Suppose that you start with this 3×3 matrix:

$$A = \begin{bmatrix} 2 & 4 & 3 \\ 4 & 5 & 2 \\ 4 & 4 & 1 \end{bmatrix}$$

Let's multiply it by this 2×2 matrix:

$$B = \begin{bmatrix} 1 & 2 \\ 2 & 3 \\ 4 & 3 \end{bmatrix}$$

The result is going to be a 3×2 matrix. To get element 0,0, you dot the first row in A with the first column in B, like this:

$$(2\ 4\ 3) \bullet (1\ 2\ 4) = (2)1 + (4)2 + (3)4 = 2 + 8 + 12 = 22$$

So the value for element 0,0 is 22. The resulting matrix currently looks like this:

$$\begin{bmatrix} 22 & - \\ - & - \\ - & - \end{bmatrix}$$

The 0,1 element (first row, second column) is given by the dot product of the first row of A with the second column of B:

$$(2\ 4\ 3) \bullet (2\ 3\ 3) = 2 \bullet 2 + 4 \bullet 3 + 3 \bullet 3 = 4 + 12 + 9 = 25$$

The resulting matrix now has two values in it:

$$\begin{bmatrix} 22 & 25 \\ - & - \\ - & - \end{bmatrix}$$

Let's keep going. The 1,0 element (second row, first column) is given by the dot product of the second row of A with the first column of B:

$$(4\ 5\ 2)\bullet(1\ 2\ 4)=4\bullet1+5\bullet2+2\bullet4=4+10+8=22$$

The resulting matrix now has a value for the second row:

$$\begin{bmatrix} 22 & 25 \\ 22 & - \\ - & - \end{bmatrix}$$

If you keep going, the rest of the elements are similar:

$$\begin{bmatrix} 2 & 4 & 3 \\ 4 & 5 & 2 \\ 4 & 4 & 1 \end{bmatrix} \begin{bmatrix} 1 & 2 \\ 2 & 3 \\ 4 & 3 \end{bmatrix} = \begin{bmatrix} 22 & 25 \\ 22 & 25 \\ 16 & 23 \end{bmatrix}$$

This method of multiplying matrices is easy to remember, and it gives some mathematical insight into the relationship between matrices and components of vectors.

The other method I'm going to show you is just an equation. The biggest advantage to this method is that it can be explained in one line. If A is an $i\times n$ matrix and B is an $n\times j$ matrix, then the following is true:

$$AB = C, \text{ if and only if}$$

$$c_{ij} = \sum_{k=0}^{n-1} a_{ik} b_{kj}$$

$$= a_{i0} b_{0j} + a_{i1} b_{1j} + \dots + a_{i(n-1)} b_{(n-1)j}$$

The Σ is a big sigma, and it stands for Sum. If you see the following

$$\sum_{k=1}^{n}$$

it means to sum up whatever is to the right of the sigma, adding n terms, the first one with k = 1, the second with k = 2, and so on, until k = n. For example,

$$\sum_{k=1}^{4} 2 = 2 + 2 + 2 + 2 = 8$$

$$\sum_{k=1}^{4} k = 1 + 2 + 3 + 4 = 10$$

Using the matrices in the previous example, you can compute the 0,0 element of C like this:

$$AB = \begin{bmatrix} 2 & 4 & 3 \\ 4 & 5 & 2 \\ 4 & 4 & 1 \end{bmatrix} \begin{bmatrix} 1 & 2 \\ 2 & 3 \\ 4 & 3 \end{bmatrix}$$

$$c_{00} = \sum_{k=0}^{3} a_{0k} b_{k0}$$

$$= a_{00} b_{00} + a_{01} b_{10} + a_{02} b_{20}$$

$$= 2 \bullet 1 + 4 \bullet 2 + 3 \bullet 4$$

$$= 2 + 8 + 12 = 22$$

Because the multiplication of two matrices is a bit more involved that the operators show so far, let's look at the code for the operator *() functions. They're shown in Listing 3.13.

Listing 3.13
Multiplying a Matrix by a Matrix

```
1     matrix2x2 matrix2x2::operator *(const matrix2x2 &rightOperand)
2     {
3         return(
4             matrix2x2(
5                 // Value for element 0,0
6                 elements[0][0]*rightOperand.elements[0][0] +
7                 elements[0][1]*rightOperand.elements[1][0],
8                 // Value for element 0,1
9                 elements[0][0]*rightOperand.elements[0][1] +
10                elements[0][1]*rightOperand.elements[1][1],
```

```
11                    // Value for element 1,0
12                    elements[1][0]*rightOperand.elements[0][0] +
13                    elements[1][1]*rightOperand.elements[1][0],
14                    // Value for element 1,1
15                    elements[1][0]*rightOperand.elements[0][1] +
16                    elements[1][1]*rightOperand.elements[1][1]));
17    }
18
19    matrix3x3 matrix3x3::operator *(const matrix3x3 &rightOperand)
20    {
21        matrix3x3 answer;
22
23        for (int i=0;i<3;i++)
24        {
25            for (int j=0;j<3;j++)
26            {
27                answer.elements[i][j] =
28                    elements[i][0]*rightOperand.elements[0][j] +
29                    elements[i][1]*rightOperand.elements[1][j] +
30                    elements[i][2]*rightOperand.elements[2][j];
31            }
32        }
33
34        return(answer);
35    }
```

In a 2×2 matrix, there are only 4 elements to deal with, so on lines 6–16 of Listing 3.13, I've explicitly written the element numbers into the code. Implementing 3×3 matrices would be too messy to write this way, so on lines 23–32, I wrote a pair of loops to handle the task.

There are a couple of features of note in matrix multiplication. The most important is probably that, except in special cases, matrix multiplication is not commutative.

$$AB \neq BA$$

However, matrix multiplication is associative and distributive.

$$(AB)C = A(BC)$$
$$A(B+C) = AB+AC$$

Transpose

Transposing a matrix involves interchanging the rows and the columns. I'll indicate the transpose like this: A^T is the transpose of matrix A. Therefore, if A is a 4×3 matrix,

$$A = \begin{bmatrix} a_{00} & a_{01} & a_{02} \\ a_{10} & a_{11} & a_{12} \\ a_{20} & a_{21} & a_{22} \\ a_{30} & a_{31} & a_{32} \end{bmatrix}$$

then its transpose is this 3×4 matrix:

$$A^T = \begin{bmatrix} a_{00} & a_{10} & a_{20} & a_{30} \\ a_{01} & a_{11} & a_{21} & a_{31} \\ a_{02} & a_{12} & a_{22} & a_{32} \end{bmatrix}$$

Determinants

The *determinant* is another way to go from a matrix to a scalar. The determinant is a little hard to explain in one try, but here's a start.

You can compute the determinant of a 2×2 matrix by multiplying the diagonal elements and subtracting them, like this:

$$A = \begin{bmatrix} a_{00} & a_{01} \\ a_{10} & a_{11} \end{bmatrix}$$
$$\det[A] = a_{00}a_{11} - a_{01}a_{10}$$

The determinant of a 3×3 matrix is a little harder. You can break it down into a sum of 2×2 determinants:

$$A = \begin{bmatrix} a_{00} & a_{01} & a_{02} \\ a_{10} & a_{11} & a_{12} \\ a_{20} & a_{21} & a_{22} \end{bmatrix}$$

$$\det[A] = a_{00}\det\begin{bmatrix} a_{11} & a_{12} \\ a_{21} & a_{22} \end{bmatrix} - a_{01}\det\begin{bmatrix} a_{10} & a_{12} \\ a_{20} & a_{22} \end{bmatrix} + a_{02}\det\begin{bmatrix} a_{10} & a_{11} \\ a_{20} & a_{21} \end{bmatrix}$$

You then plug the formula for a 2×2 matrix into this, multiply, and end up with some terms that cancel each other because of + and – signs. The resulting equation is as follows:

$$\det[A] = a_{00} \cdot a_{11} \cdot a_{22} - a_{00} \cdot a_{21} \cdot a_{12} + a_{10} \cdot a_{21} \cdot a_{02}$$
$$-a_{10} \cdot a_{01} \cdot a_{22} + a_{20} \cdot a_{01} \cdot a_{12} - a_{20} \cdot a_{11} \cdot a_{02}$$

This equation translates well into code, as Listing 3.14 demonstrates.

Listing 3.14
The Determinant() Functions for the matrix_2d and matrix_3d Classes

```
1     scalar matrix2x2::Determinant()
2     {
3         return(elements[0][0]*elements[1][1] -
4              elements[1][0]*elements[0][1]);
5     }
6
7
8     scalar matrix3x3::Determinant()
9     {
10        return(elements[0][0]*elements[1][1]*elements[2][2] -
11             elements[0][0]*elements[2][1]*elements[1][2] +
12             elements[1][0]*elements[2][1]*elements[0][2] -
13             elements[1][0]*elements[0][1]*elements[2][2] +
14             elements[2][0]*elements[0][1]*elements[1][2] -
15             elements[2][0]*elements[1][1]*elements[0][2]);
16    }
```

As you can see, the functions are a straightforward implementation of the previous formulas.

Matrix Inversion

You'll often need the inverse of a matrix. The inverse is written with a −1 in superscript, like you're taking the matrix to the −1 power, so the inverse of the matrix A is A^{-1}. The inverse of a matrix is defined like this:

$$AA^{-1} = I$$

Recall that I is the identity matrix. Therefore, multiplying a matrix by its inverse gives the identity matrix. This process mirrors the process of multiplying a scalar number by its inverse. If you multiply 2/1 by 1/2, you get 1.

The inverse matrix, in a sense, is the reverse of a matrix. It takes you to where you started; if you multiply A by B, you can get A back by multiplying AB by B⁻¹:

$$(AB)B^{-1} = A(BB^{-1}) = A$$

More trivially, the inverse of the inverse of a matrix is the original matrix:

$$(A^{-1})^{-1} = A$$

Not all matrices have an inverse. You can only find the inverse of a square matrix (same number of rows and columns) that has a determinant that is not equal to zero. In physics and computer programming, you primarily use square matrices with a nonzero determinant. You'll be able to find the inverse of most matrices. Check out this (partial) formula for calculating the inverse:

$$A^{-1} = \frac{C}{\det[A]}$$

warning

Mathematicians and physicists do not normally invert matrices with determinants. The technique is not *nearly* robust enough for general physics. I'm using it here because it's a straightforward method of matrix inversion. I *highly* recommend that you investigate matrix inversion using a Gaussian elimination algorithm. A quick search on the Internet will give you the information you need. However, be prepared to do math that is much more rigorous than any I have presented so far.

The C is called a *cofactor matrix*. I'd rather not get into how you actually compute the *general* case of the cofactor matrix. Instead, I'll give a partial formula that should suit everything we're doing just fine. If you need to work with more general matrices (especially big ones) or you're curious about how all this stuff is proven, check out a good mathematical methods book such as *Mathematical Methods for Physicists* by Arfken and Weber. You could get a linear algebra book, but the math physics books are usually more understandable and practical.

Given a 2×2 matrix A:

$$A = \begin{bmatrix} a_{00} & a_{01} \\ a_{10} & a_{11} \end{bmatrix}$$

the cofactor matrix is as follows:

$$C = \begin{bmatrix} a_{11} & -a_{01} \\ -a_{10} & a_{00} \end{bmatrix}$$

For a 3×3 matrix, it's a bit more complicated:

$$A = \begin{bmatrix} a_{00} & a_{01} & a_{02} \\ a_{10} & a_{11} & a_{12} \\ a_{20} & a_{21} & a_{22} \end{bmatrix}$$

The cofactor matrix for A is given by this:

$$C = \begin{bmatrix} a_{11}a_{22} - a_{21}a_{12} & a_{02}a_{21} - a_{01}a_{22} & a_{01}a_{12} - a_{11}a_{02} \\ a_{12}a_{20} - a_{10}a_{22} & a_{00}a_{22} - a_{02}a_{20} & a_{02}a_{10} - a_{00}a_{12} \\ a_{10}a_{21} - a_{11}a_{20} & a_{01}a_{20} - a_{00}a_{21} & a_{00}a_{11} - a_{01}a_{10} \end{bmatrix}$$

You do have to be careful when using this formula for the inverse in your programs. For one thing, you can have problems if the determinant is too close to 0, so you'll need to check for that. This form is also horrible for large matrices.

note

For large matrices, you should probably use a Gauss-Jordan elimination method. The method isn't hard, but using it involves a slightly deeper understanding of matrices than is developed here. You might try *Numerical Recipes for C++* by William Press and others.

The code for the inverse function for both the matrix classes is shown in Listing 3.15.

Listing 3.15
Matrix Inverse Functions

```
1      matrix2x2 matrix2x2::Inverse()
2      {
3          scalar determinant=Determinant();
4          if (determinant==0.0)
5          {
6              pmlib_error theError(
7                  "Can't invert a matrix that has a determinant of 0.");
8              throw theError;
9          }
10
11         return(
```

```
12                matrix2x2(
13                elements[1][1]/determinant, -elements[0][1]/determinant,
14                -elements[1][0]/determinant, elements[0][0]/determinant));
15    }
16    matrix3x3 matrix3x3::Inverse()
17    {
18        scalar determinant=Determinant();
19        if (determinant==0.0)
20        {
21            pmlib_error theError(
22                "Can't invert a matrix that has a determinant of 0.");
23            throw theError;
24        }
25
26        return(
27            matrix3x3(
28                // Value for matrix element 0,0
29                (elements[1][1]*elements[2][2] -
30                elements[1][1]*elements[1][1])/determinant,
31                // Value for matrix element 0,1
32                -(elements[0][1]*elements[2][2] -
33                elements[0][2]*elements[2][1])/determinant,
34                // Value for matrix element 0,2
35                (elements[0][1]*elements[1][2] -
36                elements[0][2]*elements[1][1])/determinant,
37                // Value for matrix element 1,0
38                -(elements[1][0]*elements[2][2] -
39                elements[0][2]*elements[2][1])/determinant,
40                // Value for matrix element 1,1
41                (elements[0][0]*elements[2][2] -
42                elements[0][2]*elements[2][0])/determinant,
43                // Value for matrix element 1,2
44                -(elements[0][0]*elements[1][2] -
45                elements[0][2]*elements[1][0])/determinant,
46                // Value for matrix element 2,0
47                (elements[0][0]*elements[1][1] -
48                elements[1][1]*elements[2][0])/determinant,
49                // Value for matrix element 2,1
50                -(elements[0][0]*elements[2][1] -
51                elements[0][1]*elements[2][0])/determinant,
52                // Value for matrix element 2,2
```

```
53                    (elements[0][0]*elements[1][1] -
54                    elements[0][1]*elements[1][0])/determinant));
55    }
```

Both these functions throw an exception if the determinant of a matrix is 0. Therefore, in your code, you need to be sure you put a try-catch statement around the call to Determinant().

Summary

Math is essential not only to physics modeling, but also to 3-D graphics. Actually, math makes up a big chunk of the game's code. This chapter presented a discussion of geometry, coordinate systems, vectors, and matrices. The math engine developed in this chapter is a good start with functionality for vectors and matrices in two and three dimensions. Of course, I'll be adding more to it as we progress and need more mathematics.

In the next chapter, you'll use some of this to actually put some stuff on the screen.

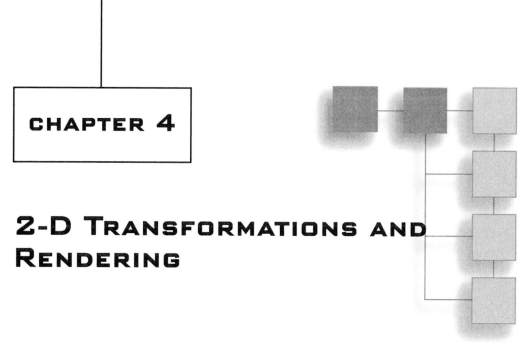

CHAPTER 4

2-D Transformations and Rendering

In Chapter 3, "Mathematical Tools for Physics and 3-D Programming," you waded through a pretty fair amount of math. This chapter shows you how to use that math for both computer graphics and physics.

2-D Transformations

Suppose that someone gave you a vector and told you the components of that vector in some coordinate system. How would you convert that vector to another coordinate system?

That's what a transformation is for. A *transformation* defines the conversion from one coordinate system to another. Transformations are usually written as capital letters. If T is the transformation, I might say that operating T on the vector **x**, which is written as T**x**, returns the components of **x** in a new coordinate system.

Say that you found an ancient map that revealed the location of an enchanted desert isle 120 miles north and 750 miles west of your location. The map was drawn using a compass and dead-reckoning, so the direction for north is magnetic north, and west is perpendicular to magnetic north. However, your GPS uses geographic north, which uses the axis of rotation of the Earth, as shown in Figure 4.1.

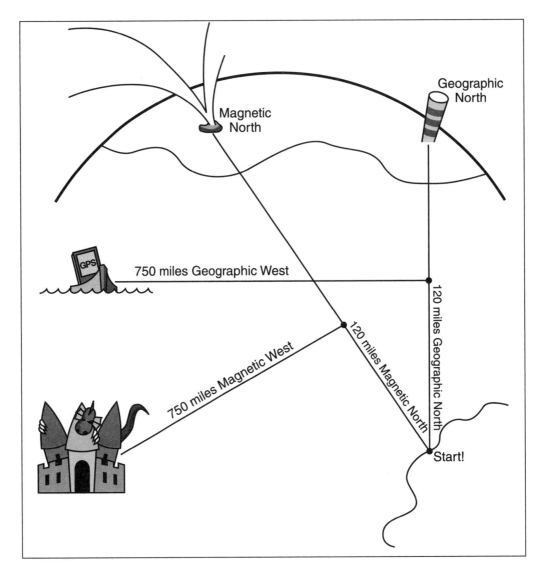

Figure 4.1
The difference between magnetic north and geographic north can cause problems in finding enchanted isles.

You'll have to find some way to convert the directions given in the magnetic north system to your coordinate system using geographic north.

Active Versus Passive Transformations

A transformation that changes the coordinate system is called a *passive transformation* because all the objects in the coordinate system are left alone. The other (opposite) kind of transformation is an *active transformation*. An active transformation leaves the coordinate system alone but changes the vectors (or whatever else is in the coordinate system).

Passive transformations are good for running around the corridors of a first-person-shooter game, such as *Quake*. The environment stays more or less the same, but I'm moving around in it and changing the coordinate system by which it's rendered.

Another way to say this is that, with passive transformations, the character that is representing you in a game never moves. You stay at the center of your world. When you walk, jump, swim, and so forth, the world moves around you, but you don't move. Most 3-D games use this technique.

Active transformations are good for objects moving around in a coordinate system, such as in a spaceship fighting game. If you're piloting the ship in the game, as in the old *Wing Commander* series, your view (your coordinate system) is fixed, but the ships attacking you are flying around everywhere. The program moves them with active transformations.

In any real game, you have to consider both kinds of transformations. Sure, you're running around the corridors in *Quake* (passive), but there are also things running around the corridors after you (active).

Here's the kicker: Active and passive transformations are just two ways of seeing the same thing. If a spaceship passes you in space from left to right, was it moving past you, or were you moving past it? An object that is actively transported to the left is the same as passively transforming the coordinate system to the right.

In this book, we're talking about physics. That means, at least for the next several chapters, that we're going to be discussing things moving around, so it will be convenient to talk about transformations in the active mode for the most part.

Computer graphics make heavy use of matrix transformations. Most of the objects that you see in games are defined as collections of points. To get the objects to move, look like they are close up, or look like they are far away, you use matrix transformations.

Physics also makes use of matrix transformations. The physics that you simulate in games is typically a simulation of the forces that are acting on objects. Those forces are usually represented as vectors in the coordinate system. Programmers generally use matrix transformations to move, rotate, or scale a force vector.

The fundamental matrix transformations are translation, rotation, and scaling. Let's take a closer look at each of these.

Translation

Translation matrices move stuff defined in coordinate systems (points, objects, force vectors, and so forth) from one place to another. You can see how translation works in Figure 4.2.

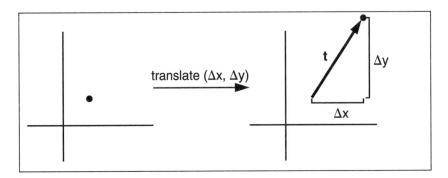

Figure 4.2
Translation of a point.

Translation is pretty easy to accomplish. Say that you want to move a point, called p, over a distance, Δx, on the x axis and up a distance, Δy, on the y axis. You can write this as a displacement vector, **t**, with components $(\Delta x, \Delta y)$. If the vector **v** is a displacement vector to your point (x, y), you can get the translated point by adding **t** to **v**.

$$\mathbf{p'} = \mathbf{v} + \mathbf{t}$$
$$p'_x = v_x + t_x$$
$$p'_y = v_y + t_y$$

The capital delta, Δ, usually means "a change in," so Δx can be thought of as a change in x. If **p** had components (x,y) before translating, then after translation, **p'** would have components $(x + \Delta x, y + \Delta y)$.

warning

When I say "up" on the y axis, I mean in the direction in which y is increasing. Be careful: In 3-D graphics, the y axis might be pointed anywhere. When you're referencing points directly on a window, the upper-left corner is the (0,0) point, which means y increasing actually points down on the screen.

What if you want the inverse transformation? That is, what if you want to translate back to the original position? It's easy. All you do is subtract that same vector **t**, and you're back to where you started.

Rotation

Just as you can translate a point from any location in a coordinate system to any other location, you can also rotate any point around any other point. However, instead of leaping into rotation of a point around an arbitrary point, let's first think about rotation around the origin, as shown in Figure 4.3. Here the point stays the same distance from the origin, but it rotates around it by the angle θ.

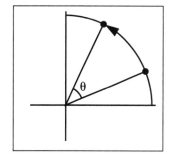

The question is this: Given a point with displacement vector **x**, rotated around the origin by an angle θ, what is the displacement vector of the point's new position? Look at Figure 4.4, which shows **x**, the angle between the two points θ, and the point at its new location. The translated point is called x', and it has the components (x', y'). I've also indicated ϕ, the angle from the x coordinate axis to the original point, **x**, and the radius, r.

Figure 4.3
Rotation of a point around the origin.

note

> Mathematicians usually like their positive angles going counterclockwise, as shown in Figure 4.4.

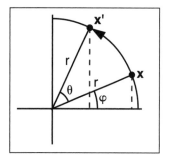

From Figure 4.4, the components of the original point are as follows:

$$x = r\cos(\varphi)$$
$$y = r\sin(\varphi)$$

and the components of the rotated point are these:

$$x' = r\cos(\varphi + \theta)$$
$$y' = r\sin(\varphi + \theta)$$

Figure 4.4
Displacement angles in a rotation.

Now what we need is a way to define the new coordinates in terms of the old ones and the rotation angle. There's a set of trigonometric identities that help us do that. Here they are:

$$\sin(a+b) = \sin(a)\cos(b) + \cos(a)\sin(b)$$
$$\cos(a+b) = \cos(a)\cos(b) - \sin(a)\sin(b)$$
$$\sin(a-b) = \sin(a)\cos(b) - \cos(a)\sin(b)$$
$$\cos(a-b) = \cos(a)\cos(b) + \sin(a)\sin(b)$$
$$\sin(-a) = -\sin(a)$$
$$\cos(-a) = \cos(a)$$
$$\cos^2(a) + \sin^2(a) = 1$$

Using these trigonometric identities, we can massage the formulas a bit:

$$x' = r(\cos(\varphi)\cos(\theta) - \sin(\varphi)\sin(\theta))$$
$$y' = r(\sin(\varphi)\cos(\theta) - \cos(\varphi)\sin(\theta))$$

Substituting the first two equations for x and y gives this:

$$x' = x\cos(\theta) - y\sin(\theta)$$
$$y' = y\cos(\theta) + x\sin(\theta)$$

That's exactly what we needed: the new coordinates in terms of the old ones and the rotation angle. This gives an easy way to calculate the coordinates of x'. However, it's even more convenient to write this as a matrix. If you define a matrix with the following components:

$$R = \begin{bmatrix} \cos(-\theta) & \sin(-\theta) \\ -\sin(-\theta) & \cos(-\theta) \end{bmatrix} = \begin{bmatrix} \cos(\theta) & -\sin(\theta) \\ \sin(\theta) & \cos(\theta) \end{bmatrix}$$

you can do the same rotation by multiplying the components of the vector **x** by R. Therefore, you could write this:

$$x' = xR$$

Or, in terms of components

$$\begin{bmatrix} x' & y' \end{bmatrix} = \begin{bmatrix} x & y \end{bmatrix} \begin{bmatrix} \cos(\theta) & \sin(\theta) \\ -\sin(\theta) & \cos(\theta) \end{bmatrix}$$

The Inverse Rotation

What about the inverse transformation? Because the rotation is a matrix, you could just find the inverse matrix using one of the standard tricks, such as the Inverse() method, in the math engine. That works, but let's think about what the rotation matrix R means for a moment.

The rotation matrix rotates the point by an angle θ. To return it to its original location, you'll have to rotate it back by that same angle θ. So the inverse matrix must be the rotation matrix, except with the angle −θ instead of θ.

$$R = \begin{bmatrix} \cos(-\theta) & \sin(-\theta) \\ -\sin(-\theta) & \cos(-\theta) \end{bmatrix} = \begin{bmatrix} \cos(\theta) & -\sin(\theta) \\ \sin(\theta) & \cos(\theta) \end{bmatrix}$$

Look at the simplified components of the inverse matrix. That matrix looks pretty similar to the rotation matrix, R, just varying by the negative signs on the sine functions. In fact, you can find one from the other by taking the transpose.

$$R^{-1} = R^{T}$$

A matrix whose inverse is equal to its transpose is called an *orthogonal matrix.* Orthogonal matrices are nice for computer games because taking the transpose is a much faster operation than taking the inverse by a general method. Taking the transpose is also a lot faster than trying to calculate those trigonometric functions again. When you do actually have to calculate trigonometric functions, consider using a look-up table to speed things up.

Rotating Around an Arbitrary Point

What if you want to rotate around a point other than the origin? If you're doing computer graphics, you'll probably want to do this fairly often; you'll want to rotate your models around their own centers rather than at the center of the coordinate system.

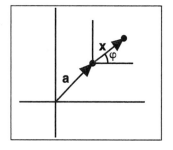

Figure 4.5
Step 1: Translating a rotation axis to the origin.

To do this, you first translate the point around which you want to rotate (the axis of rotation) to the origin, as shown in Figure 4.5.

If the vector **a** is the displacement vector from the origin of the coordinate system to the axis of rotation, and **x** is the displacement vector from the axis of rotation to the point being rotated, then the first step in rotating the point is to move the axis of rotation to the origin with the following formula:

$$\mathbf{x} - \mathbf{a}$$

This moves the point to be rotated into a position such that it will be rotated around the origin of the coordinate system. Now you can perform the next step, which is to rotate the resulting vector using the rotation matrix R, as shown in Figure 4.6. Combining this second step with the first results in this:

$$(\mathbf{x} - \mathbf{a})R$$

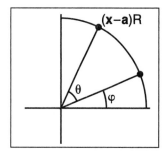

Figure 4.6
Step 2: Rotating the translated point around the origin.

Finally, you can translate the axis of rotation (and, consequently, the point being rotated) back to its original location by adding the vector **a**. This step is shown in Figure 4.7. Here's the final equation for the point rotating around the rotation axis **a**.

$$\mathbf{x}' = (\mathbf{x} - \mathbf{a})R + \mathbf{a}$$

That's all it takes to rotate any point around any other point.

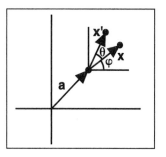

Figure 4.7
Step 3: Translating the rotation axis back to its original location.

Scaling

Scaling means changing the size of something. Scaling is much easier to accomplish than rotating. All you have to do is multiply each of the elements by a scalar. For example, to scale a vector **x**, use the following equation:

$$\mathbf{x}' = s\mathbf{x}$$

It's a little hard to see the effect of this with just one point, so Figure 4.8 shows the result of scaling several points around an axis by a factor of 2.

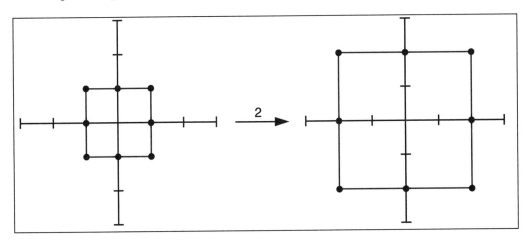

Figure 4.8
Scaling points by a factor of 2.

This is why regular numbers are called *scalars* in the context of vectors and matrices. They are actually representations of the scaling transformation.

The Matrix Representation of Scaling

You can also write a scaling transformation as a matrix. Remember the identity matrix, I, such that IA = AI = A? This has a similar effect on the coordinates of a vector: I**x** = **x**I = **x**.

$$\mathbf{x}' = s\mathbf{x} = \mathbf{x}s = (\mathbf{x}I)s = \mathbf{x}(sI) = \mathbf{x}S$$

where S is the transformation whose matrix representation is the scalar times the unit vector, sI. Here's the matrix S in components:

$$S = \begin{bmatrix} s & 0 \\ 0 & s \end{bmatrix}$$

The matrix form suggests a generalization of the scaling matrix. What if the two diagonal entries were different? That would be okay. It would just mean that we were scaling x and y values by different amounts. In that case, we would use the following scaling matrix:

$$S = \begin{bmatrix} s_x & 0 \\ 0 & s_y \end{bmatrix}$$

In components, that's

$$x' = s_x x$$
$$y' = s_y y$$

For example, this matrix

$$S = \begin{bmatrix} 4 & 0 \\ 0 & 2 \end{bmatrix}$$

would double the distances along the y axis but quadruple those on the x axis, as shown in Figure 4.9.

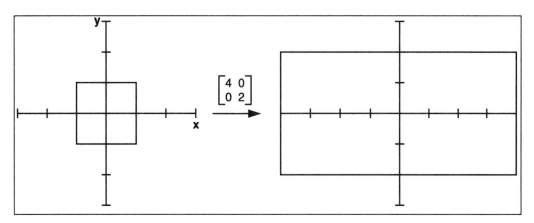

Figure 4.9
Effect of the scaling transformation with $s_x = 4$ and $s_y = 2$.

If multiplying by 3 triples the size, then dividing by 3 must third the size. Thus, the inverse of the scaling matrix is this:

$$S^{-1} = \begin{bmatrix} \dfrac{1}{s_x} & 0 \\ 0 & \dfrac{1}{s_y} \end{bmatrix}$$

Let's try it out.

$$SS^{-1} = \begin{bmatrix} s_x & 0 \\ 0 & s_y \end{bmatrix} \begin{bmatrix} \dfrac{1}{s_x} & 0 \\ 0 & \dfrac{1}{s_y} \end{bmatrix} = \begin{bmatrix} 1 & 0 \\ 0 & 1 \end{bmatrix} = I$$

Multiplying the scaling matrix by its inverse gives the identity matrix. That shows that they are, indeed, inverses of each other.

Scaling About an Arbitrary Point

Scaling expands or contracts the distances between points, but it has to expand from some origin. Imagine an expanding sphere. Points on the outside of the sphere move out quickly, but points close to the middle move out more slowly. The point in the center of the sphere doesn't move at all. This point is the *expansion point*.

Just as you would usually like to apply a rotation to the center of a 2-D object, you'll also usually want to expand an object from its center. You accomplish that in the same way that you do a rotation about an arbitrary point.

First, you translate the expansion point to the origin. Then you apply the scaling transformation. After that, you translate the expansion point back to its original location. In equations, it looks like this:

$$\mathbf{x'} = (\mathbf{x} - \mathbf{a})S + \mathbf{a}$$

where $\mathbf{x}$ is the original position of the point, $\mathbf{x'}$ is the scaled position of the point, $\mathbf{a}$ is the location of the expansion point, and S is the scaling transformation.

Combining Transformations

You can combine transformations to create new transformations. Actually, you already saw how to do it. Whenever you rotate or scale about an arbitrary point, you have to move the rotation or scaling axis to the center of the coordinate system, perform the operation, and then move the axis back. That's actually three transformations combined into one.

You can combine two rotation matrices to produce another rotation, as shown in Figure 4.10. Suppose that you have two rotations you want to perform. Let's call them R_1 and R_2. Imagine that $R_1\theta = 45°$ and $R_2 \theta = 30°$. You can combine these rotations by adding the angles. The product, R_1R_2, is a 45° rotation followed by a 30° rotation, so $R_1R_2 = R_3$ ($\theta = 75°$).

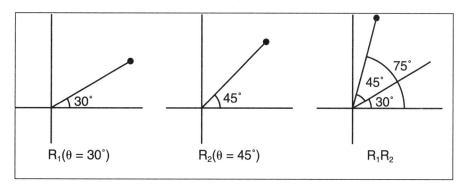

Figure 4.10
Combining rotations.

If you're expressing this in terms of matrices, you create a rotation matrix for each rotation. Next, you multiply the rotation matrices. When you then multiply the point to be rotated with the combined rotation matrix, it gives you the new location of the point. Going to all the trouble to use matrix multiplications doesn't make much sense in 2-D. However, when we get to 3-D, it will quickly become clear why all games use this method to perform their rotations.

You can combine scaling transformations the same way. If you scale something by a factor of 2 and then scale it again by a factor of 3, the object is scaled by a factor of 6. In other words, if $S_1 = 2I$ and $S_2 = 3I$, $S_1S_2 = 6I$. This is illustrated in Figure 4.11.

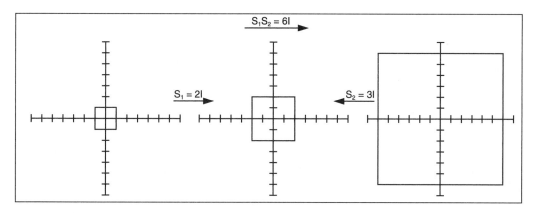

Figure 4.11
Combining scaling transformations.

You can also combine rotation and scaling. Suppose that RS is a rotation followed by a scaling. SR is a scaling followed by a rotation. Although the order of successive rotations or successive scalings doesn't matter in two dimensions, the order of combined rotations and scalings can matter if $s_x \neq s_y$ for the scaling transformation. As an example, look at Figure 4.12, where the transformations use an angle of 45° and a scaling of 4 in the x direction and 1 in the y direction. The resulting equations are as follows:

$$R = \begin{bmatrix} \cos(45) & \sin(45) \\ -\sin(45) & \cos(45) \end{bmatrix}$$

$$S = \begin{bmatrix} 4 & 0 \\ 0 & 1 \end{bmatrix}$$

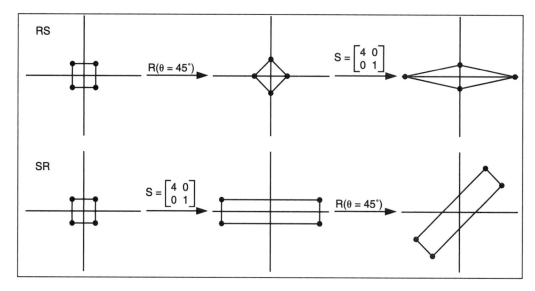

Figure 4.12
RS versus SR.

A rotation followed by this scaling and the scaling followed by the rotation give completely different results. In general, the order of transformations is important.

Implementing Transformations: Spinning a Triangle

To see how all this works, let's use the physics modeling framework introduced in Chapter 2, "Simulating 3-D with DirectX," to write a sample program. The sample will display a triangle in an xy plane. It will rotate the triangle around the origin by building and applying transformation matrices.

Using the Physics Modeling Framework

The physics modeling framework simplifies the process of getting Direct3D running for you. However, that doesn't mean it's all automatic. In particular, you have to create a project for the sample program in Visual Studio and then set the configuration options. Next, you add the functions that the framework requires.

Creating the Project

If you're doing the programming as you read through this book (which is what I recommend), you need to create a project for the sample program. The way you do that depends on the version of Visual Studio that you use. If, for instance, you have Visual Studio 7, you can use the following procedure to create a project:

1. If Visual Studio is not running, start it now. It probably displays the Start page when you run the program.

2. If you see the Start page, click the New Project button. If not, choose File from the main menu, and then click New. Now select Project.

3. At this point, you should see the New Project dialog box. In the Project Types list on the left side of the dialog box, click Visual C++ Projects.

4. In the Templates list on the right side of the dialog box, choose Win32 Project. Do not select DirectX 9 Visual C++ Wizard if you're planning to use the physics modeling framework.

5. Type the name and location (folder name) for the project. For this sample program, use the name TriSpin. Click OK.

6. In the Win32 Application Wizard, click on Application Settings. In the Application Settings tab, put a check in the check box next to the label Empty Project. This creates a bare-bones Windows program with no extra garbage that might slow down your program. Click the Finish button, and you're done.

When the Win32 Application Wizard finishes, Visual Studio usually returns to your Start page. You now have a project with no source files in it. Let's fix that by adding the framework files.

1. Copy the files PMD3DApp.h and PMD3DApp.cpp from the CD-ROM that comes with this book. Put them into the directory you just created for your project. The PMD3DApp.h and PMD3DApp.cpp files on the CD-ROM are in the Source\Chapter 4\TriSpin folder.

2. In Visual Studio, go to the Solution Explorer, point your mouse cursor at the Source Files item, and click the mouse's secondary button. The secondary button is the one under your middle finger. For right-handed people, it's the right button. If you're using the mouse left-handed, the secondary button is the left button.

3. In the menu that appears, choose Add. Then click Add Existing Item.

4. Visual Studio displays the Add Existing Item dialog box. Select PMD3DApp.cpp, and then click Open.

Now the framework is added to the project. If you want, you can use essentially the same procedure to add the file PMD3DApp.h to the Header Files item in the Source Explorer. It's not strictly necessary, but it's a good idea.

Configuring the Project

To make this generic Windows program into a DirectX application, you need to add some information to the project's configuration. First, you must add the folder containing the DirectX library files.

1. In Visual Studio, go to the Solution Explorer and point your mouse cursor at the name of the project. If you use the suggested name, it is TriSpin. Click the secondary button. In the menu that appears, choose Properties.

2. Visual Studio displays the Property Pages dialog box. In the list on the left side of the dialog box, click the Linker folder and then choose General.

3. In the list of properties, select the box to the right of Additional Library Directories. Then type the following:

    ```
    <d>:\<DXSDKDIR>\Lib
    ```

    where <d>: is the drive where you installed the DirectX SDK and <DXSDKDIR> is the directory or folder that contains the DirectX SDK.

4. In the list along the left side of the Property Pages dialog box, select Input.

5. Visual Studio displays another list of properties. One of them is called Additional Dependencies. In the box to the right of Additional Dependencies, enter the following text:

    ```
    d3dxof.lib dxguid.lib d3dx9dt.lib d3d9.lib winmm.lib  kernel32.lib user32.lib
    gdi32.lib winspool.lib
       comdlg32.lib advapi32.lib shell32.lib ole32.lib oleaut32.lib uuid.lib odbc32.lib
       odbccp32.lib
    ```

    Then click OK.

You can avoid typing all of that text in step 5 by copying and pasting it. I've provided the text for you on the CD-ROM in the Source folder. It's in a file called AdditionalDependencies.txt.

Adding the Required Functions

The final step in preparing to write the sample program is to add a file to the project that contains the functions that the physics modeling framework requires:

1. Copy the file FrameFns.cpp from the CD-ROM that comes with this book. You'll find it in the Source folder.

2. Rename the FrameFns.cpp as appropriate for your project. For this sample program, name it TriSpin.cpp.

You're now ready to start writing code.

Setting Up the Geometry

Objects in computer graphics that you see on the screen are usually defined in programs as sets of points. Each point contains a pair of x,y coordinates if you're doing 2-D graphics. In 3-D graphics, each point is defined by a set of x,y,z coordinates. The coordinate points that define objects are called *vertices*. For this sample application to display a spinning triangle, it must define both the triangle and its vertices.

Direct3D uses what Microsoft calls its *flexible vertex format*. The flexible vertex format enables you to define nearly any vertex type (within certain limits) that your application needs. A simple shape, such as a triangle, needs only a basic vertex format with some components and a color. A complex 3-D game's vertices might also have information about the normal, the material, and the texture.

Transformed and Untransformed Vertices

You can go about rendering in Direct3D in two ways. You can do the transformations yourself and then feed the Direct3D device the vertices to render directly to the screen. Or, you can tell Direct3D the transformations to apply and then feed the device the untransformed vertices of your object. Direct3D then transforms the vertices with the transformations you supplied and renders them to the screen.

There is one weird artifact left from Microsoft's insistence in Direct3D that all games be 3-D: The only *transformed* vertex format is D3DFVF_XYZRHW. It has four components: x, y, z, and w. For now, I'll just be setting the z component to 0 and the w component to 1 so that we can concentrate on 2-D graphics.

Listing 4.1 shows the vertex format that the spinning triangle program uses.

Listing 4.1
The Vertex Structure for the Spinning Triangle Program

```
1    struct vertex
2    {
3        FLOAT x,y,z;      // The untransformed, 3-D position for the vertex
4        DWORD color;      // The vertex color
5    };
```

The vertex type defined in Listing 4.1 contains members for storing the x, y, and z values of the vertex's location. It also has a member for defining a color for the vertex. When Direct3D displays shapes using this vertex type, it blends the colors from vertex to vertex. For instance, we'll see shortly that the spinning triangle program sets each vertex in the triangle to a different color. One of those colors is red, and another is blue. For each pixel in the triangle between the red and blue vertices, Direct3D determines the color of the pixel by blending the two vertex colors. Pixels closer to the red vertex have more red in their colors. Pixels closer to the blue vertex have more blue in their colors.

To get Direct3D to blend the vertex colors, the program has to tell Direct3D what the vertex contains. It does this with a set of flexible vertex format flags. All the flags start with D3DFVF_, followed by a specifier describing the vertex format. The spinning triangle program uses a vertex with an (x, y, z) coordinate and color information. The flags have to tell Direct3D that. The particular flags that the spinning triangle program uses are D3DFVF_XYZ and D3DFVF_DIFFUSE. For more information on these flags, see the topic "D3DFVF" in the DirectX 9.0 documentation.

To make these flags easier to work with, the spinning triangle program defines a constant that combines them. Here's what the definition looks like:

```
#define VERTEX_TYPE_SPECIFIER (D3DFVF_XYZ|D3DFVF_DIFFUSE)
```

The spinning triangle program uses the vertex type and the vertex specifier flags in its GameInitialization() function. You'll find this function in the file TriSpin.cpp. TriSpin.cpp is in the folder Source\Chapter04\TriSpin on the CD-ROM that comes with this book.

Listing 4.2
The GameInitialization() Function

```
1      bool GameInitialization()
2      {
3          // Initialize three vertices for a triangle.
4          vertex theVerteces[] =
5          {
6              { -1.0f,-1.0f,0.0f,0xffff0000,},
7              {  1.0f,-1.0f,0.0f,0xff0000ff,},
8              {  0.0f,1.0f,0.0f,0xffffffff,},
9          };
10
11         LPDIRECT3DVERTEXBUFFER9 tempPointer=NULL;
12         // Create the vertex buffer.
13         // If it can't be created...
```

```
14          if(FAILED(
15              theApp.D3DRenderingDevice()->CreateVertexBuffer(
16                  3*sizeof(vertex),
17                  0,VERTEX_TYPE_SPECIFIER,
18                  D3DPOOL_DEFAULT,&tempPointer,NULL)))
19          {
20              // The sample can't be run.
21              return false;
22          }
23          else
24          {
25              /* Save a pointer to the vertex buffer in the global app
26              variable. */
27              theApp.D3DVertexBuffer(tempPointer);
28          }
29
30          //
31          // Fill the vertex buffer.
32          //
33          VOID* tempBufferPointer;
34          // Lock it first.
35          if(FAILED(
36              theApp.D3DVertexBuffer()->Lock(
37                  0,3*sizeof(vertex),
38                  (void**)&tempBufferPointer,0)))
39          {
40              return false;
41          }
42          // Copy the vertices into the vertex buffer.
43          memcpy(tempBufferPointer,theVerteces,3*sizeof(vertex));
44          // Now unlock the vertex buffer.
45          theApp.D3DVertexBuffer()->Unlock();
46
47          return (true);
48      }
```

When the spinning triangle program loads, the framework calls the GameInitialization()
function. The GameInitialization() function begins by declaring an array of three vertices
for the triangle. In the declaration, it initializes the position and color of each vertex. You'll
see the code for this on lines 4–9 of Listing 4.2.

note

Using statically allocated arrays to hold the vertices is hardly the most efficient use of memory possible. You could use dynamically allocated arrays, but doing so increases the complexity of the algorithms. Here, we're worried only about putting a small 2-D triangle on the screen. Memory is not a problem, so I opted for readability and visibility. This is often a good tradeoff in game programming, where you need to manipulate data quickly.

You can perform many of the operations that Direct3D is capable of with vertex buffers. A vertex buffer is a chunk of system or graphics memory that is used for batch processing of vertices. The idea is that you fill up the vertex buffer with vertices and then call a function that takes those vertices and does something with them, such as translate, rotate, or draw them.

The vertex buffer in Direct3D is also a COM object. When your program uses a vertex buffer, it must go through the same procedure required for every COM object.

1. Declare a variable to hold the pointer to the object interface. Set it initially to NULL.

2. Call a function to create the vertex buffer.

The program creates a vertex buffer by calling the Direct3D CreateVertexBuffer() function on lines 14–18. Notice that the call to CreateVertexBuffer() uses the VERTEX_TYPE_SPECIFIER constant that the program defined earlier.

If the program successfully creates the vertex buffer, it saves a pointer to the buffer in the d3d_app object on line 27. Next, it fills the vertex buffer. To do so, it must first lock the buffer so that it has sole access. This is necessary when performing most types of operations on vertex buffers.

If the vertex buffer can be locked, the GameInitialization() function copies the vertices into the vertex buffer on line 43 of Listing 4.2. It then unlocks the vertex buffer.

Updating Frames

After the spinning triangle program performs the initialization of the geometry (triangle) it's going to display, it begins handling incoming messages. It also updates frames and renders them to the screen. The spinning triangle program is so simple that we don't need to add more message handling than the framework already provides. However, we do need to tell it how to update each frame. This is handled in the UpdateFrame() function, which is given in Listing 4.3.

Listing 4.3
The UpdateFrame() Function

```
1    bool UpdateFrame()
2    {
```

```
3          D3DXMATRIXA16 worldMatrix;
4
5          UINT  currentTime  = timeGetTime() % 1000;
6          FLOAT rotationAngle = currentTime * (2.0f * D3DX_PI) / 1000.0f;
7          D3DXMatrixRotationZ(&worldMatrix,rotationAngle);
8          theApp.D3DRenderingDevice()->SetTransform(D3DTS_WORLD,&worldMatrix);
9
10         D3DXVECTOR3 eyePoint(0.0f,3.0f,-5.0f);
11         D3DXVECTOR3 lookatPoint(0.0f,0.0f,0.0f);
12         D3DXVECTOR3 upDirection(0.0f,1.0f,0.0f);
13         D3DXMATRIXA16 viewMatrix;
14         D3DXMatrixLookAtLH(&viewMatrix,&eyePoint,&lookatPoint,&upDirection);
15         theApp.D3DRenderingDevice()->SetTransform(D3DTS_VIEW,&viewMatrix);
16
17         D3DXMATRIXA16 projectionMatrix;
18         D3DXMatrixPerspectiveFovLH(
19              &projectionMatrix,D3DX_PI/4,1.0f,1.0f,100.0f);
20         theApp.D3DRenderingDevice()->SetTransform(
21              D3DTS_PROJECTION,&projectionMatrix);
22
23         return (true);
24    }
```

Each time the framework calls the UpdateFrame() function, UpdateFrame() sets the angle of rotation. Using this angle, it builds a rotation matrix, as shown on line 7 of Listing 4.3. The UpdateFrame() function then sets that matrix as the world transformation matrix on line 8.

World matrix? What's a world matrix?

In 3-D programming, the viewer doesn't really move through the world. In actuality, the world moves around the viewer. To move the view forward, the program translates the world backward.

So what's that got to do with the triangle?

The TriSpin program calls the Direct3D helper function D3DXMatrixRotationZ() to build a rotation matrix that rotates the triangle in the xy plane. It stores the rotation matrix in the world matrix. Direct3D then uses that world matrix to rotate every vertex in the world. In the world of the TriSpin program, there are only three vertices—the ones that make up the triangle. Therefore, the entire world (one triangle) rotates around in the xy plane.

In addition to the world matrix, the UpdateFrame() function sets the view and projection matrices. The view matrix sets the position of the viewer in the 3-D world. To build the view matrix, the program uses the Direct3D helper function D3DXMatrixLookAtLH(). This function builds a view matrix in a left-handed coordinate system, which is what Direct3D uses.

The projection matrix adds perspective to scenes so that objects that are farther away look smaller. Because we're doing 2-D in this chapter, we don't need to worry about perspective. However, we still have to set the projection matrix. We do that by calling the D3DXMatrixPerspectiveFovLH() function.

note

> If you look at the TriSpin.cpp file on the CD-ROM, you'll notice that the UpdateFrame() function contains a lot of comments that are not shown in Listing 4.3. The code on the disk is heavily commented. However, in most cases, I delete the comments to save space on the printed pages of this book. If you want more information about a particular function presented in the book, it's a good idea to check the code on the CD-ROM for comments that don't appear in the book's code listings.

Rendering Frames

To render the triangle, the framework calls the RenderFrame() function. RenderFrame() must do three things to get the triangle on the screen:

1. Set the source stream that Direct3D renders from.

2. Specify the vertex format.

3. Render the triangle.

The code for the RenderFrame() function appears in Listing 4.4.

Listing 4.4
The RenderFrame() Function

```
1     bool RenderFrame()
2     {
3         // Render the vertex buffer contents.
4         theApp.D3DRenderingDevice()->SetStreamSource(
5             0,theApp.D3DVertexBuffer(),0,sizeof(vertex));
6         theApp.D3DRenderingDevice()->SetFVF(VERTEX_TYPE_SPECIFIER);
7         theApp.D3DRenderingDevice()->DrawPrimitive(D3DPT_TRIANGLESTRIP,0,1);
8
9         return (true);
10    }
```

Direct3D uses rendering streams when you draw with vertex buffers. Lines 4–5 of Listing 4.4 set the vertex buffer created in the GameInitialization() function as the source rendering stream. To parse and draw the contents of the stream, Direct3D must know the format of the vertices. This is set on line 6.

Line 7 of Listing 4.4 calls the Direct3D DrawPrimitive() function to actually do the drawing. It draws the triangle as a group of connected triangles. Drawing objects as triangle strips is a common way to render them. The vertices of most 3-D objects are typically defined as vertices of triangles. Objects in 3-D worlds are often thought of as collections of triangles.

Putting It All Together

To build and run this program, use the following procedure:

1. Start by creating a project for it, as discussed in "Creating the Project" earlier in this chapter.

2. Configure the project, as presented in "Configuring the Project" earlier in this chapter.

3. Copy the program's files from the CD-ROM into the project folder you just created. You'll find the files in the Source\Chapter4\TriSpin folder. The files you need to copy are TriSpin.cpp, PMD3DApp.h, and PMD3DApp.cpp.

4. In Visual Studio's Solution Explorer, click the mouse's secondary button on the project's Source Files folder. The secondary button is the right button if you're right handed. If you're using the mouse left handed, it's the left button.

5. In the menu that appears, select Add, and then click Add Existing Item. Add the files you copied in step 3.

6. Press F5 to build and run the program.

If you just want to see the program in action, you'll find an executable version of it on the CD-ROM. It's in the Source\Chapter04\Bin folder.

Summary

We've come a long way in this chapter. Starting from elementary notions about matrices and vectors, we derived transformations for rotation, scaling, and translation. We combined those transformations to rotate or scale around arbitrary points.

We also created and rendered a simple object. We convinced it to move and rotate around a window by using the transformations. In the next chapter, we'll see how to do it all again in 3-D.

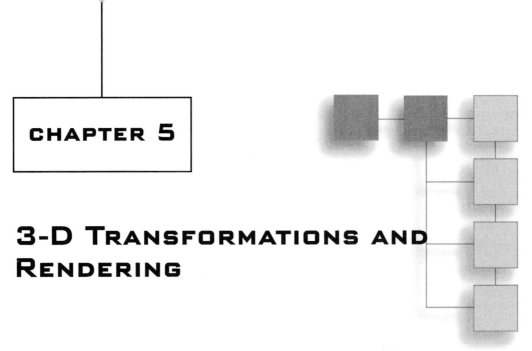

CHAPTER 5

3-D Transformations and Rendering

In this chapter, you'll move from working in 2-D to working in 3-D. The chapter explains how to do all of the transformations from Chapter 4, "2-D Transformations and Rendering," in 3-D. The process is more complex in 3-D for a variety of reasons. One of the most important is that you have to add perspective to a 3-D scene so that objects that are far away from the viewer look smaller than objects that are close. As you read through this chapter, you'll see how adding perspective affects the process of rendering.

This chapter also demonstrates how to set 3-D models of objects into a world coordinate system and render them. In the process, you'll apply the math that you picked up in earlier chapters.

3-D Transformations

From a mathematical point of view, it isn't too hard to generalize transformations to three dimensions. Recall that you can use a vector to specify any point in a coordinate system. You can treat vectors as matrices, which means you can multiply vectors and matrices to transform the vectors. So, mathematically speaking, moving from 2-D to 3-D is mostly a matter of adding a dimension to the appropriate vectors and matrices.

There is just one minor hitch. To make the process of multiplying vectors and matrices work correctly, you have to use homogenous coordinates.

Homogenous Coordinates

Homogenous coordinates add one extra dimension to the points, vectors, and matrices that your game uses. As a result, the program has to perform extra calculations. So why use them?

If your game uses homogenous coordinates, it can multiply vectors by transformation matrices in a uniform way. It also can concatenate transformation matrices by multiplying them into one resulting matrix.

To use homogeneous coordinates in 3-D, you must add one more coordinate component to every vertex in your program. So, instead of having points defined with x, y, and z coordinate components, you need to define the points with x, y, z, and w coordinate components. The w component is the reciprocal homogeneous w. Its sole purpose is to enable you to express transformations as matrices. We'll set the w coordinate to 1. It can be set to other values. However, we won't need to do that in this book.

Does this mean that you must append a 1 onto the end of every coordinate that you define?

Fortunately, the answer is no. Direct3D makes this pretty much invisible to you as the programmer. You set up your vertices with x, y, and z components. Direct3D provides functions to build transformation matrices based on homogenous coordinates. When you tell Direct3D to perform the transformation, it automatically converts your x, y, and z coordinates to x, y, z, and w coordinates, and it multiplies those with the transformation matrix.

If Direct3D handles everything automatically, why even bother talking about it?

In the next section, you'll learn how the mathematics of 3-D transformations works. That math requires the use of homogeneous coordinates.

Translations

You translate a vector in three dimensions in essentially the same way that you do it in two dimensions: by adding a displacement vector **t** representing the translation.

$$\mathbf{x}' = \mathbf{x} + \mathbf{t}$$

If you flip back to Chapter 4, you'll see that this is *exactly* the same equation used there for a translation. The only difference is that here we're going to identify the vectors as 3-D instead of 2-D.

You also use a reciprocal homogeneous w coordinate in 3-D transformations, for a total of 4 components to each vector and 16 to each 4×4 matrix transformation. Here's the matrix representation of the translation transformation:

$$T = \begin{bmatrix} 1 & 0 & 0 & 0 \\ 0 & 1 & 0 & 0 \\ 0 & 0 & 1 & 0 \\ \Delta x & \Delta y & \Delta z & 1 \end{bmatrix}$$

Notice that this is a 4×4 matrix, rather than a 3×3 matrix. The extra row and column are added to accommodate the homogeneous w coordinate. The first three entries in the bottom row contain the x, y, and z components of the translation vector. This is the change in x, y, and z, respectively. that will be applied to one or more vertices.

To translate an object in 3-D space, your game multiplies every vertex in the object by the transformation matrix. This is the same basic process used to transform vertices in 2-D space. The only differences are that a 3-D game uses vertices with 4 coordinate components rather than 2 and 4×4 matrices rather than 2×2 matrices.

The inverse transformation translates a vertex back the other direction:

$$T^{-1} = \begin{bmatrix} 1 & 0 & 0 & 0 \\ 0 & 1 & 0 & 0 \\ 0 & 0 & 1 & 0 \\ -\Delta x & -\Delta y & -\Delta z & 1 \end{bmatrix}$$

Scaling

It's easy to generalize scaling to 3-D. If you're not using homogeneous coordinates, and you're scaling every direction by the same amount (you're just expanding or contracting about a point; you're not squashing something on one axis and stretching it on another), you can still use a scalar, s:

$$x' = sx$$

The matrix form is also generalized pretty quickly. Along with the two scaling values, s_x and s_y, for scaling on the x and y axes, respectively, you have an s_z for scaling on the z axis:

$$S = \begin{bmatrix} s_x & 0 & 0 \\ 0 & s_y & 0 \\ 0 & 0 & s_z \end{bmatrix}$$

With the homogeneous coordinate, it looks like this:

$$S = \begin{bmatrix} s_x & 0 & 0 & 0 \\ 0 & s_y & 0 & 0 \\ 0 & 0 & s_z & 0 \\ 0 & 0 & 0 & 1 \end{bmatrix}$$

The inverse matrix is as follows:

$$S^{-1} = \begin{bmatrix} \dfrac{1}{s_x} & 0 & 0 & 0 \\ 0 & \dfrac{1}{s_y} & 0 & 0 \\ 0 & 0 & \dfrac{1}{s_z} & 0 \\ 0 & 0 & 0 & 1 \end{bmatrix}$$

Rotations

Rotations are a little more difficult to generalize to 3-D. Instead of there being one way to rotate around the origin, there are an infinite number of ways, each corresponding to a different rotation axis through the origin, as shown in Figure 5.1.

It turns out that all the rotations are just the sum of three. You can convince yourself of this by looking at Figure 5.2, which shows three axes for the orientation of an airplane: pitch, yaw, and roll. Not quite any three axes will do (they have to be linearly independent, for you math gurus), but there are still an infinite number of ways to choose these three axes.

This is actually good. It gives you the freedom to choose any linearly independent axes that are convenient at the time.

warning

The direction of rotation along the x, y, and z axes depends on the handedness of the coordinate system. In a right-handed coordinate system, the positive angle is counterclockwise. In a left-handed system, the positive angle is clockwise.

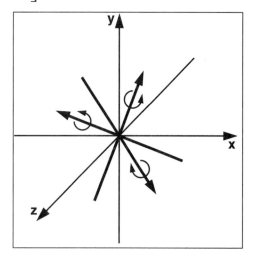

Figure 5.1
An infinite number of spin axes go through the origin in 3-D.

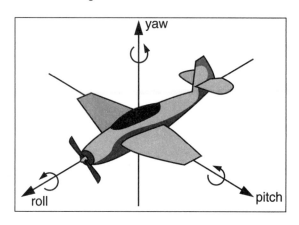

Figure 5.2
The pitch, yaw, and roll of an airplane.

Of course, in trying to convince a computer to do something, too much freedom can be a bad thing. So let's just pick a convenient set of axes to work with: the x, y, and z axes, shown in Figure 5.3.

The axes shown in Figure 5.3 form a right-handed coordinate system.

When we did rotations in 2-D, we were essentially doing rotations around the z axis, as shown in Figure 5.4, so we can get that matrix just by expanding the 2-D version.

$$R_z = \begin{bmatrix} \cos(\theta) & \sin(\theta) & 0 & 0 \\ -\sin(\theta) & \cos(\theta) & 0 & 0 \\ 0 & 0 & 1 & 0 \\ 0 & 0 & 0 & 1 \end{bmatrix}$$

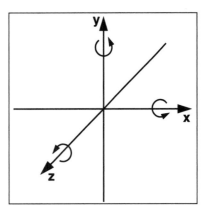

Figure 5.3
The x, y, and z rotation axes.

I'm going to write all the rotation matrices with the w coordinate. To obtain the rotation matrix without it, just get rid of the fourth row and the fourth column.

You can find the other two rotation matrices with trigonometry, as we derived the original rotation matrix.

Here's the rotation matrix about the x axis:

$$R_x = \begin{bmatrix} 1 & 0 & 0 & 0 \\ 0 & \cos(\varphi) & \sin(\varphi) & 0 \\ 0 & -\sin(\varphi) & \cos(\varphi) & 0 \\ 0 & 0 & 0 & 1 \end{bmatrix}$$

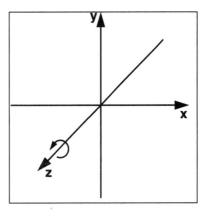

Figure 5.4
Rotations in 2-D are the same as rotations about the z axis in 3-D.

And here's the rotation matrix about the y axis:

$$R_y = \begin{bmatrix} \cos(\alpha) & 0 & -\sin(\alpha) & 0 \\ 0 & 1 & 0 & 0 \\ \sin(\alpha) & 0 & \cos(\alpha) & 0 \\ 0 & 0 & 0 & 1 \end{bmatrix}$$

The choice of θ, ϕ, and α for the angles was arbitrary. I just wanted to make the point that these three angles (and the corresponding rotation matrices) are completely independent.

You can get an arbitrary rotation by combining these three rotations with different amounts, just like the yaw, pitch, and roll can be combined to give any orientation of an airplane. To make things both simple and consistent, we'll always apply rotations in x,y,z order. That is, we'll first rotate around the x axis, then the y axis, and then the z axis. Although this simple rule is arbitrary, using it makes our rotations happen in a predictable and consistent manner.

The Inverse Rotation

You'll be glad to hear that rotation matrices in three dimensions (or any number of dimensions) are equal to the transpose. This makes it easy to write down the inverse rotations:

$$R_z^{-1} = \begin{bmatrix} \cos(\theta) & -\sin(\theta) & 0 & 0 \\ \sin(\theta) & \cos(\theta) & 0 & 0 \\ 0 & 0 & 1 & 0 \\ 0 & 0 & 0 & 1 \end{bmatrix}$$

$$R_x^{-1} = \begin{bmatrix} 1 & 0 & 0 & 0 \\ 0 & \cos(\phi) & -\sin(\phi) & 0 \\ 0 & \sin(\phi) & \cos(\phi) & 0 \\ 0 & 0 & 0 & 1 \end{bmatrix}$$

$$R_y^{-1} = \begin{bmatrix} \cos(\alpha) & 0 & \sin(\alpha) & 0 \\ 0 & 1 & 0 & 0 \\ -\sin(\alpha) & 0 & \cos(\alpha) & 0 \\ 0 & 0 & 0 & 1 \end{bmatrix}$$

If you want to use the inverse matrices to reverse a rotation, you have to be careful about the order of operations. The inverse rotation of $R_x R_y R_z$ is not $R_x^{-1} R_y^{-1} R_z^{-1}$, it's $R_z^{-1} R_y^{-1} R_x^{-1}$. You must apply the inverse rotations in reverse order.

The 3-D Pipeline

The 3-D pipeline is the complete series of transformations you have to go through to get a 3-D model rendered on the screen. Figure 5.5 shows a representation of the 3-D pipeline.

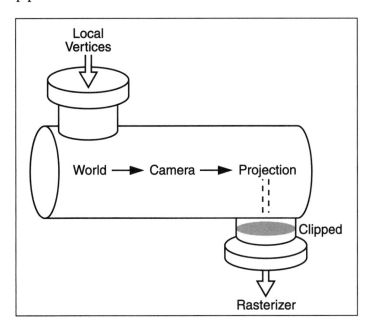

Figure 5.5
The 3-D pipeline.

Let's take a brief look at each stage of the 3-D pipeline.

Local Coordinates to World Coordinates

The objects that go into a 3-D rendering pipeline are usually defined in their own local coordinate system. Because 3-D objects are often referred to as *models*, local coordinates are also called *model coordinates*.

When you insert a model into a 3-D scene, your software must convert its vertices, which are defined in model coordinates, into the scene's coordinate system. The scene's coordinate system is usually called *world coordinates*. Converting from local or model coordinates into world coordinates can involve rotating, scaling, and translation. In the end, you have your object in some 3-D space, as shown in Figure 5.6. In Direct3D, this is called the *world transformation*.

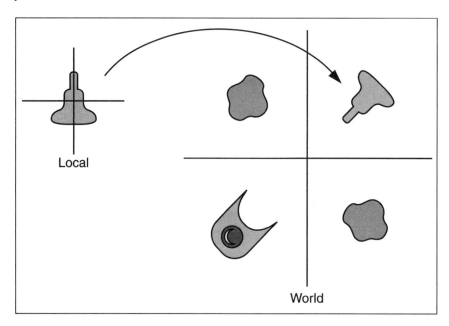

Figure 5.6
The local to world transformation.

As Figure 5.6 shows, the model starts in its own coordinate system. A set of transformations move and rotate the model into place.

World Coordinates to Viewing Coordinates

The next transformation in the pipeline is from the world coordinates to the camera coordinates, which are also called viewing coordinates. Direct3D calls this the view transformation. This transformation picks out an axis lined up nicely with the orientation of the camera. You can think of this transformation as a passive transformation to the coordinate axis local to the camera. It's shown in Figure 5.7.

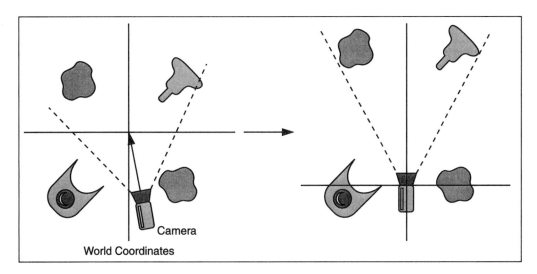

Figure 5.7
The world to camera transformation.

Moving the world to camera coordinates essentially puts the camera at the center of the world. When the game moves the viewer through the world, it actually moves the world around the camera.

Viewing Coordinates to Projection Coordinates

After the scene has been converted to camera coordinates, the 3-D pipeline then converts to a projection coordinate system. This step adds perspective to the scene and sets the field of view. At this point, the pipeline also sets a near and far clip plane. Objects beyond the far clip plane and objects nearer than the near clip plane aren't rendered. Figure 5.8 shows the expanding box, called a *viewing frustum*, that defines the perspective along with the near and far clip planes.

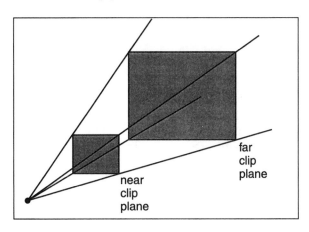

Figure 5.8
The viewing frustum with near and far clip planes.

The viewing frustum is also referred to as the view volume. Any vertices that aren't inside the viewing frustum are clipped.

Projection Coordinates to Screen Coordinates

To display the contents of the viewing frustum on the screen, everything in the frustum is scaled to screen coordinates and drawn to a buffer, called a *back buffer*. The drawing process is called *rasterization*.

Scaling to screen coordinates is necessary because the viewing frustum can be a different shape than the screen. For example, the projection of the viewing frustum onto a 2-D screen might be square. However, it's highly unlikely that the screen is square. Therefore, the pipeline must scale the viewing frustum to fit the screen.

You can spend a lot of time learning about the 3-D pipeline and maybe constructing your own. Some people specialize in it, but most of us don't need to bother. When you're writing a game, you just have to understand the basics of how the pipeline works. This gives you enough background to use the Direct3D functions that set the pipeline's transformations. Then you feed your scene into Direct3D's pipeline and let it do the rest of the work.

note

When the pipeline rasterizes 3-D objects, it rasterizes them to the back buffer. After rasterization completes, your program swaps the front and back buffers.

Rendering in 3-D

With a knowledge of 3-D transformations and the rendering pipeline, you're ready to start building your own 3-D objects and rendering them to the screen. To make your first foray into the world of 3-D a bit less intimidating, I'll present two sample programs based on the spinning triangle from Chapter 4.

Example 1: The 3-D Spinning Triangle

The sample program from Chapter 4 demonstrated how to define a triangle with Direct3D. It also showed you how to spin that triangle in the xy plane. If you go back and look at the program, you'll discover that you were really working in 3-D. I just didn't tell you that. I just sort of waved my hands at the 3-D pipeline transformations. Although the code for creating the world, viewing, and projection transformations is in the program, I really didn't explain it. The reality is that with tools like Direct3D, it's often just as easy to do 3-D graphics as it is to do 2-D graphics.

To make it easier to see that the spinning triangle program really is doing 3-D graphics, we'll revise it so that it spins the triangle around the x, y, and z axes.

You'll find the code for this example on the CD-ROM in the Source\Chapter05\ TriangleSpin3D folder. The Source\Chapter05\ folder also contains a folder called Bin. The Bin folder contains the executable version of the TriSpin3D program, called TriSpin3D.exe. If you just want to run it and see what the example looks like, double-click the file TriSpin3D.exe.

Initializing the Geometry

The initialization of the triangle's geometry is handled in the GameInitialization() function. Because the spinning triangle program from Chapter 4 was really a 3-D program, we do not need to make any changes to the initialization of the triangle. Therefore, I won't repeat the GameInitialization() function here.

Updating a Frame

To spin the triangle about the x, y, and z axes, this new version of the UpdateFrame() function creates a rotation matrix for each axis. The code is given in Listing 5.1.

Listing 5.1
Rotating in 3-D

```
1     bool UpdateFrame()
2     {
3         D3DXMATRIXA16 worldMatrix;
4         D3DXMATRIXA16 rotationX;
5         D3DXMATRIXA16 rotationY;
6         D3DXMATRIXA16 rotationZ;
7
8         UINT  currentTime  = timeGetTime() % 1000;
9         FLOAT rotationAngle = currentTime * (2.0f * D3DX_PI) / 1000.0f;
10        D3DXMatrixRotationX(&rotationX,rotationAngle);
11        D3DXMatrixRotationY(&rotationY,rotationAngle);
12        D3DXMatrixRotationZ(&rotationZ,rotationAngle);
13        D3DXMatrixMultiply(&worldMatrix,&rotationX,&rotationY);
14        D3DXMatrixMultiply(&worldMatrix,&worldMatrix,&rotationZ);
15
16        theApp.D3DRenderingDevice()->SetTransform(D3DTS_WORLD,&worldMatrix);
17        D3DXVECTOR3 eyePoint(0.0f,3.0f,-5.0f);
18        D3DXVECTOR3 lookatPoint(0.0f,0.0f,0.0f);
19        D3DXVECTOR3 upDirection(0.0f,1.0f,0.0f);
20        D3DXMATRIXA16 viewMatrix;
21        D3DXMatrixLookAtLH(&viewMatrix,&eyePoint,&lookatPoint,&upDirection);
22        theApp.D3DRenderingDevice()->SetTransform(D3DTS_VIEW,&viewMatrix);
23
24        D3DXMATRIXA16 projectionMatrix;
25        D3DXMatrixPerspectiveFovLH(&projectionMatrix,D3DX_PI/4,1.0f,1.0f,100.0f);
```

```
26        theApp.D3DRenderingDevice()->SetTransform(D3DTS_PROJECTION,&projectionMatrix);
27
28        return (true);
29    }
```

Lines 10–12 use the DirectX utility functions `D3DXMatrixRotationX()`, `D3DXMatrixRotationY()`, and `D3DXMatrixRotationZ()` to build rotation matrices. These are 4×4 matrices that use the homogenous coordinates presented earlier in this chapter. As you might expect, `D3DXMatrixRotationX()` builds a rotation matrix that rotates vertices around the x axis. `D3DXMatrixRotationY()` and `D3DXMatrixRotationZ()` do the same for the y and z axes, respectively.

note

The DirectX utility functions are not part of the DirectX API proper. Rather, they're a set of helper functions that are added on. They all rely on the DirectX API to perform their work. However, they simplify many aspects of using DirectX.

Rotating the triangle requires that the program combine the three rotation matrices into a single matrix. The `UpdateFrame()` function does this using matrix multiplication. It calls another DirectX utility function, `D3DXMatrixMultiply()`, to multiply the x rotation matrix by the y rotation matrix on line 13 of Listing 5.1. It stores the results in the variable `worldMatrix`.

On line 14, `UpdateFrame()` combines the z rotation matrix with the matrix in `worldMatrix`. It then calls the `LPDIRECT3DDEVICE9::SetTransform()` function to set the matrix in `worldMatrix` as the world matrix. When the DirectX renders the vertex buffer, it performs the transformations contained in the world matrix, which in turn transforms the local coordinates to world coordinates, as discussed previously.

Line 17 of Listing 5.1 sets the vector that defines the eye point. This is a shorthand way of setting the viewer's location in the 3-D world. The program also creates another vector, often called the lookat vector, on line 18 to specify the point at which the viewer is looking. In addition, DirectX must know which way is up for the viewer. This is like specifying which way the top of a camera is pointing. The `UpdateFrame()` function creates this vector, which 3-D programmers typically call the camera's up vector, on line 19. The use of these three vectors is illustrated in Figure 5.9.

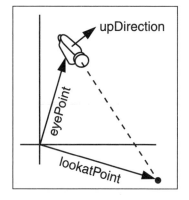

Figure 5.9
Using the three viewpoint vectors.

You must store all three of these vectors in the view matrix. Recall that the view matrix transforms world coordinates to viewing, or camera, coordinates. UpdateFrame() calls the DirectX utility function D3DXMatrixLookAtLH() to create a view matrix in the left-hand coordinate system that DirectX uses. On line 22, UpdateFrame() stores the view matrix so that DirectX will use it when the frame is rendered.

The last task that UpdateFrame() performs is to set the projection matrix on lines 24–26. As you might guess by now, there's a DirectX utility function for that, too. It's named D3DXMatrixPerspectiveFovLH(). This function builds a projection matrix that adds perspective and defines the field of view in DirectX's left-hand coordinate system. UpdateFrame() saves this matrix as the projection matrix on line 26.

Rendering a Frame

Rendering a frame in this version of the spinning triangle program is done exactly as it was in Chapter 4. Therefore, I won't bother presenting the code. Instead, let's move on to another sample program that demonstrates a few more features of 3-D programming.

Example 2: The Spinning Pyramid

The second sample program for this chapter demonstrates how to extend the geometry of triangle strips into 3-D. It creates a three-sided pyramid and spins the pyramid around the x, y, and z axes.

Initializing the Geometry

Of course, creating a pyramid rather than a simple triangle requires changes to the GameInitialization() function. The new code is given in Listing 5.2.

Listing 5.2
Creating a Three-Sided Pyramid

```
1      bool GameInitialization()
2      {
3          const int TOTAL_VERTICES = 6;
4
5          // Initialize six vertices for rendering the figure.
6          vertex theVerteces[TOTAL_VERTICES] =
7          {
8              { -1.0f,-1.0f,0.0f,0xffff0000,},
9              {  1.0f,-1.0f,1.0f,0xff0000ff,},
10             {  0.0f,1.0f,0.0f,0xffffffff,},
11             {  1.0f,-1.0f,-1.0f,0xff00ff00,},
12             { -1.0f,-1.0f,0.0f,0xffff0000,},
13             {  1.0f,-1.0f,1.0f,0xff0000ff,},
```

```
14        };
15
16        LPDIRECT3DVERTEXBUFFER9 tempPointer=NULL;
17        // Create the vertex buffer.
18        if(FAILED(theApp.D3DRenderingDevice()->CreateVertexBuffer(
19            TOTAL_VERTICES*sizeof(vertex),
20            0,VERTEX_TYPE_SPECIFIER,
21            D3DPOOL_DEFAULT,&tempPointer,NULL)))
22        {
23            return false;
24        }
25        else
26        {
27            theApp.D3DVertexBuffer(tempPointer);
28        }
29
30        // Fill the vertex buffer.
31        VOID* tempBufferPointer;
32        if (FAILED(theApp.D3DVertexBuffer()->Lock(
33            0,
34            TOTAL_VERTICES*sizeof(vertex),
35            (void**)&tempBufferPointer,0)))
36        {
37            return false;
38        }
39        memcpy(
40            tempBufferPointer,
41            theVerteces,
42            TOTAL_VERTICES*sizeof(vertex));
43        theApp.D3DVertexBuffer()->Unlock();
44
45        return (true);
46    }
```

Like previous incarnations of this program, the spinning pyramid example uses a triangle strip. It defines six vertices for the pyramid. Notice that vertices 5 and 6 repeat vertices 1 and 2, respectively. This is done so that all faces of the pyramid are drawn. Vertices 1, 2, and 3 form the first face. The second face is made from vertices 2, 3, and 4. DirectX draws the third face from vertices 3, 4, and 5. Finally, it draws the fourth face from vertices 4, 5, and 6.

After the GameInitialization() function defines the vertices, it creates the vertex buffer on lines 16–21 and stores the vertex buffer pointer into the d3d_app object. It then fills the vertex buffer on lines 31–43.

Updating a Frame

No changes were required to the UpdateFrame() function. However, I did slow down the rotation of the pyramid and move the eye point. Listing 5.3 gives the new code for UpdateFrame().

Listing 5.3
Minor Adjustments to the UpdateFrame() Function

```
1     bool UpdateFrame()
2     {
3         D3DXMATRIXA16 worldMatrix;
4         D3DXMATRIXA16 rotationX;
5         D3DXMATRIXA16 rotationY;
6         D3DXMATRIXA16 rotationZ;
7
8         UINT  currentTime  = timeGetTime() % 4000;
9         FLOAT rotationAngle = currentTime * (2.0f * D3DX_PI) / 4000.0f;
10        D3DXMatrixRotationX(&rotationX,rotationAngle);
11        D3DXMatrixRotationY(&rotationY,rotationAngle);
12        D3DXMatrixRotationZ(&rotationZ,rotationAngle);
13        D3DXMatrixMultiply(&worldMatrix,&rotationX,&rotationY);
14        D3DXMatrixMultiply(&worldMatrix,&worldMatrix,&rotationZ);
15
16        theApp.D3DRenderingDevice()->SetTransform(
17            D3DTS_WORLD,
18            &worldMatrix);
19
20        D3DXVECTOR3 eyePoint(0.0f,1.0f,-5.0f);
21        D3DXVECTOR3 lookatPoint(0.0f,0.0f,0.0f);
22        D3DXVECTOR3 upDirection(0.0f,1.0f,0.0f);
23        D3DXMATRIXA16 viewMatrix;
24        D3DXMatrixLookAtLH(
25            &viewMatrix,
26            &eyePoint,
27            &lookatPoint,
28            &upDirection);
29        theApp.D3DRenderingDevice()->SetTransform(
30            D3DTS_VIEW,&viewMatrix);
31
32        D3DXMATRIXA16 projectionMatrix;
33        D3DXMatrixPerspectiveFovLH(
34            &projectionMatrix,D3DX_PI/4,1.0f,1.0f,100.0f);
35        theApp.D3DRenderingDevice()->SetTransform(
```

```
36              D3DTS_PROJECTION,&projectionMatrix);
37
38         return (true);
39    }
```

Rendering a Frame

There is one small but important change required in the RenderFrame() function. First, let's look at the code in Listing 5.4. Then I'll explain the change.

Listing 5.4
Drawing the Three-Sided Pyramid

```
1     bool RenderFrame()
2     {
3          // Render the vertex buffer contents.
4          theApp.D3DRenderingDevice()->SetStreamSource(
5               0,
6               theApp.D3DVertexBuffer(),
7               0,
8               sizeof(vertex));
9          theApp.D3DRenderingDevice()->SetFVF(VERTEX_TYPE_SPECIFIER);
10         theApp.D3DRenderingDevice()->DrawPrimitive(
11              D3DPT_TRIANGLESTRIP,0,4);
12
13         return (true);
14    }
```

If you look on line 11 of Listing 5.4, you'll see that the last parameter to the DirectX DrawPrimitive() function is now 4. When your program is drawing triangle strips with the DrawPrimitive() function, it must tell DrawPrimitive() how many faces (triangles) to draw. In the spinning triangle example, it drew only one face. In this case, it must draw four faces to get the full pyramid.

Back-Face Culling

Previous sample programs displayed only a simple triangle. To see both sides of the triangle, the function InitD3D() in the PMD3DApp.cpp file disabled back-face culling. If your program is drawing solid figures, such as the three-sided pyramid, you do not want to see both the front and back of every triangle. Instead, you want the program to display only the front face of each triangle. Therefore, I've modified InitD3D() so that it no longer disables back-face culling. Listing 5.5 presents the new code.

Listing 5.5
InitD3D() No Longer Disables Back-Face Culling

```
1    HRESULT InitD3D(HWND hWnd)
2    {
3        HRESULT hr = S_OK;
4        D3DPRESENT_PARAMETERS d3dpp;
5
6        // Create the D3D object.
7        if((theApp.direct3D = Direct3DCreate9(D3D_SDK_VERSION))==NULL)
8        {
9            // If the object wasn't created...
10           hr = E_FAIL;
11       }
12       else
13       {
14           // If the D3D object was created...
15           // Set up the structure used to create the D3DDevice.
16           ZeroMemory(&d3dpp,sizeof(d3dpp));
17           d3dpp.Windowed = TRUE;
18           d3dpp.SwapEffect = D3DSWAPEFFECT_DISCARD;
19           d3dpp.BackBufferFormat = D3DFMT_UNKNOWN;
20       }
21
22       // Create the D3DDevice.
23       // Can the device use the HAL?
24       if ((hr==S_OK) &&
25           (FAILED(theApp.direct3D->CreateDevice(
26               D3DADAPTER_DEFAULT,D3DDEVTYPE_HAL,hWnd,
27               D3DCREATE_HARDWARE_VERTEXPROCESSING,
28               &d3dpp,&theApp.d3dDevice))))
29       {
30           // If not, maybe it can use software emulation...
31           if(FAILED(theApp.direct3D->CreateDevice(
32               D3DADAPTER_DEFAULT,
33               D3DDEVTYPE_REF,
34               hWnd,
35               D3DCREATE_HARDWARE_VERTEXPROCESSING,
36               &d3dpp,
37               &theApp.d3dDevice)))
38           {
```

```
39                    // If not, too bad.
40                    hr = E_FAIL;
41                }
42            }
43
44        if (hr==S_OK)
45        {
46            /* Turn off D3D lighting, since we are providing our own
47            vertex colors.*/
48            theApp.d3dDevice->SetRenderState(D3DRS_LIGHTING,FALSE);
49        }
50
51        return hr;
52    }
```

If you examine lines 44–49, you'll see that I deleted the statement that turned off back-face culling. By default, Direct3D turns back-face culling on.

Summary

This chapter touched on 3-D transformations, the 3-D pipeline, and rendering some simple models. We've covered a lot of ground—some of it carefully and some of it with blinders.

We're almost ready to start in with some real physics, but we must take care of one task first. Games don't use the simple models shown in the examples so far. They use complex objects defined by 3-D meshes. Therefore, the next task is to learn how to load and display meshes.

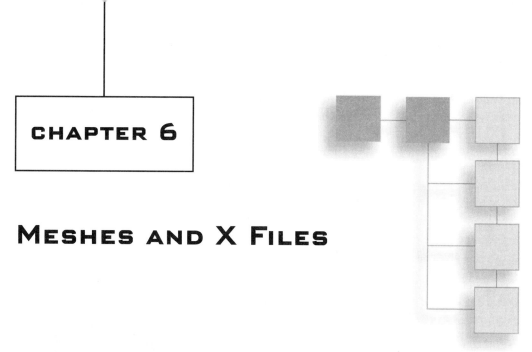

CHAPTER 6

MESHES AND X FILES

This chapter is called "Meshes and X Files," but it's really about making things look good. Physics modeling became important in the computer games industry when advances in computer graphics made games look realistic. Realistic-looking objects have to move in a realistic way.

You're not going to be able to create tons of realistic objects by programming them directly into the computer with a few lines of C++ code. Instead, you'll build them in a 3-D editor such as Milkshape 3D from chUmbaLum sOft, 3ds max from Discreet, or Caligari trueSpace. Then you'll convert the objects to a format that the game uses.

These models use triangles as their primitives because a triangle is the simplest possible plane figure. Each triangle is formed from three vertices. All three vertices are guaranteed to be in the same plane. The space inside the triangle's vertices is called its *face*.

DirectX specifies a file format for saving 3-D objects. It's called the X file format. Our graphics engine is going to use X files for its 3-D objects.

note

> We'll only be doing enough with meshes, materials, and textures to get us into doing physics. If you really want to get into texturing (which I recommend for realistic games), read *Special Effects Game Programming with DirectX* by Mason McCuskey (Premier Press) or *The Dark Side of Game Texturing* by David Franson (Premier Press).

All we need to do with X files is to get some models and load them. You can make an X file yourself in a 3-D modeler or get it from a Web site that gives away free models. A good place to start is the Free Stuff section at http://www.3Dcafe.com.

An X file contains a mesh. It might also contain textures or materials. Before we can load the mesh, we're going to have to get some background on how to use textures and materials.

Textures

Textures are bitmaps that can be glued to a triangle's face like wallpaper. In the hands of a skilled artist, textures can greatly add to the realism of a model. If you look at one of your favorite video game characters, you'll notice that much of the sense of depth and structure you see in the characters isn't from adding more vertices. Instead, it comes from using textures to give the illusion of structure. It's a nice trick if you can pull it off.

Textures are mapped onto a mesh by using *texture coordinates*. Figure 6.1 shows a texture with texture coordinates (u,v). The texture coordinates range from (0,0) in the upper left to (1,1) in the lower right.

Each vertex of a mesh is assigned a texture coordinate. If you want the texture to stretch over the entire face of a polygon, you match the corners of the texture to the corners of the polygon. For example, the texture in Figure 6.1 stretches over the entire rectangle it's applied to. Suppose that the corners of the rectangle are at (−1.5,1), (1.5,1), (1.5,−1), and (−1.5,−1) starting at the upper left and moving clockwise around the vertices. To get the texture to stretch over the entire rectangle, you would assign the upper-left vertex the texture coordinate of (0,0). Doing this matches up the upper-left corner of the texture to the upper-left corner of the rectangle. The upper-right vertex would get the texture coordinate (1,0), and the texture coordinate (1,1) would be assigned to the lower-right vertex. Finally, you would assign (0,1) as the texture coordinate to the lower-left vertex.

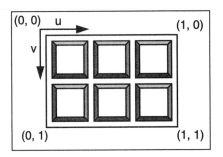

Figure 6.1
A texture with associated coordinates.

After you apply a texture, DirectX textures the faces of a polygon by interpolating between the vertices. Just as the elements in a bitmap are called *pixels* (picture elements), the elements of a texture are called *texels* (texture elements). Applying a texel onto each location of the face accomplishes the interpolation.

As an example, look at the three vertices in Figure 6.2. The top vertex is assigned a texture coordinate of (0,0), so the (0,0) component of the texture in Figure 6.1 is mapped on to it. The right vertex has

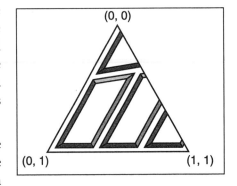

Figure 6.2
A textured triangle.

texture coordinates (1,1), and the left vertex has texture coordinates (0,1). After these texture points are set, the face is textured by interpolation.

Notice how the texture distorts when you ask DirectX to map a square texture to a triangular polygon. Most textures are square. Usually, you map them to square polygons to keep them from distorting. That's not always the case, but it's common.

Creating Textures from Files

If you have a bitmap stored in a file, you can create a texture from the file. First, you need a pointer to a texture:

```
LPDIRECT3DTEXTURE9 pTexture = NULL;
```

To actually create the texture, you'll use a Direct3D utility function with the easy-to-remember name D3DXCreateTextureFromFile().

This function handles several different file types, listed in Table 6.1. Note that the D3DXCreateTextureFromFile() function doesn't support .gif, .pcx, or .tif.

Table 6.1 Files Types Supported by D3DXCreateTextureFromFile()

Extension	File Type
.bmp	Windows device-independent bitmaps
.dds	DirectDraw Surfaces
.jpg	Joint Photographic Experts Group
.png	Portable Network Graphics
.tga	Targa

Say that you want to create a texture from a file, lava.jpg. One line will do it:

```
D3DXCreateTextureFromFile( pDevice, "lava.jpg", pTexture);
```

If you want more control over how DirectX applies the texture, you can use the D3DXCreateTextureFromFileEx() function. It takes 14 parameters! In general, I recommend sticking with D3DXCreateTextureFromFile() unless you have a compelling reason not to.

Setting the Texture

Your average 3-D game has to deal with numerous textures, so you need some way to specify which texture is active before rendering. You do this with the IDirect3DDevice9::SetTexture() function.

The second parameter to `IDirect3DDevice9::SetTexture()` is the pointer to the texture you created. The first is an index for the texture that enables you to set up to eight textures for a device. It's used for *multiple texturing*, which is a more advanced graphics technique that we're not going to bother with. We'll set it to 0.

With that said, setting the texture is easy:

```
pDevice -> SetTexture(  0, pTexture );
```

Materials

In Direct3D, the material specifies how an object looks under light. It has five properties, encapsulated in the `D3DMATERIAL9` structure:

```
typedef struct _D3DMATERIAL9 {
    D3DCOLORVALUE Diffuse;
    D3DCOLORVALUE Ambient;
    D3DCOLORVALUE Specular;
    D3DCOLORVALUE Emissive;
    float Power;
} D3DMATERIAL;
```

The *diffuse color* is the color that the object will appear if you shine a light onto it. The amount of diffuse light that is reflected depends on the angle of the incident light with respect to the surface.

The *ambient color* is the color that the object will appear under ambient light—that is, completely scattered light in a room that doesn't seem to come from a definite source.

Diffuse and ambient color determine the basic color of an object. Usually, diffuse and ambient should be set to the same color to correspond with the real world.

The *specular color* is the color of the shiny parts of an object. Usually, you'll want to set the specular color to white. Increasing the value of the `Power` structure member increases the sharpness of the specular highlights.

The *emissive color* makes an object appear to be glowing. An object that has an emissive color doesn't shine light onto other objects.

All you need to do to set a color is to declare one of these structures, fill it out, and send it to the `IDirect3DDevice9::SetMaterial()` method:

```
D3DMATERIAL9 Material;
// Set the colors in the materials structure.
pDevice->SetMaterial( &Material );
```

Loading a Mesh

Loading a mesh isn't too difficult using the D3DXLoadMeshFromX() function. This function creates buffers to hold the materials and textures it finds in the X file. Before you can load a mesh, you must declare pointers to the materials buffer and the mesh interface and set a DWORD to hold the number of materials:

```
LPD3DXMESH theMesh = NULL;
LPD3DXBUFFER materialsBuffer = NULL;
DWORD numMaterials = 0l;
```

Now you can load the mesh into memory:

```
D3DXLoadMeshFromX(
    meshFileName,
    D3DXMESH_MANAGED,
    d3dDevice,
    NULL,
    & materialsBuffer,
    NULL,
    & numMaterials, & theMesh) ) )
```

The meshFileName parameter is the file name of the X file.

Extracting Textures and Materials

At this point, the file has been loaded, but we still need to extract the textures and materials from the materials buffer. That's because the materials buffer contains both the D3DMATERIAL9 structure with information about the material's light properties and the name of the file containing the texture.

To extract the textures and materials from the materials buffer, we need to declare arrays for textures and materials:

```
D3DMATERIAL9 *pMaterials;
LPDIRECT3DTEXTURE9 *pTextures;
// Create new textures and materials arrays.
pTextures = new LPDIRECT3DTEXTURE9[numMaterials];
pMaterials = new D3DMATERIAL9[numMaterials];
```

We also need a pointer to the beginning of the materials buffer. We can do this with the ID3DXBuffer::GetBufferPointer() method:

```
// Get a pointer to the materials buffer.
D3DXMATERIAL* pMatBufferPointer
    = (D3DXMATERIAL*)pMaterialBuffer->GetBufferPointer();
```

Now you loop through each of the materials in the materials buffer. The total number of materials in the buffer is specified in numMaterials. As your program iterates through the buffer, it fills the pMaterials array and loads texture files into the pTextures array. If the materials buffer loaded from the X file doesn't specify a texture, set the texture pointer to NULL:

```
1     // Count through the materials.
2     for (DWORD i = 0;i<numMaterials;i++ )
3     {
4         // Set pMaterials to extract textures from the buffer.
5         pMaterials[i] = pMatBufferPointer[i].MatD3D;
6         // Set the ambient equal to diffuse.
7         // Usually, ambient is set equal to zero, which
8         // makes the models look dark in Direct3D.
9         pMaterials[dwMatCount].Ambient = pMaterials[dwMatCount].Diffuse;
10        // Load the textures.
11        // If the X file specifies a texture...
12        if(pMatBufferPointer[dwMatCount].pTextureFilename)
13        {
14            // Load it.
15            if (FAILED(D3DXCreateTextureFromFile(
16                d3dDevice,
17                pMatBufferPointer[i].pTextureFilename,
18                &pTextures[i])))
19            {
20                // If the load doesn't work, set it to NULL.
21                pTextures[i] = NULL;
22            }
23        }
24        // If there is still no texture, set it to NULL.
25        else
26        {
27            pTextures[i] = NULL;
28        }
29    }
```

You might have noticed one interesting oddity in the code. I manually set the ambient color equal to the diffuse color. As I mentioned before, this is normally what you want for the world to look normal. Furthermore, it turns out that for several of the models you might want to load, the ambient color is set to black. This is going to make your models look awfully dark in Direct3D.

After you've extracted the textures and materials, you're done with the materials buffer, so release it:

```
pMaterialBuffer->Release();
```

Rendering the Mesh

The mesh is divided into subsets, each with its own material and texture. Your program will have to loop through each of these subsets and render each one separately:

```
// Count through the material subsets.
for ( DWORD i = 0;i<numMaterials;i++ )
{
    // Set the material and texture for this subset.
    d3dDevice->SetMaterial(&pMaterials[i]);
    d3dDevice->SetTexture(0,pTextures[i]);
    // Draw it
    pMesh->DrawSubset(i);
}
```

This function is pretty straightforward because we did all the hard work when loading the mesh. Just set the texture and material, and then ask the mesh to draw that subset.

Cleaning Up the Mesh

When you're finished with the mesh, you need to clean up the memory. First, release the memory for the materials array:

```
delete[] pMaterials;
```

Then release the interface to each of the textures:

```
for( DWORD i = 0;i< numMaterials;i++ )
{
        if(pTextures[i] )
            pTextures[i]->Release();
    }
```

After you've released those interfaces, you're done with the textures array, so you can delete it. You can also delete the materials array:

```
delete []pMaterials;
```

Finally, release the interface to the mesh:

```
pMesh->Release();
```

The d3d_mesh Class

I've encapsulated all this functionality into a class called d3d_mesh. This class can load, render, and clean up a mesh.

In addition, the d3d_mesh class handles a common feature of most games. It's not uncommon in games to display many copies of an object. The next time you're playing a game, look around the scene. Are torches hanging from the wall? There's really only one torch mesh in memory. The game uses the same mesh for many torches.

The d3d_mesh class contains special provisions for using the same mesh for many objects in a scene. I'll explain them in detail in the later section called "Reference Counting in the d3d_mesh Class."

Listing 6.1 gives the definition of the d3d_mesh class.

Listing 6.1
The d3d_mesh Class

```
1      class d3d_mesh
2      {
3      private:
4          class mesh_data
5          {
6          public:
7              LPD3DXMESH theMesh;
8              D3DMATERIAL9 *allMaterials;
9              LPDIRECT3DTEXTURE9 *allTextures;
10             int totalMaterials;
11
12             int referenceCount;
13
14             //Public functions
15             mesh_data();
16             ~mesh_data();
17
18         };
19
20         mesh_data *meshData;
21
22     public:
23         d3d_mesh();
24         d3d_mesh(
25             d3d_mesh &sourceMesh);
26         ~d3d_mesh();
```

```
27
28          d3d_mesh &operator = (
29              d3d_mesh &sourceMesh);
30
31          bool Load(
32              std::string fileName);
33          bool Render();
34      };
```

The d3d_mesh class in Listing 6.1 encapsulates the information needed to load and render a mesh. Notice that it contains another class. This is a common technique in professional C++ programs. However, I usually avoid it in examples because it can rapidly become complex. The reason I use it here is to implement a scheme called *reference counting*. Reference counted objects store data like regular objects. However, they also let other objects refer to their data with a pointer. They keep a count of how many objects are pointing at their data. That way, their data doesn't get deleted until there are no other objects pointing at it. That's the purpose of the mesh_data class.

Both the mesh_data and d3d_mesh classes have the member functions they need to accomplish their tasks. All the d3d_mesh class's member functions access the data using a dynamically allocated instance of the mesh_data class. Let's look at how the d3d_mesh class works.

Loading a Mesh

To load a mesh, your program calls the d3d_mesh class's Load() function, which appears in Listing 6.2.

Listing 6.2
The d3d_mesh::Load() Function

```
1       bool d3d_mesh::Load(std::string fileName)
2       {
3           bool meshLoaded=false;
4           LPD3DXBUFFER tempMaterialbuffer=NULL;
5           D3DXMATERIAL *materialBuffer=NULL;
6
7           HRESULT hr = D3DXLoadMeshFromX(
8               fileName.c_str(),
9               D3DXMESH_SYSTEMMEM,
10              theApp.D3DRenderingDevice(),
11              NULL,
12              &tempMaterialbuffer,
13              NULL,
14              (DWORD *)&meshData->totalMaterials,
```

```
15              &meshData->theMesh);
16
17          // If the mesh was loaded...
18          if (hr==D3D_OK)
19          {
20              // Get the materials buffer.
21              materialBuffer =
22                  (D3DXMATERIAL *)tempMaterialbuffer->GetBufferPointer();
23              meshLoaded=true;
24          }
25
26          if (meshLoaded==true)
27          {
28              // Allocate the array of materials.
29              meshData->allMaterials =
30                  new D3DMATERIAL9 [meshData->totalMaterials];
31
32              // If the array was not allocated...
33              if (meshData->allMaterials==NULL)
34              {
35                  meshLoaded=false;
36              }
37          }
38
39          if (meshLoaded==true)
40          {
41              // Allocate the array of textures.
42              meshData->allTextures =
43                  new LPDIRECT3DTEXTURE9 [meshData->totalMaterials];
44
45              // If the array was not allocated...
46              if (meshData->allTextures==NULL)
47              {
48                  // Free the array of materials.
49                  delete [] meshData->allMaterials;
50
51                  meshLoaded=false;
52              }
53          }
54
55          if (meshLoaded==true)
56          {
```

```
57                   for(int i=0;(i<meshData->totalMaterials);i++ )
58                   {
59                       // Copy the material.
60                       meshData->allMaterials[i]=materialBuffer[i].MatD3D;
61
62                       /* Set the ambient color for the material to be the same as the
63                       diffuse color. This is typical for realistic rendering. */
64                       meshData->allMaterials[i].Ambient =
65                           meshData->allMaterials[i].Diffuse;
66
67                       // If there is a texture named in the X file...
68                       if ((materialBuffer[i].pTextureFilename != NULL) &&
69                           (lstrlen(materialBuffer[i].pTextureFilename) > 0))
70                       {
71                           // Load the texture.
72                           if(FAILED(D3DXCreateTextureFromFile(
73                               theApp.D3DRenderingDevice(),
74                               materialBuffer[i].pTextureFilename,
75                               &meshData->allTextures[i])))
76                           {
77                               /* If the texture couldn't be loaded, set the return
78                               value to indicate an error. */
79                               meshLoaded=false;
80                           }
81                       }
82                       // Else there is no texture...
83                       else
84                       {
85                           meshData->allTextures[i] = NULL;
86                       }
87                   }
88
89               // Finished with the materials buffer
90               tempMaterialbuffer->Release();
91
92           }
93       return (meshLoaded);
94   }
```

The first thing to notice about the Load() function is that it stores its data in its meshData member. Again, this is for reference counting, which I'll explain in just a bit.

The Load() function requires only one parameter: the name of the X file to load. After declaring some variables it needs, the Load() function calls the D3DXLoadMeshFromX() function to load the X file on lines 7–15 of Listing 6.2. If the X file was loaded, Load() gets a pointer to the materials buffer on lines 21–22.

Next, Load() allocates an array of material structures on lines 29–30. If there's memory for the array, it also allocates an array of pointers to textures on lines 42–43. If that allocation was successful, the Load() function loops through the list of materials on lines 57–87. In the loop, Load() copies the material from the materials buffer into the array of materials in the current object. It sets the ambient color equal to the diffuse color on lines 64–65. If a texture is associated with the current material, the Load() function attempts to load it. If the texture can't be loaded, there's something wrong, and an error condition is set. This error condition is later returned to the calling function. If no texture is associated with the material, Load() simply sets the texture pointer to NULL.

warning

The d3d_mesh::Load() function does not load all types of DirectX meshes that X files might contain. It loads basic meshes that we'll use throughout the rest of the book. For more information on X files and loading meshes, I recommend *Beginning Direct3D Game Programming* by Wolfgang F. Engle (Premier Press). It's one of the few books on the market that really explains X files and how to use them.

Rendering a Mesh

Rendering a mesh is easier than loading it. As mentioned previously, meshes contain subsets. Therefore, to render a mesh, your program has to iterate through each subset and perform the following steps:

1. Set the material for the subset.

2. Set the texture (if there is one) for the subset.

3. Render the subset.

The d3d_mesh::Render() function in Listing 6.3 shows how to accomplish these steps.

Listing 6.3
The d3d_mesh::Render() Function

```
1     bool d3d_mesh::Render()
2     {
3         bool meshRendered=true;
4
5         /* Meshes are divided into subsets, one for each material. Each
6         mesh subset needs to be rendered individually. */
7         for(DWORD i=0;i<(DWORD)meshData->totalMaterials;i++ )
8         {
9             // Set the material and texture for this subset.
```

```
10              if (theApp.D3DRenderingDevice()->SetMaterial(
11                  &meshData->allMaterials[i]) != D3D_OK)
12              {
13                  meshRendered=false;
14              }
15
16              if (theApp.D3DRenderingDevice()->SetTexture(
17                  0,meshData->allTextures[i]) != D3D_OK)
18              {
19                  meshRendered=false;
20              }
21
22              // Draw the mesh subset.
23              meshData->theMesh->DrawSubset(i);
24          }
25
26      return (meshRendered);
27  }
```

The Render() function in Listing 6.3 follows the three steps for rendering a mesh in Direct3D. It uses a loop, beginning on line 7, to iterate through the mesh subsets. Each time through the loop, the Render() function calls the Direct3D LPDIRECT3DDEVICE9::SetMaterial() function to set the subset's material.

Next, the Render() function calls LPDIRECT3DDEVICE9::SetTexture() to set the subset's texture. Finally, it calls the DrawSubset() function to render the subset of the mesh.

Optimization in the Render() Function

I purposely omitted an optimization in the d3d_mesh::Render() function. The if statement on lines 16–20 should be enclosed in another if statement that tests whether allTextures[i] equals NULL. If it does, the Render() function should not call SetTexture() because there is no texture for the subset. This speeds up rendering whenever the subset doesn't have a texture.

So why did I omit the extra if statement?

I omitted it because I knew in advance that all the meshes I'd be using for this book had textures for subsets. If the subset doesn't have a texture, something's wrong. Also, I tend to omit error checking and optimizations in these samples whenever I can get away with it so that I can keep the code simple and uncluttered.

I'm pointing this out because you might want to use this code for an actual game. If you do, it's possible that some of your meshes might not have textures. If there's any chance that's the case, you need to put the extra if statement into this code. Doing so helps optimize performance.

Reference Counting in the d3d_mesh Class

As mentioned previously, multiple objects often share the same mesh in games. To accommodate that, the d3d_mesh class implements reference counting. Here's how it works.

Rather than store the mesh's data in the d3d_mesh class, the data is stored in a helper class called mesh_data. The d3d_mesh class contains a dynamically allocated object of type mesh_data. Multiple d3d_mesh objects in the program can point to the same mesh_data object. The mesh_data object keeps track of how many d3d_mesh objects are pointing at it, as shown in Figure 6.3.

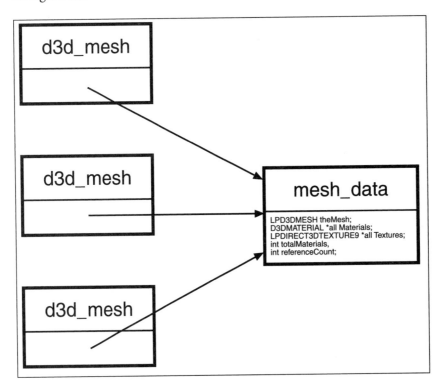

Figure 6.3
Multiple d3d_mesh objects pointing to a single mesh_data object.

In Figure 6.3, the three d3d_mesh objects contain pointers, which are represented graphically by arrows. All three objects share the same data by pointing at the same mesh_data object. The mesh_data object contains a data member called referenceCount that it uses to keep track of how many d3d_mesh objects are pointing to it.

To understand how this reference counting technique works, let's start by looking again at the d3d_mesh class. It's repeated in Listing 6.4 for your convenience.

Listing 6.4
The d3d_mesh Class

```
1     class d3d_mesh
2     {
3     private:
4         class mesh_data
5         {
6         public:
7             LPD3DXMESH theMesh;
8             D3DMATERIAL9 *allMaterials;
9             LPDIRECT3DTEXTURE9 *allTextures;
10            int totalMaterials;
11
12            int referenceCount;
13
14            //Public functions
15            mesh_data();
16            ~mesh_data();
17
18        };
19
20        mesh_data *meshData;
21
22    public:
23        d3d_mesh();
24        d3d_mesh(
25            d3d_mesh &sourceMesh);
26        ~d3d_mesh();
27
28        d3d_mesh &operator = (
29            d3d_mesh &sourceMesh);
30
31        bool Load(
32            std::string fileName);
33        bool Render();
34    };
```

The class definition of the mesh_data class appears in the private section of the d3d_mesh class. This is so that the d3d_mesh class is the only class that can use an object of type mesh_data. The mesh_data class contains the mesh's data as *public* member data, which is unusual in good C++ programming. Data should almost never be public, but this is a notable exception. Because the mesh_data class definition is accessible only to the d3d_mesh class, and because the d3d_mesh class needs rapid access to the members of the mesh_data class, I've made the members of the mesh_data class public.

warning

Experienced C++ programmers might point out that you could make the member data in the mesh_data class private without slowing down access by providing public inline member functions for getting and setting the data. This is quite true. C++ substitutes the code of inline member functions directly into the program, similar to C preprocessor macro expansion.

If you're implementing a reference counted class that is more complex than the mesh_data class, I strongly recommend that you make the member data private and provide access through public member functions. Although it makes the code a bit wordier, it provides safer access to the data.

The mesh_data class also has some member functions. Specifically, it has a constructor and a destructor. Listing 6.5 gives their code.

Listing 6.5
The Member Functions of the mesh_data Class

```
1     inline d3d_mesh::mesh_data::mesh_data()
2     {
3         theMesh=NULL;
4         allMaterials=NULL;
5         allTextures=NULL;
6         totalMaterials=0;
7         referenceCount=1;
8     }
9
10
11    inline d3d_mesh::mesh_data::~mesh_data()
12    {
13        if (allMaterials!=NULL)
14        {
15            delete [] allMaterials;
16        }
17
18        if (allTextures!=NULL)
19        {
20            for (int i=0;i<totalMaterials;i++)
21            {
22                if (allTextures[i]!=NULL)
23                {
```

```
24                    allTextures[i]->Release();
25                }
26            }
27          delete [] allTextures;
28      }
29
30      if (theMesh!=NULL)
31      {
32          theMesh->Release();
33          theMesh=NULL;
34      }
35  }
```

Whenever a game creates a d3d_mesh object and consequently a mesh_data object, it needs to initialize the mesh's data to NULL or 0. The mesh_data constructor performs this initialization. It also initializes the reference count to 1 because, if a mesh_data object gets created, at least one d3d_mesh object refers to it.

The only function that should set the mesh's data to anything other than the initial values is the d3d_mesh::Load() function. For this implementation, the mesh's data should not change as the program runs. That's not true for every type of application you might want to create. For instance, one technique for generating terrain is to load a flat mesh with its materials and textures and then displace the y coordinates of some of the vertices to get hills and valleys. In that case, your program must be able to access the individual vertices. We don't need that capability here, so we won't worry about it.

Whenever a mesh_data object is deleted, the program calls the destructor, which appears on lines 11–35. The destructor goes through the steps described previously in "Cleaning Up the Mesh." First, it deletes the array of materials. Recall that this is an array of structures, so they can just be freed. The textures, on the other hand, are contained in an array of pointers to COM objects. Therefore, the destructor has to loop through the array and call the COM Release() function on every texture. The loop appears on lines 20–26 of Listing 6.5. After all the textures are released, the destructor deletes the array of pointers on line 27. Finally, the destructor ends by releasing the mesh.

The functions that do the reference counting are the constructor, the copy constructor, the destructor, and the assignment operator in the d3d_mesh class. These are shown in Listing 6.6.

Listing 6.6
The Reference Counting Functions

```
1      inline d3d_mesh::d3d_mesh()
2      {
3          /* At this point, this function does not check the allocation.
```

```
4            That is added later. */
5            meshData = new mesh_data();
6        }
7
8        inline d3d_mesh::d3d_mesh(
9            d3d_mesh &sourceMesh)
10       {
11           meshData = sourceMesh.meshData;
12           sourceMesh.meshData->referenceCount++;
13       }
14
15       inline d3d_mesh &d3d_mesh::operator = (
16               d3d_mesh &sourceMesh)
17       {
18           // If they're not already the same...
19           if (meshData!=sourceMesh.meshData)
20           {
21               // The current data is going away. Decrement the count.
22               meshData->referenceCount--;
23
24               // If this is the last object referring to the data...
25               if (meshData->referenceCount==0)
26               {
27                   delete meshData;
28               }
29
30               // Make this point at the source data.
31               meshData = sourceMesh.meshData;
32
33               // Add a reference to the source data.
34               sourceMesh.meshData->referenceCount++;
35
36           }
37           return (*this);
38       }
39
40       inline d3d_mesh::~d3d_mesh()
41       {
42           // Decrement for this destruction.
43           meshData->referenceCount--;
44
45           // If this is the last object using the data...
```

```
46          if (meshData->referenceCount==0)
47          {
48              delete meshData;
49          }
50      }
```

When a program creates a d3d_mesh object, it calls the d3d_mesh constructor, which is given on lines 1–6 of Listing 6.6. All the constructor does is allocate a mesh_data object and save its address in its meshData member. As mentioned previously, the mesh_data constructor initializes the data members and sets the reference count to 1. The program can then load and render a mesh.

warning

To keep the focus of this discussion on reference counting and rendering meshes, I've omitted any error handling in the d3d_mesh constructor. Never do this in an actual game because it's an invitation for disaster. I'll add the error handling in later chapters.

The copy constructor and assignment operator enable some of the objects in your program to share the same mesh. The copy constructor is easy; because it is creating a new object, there is no possibility that the new object already references a mesh. Therefore, the copy constructor simply sets the meshData pointer of the new object to hold the same address as the meshData pointer in the object being copied. This adds a reference to the mesh_data object, so the copy constructor increments its reference count.

Suppose that your program declares three d3d_mesh variables called mesh1, mesh2, and mesh3. Now imagine that it loads a mesh into mesh1. Next, it contains the following statement:

mesh3=mesh2=mesh1;

This causes the d3d_mesh class's assignment operator to be called. The code is given on lines 15–38 of Listing 6.6. This operator's job is more complex than the copy constructor's. First, it's possible that the source object and the destination object might be the same. In other words, the program might contain a statement such as this:

mesh1=mesh1;

No program should contain a statement like this, but that doesn't stop it from happening. The if statement on line 19 of Listing 6.6 prevents the assignment operator function from doing anything if the source and destination objects already point to the same mesh_data object.

If the source and destination objects do not point to the same mesh_data object, the assignment operator function decrements the reference count of the destination object. It does this because the destination of the assignment will no longer point to the same data it did before the assignment. Instead, it will point to the same data as the source object.

Decrementing the reference count might mean that no more d3d_mesh objects are referring to the mesh_data object. If that's the case, the assignment operator function deletes the mesh_data object on lines 25–28.

Next, the assignment operator function sets the meshData member to point to the same mesh_data object as the object being copied. It does this on line 31. Also, it increments the reference count because another d3d_mesh object now points at the mesh_data object. The assignment operator function ends as it should—by returning a copy of the destination object.

The only remaining task in reference counting is to handle the final deletion of a d3d_mesh object. The destructor for the d3d_mesh class is shown on lines 40–50. When a d3d_mesh object is deleted, it no longer points to the mesh data. Therefore, the destructor decrements the reference count on line 43. If no other d3d_mesh objects point to the mesh_data object, the mesh_data object. can be deleted. The mesh_data object destructor handles the task of cleaning up the mesh as Direct3D requires.

tip

This reference counting technique is based on the one that appears in Article 29 of the book *More Effective C++* by Scott Meyers (Addison-Wesley). I consider it and its companion book *Effective C++* to be required reading for all C++ programmers. I cannot emphasize enough how much reading these two books will help your C++ programming.

Summary

I've included a sample program for this chapter that shows how to use the d3d_mesh class. It's on the CD-ROM in the folder Source\Chapter06\MeshSpin. The program uses the tiger mesh that comes with the DirectX SDK. When you build the sample program, copy the files tiger.x and tiger.bmp from the SDK's Media folder into the folder that contains the project. You should get a nice spinning tiger on a blue background.

Now you've graduated from drawing objects made up of simple triangles to drawing complex objects made up of meshes and textures. With this knowledge, you can move on to simulating 3-D objects in motion.

PART TWO

3-D OBJECTS, MOVEMENT, AND COLLISIONS

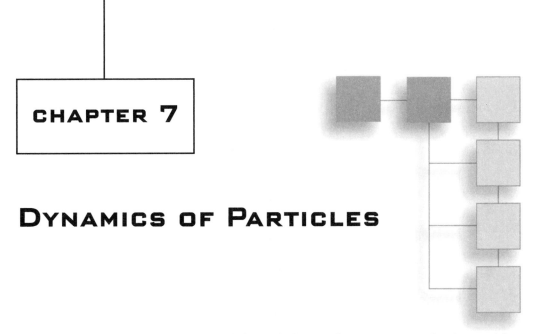

CHAPTER 7

DYNAMICS OF PARTICLES

This chapter presents the core of classical physics: the movements of point particles. This topic covers a lot of ground and allows for some pretty good effects, but it's also the starting point for generalizing to the rigid and deformable bodies that are going to become a significant threat to our sanity later on. In addition, this chapter introduces a few forces that you might run into and some others that can really jack up the realism in your game. Oh, and it covers calculus as well. Hold on tight!

Point Particles

The objects we're going to look at in this chapter are smaller than the distances over which they move. Think of a car driving down a freeway. If you look up close, as in Figure 7.1, the car has some orientation and length, people move around inside, and maybe the hubcap falls off. As the car drives down the road, the tires turn. Many forces act on the car, including air resistance, winds blowing the car toward one side or the other, friction between the tires and the road, and so on.

All of that is a lot to try and model. Physicists, and programmers simulating physics, generally start by simplifying the situation. The first step is to back off a bit. In Figure 7.2, we see the big picture. The car looks like a point. All the local complication has been lost to distance. Instantaneously, the whole situation can be described by one vector that gives the position of the car relative to some coordinate system. It's simple.

Figure 7.1
A car driving down the freeway looks complicated up close.

147

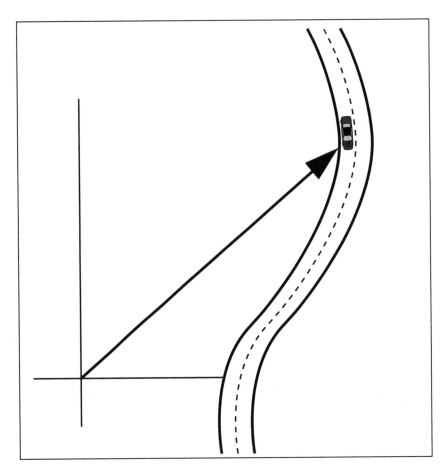

Figure 7.2
The same car, as seen from far away, can be described completely with one
vector in a given instant.

When I talk about a point particle, this is what I mean: Ignore the orientation, ignore anything happening internally, and concentrate only on those properties that affect the position.

tip

The key to good physics modeling (and fast code) is knowing what you can ignore in a calculation.

1-D Kinematics

Kinematics is the study of motion in the absence of forces. Let's start our study of kinematics by considering point particles in one dimension. These particles are constrained to move on a line. Particles that are moving along lines with no forces might not seem like the most fascinating thing to look at, but it's a good start, and the subtleties can sometimes be pretty slippery. Let's take a look.

Velocity

The study of kinematics usually starts with velocity. *Velocity* is the amount of distance traveled over some period of time. You can write the equation for velocity like this:

$$v = \frac{\Delta x}{\Delta t}$$

where v is the average velocity, Δx is the distance traveled, and Δt is the time it took to travel the distance.

note

Velocity is measured in miles per hour (mph) in the U.S. and in meters per second (m/s) everywhere else. One meter per second is about two miles per hour.

Imagine that our car has passed the "Welcome to Kansas" sign and is now traveling along a long, straight piece of road at a prodigious velocity (see Figure 7.3). For those who've never been to Kansas, it's very flat, so it makes a good setting for our example. A police officer, sitting in her car behind a bush 500 meters from the state border, starts her stopwatch when the car passes the border and stops it when the car passes the bush. She sees that 10 seconds have passed, so she can compute the average velocity of the car over that distance.

Figure 7.3
A car speeds down the road in Kansas.

$$v = \frac{\Delta x}{\Delta t} = \frac{500 \text{ meters}}{10 \text{ seconds}} = 50 \ \frac{\text{meters}}{\text{second}}$$

50 meters per second is more than 100 mph, which is somewhat faster than the speed limit in Kansas. The officer feels justified in pulling the car over.

Velocity as a Derivative

The police officer adjusts her sunglasses and saunters up to the car window. The driver of the car sighs and rolls down his window to begin the ritual. On cue, the cop says, "Do you know how fast you were going?" The driver shakes his head, and the cop continues. "I clocked you going more than 100 miles per hour." The driver says, "That's impossible! I was only going to drive for 20 minutes! How could I drive 100 miles in an hour when I wasn't driving for an hour?"

How could the police officer answer this argument? Well, a real traffic cop wouldn't have to, but maybe this cop is a physics student trying to supplement her stipend. The policewoman says, "What I mean is that if you kept going for an hour, you'd have driven 100 miles." The driver replies, "But I was braking and slowing down, so if I'd have kept going, I wouldn't have made 100 miles."

note

My little story about the cop and driver was adapted from *The Feynman Lectures on Physics* by Richard Feynman (the Great Feynman), Robert Leighton, and Matthew Sands. Feynman is one of the greatest physicists of all time and one of its greatest teachers. His *Lectures*, a three-volume set, might be the best book ever written on introductory physics.

The point here is that our formula for velocity, $v = \frac{\Delta x}{\Delta t}$, is good only for computing an average velocity over some distance. This average velocity isn't what we usually mean by velocity; we mean some instantaneous velocity—the velocity at some moment.

Look at Figure 7.4, a graph of the braking car. The curving line represents the distance that the car has traveled at any given time. Because the vertical axis is distance and the horizontal axis is time, the slope of any line on this graph is the speed. Velocity is a vector. It has magnitude and direction. Speed is the magnitude of the velocity vector. It is a scalar quantity that is always positive.

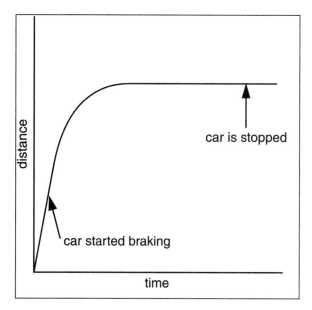

Figure 7.4
Distance versus time for a braking car.

Notice from this figure that as the car slows down, the distance it covers becomes smaller. When the car is stopped, it doesn't matter how much time goes by—the distance traveled doesn't increase.

Let's try to measure the speed at some instant in time. You can get a first estimate for the speed by choosing a Δt centered around the time you would like to know the speed, as in Figure 7.5. Using the graph, you can find the distance measurements at the beginning and end of the time span, Δt. That gives you Δx. The average speed over that time is then $\Delta x / \Delta t$.

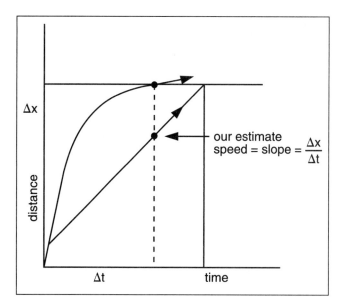

Figure 7.5
Estimating the speed.

You can see that there's quite a difference between the average speed and the actual speed at the time the car was clocked if you compare the slope of the original line to the slope of our estimate. The slope of a line equals the *rise* (change in the vertical axis) of a line divided by the *run* (change in the horizontal axis). A horizontal line has a slope of 0 because the rise is 0. A line running at a 45° angle has a slope of 1. A vertical line has an undefined slope because the run is 0 (slope = [rise] / 0 = undefined). In this case, the distance is on the vertical axis, so the rise is Δx. The horizontal axis is time, so Δt is the run.

You might have already figured out that we can get a better estimate by making Δt smaller. This works really well; look at Figure 7.6.

You can keep repeating this process, making the Δt smaller and smaller and getting better and better estimates for the speed at that moment. This is a method we'll use a lot for our physics models. We can make the solutions more exact by taking smaller time steps.

You can even ask what happens in the limit as Δt goes to 0.

$$v = \lim_{\Delta t \to 0} \frac{\Delta x}{\Delta t}$$

This is the instantaneous speed we've been looking for. This infinitely small Δt is written dt, and the infinitely small

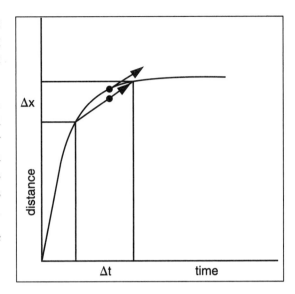

Figure 7.6
Get a better estimate of the speed by using a smaller Δt.

Δx that results is written dx. Using this notation, you can write the previous equation like this:

$$v = \lim_{\Delta t \to 0} \frac{\Delta x}{\Delta t} = \frac{dx}{dt}$$

The quantity dx / dt is called "the derivative of x with respect to t." The process of getting the value of the derivative is called *differentiation*.

note

This is an *extremely* fast and loose introduction to differential calculus. "Nonrigorous" doesn't even begin to describe it. For a more mathematical introduction, check out any introductory text in calculus. A nice one is Gerald Bradley and Karl Smith's book, descriptively titled *Calculus*. For a more rigorous treatment (and a certain amount of masochistic pleasure), check out an introduction to analysis. My favorite is *Yet Another Introduction to Analysis* by Victor Bryant.

Often, we can ignore differentiation because we can use the computer to make good numerical approximations for us.

Acceleration

Remember the braking car? A braking car is slowing down; that is, the speed of the car is changing with time. *Acceleration* is the rate of change of the speed with respect to time, just as *speed* is the rate of change of distance with respect to time.

You can write the average acceleration just like you might expect:

$$a = \frac{\Delta v}{\Delta t}$$

where a is the average acceleration, Δs is the change in speed, and Δt is the time period it underwent that change. The units of acceleration are m/s².

Here's an example. Let's say that you can go from 0 to 32 m/s in 4 seconds on your new motorcycle. Your average acceleration over that time is as follows:

$$a = \frac{32\frac{m}{s}}{4s} = 8\frac{m}{s^2}$$

Now let's try it in reverse. Say that your acceleration is 4 m/s² for 5 seconds. You can compute your speed by rearranging the equation for acceleration:

$$a = \frac{\Delta v}{\Delta t}$$

$$v = a\Delta t = (4\frac{m}{s^2})(5s) = 20\frac{m}{s}$$

You can get the instantaneous acceleration by taking the limit as Δt goes to 0.

$$a = \lim_{\Delta t \to 0} \frac{\Delta v}{\Delta t} = \frac{dv}{dt}$$

The instantaneous acceleration shows the acceleration at any given moment.

Forces

Most of the ancients in the West thought that moving things naturally come to a stop. This seems to be borne out by experience. Anyone who's ever tried to move heavy furniture will vouch that getting it moving is no guarantee that it will keep moving. However, the ancients had some problems with their theory. Great thinkers throughout history observed these problems and tried to sort them out.

Galileo came up with a successful alternative theory called the *principle of inertia*. His theory states that something moving at a constant speed will continue to move at that speed unless acted upon. This took a certain amount of imagination because almost everything in this world does stop unless you keep pushing it, but Galileo realized that this slowing was due to friction between surfaces rather than the inherent nature of things.

Sir Isaac Newton later formulated this same idea in a more precise way. He called it his first law of motion. Newton's second law asks the next logical question. If objects that aren't acted upon continue to travel at the same speed forever, what happens if objects *are* acted upon? The answer is that the force is equal to the mass of an object times its acceleration:

$$F = ma$$

Most objects have some mass, which is a measure of how hard it is to change the velocity of an object; you have to push a more massive object harder than a less massive object to get it to change speed. This formula assumes that the mass of an object does not change over time.

For example, we can use this formula to calculate the forces acting on a car as it travels down the road. But nothing must fall off the car. You might point out that the mass of the car decreases over time because it burns up its fuel. You're right. However, the change in the car's mass is small enough to be ignored in 3-D simulations.

The formula F=ma is the way most people remember the second law for Newtonian mechanics because it's so useful. If I give you the force, you can use the second law to find the acceleration, use the acceleration to find the velocity, and use the velocity to find the distance traveled.

note

> You might have heard that the mass isn't constant in special relativity. Don't worry about it. Unless you're specifically trying to simulate special relativity (I don't know of any games that do), you can assume that mass is constant.

The only trick is to find the forces. In modern physics, there are really only four forces: gravitational, electromagnetic, weak nuclear, and strong nuclear. In theory, you should be able to calculate any problem by properly treating these four forces. In reality, doing this is much too complicated.

What you do in practice is measure the type of force in several situations and look for an equation that describes the results well under some subset of conditions. For example, if you stretch a spring, you'll notice that it applies a force against you, as shown in Figure 7.7.

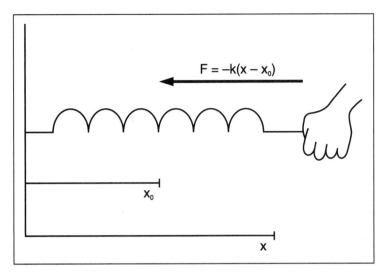

Figure 7.7
Forces on a stretched spring.

You can model this force with this equation:

$$F = -k(x - x_0)$$

where x is the position of the end of the spring and x_0 is the position of the spring at equilibrium. k is a constant that's called the spring constant.

This equation says that if you increase the distance between x and x_0, ($x - x_0$), the force grows larger, which corresponds to our experience with springs. The value of k depends on the stiffness of the spring.

2-D and 3-D Kinematics

All of the equations we've been talking about are extended easily to more dimensions.

Look at the first kinematic equation:

$$v_x = \frac{dx}{dt}$$

If x is the distance along the x axis of a 2-D Cartesian coordinate system, this equation describes the velocity of the particle in the x direction, as shown in Figure 7.8. You can treat the motion along the y axis completely independently, like this:

$$v_y = \frac{dy}{dt}$$

When you're working in three dimensions, the same is true of motion along the z axis.

$$v_z = \frac{dz}{dt}$$

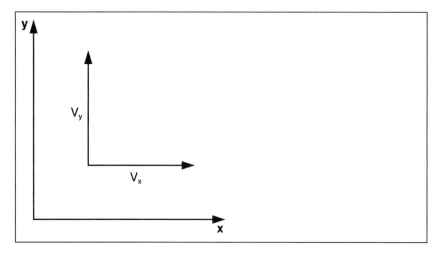

Figure 7.8
Velocities along the x and y axes.

Now, look at this. If **v** is the vector whose components in a 2-D coordinate system are (v_x, v_y), and **x** has components (x, y), you can write these two equations together:

$$\mathbf{v} = \frac{d\mathbf{x}}{dt}$$

In components, that's

$$\begin{bmatrix} v_x \\ v_y \end{bmatrix} = \frac{d\begin{bmatrix} x \\ y \end{bmatrix}}{dt} = \begin{bmatrix} \dfrac{dx}{dt} \\ \dfrac{dy}{dt} \end{bmatrix}$$

Now that you have this equation in vector form, you can guarantee that it holds in all dimensions and coordinate systems. In three dimensions, then, the equation is still this:

$$\mathbf{v} = \frac{d\mathbf{x}}{dt}$$

and the components are usually written like this:

$$\begin{bmatrix} v_x \\ v_y \\ v_z \end{bmatrix} = \frac{d\begin{bmatrix} x \\ y \\ z \end{bmatrix}}{dt} = \begin{bmatrix} \dfrac{dx}{dt} \\ \dfrac{dy}{dt} \\ \dfrac{dz}{dt} \end{bmatrix}$$

The velocity vector, being a vector, has both a direction and a magnitude. The direction is the direction the point particle is moving, and the magnitude is the speed, as shown in Figure 7.9:

$$\text{speed} = |v| = v$$

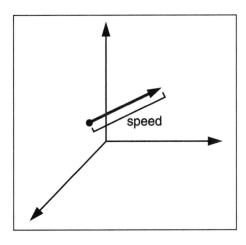

Figure 7.9
The velocity vector of a point particle can be resolved into direction and speed.

You can generalize all the other equations I've mentioned in the same way by expressing them as vectors, as shown here:

$$v = \frac{dx}{dt}$$

$$a = \frac{dv}{dt}$$

$$F = ma$$

These equations express velocity, acceleration, and force as vectors. You might ask, "So what?"

The answer is that when you're programming 3-D scenes that involve complex systems of moving objects, you can often calculate how the objects behave by treating them as if they were point particles. This generalization provides a simple way to find the linear velocity and acceleration of each object, as well as forces acting on each one. Being able to express velocity, acceleration, and force as vectors means that you can express them as matrices.

Again, you might ask, "So what?"

Recall that 3-D objects in software are defined as meshes that are really a collection of vertices. As an object in a 3-D scene moves, every vertex in the mesh has to move. That means a game must apply the concepts of velocity, acceleration, and force to each vertex in the mesh. Complex objects can involve meshes containing 200,000 triangles with as many as 600,000 vertices!

How can a program possibly calculate the movement of every vertex of an object that complex?

It doesn't. It treats the object as a point and uses vectors representing the forces acting on the object to calculate the velocity and acceleration of the point object. It then expresses velocity and acceleration as matrices. Moving every vertex in the object becomes a matter of doing a matrix multiplication on each vertex. This moves the entire object in a way that realistically simulates the physics of our universe.

The Modeling Point Masses

Now that we have the physics we need, we can write code that models the physics of point masses. This requires that we first create a class for point masses. Next, we'll put the point mass into an environment that is free of gravity and friction. This enables us to see how point masses move with just one external force acting on them. Later chapters demonstrate how to add gravity and friction.

The sample program will display a nice bowling ball moving from left to right across the program's window. Because we're not yet looking at rotational kinematics, the same program doesn't make the ball roll.

Introducing the d3d_point_mass Class

A class that models point masses must store information about its mass, its location, and the forces acting on it. Listing 7.1 presents the definition of the d3d_point_mass class.

note

> You can find the code for this sample program on the CD-ROM that comes with this book. It's in the folder Source\Chapter07\PointMass. If you want to take a quick look at the program in action, you'll find the executable version of it in Source\Chapter07\Bin.

Listing 7.1
The d3d_point_mass Class

```
1     class d3d_point_mass
2     {
3     private:
4         d3d_mesh objectMesh;
5
6         scalar mass;
7         vector_3d centerOfMassLocation;
8         vector_3d linearVelocity;
9         vector_3d linearAcceleration;
```

```
10          vector_3d sumForces;
11
12          D3DXMATRIX worldMatrix;
13
14    public:
15          d3d_point_mass();
16
17          bool LoadMesh(
18              std::string meshFileName);
19
20          void Mass(
21              scalar massValue);
22          scalar Mass(void);
23
24          void Location(
25              vector_3d locationCenterOfMass);
26          vector_3d Location(void);
27
28          void LinearVelocity(
29              vector_3d newVelocity);
30          vector_3d LinearVelocity(void);
31
32          void LinearAcceleration(
33              vector_3d newAcceleration);
34          vector_3d LinearAcceleration(void);
35
36          void Force(
37              vector_3d sumExternalForces);
38          vector_3d Force(void);
39
40          bool Update(
41              scalar changeInTime);
42          bool Render(void);
43    };
```

The d3d_point_mass class defines private data members that contain the object's mesh, mass, center of mass, and properties of movement. This class also defines a special data member just for working with Direct3D. If you look on line 12, you'll see a member called worldMatrix. The world matrix was explained in Chapter 4, "2-D Transformations and Rendering." Direct3D uses the world matrix to update the position and orientation of objects in 3-D space. If your program has multiple d3d_point_mass objects moving through a scene, each one needs a different world matrix to track its position and orientation. The d3d_point_mass class sets its world matrix each time the program calls its Update() function. In its Render() function, the d3d_point_mass class uses the world matrix to animate the point mass.

In addition to the private member data, the d3d_point_mass class defines its public member functions on lines 15–42. Most of them simply set or get the member data. The LoadMesh(), Update(), and Render() functions do the real work for the class. The LoadMesh() function is so simple that its defined as an inline member function in the file PMPointMass.h. It's shown in Listing 7.2.

Listing 7.2
The LoadMesh() Function

```
1      inline bool d3d_point_mass::LoadMesh(
2          std::string meshFileName)
3      {
4          assert(meshFileName.length()>0);
5
6          return (objectMesh.Load(meshFileName));
7      }
```

The LoadMesh() function uses the d3d_mesh::Load() function to load the mesh that gives its appearance.

tip

On line 4 of Listing 7.2, the LoadMesh() function uses an assert() to ensure that the length of the file name is greater than 0. If a program calls this function with an empty file name, the program does not have enough error checking in it. That's a programmer error rather than a runtime error. This function uses the assert() to make sure the programmer catches the error before the software is released. In general, that's how software should guard against programmer errors in parameters.

The Update() function has to work a little harder. It appears in Listing 7.3.

Listing 7.3
The Update() Function

```
1      bool d3d_point_mass::Update(
2          scalar changeInTime)
3      {
4          //
5          // Begin calculating linear dynamics.
6          //
7
8          // Find the linear acceleration.
```

```
9          // a = F/m
10         assert(mass!=0);
11         linearAcceleration = sumForces/mass;
12
13         // Find the linear velocity.
14         linearVelocity += linearAcceleration * changeInTime;
15
16         // Find the new location of the center of mass.
17         centerOfMassLocation += linearVelocity * changeInTime;
18
19         //
20         // End calculating linear dynamics.
21         //
22
23         // Create the translation matrix.
24         D3DXMatrixTranslation(
25             &worldMatrix,
26             centerOfMassLocation.X(),
27             centerOfMassLocation.Y(),
28             centerOfMassLocation.Z());
29
30         return(true);
31     }
```

The d3d_point_mass class's Update() function calculates the linear dynamics of a point mass. For now, it ignores real-world factors such as rotation, friction, and gravity. However, the implementation here forms a solid basis for implementing those real-world factors.

The Update() function begins by asserting that the mass of the object is not zero. This is an important assertion because it catches a common programmer error. The mass should never be zero or negative because that's physically impossible.

warning

In physics simulations, we often ignore the mass of some objects in the system. This helps keep the calculations simple enough to be manageable. If you're using this technique in a game, don't use the d3d_point_mass class to simulate a massless objects. That's not what it's for.

On line 11 of Listing 7.3, the Update() function rearranges the formula **F=ma** into **a=F/m** so that it can find the acceleration of the point mass. In each frame of the game, your program has to calculate the forces acting on the point mass. It then calls the d3d_point_mass::Force() function to set the sum of all the forces. When the program invokes the d3d_point_mass::Update() function, Update() uses the force to calculate the object's reaction.

Next, Update() uses the acceleration to find the new velocity of the object at the end of the time period specified by the parameter changeInTime. On line 17, Update() uses the velocity (and the time) to find the new location of the object's center of mass.

The calculations on lines 11, 14, and 17 are fairly straightforward because of the tools we developed in Chapter 3, "Mathematical Tools for Physics and 3-D Programming." The vectors presented there make these calculations easy. The next step is to convert to matrices so that the program can use the transformations presented in Chapters 4 and 5, "3-D Transformations and Rendering." This begins on line 24 of Listing 7.3.

On lines 24–28, the Update() function invokes the Direct3D D3DXMatrixTranslation() utility function to build a translation matrix. It builds the matrix from the x, y, and z locations of the object's center of mass. The D3DXMatrixTranslation() function stores the translation matrix into the d3d_point_mass object's world matrix. The program uses the world matrix when it calls the d3d_point_mass::Render() function, which is presented in Listing 7.4.

Listing 7.4
The Render() Function

```
1       bool d3d_point_mass::Render(void)
2       {
3           // Save the world transformation matrix.
4           D3DXMATRIX saveWorldMatrix;
5           theApp.D3DRenderingDevice()->GetTransform(
6               D3DTS_WORLD,
7               &saveWorldMatrix);
8
9           // Apply the world transformation matrix for this object.
10          theApp.D3DRenderingDevice()->SetTransform(
11              D3DTS_WORLD,&worldMatrix);
12
13          // Now render the object with its transformations.
14          bool renderedOK=objectMesh.Render();
15
16          // Restore the world transformation matrix.
17          theApp.D3DRenderingDevice()->SetTransform(
18              D3DTS_WORLD,
19              &saveWorldMatrix);
20
21          return (renderedOK);
22      }
```

To render just one d3d_point_mass object, the Render() function needs a world transformation matrix for that specific object. It uses that world matrix to position the d3d_point_mass object in 3-D space. However, Direct3D allows only one world matrix at a time. Therefore, the Render() function must perform the following steps:

1. Save the existing world matrix.
2. Set the d3d_point_mass object's world matrix as the current world matrix.
3. Render the d3d_point_mass object's mesh.
4. Restore the existing world matrix saved in step 1.

Using these steps, the Render() function can position the d3d_point_mass object in the world and render it without disturbing the contents of the existing world matrix. If the Render() function did not save and then restore the existing world matrix, the translation for the current d3d_point_mass object might get applied to other objects in the scene. The results could be undesirable, to say the least.

Listing 7.4 shows that the Render() function for the d3d_point_mass class follows these steps exactly. The function begins by declaring a temporary variable to save the existing world matrix into. Next, it calls the Direct3D GetTransform() function to store the current world matrix in the variable. On lines 10–11, it sets the d3d_point_mass object's world matrix as the current world matrix. It renders the mesh by calling the d3d_mesh::Render() function on line 14. Lines 17–19 restore the existing world matrix.

Using the d3d_point_mass Class

Okay, so now we have a d3d_point_mass class that's just waiting to be used. Let's use it. However, before we do, I want to take a moment to talk briefly about lighting in Direct3D. We'll use some of Direct3D's lighting capabilities to get a decent-looking bowling ball in the sample program.

Enabling Direct3D Lighting

One of the ways we make 3-D objects in our games look better is by using Direct3D's lighting capabilities. At this point, I could launch into a big discussion of how light behaves in nature and how Direct3D simulates it. But I won't. Although light is an aspect of physics, it's not the focus of this book. What we're trying to do here is get things to behave as they would in the real world. Making things look nice is the subject of another book.

note

Color, lighting, and materials are subjects that are closely related to texturing. Games require a knowledge of all of these subjects to look professional. A good introduction to all of them is Mason McCuskey's *Special Effects Game Programming with DirectX* (Premier Press).

For our purposes, all we really need to know is that DirectX does a lot of the work of lighting 3-D scenes for us. It defines several different types of lights. Among these are ambient light and diffuse light. At this point, we'll only worry about diffuse light.

The color that we see on the screen when Direct3D displays a 3-D object depends on the color of the object's material and the color of the light. If the program adds a texture, that factors in as well. However, let's set that aside for now.

The bowling ball used in the sample program is blue. What we want is for the ball to look blue and to look round. Using diffuse lighting can get us that. Let's make some minor changes to the framework so that we can use diffuse lighting.

First, we have to change the InitD3D() function in D3DApp.cpp so that it uses Direct3D's lighting. Look at the source code on the CD-ROM. Open the file D3DApp.cpp in the folder Source\Chapter07\PointMass and find the InitD3D() function. Right near the end of the function is a line of code that reads

```
theApp.d3dDevice->SetRenderState(D3DRS_LIGHTING,theApp.enableD3DLighting);
```

In previous chapters, we had lighting turned off, so that line read

```
theApp.d3dDevice->SetRenderState(D3DRS_LIGHTING,TRUE);
```

Now we're passing that information to the framework in the OnAppLoad() function. Listing 7.5 presents the code for OnAppLoad().

Listing 7.5
The New Version of OnAppLoad()

```
1      bool OnAppLoad()
2      {
3            window_init_params windowParams;
4            windowParams.appWindowTitle = "Point Mass Test";
5            windowParams.defaultX=100;
6            windowParams.defaultY=100;
7            windowParams.defaultWidth = 400;
8            windowParams.defaultHeight = 400;
9
10           d3d_init_params d3dParams;
11           d3dParams.renderingDeviceClearFlags = D3DCLEAR_TARGET | D3DCLEAR_ZBUFFER;
12           d3dParams.surfaceBackgroundColor = D3DCOLOR_XRGB(50,50,50);
13           d3dParams.enableAutoDepthStencil = true;
14           d3dParams.autoDepthStencilFormat = D3DFMT_D16;
15           d3dParams.enableD3DLighting = true;
16
17           // This call must appear in this function.
```

```
18        theApp.InitApp(windowParams,d3dParams);
19
20        return (true);
21    }
```

Remember your framework requires the OnAppLoad() function. In this sample program, you'll find it in the file PointMassTest.cpp.

As in Chapter 6, "Meshes and X Files," the programs pass the startup parameters for Windows and Direct3D into the framework using the d3d_init_params structure. I added some structure members that enable games to specify the default position and size. I also added a member that lets them turn Direct3D lighting on or off when the game starts. Here's the new structure definition:

```
struct d3d_init_params
{
    DWORD renderingDeviceClearFlags;
    D3DCOLOR surfaceBackgroundColor;
    bool enableAutoDepthStencil;
    D3DFORMAT autoDepthStencilFormat;
    bool enableD3DLighting;
};
```

Line 15 of OnAppLoad() in Listing 7.5 sets the enableD3DLighting member to true. OnAppLoad() passes the structure to the framework's InitApp() function. InitApp() is a member of the d3d_app class. It's on the CD-ROM in the file PMD3DApp.h, which is in the folder Source\Chapter07\PointMass. The code for the InitApp() function is also given in Listing 7.6.

Listing 7.6
The New InitApp() Function

```
1     inline bool d3d_app::InitApp(
2         window_init_params windowParams,
3         d3d_init_params d3dParams)
4     {
5         // Set the initial window parameters.
6         windowTitle=windowParams.appWindowTitle;
7         defaultX = windowParams.defaultX;
8         defaultY = windowParams.defaultY;
9         defaultHeight = windowParams.defaultHeight;
10        defaultWidth = windowParams.defaultWidth;
11
12        // Set the initial D3D parameters.
13        deviceClearFlags = d3dParams.renderingDeviceClearFlags;
14        backgroundColor = d3dParams.surfaceBackgroundColor;
```

```
15              enableAutoDepthStencil = d3dParams.enableAutoDepthStencil;
16              autoDepthStencilFormat = d3dParams.autoDepthStencilFormat;
17              enableD3DLighting = d3dParams.enableD3DLighting;
18
19              appInitialized=true;
20              return(appInitialized);
21      }
```

As you can see from Listing 7.6, the new version of the InitApp() function simply copies the information it received in the structure into some new members of the d3d_app class. Let's look at Listing 7.7 to see the new definition of the d3d_app class.

Listing 7.7
The New d3d_app Class Definition

```
1       class d3d_app
2       {
3       private:
4           // App properties
5           bool appInitialized;
6
7           // Window properties
8           std::string windowTitle;
9           int defaultX, defaultY;
10          int defaultHeight,defaultWidth;
11
12          // D3D properties
13          LPDIRECT3D9             direct3D; // Used to create the D3DDevice
14          LPDIRECT3DDEVICE9       d3dDevice; // Our rendering device
15          LPDIRECT3DVERTEXBUFFER9 vertexBuffer; // Buffer to hold vertices
16          DWORD deviceClearFlags;
17          D3DCOLOR backgroundColor;
18          bool enableAutoDepthStencil;
19          D3DFORMAT autoDepthStencilFormat;
20          bool enableD3DLighting;
21
22      public:
23          d3d_app();
24          bool InitApp(
25              window_init_params windowParams,
26              d3d_init_params d3dParams);
27
28          LPDIRECT3DDEVICE9 D3DRenderingDevice(void);
```

```
29
30         LPDIRECT3DVERTEXBUFFER9 D3DVertexBuffer(void);
31         void D3DVertexBuffer(
32             LPDIRECT3DVERTEXBUFFER9 vertexBufferPointer);
33
34         DWORD RenderingDeviceClearFlags(void);
35         D3DCOLOR BackgroundSurfaceColor(void);
36
37         friend INT WINAPI AppMain(
38             HINSTANCE hInst,
39             HINSTANCE,
40             LPSTR,
41             INT);
42         friend HRESULT InitD3D(
43             HWND hWnd);
44         friend VOID CleanupD3D();
45     };
```

As you look at Listing 7.7, notice in particular that there are new members on lines 9–10 and 20. These accommodate the new information being passed in through the InitApp() function. As I mentioned earlier, this information is used in the InitD3D() function.

Okay, so now we have Direct3D lighting activated, and we're ready to start tossing a bowling ball around. Let's get back to our discussion of how to use the d3d_point_mass class for modeling physics.

Initializing a d3d_point_mass Object

If you look at the GameInitialization() function in the file PointMassTest.cpp, you'll see that it initializes a d3d_point_mass object. The declaration of the d3d_point_mass object, which looks like this:

```
d3d_point_mass theObject
```

appears near the top of the file. Take a look at Listing 7.8 to see how the GameInitialization() function sets up the d3d_point_mass object.

Listing 7.8
The GameInitialization() Function
```
1     bool GameInitialization()
2     {
3         // Load the ball's mesh.
4         theObject.LoadMesh("bowlball.x");
5
6         // Set its starting location.
```

```
7              theObject.Location(vector_3d(-5.0f,0.0,0.0));
8
9              // Set the mass.
10             theObject.Mass(10);
11
12             D3DLIGHT9 light;
13             ZeroMemory( &light, sizeof(light) );
14             light.Type = D3DLIGHT_DIRECTIONAL;
15
16             D3DXVECTOR3 vecDir;
17             vecDir = D3DXVECTOR3(0.0f, -1.0f, 1.0f);
18             D3DXVec3Normalize( (D3DXVECTOR3*)&light.Direction, &vecDir );
19
20             // Set directional light diffuse color.
21             light.Diffuse.r = 1.0f;
22             light.Diffuse.g = 1.0f;
23             light.Diffuse.b = 1.0f;
24             light.Diffuse.a = 1.0f;
25             theApp.D3DRenderingDevice()->SetLight( 0, &light );
26             theApp.D3DRenderingDevice()->LightEnable( 0, TRUE );
27             theApp.D3DRenderingDevice()->SetRenderState(
28                  D3DRS_DIFFUSEMATERIALSOURCE,
29                  D3DMCS_MATERIAL);
30
31             return (true);
32      }
```

The GameInitialization() function in the sample program for this chapter accomplishes three basic tasks. On line 4 of Listing 7.8, it loads the point mass's mesh. The mesh is a bowling ball that is defined in the file bowlball.x. This file is with the sample program in the folder Source\Chapter07\PointMass.

The second task that GameInitialization() performs is to set the properties of the point mass. It sets the starting location of the bowling ball to the left of the program's window. It isn't displayed initially. GameInitialization() also sets the mass of the bowling ball. I've set it to 10 kilograms (22 pounds), which is a fairly hefty weight for a bowling ball.

The GameInitialization() function's final task is to set up diffuse lighting for Direct3D. On line 12, it declares a D3DLIGHT9 variable. It calls the Windows ZeroMemory() function to initialize the light. On line 14, it sets the light type as directional. GameInitialization() uses a D3DXVECTOR3 variable on lines 16–18 to define a vector that specifies where the light points. The light color is set to white on lines 21–24. Line 25 tells Direct3D to use the light, and line 26 tells it to turn the light on. Lines 27–29 make Direct3D combine the light color and the ball's material color to get the final color.

Well, everything's ready. We have a point mass with a mesh. We have our lights set up. I suppose this is a good time to make some pithy joke that transitions us to the next section that involves the phrase, "Lights, camera, action." Unfortunately, I can't think of one. So please just read the next section.

Updating a d3d_point_mass Object

When the program runs, it updates the point mass for each frame of animation. As presented in previous chapters, the update is done in the required function UpdateFrame(). To see the code for UpdateFrame(), refer to Listing 7.9.

Listing 7.9
The UpdateFrame() Function

```
1    bool UpdateFrame()
2    {
3        // Set up the view matrix as in previous examples.
4        D3DXVECTOR3 eyePoint(0.0f,3.0f,-5.0f);
5        D3DXVECTOR3 lookatPoint(0.0f,0.0f,0.0f);
6        D3DXVECTOR3 upDirection(0.0f,1.0f,0.0f);
7        D3DXMATRIXA16 viewMatrix;
8        D3DXMatrixLookAtLH(&viewMatrix,&eyePoint,&lookatPoint,&upDirection);
9        theApp.D3DRenderingDevice()->SetTransform(D3DTS_VIEW,&viewMatrix);
10
11       // Set up the projection matrix as in previous examples.
12       D3DXMATRIXA16 projectionMatrix;
13       D3DXMatrixPerspectiveFovLH(&projectionMatrix,D3DX_PI/4,1.0f,1.0f,100.0f);
14       theApp.D3DRenderingDevice()->SetTransform(D3DTS_PROJECTION,&projectionMatrix);
15
16       //
17       // Apply a one-time force to the ball.
18       //
19       // This initialization is done only once.
20       static bool forceApplied = false;
21
22       // If the force has not yet been applied...
23       if (!forceApplied)
24       {
25           // Apply a force.
26           theObject.Force(vector_3d(2.0f,0.0,0.0));
27           forceApplied = true;
28       }
29       // Else the force was already applied...
30       else
```

```
31        {
32            // Set it to zero.
33            theObject.Force(vector_3d(0.0,0.0,0.0));
34        }
35
36        /* Set the parameter to a value between 0 and 1 for smoother
37        animation. */
38        theObject.Update(1);
39
40        return (true);
41    }
```

The UpdateFrame() function starts off similarly to the UpdateFrame() functions from previous chapters. It first sets up the matrices that Direct3D requires. When that's done, it applies a one-time force to the bowling ball to make it move. To do so, UpdateFrame() declares a static variable.

You might know that in C++, static variables in functions are initialized the first time the program calls the function. After that, the initialization is never performed. Using a static variable here helps the program keep track of whether the force has been applied. If it hasn't, the value of forceApplied is false. That causes the if statement, which begins on line 23, to set the force acting on the bowling ball on line 26. It also sets the variable forceApplied to true.

note

Notice that the force is applied in the positive x direction. That makes the bowling ball move toward the right. Its initial position was set as off-screen to the left. Therefore, when the program runs, the ball moves across the program's window from left to right. After the ball disappears off the right end of the window, close the program. You won't see it do anything else.

The next time that the framework calls the UpdateFrame() function, forceApplied will still be true. When it is, the program executes the else clause of the if statement. The else clause sets the force to zero. The result is that the ball gets a push the first time the UpdateFrame() function executes. After that, no other forces act on the ball. The ball just keeps moving into virtual infinity for as long as you let the program run. It's nice to know that our simulation acts in accordance with Newton's laws. It tells us that we're writing the program correctly.

The last thing that the UpdateFrame() function does is to call the d3d_point_mass::Update() function on the bowling ball. The d3d_point_mass::Update() function updates the ball's position based on the force acting on it (if any), the current velocity (if any), and the current acceleration (if any). If you want to look again at the d3d_point_mass::Update() function, it's back in Listing 7.3.

Rendering a d3d_point_mass Object

Rendering the bowling ball is really, really tough. If fact, it's excruciating. Are you ready for it? Okay, look at Listing 7.10.

Listing 7.10
Too Tough for Me, Baby

```
1      bool RenderFrame()
2      {
3            theObject.Render();
4            return (true);
5      }
```

Wow! That was a killer! Okay, so I'm a ham. If you're new to computer graphics, you just can't appreciate how wonderful it is to have something this short that renders a complex object like a bowling ball. I started in graphics more than 20 years ago. Back then, I had to write my own renderer to get anything displayed. It was in Assembly Language. If you don't know what that means, you're very, very lucky. Those were sometimes painful years.

In any case, Listing 7.10 shows that all the RenderFrame() function does is call the d3d_point_mass class's Render() function. That function, in turn, uses the d3d_mesh function to apply the world matrix created by rendering the d3d_point_mass class's Update() function. It also calls the d3d_mesh::Render() function to render the point mass's mesh. Because the underlying functions do so much, there's not really a lot for the RenderFrame() function to do. In other words, when you're using the d3d_point_mass class, you just have to set it up, apply a force, and let it go. There's really little else to do. Nice.

Point Masses in Games

How often do we *really* use point masses in games? Constantly. And there are more uses coming. As processing power increases, point masses will become much more important in games. Let me give you an example.

Suppose that you're writing a game that lets the player shoot a wall. Such games do not use point masses. When the bullet hits, these games apply a texture to the wall to show the bullet hole and discoloration caused by the gunpowder. But the wall's not really damaged. That's okay, but games are getting better.

Some games use what are called particle systems to simulate small fragments of the wall flying around the room. The fragments disappear after a specified period of time. Again, though, the wall is not really damaged.

If you have the processing power, you can simulate the player shooting a hole in the wall. However, the program has to keep track of how much force actually hits the wall. If the player is standing far away, his bullet shouldn't get through the wall. If he's close, the bullet should penetrate and leave a hole. That takes point masses.

More complex objects are often composed of point masses. Any time you're creating an object that's made of heavy things connected by much lighter things, you can use a collection of point masses. If you do, you can blow it up nicely. All the point masses fly apart in a satisfying way. Toss in some nifty explosion effects, and you've got a game.

Summary

That's it for the kinematics of point particles. We've come a long way! Starting with some basic ideas about point particles and speed, we built a system to model them and took it out for a spin. Excellent.

We haven't yet looked at forces like gravity, deflection, drag, and friction, but we will soon. At this point, we have a pretty realistic model of a ball, so let's leave it at that.

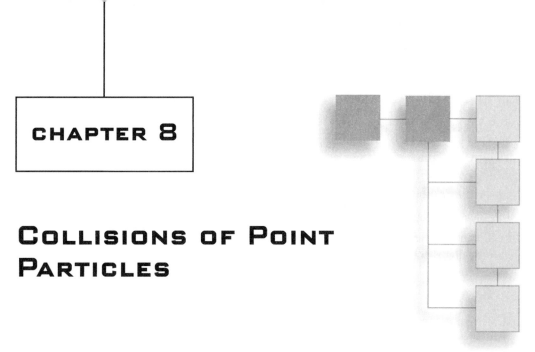

CHAPTER 8

COLLISIONS OF POINT PARTICLES

So far, the point masses created in the previous chapter move around under any force you might care to give them. We could keep adding forces, making the model more realistic (and complicated!), but we would still be lacking something fundamental because the balls don't interact. In this chapter, we'll do something about that.

However, before we dive into collisions, it's important to understand that simulating collisions is really a combination of two distinct problems. The first is collision detection. To be able to react to collisions, games have to know that a collision has occurred. It sounds simple, but it's not. Collision detection is complex.

In any case, collision detection is a programming problem, not a physics problem. It's definitely not the focus of this book. Therefore, I'll give an overview of collision detection and move on to the second problem associated with collisions: collision response.

Collision response *is* a physics problem. When we talk about collision response, we're speaking of how objects react when they collide. That's determined strictly by physics. After the overview of collision detection, we'll look at collision response for point masses.

Collision Detection

Computer Science departments are full of professors and grad students trying to work out newer, faster, better collision algorithms. Consequently, there's a tremendous bulk of literature on the subject that you could spend the rest of your life sifting through. In computer games, simple solutions are usually the best, so we'll look at the most common methods of collision detection.

Bounding Spheres

This is the easiest type of collision detection. Fit a sphere around your object, and shrink the radius until it fits as tightly as possible, as in Figure 8.1. If anything comes within this sphere, you assume that the object has collided with it.

For example, you can use this method when testing for collisions between objects and a ground plane. Here's the algorithm:

1. First check to see if the object is above the plane. If it is, proceed to step 2.

2. Test to determine whether the distance from the center of the point mass to the ground is less than the radius of the bounding sphere. If it is, proceed to step 3. Otherwise, skip step 3 and repeat this algorithm for the next object in the scene.

3. The object has collided with the ground. React to the collision.

This method works just as well with any planar surface, such as walls. Figure 8.2 applies this algorithm to collisions with walls.

The objects in question do not have to be balls. They can be any shape that you can fit into a sphere.

Your game applies a variation of this algorithm to collisions with other point masses. Two objects are said to have collided if their bounding spheres overlap, as in Figure 8.3.

To detect whether a collision has taken place, you need the radii of the two bounding spheres and the position vectors of the objects. You then compare the distance between the bounding spheres of two objects to the sum of their radii, as in Figure 8.4. If the separation between the two objects is less than the sum of the radii, a collision has taken place.

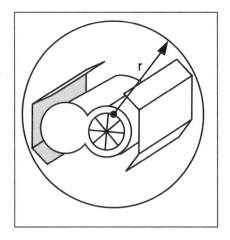

Figure 8.1
An object with a bounding sphere.

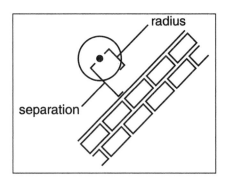

Figure 8.2
Detecting a ball colliding with a wall.

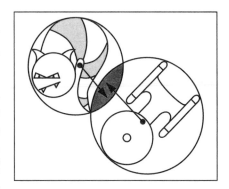

Figure 8.3
Two objects with bounding spheres colliding.

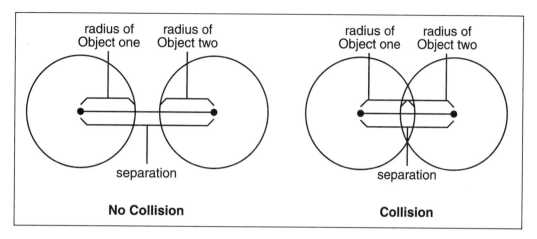

Figure 8.4
Comparing the separation between two objects to the sum of their radii.

Using vectors makes these calculations easy. Suppose that you're creating a pool game, and you want to write a function for detecting whether two balls have collided. If you have the positions of the centers of the balls as vectors, you can compute the distance between them by subtracting the vectors. Figure 8.5 illustrates this.

Subtracting P_2 from P_1 in Figure 8.5 gives a vector specifying the distance between the two centers of mass. Now your program can find the magnitude of the distance vector. Compare it to the sum of the radii of the bounding spheres. If the distance is less than the sum of the radii, the balls have collided. If not, there is no collision.

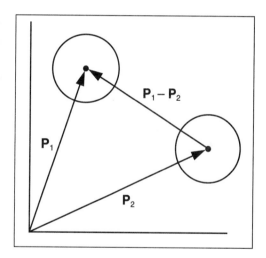

Figure 8.5
Computing the separation vector between two objects.

To make this a little clearer, look at the following code fragment. It takes two d3d_point_mass objects—ball1 and ball2—calculates the separation vector, and compares the length of the separation vector with the sum of the radii.

```
// Calculate the vector between the spheres.
vector_3d distance = ball1. Location() - ball2.Location();
// Compute the actual separation distance.
scalar magnitude = distance.Norm();
```

```
// Calculate the distance at which a collision occurs.
scalar minDistance = (ball1.Radius() + ball2.Radius());
if (magnitude < minDistance)
{
    // A collision occurred, so we have to handle it.
}
```

This algorithm works great, except that it's incredibly slow! Remember that you're going to have to calculate this for every pair of particles in the region. It's the square root in the norm calculation that kills you: It takes about 70 times as long as multiplying floats. Here's a look at that vector_3d::Norm() method I used to calculate the norm:

```
inline scalar vector_3d::Norm(void)
{
    return(sqrtf(x*x + y*y + z*z));
}
```

You could speed this up in several ways, including taking fast numerical approximations of the square root. Clever readers might have noticed an even faster optimization: not taking the square root at all!

If I have two numbers x and y, if x is greater than y, then x^2 had better be greater than y^2. The same concept holds here: Instead of comparing the separation distance to the sum of the radii, I'll compare the *square* of the separation with the *square* of the sum of the radii.

Here's some code that uses this optimization:

```
// Calculate the vector between the spheres.
vector_3d distance = ball1. Location() - ball2.Location();
// Compute the actual separation distance.
scalar magnitude = distance. NormSquared();
// Calculate the distance at which a collision occurs.
scalar minDistance = (ball1.Radius() + ball2.Radius());
// Square the minimum distance.
minDistance*=minDistance;
if (magnitude < minDistance)
{
    // A collision occurred, so we have to handle it.
}
```

In this case, we used the vector_3d::NormSquared() method. It's exactly like the vector_3d::Norm function, except that it doesn't compute that square root.

```
inline scalar vector_3d::NormSquared(void)
{
    return(x*x + y*y + z*z);
}
```

We do have to calculate an extra floating-point multiplication this way, when we square the sum of the radii. However, because that calculation is lightning fast compared to finding the square root, it's definitely worth it.

Using bounding spheres is often the best way to detect collisions. It's simple, it's fast, and it gives great results for many applications. Even when you want to use more sophisticated collision detection algorithms, it's usually worth it to try a bounding sphere first to see whether it's even worth the CPU cycles to try the more complicated method.

Bounding Cylinders

Instead of using bounding spheres, you can try some more complicated shapes. Bounding cylinders work great for games in which most objects are oriented about the same way toward some surface. Good examples are *Doom*-type games where most characters manage to stay standing upright even under a barrage of bullets. Every character stays oriented in the same direction with respect to the floor. Figure 8.6 shows such a character bounded by a cylinder.

To detect collisions, you have to check the top and bottom of the cylinder, as well as its radius. The first step to putting this in code is to add the dimensions to the d3d_point_mass class. Figure 8.7 shows those dimensions in relation to the position of the object.

Figure 8.6
An object in a bounding cylinder.

Testing for collision between bounding cylinders is a two-step process. In the first step, you assume that the bounding cylinders are always oriented as shown in Figures 8.6 and 8.7. That enables you to reduce this to a 2-D problem rather than a 3-D problem. The radius of the bounding cylinder is always in the xz plane. The first step is to treat the objects as circles in the xz plane. Find the distance between the centers of the circles. If the distance is greater than the sum of the radii, there is no collision. However, if the distance is less, there might be a collision.

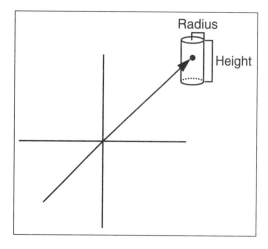

Figure 8.7
Dimensions of the bounding cylinder.

The next step to determining whether there has been a collision is to check whether the vertical distances overlap, as in Figure 8.8.

What matters is whether the top of one cylinder is vertically between the top and bottom of the other cylinder. If it is, the program must handle the collision. If not, there is no collision even though the radii overlap. This occurs, for instance, when the characters in a multiplayer game are on different floors of a building and one walks over the top of the other.

Bounding Boxes

Now that we've done bounding spheres and bounding cylinders, it probably won't surprise you that we can also detect collisions using bounding boxes, as shown in Figure 8.9. You can use bounding boxes in two and three dimensions.

When you use a bounding sphere or a bounding cylinder, you're assuming that the object has that shape, more or less. That might be just fine, but sometimes it can create problems. Look at Figure 8.10, which shows a 2-D polygon. Although a circular bounding area works, it encloses an awful lot that isn't part of the polygon. In this case, a bounding box works much better.

Here's how you check whether two boxes have collided. Pick a vertex on one box. Then see if that vertex is inside the other bounding box. If it is, the boxes have collided, as in Figure 8.11. If it isn't, check the next vertex until you run out of vertices. There are eight vertices in a box.

Note that you'll have to check all the vertices for *both* boxes to avoid errors. In Figure 8.11, if you check only the vertices of the box on the left, you won't find a collision.

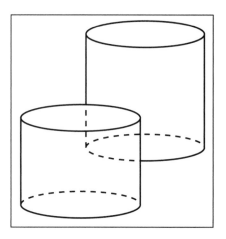

Figure 8.8
Checking on the overlap of bounding cylinders in the vertical direction.

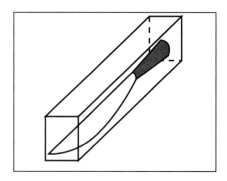

Figure 8.9
A bounding box.

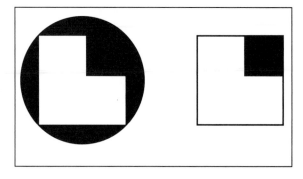

Figure 8.10
Choose the shape of your bounding region to fit the object.

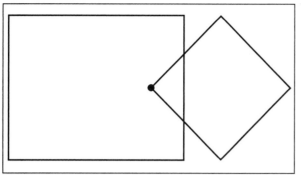

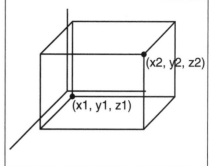

Figure 8.11
Two bounding boxes are colliding if the vertex of one is inside the other.

Figure 8.12
A box sitting flat in a Cartesian plane can be defined with two points.

You can define a box with two vertices in a Cartesian coordinate system, as shown in Figure 8.12, as long as the box is constrained to sit flat. I'll call these vertices (x1, y1, z1) and (x2, y2, z2). Checking whether a vertex (x, y, z) is in this box is pretty easy. It's much like the check you just did on the top and bottom of the cylinder, but in all three directions.

```
if( x >= x1 && x <= x2) // Contained on the x axis
    if( y >= y1 && y <= y2) // Contained on the y axis
        if( z >= z1 && z <= z2) // Contained on the z axis
            ( /* The Point is Contained */ )
```

Bounding boxes take quite a bit more CPU time to calculate than bounding spheres or cylinders, but they're often helpful. One of these three methods will serve most of the time.

note

A bounding box that is constrained to sit flat is called an axis-aligned bounding box (AABB). You'll see this term a lot in game programming literature.

Optimization with Spatial Partitioning

You can calculate the number of possible collisions, N_c, you have to deal with in each frame with this formula, where n is the number of objects:

$$N_c = \frac{n!}{2!(n-2)!}$$

For large n, this number is approximately equal to half the square of n. That is $N_c \approx n^2 / 2$.

Factorials

The ! sign is a *factorial*. This is a little hard to explain in words, so let me give you a formula and some examples.

$$n! = \prod_{k=1}^{n} k$$

The factorial of zero is defined to be one ($0! = 1$). Here are a few examples:

$$3! = 3 \times 2 \times 1 = 6$$
$$5! = 5 \times 4 \times 3 \times 2 \times 1 = 120$$
$$6!/4! = (6 \times 5 \times 4 \times 3 \times 2 \times 1)/(4 \times 3 \times 2 \times 1) = 6 \times 5 = 30$$

Table 8.1 lists the number of collisions you need to check for several values of n. You can see from the table that the number grows large quickly as you increase the objects. 10,000 objects wouldn't be ridiculous for a game once the bullets started flying. That's almost 50 million possible collisions! This makes collision algorithms a good place to optimize.

Table 8.1 Number of Possible Collisions

Number of Objects	Number of Possible Collisions
2	1
4	6
10	45
20	190
100	4950
1,000	499,500
10,000	49,995,000

Still, making faster collisions isn't going to solve the fundamental problem here. The only way to do that is to reduce the number of collisions you have to deal with.

One way to do this is called *spatial partitioning*. The idea is to divide the universe into cells, as in Figure 8.13. You only need to check for collisions in those regions near the player.

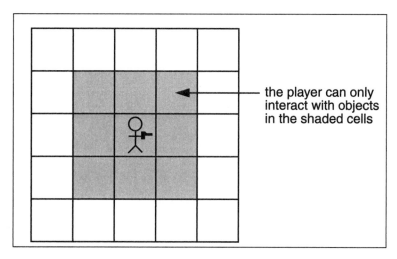

the player can only interact with objects in the shaded cells

Figure 8.13
Spatial partitioning can speed up collision detection.

tip

You can also use spatial partition to clip graphics. Why calculate and render things the player can't see?

Let's say that you've divided your world into a $10 \times 10 \times 10$ grid of cells. That's 1,000 cells. If there are 10,000 objects, each cell will average 10 objects. If the player can only interact with objects in the closest $3 \times 3 \times 3$ block of cells, you only have to calculate collisions for these 27 cells. That's about 270 objects, or 270!/2!269! $\approx$ 36,500 possible collisions. 36,500 is quite an improvement over 50 million!

Collision Response

What happens when the objects actually do collide?

Massive confusion—that's what happens. Things squish together. Cracks form, and chips of material go hurtling away. Sound erupts, and sparks fly. The objects heat up, and the air gets more turbulent.

Can we hope to model all this?

No way.

Here's what we're going to do instead. Consider a one-dimensional collision between two objects, as in Figure 8.14. Two objects with masses m_1 and m_2 fly in with some velocities v_1 and v_2, stuff happens, and the two objects fly out with different velocities v_1' and v_2'. The question becomes this: Given the masses and incoming velocities, what are the outgoing velocities?

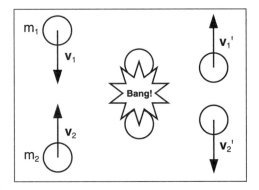

Figure 8.14
A collision between two objects.

We're going to assume that the collision (that is, all of this nasty, hard-to-model stuff in the middle) is short and ask ourselves if there are relationships between the velocities of the objects coming in and their velocities going out. It turns out that there are.

Conservation of Momentum

There's another way we can write Newton's second law. It looks like this:

$$\mathbf{F} = \frac{d\mathbf{p}}{dt}$$

where $\mathbf{F}$ is the force and $\mathbf{p}$ is the momentum. What is *momentum*? It's usually just defined in physics books as the product of the mass of an object times its velocity. However, a professor friend of mine says that momentum is inertia in motion. That's the best conceptual definition of momentum that I've ever encountered.

$$\mathbf{p} = m\mathbf{v}$$

Imagine that we have a system of particles, each with its own momentum, all in a big box in space. They're flying past each other, doing whatever, but we aren't applying forces to them from the outside. If we add up the momentum of all the particles, we have the momentum for the system. Now, using Newton's second law,

$$\frac{d\mathbf{p}}{dt} = 0$$

The only solution to this equation is that the momentum is constant. This leads us to a nice general principle that the momentum of this type of system must be constant for all time. That is, if the equation

$$\frac{\Delta\mathbf{p}}{\Delta t} = 0$$

is true for a system, then

$$\Delta\mathbf{p} = 0$$

The reason for this is that dividing by 0 is undefined, so Δt cannot be 0. Therefore, it must be Δ that's 0. This gives the equation:

$$\mathbf{p}' = \mathbf{p} + \Delta\mathbf{p}$$
$$\mathbf{p}' = \mathbf{p}$$

This is a mathematical way of stating the principle of the Conservation of Momentum. Formally, here's the way that the conservation of momentum works: In a system with no outside forces applied, the momentum is constant.

We can apply conservation of momentum to the collision problem. Because the momentum is constant, the sum of the momenta before and after the collision must be equal.

$$\mathbf{p}_1 + \mathbf{p}_2 = \mathbf{p}_1' + \mathbf{p}_2'$$

where $\mathbf{p}_1$ is the momentum of particle one before the collision, $\mathbf{p}_1'$ is the momentum of particle one after the collision, and similarly for the second particle. I'm assuming there aren't little bits flying off that could carry momentum away.

Plugging in $\mathbf{p} = mv$ for each particle, we get this:

$$m_1\mathbf{v}_1 + m_2\mathbf{v}_2 = m_1\mathbf{v}_1' + m_2\mathbf{v}_2'$$

Because we're doing a one-dimensional collision, we can write this as follows:

$$m_1 v_1 + m_2 v_2 = m_1 v_1' + m_2 v_2'$$

This is really a great result. We have a nice relationship between the velocities before the collision and the velocities afterward that's independent of anything that happens during the actual collision.

Still, it's not enough to actually solve for the motion. It leaves us with only one equation, and we would like to be able to solve for both v_1' and v_2'.

Energy

To talk much more about collisions, I'm going to have to say a little something about energy and the related concept of work. If you keep pushing on something with a constant force while it moves over some distance, as in Figure 8.15, it moves faster and faster. This takes some effort. That effort is called *work*, and it's given by the dot product of force and distance.

$$W = \mathbf{F} \bullet \mathbf{x}$$

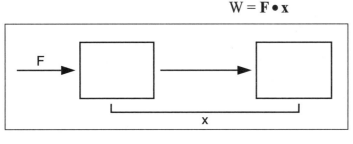

Figure 8.15
Applying a force over a distance.

Let's say that we're accelerating something from rest at a position $\mathbf{x} = \mathbf{0}$, at a constant acceleration to some velocity $\mathbf{v}$ in a time t. In this case, we can use the following equations:

$$\mathbf{x} = (\frac{1}{2})\mathbf{a}t^2$$

$$\mathbf{v} = \mathbf{a}t$$

We also have Newton's second law:

$$\mathbf{F} = m\mathbf{a}$$

Combining all these, we can solve for the work required to accelerate an object of mass m to a speed $\mathbf{v}$.

$$
\begin{aligned}
W &= \mathbf{F} \bullet \mathbf{x} \\
&= m\mathbf{a} \bullet \mathbf{x} \\
&= m\mathbf{a} \bullet \left(\frac{1}{2}\right)\mathbf{a}t^2 \\
&= \left(\frac{1}{2}\right)m(\mathbf{a} \bullet \mathbf{a})\, t^2 \\
&= \left(\frac{1}{2}\right)m(\mathbf{a}t \bullet \mathbf{a}t) \\
&= \left(\frac{1}{2}\right)m(\mathbf{v} \bullet \mathbf{v}) \\
&= \left(\frac{1}{2}\right)mv^2
\end{aligned}
$$

Most of this is just simple substitution. It also uses the fact that a vector dotted with itself gives the square of the norm of the original vector.

warning

Don't forget that the norm of a vector **v** can be written in two ways: v or |v|.

This equation might look familiar to you if you've had a physics class. This quantity is called the *kinetic energy*. It's the energy of a body in motion. I'm going to write the kinetic energy as a capital K, like this:

$$K = \left(\frac{1}{2}\right)mv^2$$

Work can then be reinterpreted as the change in energy of a system due to forces on it. If there are no forces on a system, there is no work done, and the energy is constant. This principle is called the *Conservation of Energy*.

Elastic Collisions

Now let's get back to collisions. Recall that applying the conservation of momentum gave this equation:

$$m_1 v_1 + m_2 v_2 = m_1 v_1' + m_2 v_2'$$

In this equation, m_1 and m_2 are the masses, v_1 and v_2 are the velocities before the collisions, and v_1' and v_2' are the velocities afterward.

Conservation of energy says the sum of the energies before the collision is equal to the sum of the energies afterward. If I assume that all the energy from before the collision goes into the motion of the balls afterward, I can write this:

$$K_1 + K_2 = K_1' + K_2'$$

where the Ks are the kinetic energies of the objects before and after the collision.

If you plug in the definition for K, K = (1/2)mv², you get this:

$$\left(\frac{1}{2}\right)m_1 v_1^2 + \left(\frac{1}{2}\right)m_2 v_2^2 = \left(\frac{1}{2}\right)m_1 v_1'^2 + \left(\frac{1}{2}\right)m_2 v_2'^2$$

note

The preceding equation works in one, two, or three dimensions.

Now we have two equations and two unknowns, so we can solve for the final velocities. The algebra is easy because we're working with scalars, but it's a little tedious to print in a book, so I'm just going to give you the result:

$$v_1' = \frac{(m_1 - m_2)v_1}{m_1 + m_2} + \frac{2m_2v_2}{m_1 + m_2}$$

$$v_2' = \frac{(m_2 - m_1)v_2}{m_1 + m_2} + \frac{2m_1v_1}{m_1 + m_2}$$

Inelastic Collisions

Let's say that the two colliding objects are lumps of clay, as in Figure 8.16. Then, when we throw them together, they're going to stick into one massive blob with mass m_1+m_2.

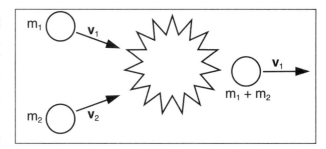

Figure 8.16
An inelastic collision.

With this setup, we can write the conservation of momentum like this:

$$m_1v_1 + m_2v_2 = (m_1+m_2)v'$$

where v' is the velocity of the final blob. Rearrange to solve for the final velocity.

$$v' = m_1v_1 + \frac{m_2v_2}{m_1 + m_2}$$

Nice! For an inelastic collision, you can completely solve the collision without talking about the energy at all.

note

Inelastic collisions do come up in games. When you lodge a bullet into an alien abdomen, bullet and alien are joined and go flying off in the same direction.

One thing might seem a little strange. If we got the elastic collision result just by assuming energy and momentum conservation, why do we get a different result for this inelastic collision?

The answer is that in an inelastic collision, not all the energy goes into the final motion of the objects. When the lumps of clay stuck together, they were deformed, and heat was generated inside them. Energy was still conserved, but we didn't track all of it.

The Coefficient of Restitution

Look again at the equations for an elastic collision, the conservation of energy and momentum:

$$m_1 v_1 + m_2 v_2 = m_1 v_1' + m_2 v_2'$$

$$\left(\frac{1}{2}\right) m_1 v_1^2 + \left(\frac{1}{2}\right) m_2 v_2^2 = \left(\frac{1}{2}\right) m_1 v_1'^2 + \left(\frac{1}{2}\right) m_2 v_2'^2$$

Let me rearrange these two equations a little:

$$m_1 (v_1 - v_1') = -m_2 (v_2 - v_2')$$

$$m_1 (v_1 - v_1')(v_1 + v_1') = -m_2 (v_2 - v_2')(v_2 + v_2')$$

If you divide the second of these by the first and do a little rearrangement, you get this:

$$\frac{-(v_1' - v_2')}{v_1 - v_2} = 1 \qquad \text{(elastic)}$$

That is, the difference in velocities before the event is equal to and opposite of the difference afterward.

What does this quantity look like for the inelastic collision? In the end, the two particles become one, so $v_1' = v_2'$; therefore, this quantity is 0.

$$\frac{-(v_1' - v_2')}{v_1 - v_2} = 0 \qquad \text{(inelastic)}$$

Collisions in the real world aren't perfectly elastic or inelastic. Most of them take up some energy in the jumble of the collision, but the objects don't remain stuck together. To describe these circumstances, we're going to define the *coefficient of restitution*, e.

$$e = \frac{-(v_1' - v_2')}{v_1 - v_2}$$

If $e = 0$, it's a completely inelastic collision; if $e = 1$, it's perfectly elastic. We'll usually pick something in between, generally just by our intuition about how something should behave. For billiard balls, you'd pick something near 1; billiard balls don't deform because they don't heat much. For nerf balls, the coefficient of restitution needs to be something closer to 0—maybe 0.2.

note

You can get a fun little effect by setting the coefficient of restitution greater than 1. This system doesn't just conserve energy—every collision makes energy!

Collision Equations

Using the coefficient of restitution and momentum conservation, we can derive the final equations we'll use for calculating collisions in the physics model. Here are the two together:

$$e = \frac{-(v_1' - v_2')}{v_1 - v_2}$$

$$m_1 v_1 + m_2 v_2 = m_1 v_1' + m_2 v_2'$$

By rearrangement and substitution, you can solve for v_1' and v_2'.

$$v_1' = \frac{(m_1 - e m_2) v_1 + (1 + e) m_2 v_2}{m_1 + m_2}$$

$$v_2' = \frac{(m_2 - e m_1) v_2 + (1 + e) m_1 v_1}{m_1 + m_2}$$

This is exactly what we've been looking for: an equation that will describe any linear collision. Try plugging in $e = 0$ and $e = 1$ as a check to make sure you get the collision equations for inelastic and elastic collisions.

Point Particle Collisions in Two and Three Dimensions

This section ought to be short. Why? Because, in general, exact solution of collisions in two and three dimensions is too complex. Usually you don't have enough information to solve the two- and three-dimensional equations, except for inelastic collisions. In elastic collisions in two and three dimensions, you need to know additional details about the collision, such as the force law of the interaction between the bodies (for example, Newton's law of gravitation) or the detailed shape of the colliding bodies.

Collisions of Spheres

Because point particle collisions are generally too difficult, we're going to turn our attention to spheres. Suppose that we have two massive, uniform spheres undergoing a frictionless collision, as in Figure 8.17. They come in with velocities $\mathbf{v_1}$ and $\mathbf{v_2}$ and leave with velocities $\mathbf{v_1}'$ and $\mathbf{v_2}'$. Note that the point of contact has to be on a line connecting the centers of the spheres. This line is perpendicular to the surfaces of the spheres.

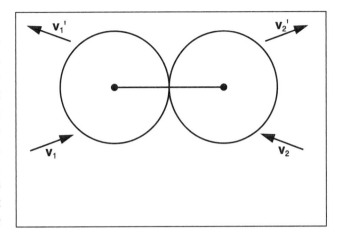

Figure 8.17
Two spheres colliding.

Because this is the only point of contact, the line acts as a line of action for the two spheres. In other words, we can treat the collision problem as one dimensional along this line. The technical reason we can do this is that there is no change in momentum perpendicular to the line of action.

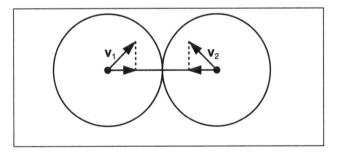

Figure 8.18
To convert this problem to a linear collision, project the initial velocity vectors onto the line of action.

To find the equivalent one-dimensional problem for this collision, all we have to do is project the initial velocities of the spheres onto the line of action, as in Figure 8.18. Using these projected velocities, you solve the problem using the equations we derived for the linear collision.

You can find the unit vector for this line of action by normalizing the displacement vector between the centers of the two spheres. Find the displacement vector by subtracting the position vectors of the spheres, as shown in Figure 8.19.

After you have the unit vector, which can be represented by $\hat{\mathbf{n}}$, the projection, v_{1p}, of $\mathbf{v}_1$ is $\mathbf{v}_1 \cdot \hat{\mathbf{n}}$ and the projection, v_{2p}, of $\mathbf{v}_2$ is $\mathbf{v}_2 \cdot \hat{\mathbf{n}}$. These projected velocities are plugged into the linear collision equations.

$$v'_{1p} = \frac{(m_1 - em_2)v_{1p} + (1+e)m_2v_{2p}}{m_1 + m_2}$$

$$v'_{2p} = \frac{(m_2 - em_1)v_{2p} + (1+e)m_1v_{1p}}{m_1 + m_2}$$

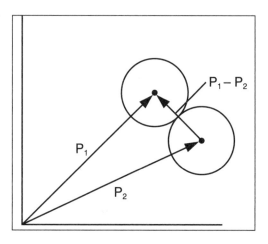

Figure 8.19
The displacement vector between the spheres is the difference of the spheres' position vectors.

where v_{1p}' and v_{2p}' are the projections of the velocity vectors after the collision, as shown in Figure 8.20. From these projections, you can calculate the final velocities of the spheres by subtracting the old $\hat{\mathbf{n}}$ component and adding the new one. Calculating the final velocities takes you back into three dimensions, which is what 3-D games require.

$$\mathbf{v}'_1 = \mathbf{v}_1 + (v'_{1p} - v_{1p})\hat{\mathbf{n}}$$

$$\mathbf{v}'_2 = \mathbf{v}_2 + (v'_{2p} - v_{2p})\hat{\mathbf{n}}$$

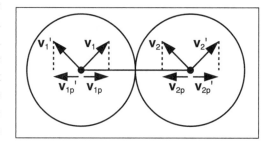

Figure 8.20
The projections of the velocity vectors before and after the collision.

Implementation

With all this background, implementation should be a snap.

We're going to treat the collision of two spheres, so we'll use bounding spheres for the collision detection scheme. Everything else follows directly from the equations and line of reasoning that we just completed.

The first task of implementing collision detection and response is to update the d3d_point_mass class. Next, we need to set up the simulation. The new aspects of the simulation require that we modify the UpdateFrame() function. During each update, the program must check for collisions and handle them when they occur. Finally, it can render the frame. Let's look at each of these tasks.

note

The code for this chapter's sample program is on the CD-ROM that comes with this book. Look for it in the folder Source\Chapter08\ParticleBounce. If you want to view the working program, you can find its .EXE file in the folder Source\Chapter08\Bin.

Modifying the d3d_point_mass Class

The d3d_point_mass class requires only minor modifications for handling collisions. Listing 8.1 gives the new version.

Listing 8.1
The d3d_point_mass Class for Handling Collisions

```
1      class d3d_point_mass
2      {
3      private:
4          d3d_mesh objectMesh;
5
6          scalar mass;
7          vector_3d centerOfMassLocation;
8          vector_3d linearVelocity;
9          vector_3d linearAcceleration;
10         vector_3d sumForces;
11
12         scalar radius;
13         scalar coefficientOfRestitution;
14
15         D3DXMATRIX worldMatrix;
16
17     public:
18         d3d_point_mass();
19
20         bool LoadMesh(
21             std::string meshFileName);
22
23         void Mass(
24             scalar massValue);
25         scalar Mass(void);
26
27         void Location(
```

```
28                 vector_3d locationCenterOfMass);
29         vector_3d Location(void);
30
31         void LinearVelocity(
32             vector_3d newVelocity);
33         vector_3d LinearVelocity(void);
34
35         void LinearAcceleration(
36             vector_3d newAcceleration);
37         vector_3d LinearAcceleration(void);
38
39         void Force(
40             vector_3d sumExternalForces);
41         vector_3d Force(void);
42
43         void BoundingSphereRadius(
44             scalar sphereRadius);
45         scalar BoundingSphereRadius(void);
46
47         void Elasticity(scalar elasticity);
48         scalar Elasticity(void);
49
50         bool Update(
51             scalar changeInTime);
52         bool Render(void);
53     };
```

Lines 12 and 13 of Listing 8.1 show that the d3d_point_mass class now has private data members that store the radius of the mass's bounding sphere and the mass's coefficient of restitution. Lines 43–48 give the prototypes for the member functions that programs use to get and set these values. Other than the addition of these two data members and four member functions, no other changes to the d3d_point_mass class are needed.

Setting Up the Simulation

The code that's specific to this simulation is on the CD-ROM in the file ParticleBounce.cpp. The GameInitialization() function, which is required by the framework, is similar to the version that appeared in Chapter 7, "Dynamics of Particles." The code for this version is presented in Listing 8.2.

Listing 8.2
Initializing the Colliding Bowling Balls

```
1     bool GameInitialization()
2     {
```

```
3          // Load the first ball's mesh.
4          allParticles[0].LoadMesh("bowlball.x");
5
6          // Set the first ball's mass.
7          allParticles[0].Mass(10);
8
9          // Set the first ball's coefficient of restitution.
10         allParticles[0].Elasticity(0.9f);
11
12         // Set the radius of the bounding sphere.
13         allParticles[0].BoundingSphereRadius(0.75f);
14
15         // Let both balls share the same mesh and other properties.
16         allParticles[1]=allParticles[0];
17
18         // Set the first ball's starting location.
19         allParticles[0].Location(vector_3d(-5.0f,0.0,0.0));
20
21         // Set the second ball's starting location.
22         allParticles[1].Location(vector_3d(0.0,-5.0f,0.0));
23
24         // Set the initial forces on the balls.
25         allParticles[0].Force(vector_3d(2.0f,0.0,0.0));
26         allParticles[1].Force(vector_3d(0.0,2.0f,0.0));
27
28         //
29         // Set up a diffuse directional light.
30         //
31         D3DLIGHT9 light;
32         ZeroMemory( &light, sizeof(light) );
33         light.Type = D3DLIGHT_DIRECTIONAL;
34
35         D3DXVECTOR3 vecDir;
36         vecDir = D3DXVECTOR3(0.0f, -1.0f, 1.0f);
37         D3DXVec3Normalize((D3DXVECTOR3*)&light.Direction,&vecDir);
38
39         // Set the directional light diffuse color.
40         light.Diffuse.r = 1.0f;
41         light.Diffuse.g = 1.0f;
42         light.Diffuse.b = 1.0f;
43         light.Diffuse.a = 1.0f;
44         theApp.D3DRenderingDevice()->SetLight( 0, &light );
```

```
45        theApp.D3DRenderingDevice()->LightEnable( 0, TRUE );
46        theApp.D3DRenderingDevice()->SetRenderState(
47            D3DRS_DIFFUSEMATERIALSOURCE,
48            D3DMCS_MATERIAL);
49
50        return (true);
51    }
```

This version of the GameInitialization() function begins by loading the mesh for the first point mass. It uses the bowling ball mesh, as in Chapter 7. It sets the mass to 10 kilograms on line 7. On line 10, GameInitialization() sets the ball's coefficient of restitution to 0.9. This is much bouncier than a real bowling ball.

tip

I recommend that you try running this program with various values of the coefficient of restitution.

Line 13 of Listing 8.2 sets the bounding sphere for the first ball. Line 16 copies all the initialized data into the second ball. The result is that they share the same mesh and have the same mass, bounding sphere radius, and coefficient of restitution.

Next, the GameInitialization() function sets the starting location of the first ball so that it's off the left edge of the program's window. On line 22, it sets the starting location of the second ball so that it's below the bottom of the window. Lines 25–26 set the initial forces on the balls such that they both fly toward the origin (the middle of the window) at the same speed. This guarantees that they'll hit each other.

The rest of the GameInitialization() function sets up the lighting, as was done in Chapter 7.

Updating a Frame

The UpdateFrame() function must now test for collisions between the flying bowling balls. If a collision occurs, it must calculate the forces to apply to the balls. I've isolated those calculations into a separate function that's discussed in the next section. For now, look at Listing 8.3 to see how UpdateFrame() detects collisions.

Listing 8.3
UpdateFrame() Tests for Collisions

```
1    bool UpdateFrame()
2    {
3        // Set up the view matrix, as in previous examples.
4        D3DXVECTOR3 eyePoint(0.0f,3.0f,-5.0f);
5        D3DXVECTOR3 lookatPoint(0.0f,0.0f,0.0f);
6        D3DXVECTOR3 upDirection(0.0f,1.0f,0.0f);
```

```
7        D3DXMATRIXA16 viewMatrix;
8        D3DXMatrixLookAtLH(&viewMatrix,&eyePoint,&lookatPoint,&upDirection);
9        theApp.D3DRenderingDevice()->SetTransform(D3DTS_VIEW,&viewMatrix);
10
11       // Set up the projection matrix, as in previous examples.
12       D3DXMATRIXA16 projectionMatrix;
13       D3DXMatrixPerspectiveFovLH(
14           &projectionMatrix,D3DX_PI/4,1.0f,1.0f,100.0f);
15       theApp.D3DRenderingDevice()->SetTransform(
16           D3DTS_PROJECTION,&projectionMatrix);
17
18       // These initializations are done only once.
19       static bool forceApplied = false;
20       static vector_3d noForce(0.0,0.0,0.0);
21
22       // If the force has not yet been applied...
23       if (!forceApplied)
24       {
25           forceApplied = true;
26       }
27       // Else the force was already applied...
28       else
29       {
30           // Set the forces to 0.
31           allParticles[0].Force(noForce);
32           allParticles[1].Force(noForce);
33       }
34
35       //
36       // Test for a collision.
37       //
38       // Find the distance vector between the balls.
39       vector_3d distance =
40           allParticles[0].Location() - allParticles[1].Location();
41       scalar distanceSquared = distance.NormSquared();
42
43       // Find the square of the sum of the radii of the balls.
44       scalar minDistanceSquared =
45           allParticles[0].BoundingSphereRadius() +
46           allParticles[0].BoundingSphereRadius();
47       minDistanceSquared *= minDistanceSquared;
48
```

```
49          // Set this to a value between 0 and 1 for smoother animation.
50          scalar timeInterval = 1.0;
51
52          // If there is a collision...
53          if (distanceSquared < minDistanceSquared)
54          {
55              // Handle the collision.
56              HandleCollision(distance,timeInterval);
57          }
58
59          allParticles[0].Update(timeInterval);
60          allParticles[1].Update(timeInterval);
61
62          return (true);
63      }
```

In Listing 8.3, the UpdateFrame() function takes care of the typical Direct3D overhead on lines 4–14. On line 19, it declares the variable forceApplied, which is used in the same manner that it was in Chapter 7. Line 20 declares a static vector_3d variable that UpdateFrame() uses to initialize the force vectors on lines 28–29. Collision testing begins on line 39.

To determine whether there has been a collision, the UpdateFrame() function calculates the square of the distance between the centers of the two bowling balls. The code for this is on lines 39–41. Next, UpdateFrame() adds the radii of the balls' bounding spheres on lines 44–46. It squares that value on line 47. On line 53, it uses these two squared values to test for a collision. If a collision occurs, UpdateFrame() calls the HandleCollision() function on line 56. As we'll soon see, HandleCollision() calculates the forces that are acting on the point masses. When the d3d_point_mass::Update() function is called on lines 59–60, the forces of the collision move the point masses.

Handling Collisions

Calculating the forces that result from a collision is the job of the HandleCollision() function. This is a helper function that the physics modeling framework does not require. The code for it is in the file ParticleBounce.cpp. It's also shown in Listing 8.4.

Listing 8.4
The HandleCollision() Function

```
1       void HandleCollision(
2           vector_3d separationDistance,
3           scalar changeInTime)
4       {
5           //
6           // Find the outgoing velocities.
```

```
 7          //
 8          /* First, normalize the displacement vector because it's
 9          perpendicular to the collision. */
10          vector_3d unitNormal =
11              separationDistance.Normalize(FLOATING_POINT_TOLERANCE);
12
13          /* Compute the projection of the velocities in the direction
14          perpendicular to the collision. */
15          scalar velocity1 =
16              allParticles[0].LinearVelocity().Dot(unitNormal);
17          scalar velocity2 =
18              allParticles[1].LinearVelocity().Dot(unitNormal);
19
20          // Find the average coefficient of restitution.
21          scalar averageE =
22              (allParticles[0].Elasticity()*allParticles[1].Elasticity())/2;
23
24          // Calculate the final velocities.
25          scalar finalVelocity1 =
26              (((allParticles[0].Mass() -
27              (averageE * allParticles[1].Mass())) * velocity1) +
28              ((1 + averageE) * allParticles[1].Mass() * velocity2)) /
29              (allParticles[0].Mass() + allParticles[1].Mass());
30          scalar finalVelocity2 =
31              (((allParticles[1].Mass() -
32              (averageE * allParticles[0].Mass())) * velocity2) +
33              ((1 + averageE) * allParticles[0].Mass() * velocity1)) /
34              (allParticles[0].Mass() + allParticles[1].Mass());
35          allParticles[0].LinearVelocity(
36              (finalVelocity1 - velocity1) * unitNormal +
37              allParticles[0].LinearVelocity());
38          allParticles[1].LinearVelocity(
39              (finalVelocity2 - velocity2) * unitNormal +
40              allParticles[1].LinearVelocity());
41
42          //
43          // Convert the velocities to accelerations.
44          //
45          vector_3d acceleration1 =
46              allParticles[0].LinearVelocity() / changeInTime;
47          vector_3d acceleration2 =
48              allParticles[1].LinearVelocity() / changeInTime;
```

```
49
50         // Find the force on each ball.
51         allParticles[0].Force(
52              acceleration1 * allParticles[0].Mass());
53         allParticles[1].Force(
54              acceleration2 * allParticles[1].Mass());
55     }
```

The problem of calculating the collision forces can be approached in many ways. Earlier in this chapter, we used the conservation of momentum, energy, and work as a means for obtaining formulas for the outgoing velocities of particles after a collision. If we realize that each frame covers a specific amount of time, we can use those formulas to calculate the change in velocity during a period of time. Well, that's the definition of acceleration—the change in velocity divided by the change in time. Knowing the acceleration of a point mass enables us to use the formula F=ma. We really get a lot of mileage out of that formula.

The HandleCollision() function calculates the outgoing velocities of the point masses after the collision using the formulas we derived previously. I've repeated them here for your convenience.

$$\mathbf{v}_1' = \mathbf{v}_1 + (v_{1p}' - v_{1p})\hat{\mathbf{n}}$$
$$\mathbf{v}_2' = \mathbf{v}_2 + (v_{2p}' - v_{2p})\hat{\mathbf{n}}$$

To use these equations, the HandleCollision() function must have a unit vector that points along the action of the collision. HandleCollision() obtains the unit vector by invoking the vector_3d::Normalize() function on lines 10–11. It gets the distance vector through its separationDistance parameter from the UpdateFrame() function.

After it has the unit normal vector, HandleCollision() dots it with the velocity vectors of the particles. This gives the component of the velocity vectors in the direction of action of the collision.

To calculate the final velocity, HandleCollision() must use the coefficient of restitution. To enable maximum flexibility, the d3d_point_mass class enables each point mass to store its own coefficient of restitution. That allows you to make some objects bouncier than others. However, when a collision occurs, there is only one coefficient of restitution that can be used for the pair of objects. Therefore, HandleCollision() averages the coefficient of restitution for the pair of objects and uses that. The code is given on lines 21–22.

tip

For even better results, you could use an average weighted by the masses of the objects involved in the collision.

The final velocities are calculated on lines 24–40. After the HandleCollision() function has these velocities, it can calculate the accelerations produced by the collision. That happens on lines 45–48. Using the accelerations, HandleCollision() determines the forces acting on the point masses using the formula **F=ma**.

Rendering a Frame

Chapter 7 demonstrated how hard rendering a frame *isn't*. If we've modeled all the physics correctly and used the physics to calculate the translation matrix for Direct3D, rendering is easy. In this chapter, rendering requires the addition of only one more line of code. Listing 8.5 shows what it is.

Listing 8.5
Rendering the Colliding Bowling Balls

```
1       bool RenderFrame()
2       {
3           allParticles[0].Render();
4           allParticles[1].Render();
5           return (true);
6       }
```

The only additional work that the RenderFrame() function has to do is to call the d3d_point_mass::Render() function for two objects instead of just one. It doesn't even break a sweat.

Summary

In this chapter, you learned several ways of detecting collisions between objects. Sure, there's more to learn on the subject, but this is a good start. We talked a lot about the physics of collisions. This understanding is going to be helpful when we're trying to come to grips with rigid body collisions. Finally, we put together a program with two spheres bumping off each other. As we move into the later chapters of the book, you might be surprised at how much you can do with the straightforward physics you learned in this chapter.

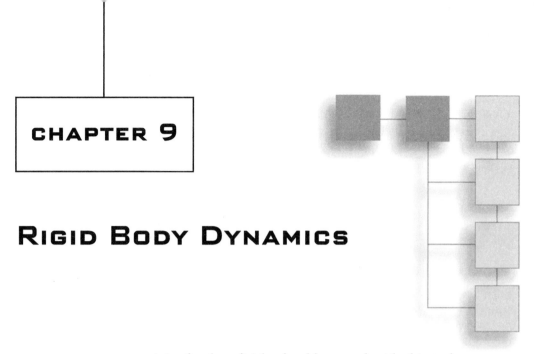

CHAPTER 9

Rigid Body Dynamics

In a computer game, it is often beneficial to be able to work with objects that are more complicated than the triangles and spheres we've been using so far. You undoubtedly will want the ability to simulate cars that can turn (or turn over), dragons that can dive and swoop, or characters that can throw furniture when they throw tantrums.

The goal of this chapter is to build a general physical model for dealing with these sorts of complicated solid objects.

Rigid Bodies

The golden rule of simulation (or physics calculation, for that matter) is "Simplify." The goal is to get the most out of the simplest set of assumptions.

Any ordinary object is enormously complicated. Most things are composed of a tremendous number of atoms, all interacting in complicated ways. There's no way we can model that for a human-size object.

So here's what we do instead. You might have noticed that a lot of the objects around you hold their shape for a while. Your toaster generally looks the same today as it looked yesterday morning, unless you melted it or something. We're going to call all of these objects *rigid bodies* and make the assumption that these objects have the same shape, now and forever or until they blow up.

Any real object doesn't really hold its shape. A tennis ball gets squished to half its volume when it's hit with a racket. If you take a baseball bat or a blowtorch to your toaster, it'll change shape, too. But you can model many objects as rigid bodies.

A good way to think about solid objects is to imagine them as a set of point particles, as in Figure 9.1. The set of barbells in Figure 9.1 is composed of two point particles. You can ignore the mass of the bar between them. Each of these point particles has a mass and forces acting on it, including forces from the other particles.

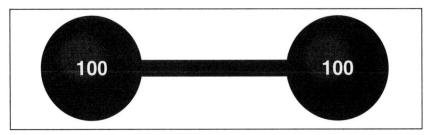

Figure 9.1
You can envision a solid object as a set of point particles.

In a rigid body, the distance between the particles is constant. That means that the position of each of the points with respect to the others is constant. In other words, the object holds its shape and is rigid.

As it turns out, this model is quite useful. It leads naturally to a set of concepts that make calculating real-world objects much easier.

The Center of Mass

If you toss a ball into the air, it follows a nice parabolic path, as in Figure 9.2. The path followed by a tomahawk tossed into the air looks enormously more complicated. It flops all around, as shown in Figure 9.3. However, if you look close, you'll notice that one spot on the tomahawk follows that same parabolic path. That spot is called the *center of mass*. Let's see if we can find it.

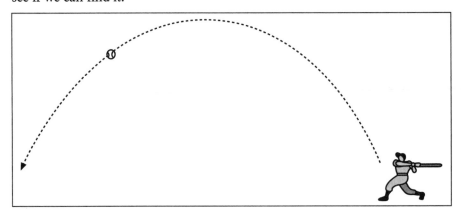

Figure 9.2
A hit ball follows a parabolic path.

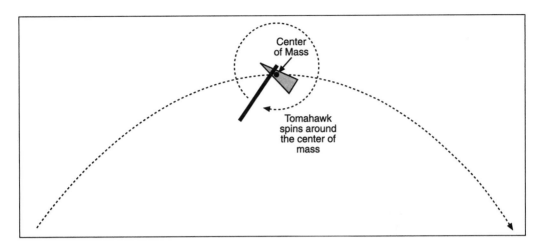

Figure 9.3
The center of mass of a tossed tomahawk follows a parabolic path.

The objects are composed of lots of little particles, each with its own mass and forces acting on it. Therefore, we can write the force on the *i*th particle as follows:

$$\mathbf{F}_i = m_i \mathbf{a}_i = \frac{m_i d^2 \mathbf{x}_i}{dt^2} = \frac{d^2 m_i \mathbf{x}_i}{dt^2}$$

where m_i is the mass on the *i*th particle, and $\mathbf{x}_i$ is its position, as shown in the following equation:

$$\mathbf{F} = \sum_i \mathbf{F}_i$$

$$= \sum_i d^2 m_i \frac{\mathbf{x}_i}{dt^2}$$

$$= \frac{d^2}{dt^2} \sum_i m_i \mathbf{x}_i$$

This is another way to view the equation **F=ma**. In this case, I've broken it down to derivatives. Acceleration is the second derivative of the displacement over time. We have this equation right where we want it. If we define the center of mass, $\mathbf{X}_{cm}$, as this:

$$\mathbf{X}_{cm} = \frac{1}{M} \sum_i m_i \mathbf{x}_i$$

where M is the total mass of the rigid body, we can write a nice, simple equation for the total force on the body:

$$\mathbf{F} = \frac{Md^2\mathbf{X}_{cm}}{dt^2}$$

This is exactly like Newton's law for a point particle. This means that as far as the total movement of the body and the total force on it, the rigid body acts as a point particle, as long as we measure from the center of mass. We still have to deal with rotations of the rigid body. However, as far as the overall motion of rigid bodies, we already covered it in the previous two chapters on point particles. The rotation can be treated completely separately.

tip

You can often simplify your calculations by making the center of your mesh the same as the center of mass of your object.

2-D Rigid Body Rotation

Okay, so the overall position and velocity of the rigid body is taken care of. Just treat the center of mass as a point particle. It's cake. What about the rotational motion?

It probably won't shock you to hear that this is a little more difficult. For the moment, I'm going to talk about rotations in a plane, where I can introduce the notions without the heinous math. Because the objects are constrained to move in a plane, the only way they're allowed to rotate is around the axis that points out of the screen. Figure 9.4 shows a rigid body that behaves in this way.

Rigid bodies that are constrained to move in a plane come up quite a bit, even in 3-D games. If you're pushing objects across a floor, you can model them with 2-D mechanics as long as they don't leave the surface. You can

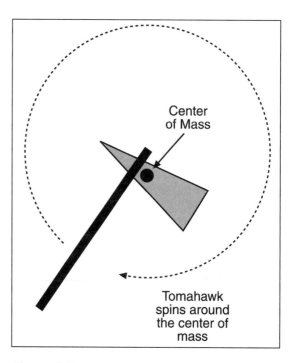

Figure 9.4
A rigid body that rotates in a plane around the z axis.

also use these constrained rigid bodies for wheels and gears, as long as they don't fall over anything. The mathematics is considerably easier for the computer than 3-D, so use this technique when you can.

For objects that are constrained to move in a plane, a single scalar, θ, can represent the rotation of the object, as shown in Figure 9.5. We'll measure this angle in radians.

In analogy with 1-D kinematics, we can define angular velocity, ω, and angular acceleration, α:

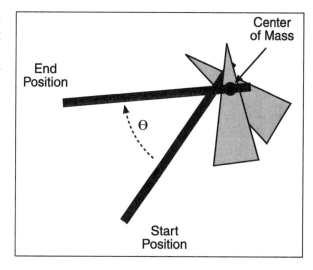

Figure 9.5
The rotation of a 2-D rigid body is represented by an angle θ.

$$\omega = \frac{d\theta}{dt}$$

$$\alpha = \frac{d\omega}{dt} = \frac{d^2\theta}{dt^2}$$

The units of angular velocity are radians per second (rad/s), and the units of angular acceleration are rad/s².

Point Particles of a 2-D Rigid Body

This section asks the question: If I know everything about the rigid body (the position, the velocity, the acceleration, the angular velocity, and the angular acceleration), what are the velocity and acceleration of a point particle on the rigid body? This is an important question because the utility of the rigid body model rests on being able to apply outside forces to it at different locations.

Consider a local coordinate system—one traveling at the same speed as the center of mass. The rigid body is rotating by an angle θ. Focus your attention on one point on the rigid body at a distance r from the center of mass. As the body rotates, it sweeps out an arc length (arcLength).

By the definition of a radian,

$$\theta = \frac{\text{arcLength}}{r}$$

If you differentiate this equation with respect to time, you get an equation for the angular velocity.

$$\frac{d\theta}{dt} = \frac{d}{dt}\left(\frac{\text{arcLength}}{r}\right)$$

$$\omega = \left(\frac{1}{r}\right)\frac{d\ \text{arcLength}}{dt}$$

darcLength/dt is the *tangential velocity*, pictured in Figure 9.6. For the rigid body, the tangential velocity is the total velocity of the particle in local coordinates, so we'll call it v.

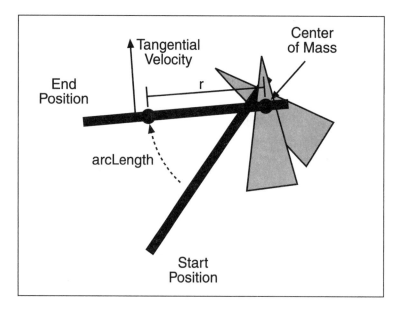

Figure 9.6
The tangential velocity of a point particle on a 2-D rigid body.

You can pull the $(1/r)$ out of the derivative because the distance of the point particle from the center of mass is a constant for a rigid body. All the distances between particles on a rigid body are constant. Constants don't change when you take a derivative.

$$v = r\omega$$

To get the tangential acceleration of the particle, differentiate this equation one more time:

$$\frac{dv}{dt} = \frac{r\,d\omega}{dt}$$

$$a_t = r\alpha$$

I was careful to say the *tangential* acceleration, because there's another acceleration here: the centripetal acceleration. As shown in Figure 9.7, the tangential acceleration changes the magnitude of the velocity of the point particle, whereas the centripetal acceleration changes its direction. For now, we're mostly going to be concerned with the tangential component of the acceleration, but we'll eventually want a good understanding of both.

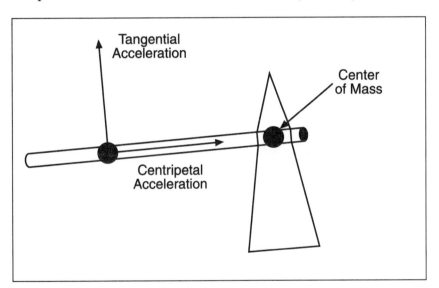

Figure 9.7
The tangential and centripetal acceleration.

The centripetal acceleration corresponds to a centripetal force. The centripetal force causes the point particle to turn from its straight path. If you were sitting on the rotating point particle, you'd feel a force throwing you out from the particle, opposite to the direction of the centripetal force. You'd feel this force because you aren't a rigid body securely affixed to the rotating particle, and your body tends to move in straight-line motion if not constrained otherwise. Because the force is due only to your reference frame, it's called a *fictional force*. This fictional force is known as the *centrifugal force*.

Here's a quick derivation of the centripetal acceleration, using finite differences. Over some small time interval δt, the centripetal acceleration changes the direction of the velocity vector but not its magnitude, as shown in Figure 9.8. In the figure, the change in velocity due to the centripetal acceleration is called δv. δv equals the product of the centripetal acceleration and δt.

$$\Delta v = a_c \Delta t$$

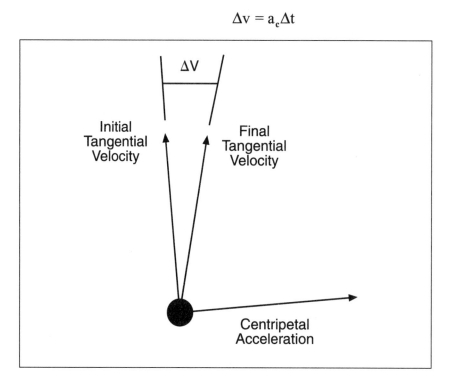

Figure 9.8
Tangential velocity changes due to centripetal acceleration.

The tangential velocity's change in direction occurs as the particle moves in a circle. Specifically, it occurs as the particle on the rigid body sweeps out an arc. Remember arcLength from earlier formulas in this chapter? That specifies the arc through which the particle moves. That means you can say this:

$$\frac{\Delta arcLength}{r} = \frac{\Delta v}{v}$$

The tangential velocity is defined as the derivate of the arc length, so, in finite differences, we can express that this way:

$$\Delta arcLength = v\Delta t$$

To solve for the centripetal acceleration, plug in for $\delta arcLength$ and δv:

$$a_c = \frac{\Delta v}{\Delta t}$$
$$= \frac{v\Delta arcLength}{r\Delta t}$$
$$= \frac{v^2\Delta t}{r\Delta t}$$
$$= \frac{v^2}{r}$$

This enables us to find the centripetal acceleration in terms of a point particle's tangential velocity and its distance from the rigid body's center of mass.

Torque and the Moment of Inertia

There's a reason that doorknobs are as far from the door hinge as possible. Try pushing on a door near the hinges. Sure, you can move it, but it takes more effort.

Torque embodies this concept for a rigid body. The torque τ is defined as follows:

$$\boldsymbol{\tau} = \mathbf{r} \times \mathbf{F}$$

Here, $\mathbf{r}$ is the distance from the center of mass to the point we're applying the force, $\mathbf{F}$. If we've constrained the object to move in a plane, the torque must always point in the same direction, so we can get away with using scalars.

$$\tau = rF\sin(\theta)$$

θ is the angle between the $\mathbf{r}$ vector and the $\mathbf{F}$ vector. If the force is tangential to the radius (like the force of the ground against a rolling wheel), we can even write this:

$$\tau = rF_t$$

Okay, now that we've defined this concept, let's connect it to the mechanics we already know. Let's take the torque on the ith point particle of a rigid body.

$$\tau_i = r_i F_{ti}$$

The tangential force on the particle is equal to its mass times its tangential acceleration, from Newton's second law:

$$\mathbf{F}_{ti} = m_i \mathbf{a}_{ti}$$

Therefore, the torque on the particle is this:

$$\tau_i = r_i m_i a_{ti}$$

In the previous section, we found that $a_t = \alpha r$, where α is angular acceleration:

$$\tau_i = r_i m_i r_i \alpha = r_i^2 m_i \alpha$$

To get to the total torque, sum the torques on each of the point particles in the rigid body:

$$\tau = \sum_i \tau_i$$

$$\tau = \alpha \sum_i r_i^2 m_i$$

$$\tau = \left(\sum_i r_i^2 m_i \right) \alpha$$

The summation in parentheses is called the *moment of inertia*, usually written I.

$$\tau = I\alpha$$

This equation is the rotational analog of Newton's second law, F = ma. Because the second law for rotations is the same form as the second law for point particles, the equations have the same solutions. How convenient!

Calculating the Moment of Inertia

Using Newton's second law for rotations means that you have to calculate the moments of inertia for each rigid body. For many shapes, you can just sum over the point particles that make up the rigid body using the formula for the moment of inertia:

$$I = \sum_i r_i^2 m_i$$

You can solve for the moments of inertia of solids by making the point particles that compose the solid small and close together. If you make the point particles infinitesimally small, the sum in the previous equation becomes an integral that you can solve to get the moment of inertia:

$$I = \int r^2 dm$$

Figure 9.9 lists the moments of inertia of some common shapes derived this way.

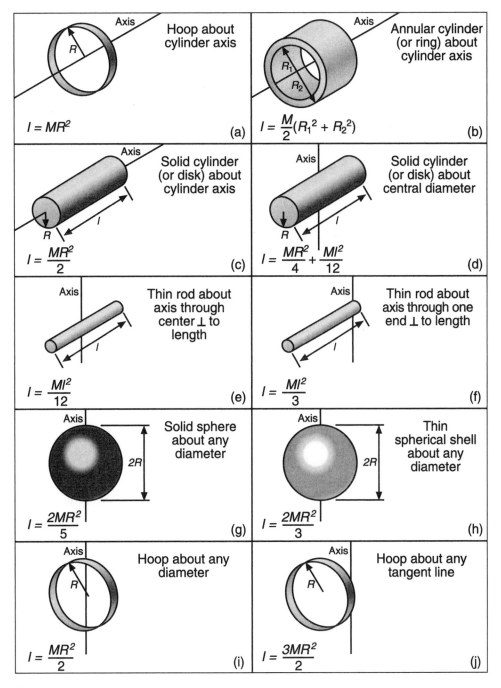

Figure 9.9
Some moments of inertia.

If you know the moment of inertia of an element about one axis, you can find its moment of inertia around a parallel axis using the *parallel axis theorem*:

$$I = I_{cm} + Mh^2$$

Here, I_{cm} is the center of mass of the element, M is its mass, and h is the distance to the new axis, as shown in Figure 9.10.

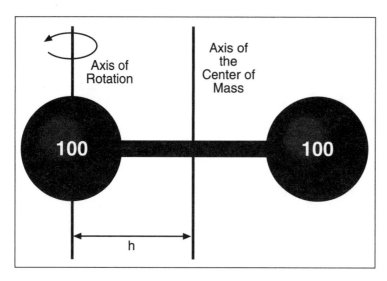

Figure 9.10
The parallel axis theorem.

Figure 9.10 shows a barbell rotating around its center of mass. However, the barbell is a rigid body composed of two heavy point particles. Using the sphere on the left as an example, the figure illustrates that the point particles are rotating around an off-center axis. The off-center axis is at a distance h from the axis that passes through the center of mass of the barbell.

Using the parallel axis theorem, you can calculate the moment of inertia of a rigid body composed of more simple rigid bodies. Moments of inertia add, but only if they're about the same axis, so you'll need to use the parallel axis theorem to convert the moments of inertia about the center of mass of each element to moments of inertia about the center of mass of the rigid body.

An Example Using the Parallel Axis Theorem

Let's try computing the moment of inertia about the center of mass of the rigid body in Figure 9.11. This rigid body is composed of three elements: two solid spheres and a hoop, arranged as shown in the figure. Each of the spheres has a mass of 200 kg and a radius of 1 m. The hoop has a mass of 100 kg and a radius of 1 m. The entire rigid body is constrained to move in a plane, so we can analyze it as a 2-D rigid body.

note

We'll often use simplified models like the one in this section to calculate the physical response of our rigid bodies. To make the action look realistic, the physics model of your object should correspond to the mesh.

The first thing we need to do is compute the center of mass. Here's the definition of the center of mass again:

$$X_{cm} = \left(\frac{1}{M}\right)\sum_i m_i x_i$$

Figure 9.11
A rigid body composed of simpler shapes.

For this example, let's set the origin of the coordinate system at the middle of the hoop. The total mass, M, is 200 kg + 200 kg + 100 kg = 500 kg. Using Figure 9.11, we can compute the center of mass in the x and y directions, X_{cm} and Y_{cm}.

$$
\begin{aligned}
X_{cm} &= \left(\frac{1}{M}\right)\sum_i m_i x_i \\
&= \left(\frac{1}{500\ \text{kg}}\right)\left(200\ \text{kg}\bullet 0\ \text{m} + 200\ \text{kg}\bullet 0\ \text{m} + 100\ \text{kg}\bullet 0\ \text{m}\right) \\
&= 0\ \text{m} \\
Y_{cm} &= \left(\frac{1}{M}\right)\sum_i m_i y_i \\
&= \left(\frac{1}{500\ \text{kg}}\right)\left(200\ \text{kg}\bullet(-2\ \text{m}) + 200\ \text{kg}\bullet 2\ \text{m} + 100\ \text{kg}\bullet 0\ \text{m}\right) \\
&= 0\ \text{m}
\end{aligned}
$$

This confirms what you probably knew intuitively: The center of mass is at (0,0).

Now, use the parallel axis theorem to figure the moment of inertia from each element around the center of mass of the rigid body. The distance from the center of mass of each element to the center of mass of the rigid body is listed in Table 10.1.

Table 10.1 The Distance of Each Element from the Center of Mass

Element	Distance
Bottom sphere	2 m
Top sphere	2 m
Hoop	0 m

We'll need the moment of inertia of each element around its center of gravity. The moment of inertia of a sphere around any diameter is $(2/5)MR^2$, so the moment of inertia of each of these spheres is 80 kg m². The moment of inertia of a hoop through the central axis is MR^2, so our hoop has a moment of inertia of 100 kg m².

That's all the information that we need. Just apply the parallel axis theorem. The two spheres give the same result:

$$I = I_{cm} + Mh^2$$

$$I_{sphere} = 80 \text{ kg m}^2 + 200 \text{ kg } (2 \text{ m})^2 = 880 \text{ kg m}^2$$

$$I_{hoop} = 100 \text{ kg m}^2 + 100 \text{ kg } (0 \text{ m})^2 = 100 \text{ kg m}^2$$

The total moment of inertia of the rigid body is the sum of these:

$$I = 2I_{sphere} + I_{hoop}$$

$$= 2(880 \text{ kg m}^2) + 100 \text{ kg m}^2$$

$$= 1,860 \text{ kg m}^2$$

Rigid Bodies in 3-D

Now that you're a master of rigid bodies in 2-D, it's time to add that crucial extra dimension. Although you can write plenty of games entirely with 2-D rigid bodies, more and more games are completely 3-D. You can't build a flight simulator without 3-D.

The mathematics for 3-D rigid bodies can be a little slippery, so we'll build it up bit by bit. Let's start by talking about the rotation of a 3-D rigid body around an arbitrary axis. At any given instant, a rigid body is rotating about some rotation axis with an angular velocity, as shown in Figure 9.12. You can encode this information in an angular velocity vector, ω, which points along the axis of rotation and whose magnitude is the angular speed.

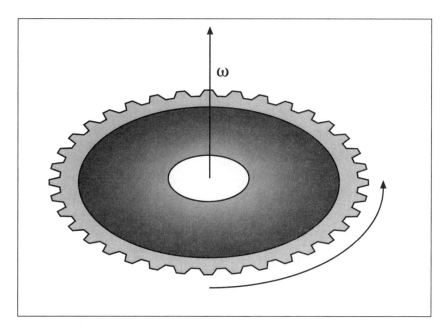

Figure 9.12
The angular velocity vector represents angular velocity around an arbitrary axis.

note

Why did I start with the angular velocity instead of a vector corresponding to the orientation, in analogy to the orientation scalar θ in two dimensions? Because the relationship between the orientation vector and the angular velocity vector isn't as simple as it was in 2-D. In fact, ω isn't the derivative of any vector. Almost everything else (angular velocity, angular acceleration, and torque) is analogous, so we'll start with these.

The angular acceleration vector, α, is the time derivative of the angular velocity.

$$\alpha = \frac{d\omega}{dt}$$

So far, so good. This should look pretty familiar. We've just promoted everything to vectors. The next thing that we did in the 2-D case was relate the angular velocity and angular acceleration to the velocities and accelerations of the point particles that make up the rigid body in the body's rest frame. Let's try to do that here.

The velocity of a particle, $\mathbf{v}$, at position $\mathbf{r}$ from the center of mass is given by the following equation:

$$\mathbf{v} = \boldsymbol{\omega} \times \mathbf{r}$$

You can reduce the rotation about an arbitrary axis to the two-dimensional case by projecting the **r** vector onto a plane that's perpendicular to the axis of rotation. This distance is r sin θ, where θ is the angle between the two vectors. In the previous section, we derived the velocity for the 2D case: v = ωr, which is consistent with the magnitude of a cross product.

$$|\mathbf{a} \times \mathbf{b}| = ab \sin(\theta)$$
$$|\mathbf{v}| = |\boldsymbol{\omega} \times \mathbf{r}|$$
$$|\mathbf{v}| = \omega r \sin(\theta)$$

The velocity must be perpendicular to both the radius and the orientation axis, by definition.

Now you can find the acceleration of the point particle on the rigid body by taking the time derivative of the velocity vector:

$$\mathbf{a} = \frac{d\mathbf{v}}{dt}$$
$$= \frac{d(\boldsymbol{\omega} \times \mathbf{r})}{dt}$$
$$= \frac{d\boldsymbol{\omega}}{dt} \times \mathbf{r} + \boldsymbol{\omega} \times \frac{d\mathbf{r}}{dt}$$
$$= \boldsymbol{\alpha} \times \mathbf{r} + \boldsymbol{\omega} \times (\boldsymbol{\omega} \times \mathbf{r})$$

The first term of the acceleration is the tangential acceleration, and the second term is the centripetal acceleration. Try comparing them to the expressions found in the 2-D case.

$$\mathbf{a}_t = \boldsymbol{\alpha} \times \mathbf{r}$$
$$\mathbf{a}_c = \boldsymbol{\omega} \times (\boldsymbol{\omega} \times \mathbf{r})$$

note

This might not make much sense if you haven't had some vector calculus. It might not make much sense even if you have. I admit to balking at teaching vector calculus in this book, but if you want an introduction, you might try *Div, Grad, Curl, and All That* by H.M. Schey. For an approach to this problem, check out the grand old mechanics text, *Classical Mechanics*, by Herbert Goldstein. Get the second edition if you can find it; in my humble opinion, it's superior to the third.

Because we have vector expressions for the velocity and acceleration of the point particle in a coordinate system at rest to the rigid body, we can easily find the velocity and acceleration in world coordinates. All we have to do is add them to the velocity and acceleration of the center of mass of the rigid body:

$$\mathbf{v}_{world} = \mathbf{v}_{cm} + \boldsymbol{\omega} \times \mathbf{r}$$

$$\mathbf{a}_{world} = \mathbf{a}_{cm} + \boldsymbol{\alpha} \times \mathbf{r} + \boldsymbol{\omega} \times (\boldsymbol{\omega} \times \mathbf{r})$$

Torque in 3-D

We defined torque in three dimensions, so its definition stays the same:

$$\boldsymbol{\tau} = \mathbf{r} \times \mathbf{F}$$

That's a relief after the last section, but wait until you see what happens next!

We're going to take the same tack that we did before. We'll look at the torque on the *i*th point particle of the rigid body. First, we'll plug in an expression for the applied force, $\mathbf{F}$:

$$\mathbf{F}_i = m_i \mathbf{a}_{ti}$$

$$\boldsymbol{\tau}_i = \mathbf{r}_i \times m_i \mathbf{a}_{ti}$$

$$= m_i \mathbf{r}_i \times \mathbf{a}_{ti}$$

The applied force corresponds to the tangential acceleration. The centripetal acceleration is a result of forces leveraged by the structure of the rigid body.

Now we can plug in the expression we found in the previous section for the tangential acceleration:

$$\mathbf{a}_{ti} = \boldsymbol{\alpha} \times \mathbf{r}_i$$

$$\boldsymbol{\tau}_i = \mathbf{r}_i \times m_i \mathbf{a}_{ti}$$

$$= m_i \mathbf{r}_i \times \boldsymbol{\alpha} \times \mathbf{r}_i$$

The next step is to sum all the torques on each point particle to get the total torque for the system:

$$\boldsymbol{\tau} = \sum_i \boldsymbol{\tau}_i$$

$$= \sum_i m_i \mathbf{r}_i \times \boldsymbol{\alpha} \times \mathbf{r}_i$$

Then, in the 2-D case, we noted that we could pull out the angular acceleration and leave ourselves a nice scalar term that we called the moment of inertia. However, it isn't so easy in three dimensions! How are we going to pull that α vector out of there?

Let's look at the components. I'll call the components of $\mathbf{r_i}$ (x,y,z). I'm suppressing the i subscript to make the equation more readable, but don't forget that you're still summing over every particle in the rigid body. The components of α are (α_x, α_y, α_z). Watch out! This is going to be ugly!

$$\tau = \sum_i m_i \left\{ \begin{array}{l} \left[+(y^2 + z^2)\alpha_x - xy\alpha_y - xz\alpha_z \right]\hat{\mathbf{x}} + \\ \left[-xy\alpha_x + (z^2 + x^2)\alpha_y - yz\alpha_z \right]\hat{\mathbf{y}} + \\ \left[-xz\alpha_x - yz\alpha_y + (x^2 + y^2)\alpha_z \right]\hat{\mathbf{z}} \end{array} \right\}$$

tip

Looking at components should always be a last resort when you're doing vector analysis, mostly because the algebra is messy and you can't see anything. There's probably a more clever way to do this. If anybody knows one, please publish it immediately.

This probably doesn't look like anything in particular, but let's make some substitutions and then see what you think. Here are the new terms:

$$I_{xx} = \sum_i (y_i^2 + z_i^2)m_i$$

$$I_{yy} = \sum_i (z_i^2 + x_i^2)m_i$$

$$I_{zz} = \sum_i (x_i^2 + y_i^2)m_i$$

$$I_{xy} = I_{yx} = \sum_i (x_i y_i)m_i$$

$$I_{xz} = I_{zx} = \sum_i (x_i z_i)m_i$$

$$I_{yz} = I_{zy} = \sum_i (y_i z_i)m_i$$

Here's the expression for the torque with the new terms:

$$\boldsymbol{\tau} = (+I_{xx}\alpha_x - I_{xy}\alpha_y - I_{xz}\alpha_z)\hat{\mathbf{x}} + (-I_{yx}\alpha_x + I_{yy}\alpha_y - I_{yz}\alpha_z)\hat{\mathbf{y}} + (-I_{zx}\alpha_x - I_{zy}\alpha_y + I_{zz}\alpha_z)\hat{\mathbf{z}}$$

This look familiar to anybody? These are the components of a *matrix* multiplied by the components of a vector. In other words, if we call **I** the matrix whose components are given by the new terms, we can write this:

$$\boldsymbol{\tau} = \begin{bmatrix} I_{xx} & -I_{xy} & -I_{xz} \\ -I_{yx} & I_{yy} & -I_{yz} \\ -I_{zx} & -I_{zy} & I_{zz} \end{bmatrix} \begin{bmatrix} \alpha_x \\ \alpha_y \\ \alpha_z \end{bmatrix}$$

$$= \mathbf{I}\boldsymbol{\alpha}$$

Wow! The geometric object whose components in some coordinate system are a square matrix is called a *tensor*. This makes **I** the *moment of inertia tensor*. It allows us to write a rotational analog in three dimensions to Newton's second law.

note

Although I've used the same notation for a vector and a tensor, you can tell that I is a tensor from the way it's used. There is no operation on vectors written by putting the vectors next to each other with no operator symbol.

The equation of motion as I've written it is perfectly valid, but it has a drawback for numerical use. Because it's calculated in a nonrotating coordinate system, the moment of inertia tensor can change from frame to frame, which is a computational disaster.

What we're going to do is move into a coordinate system that is rotating with an angular velocity of ω. This is pretty easy to accomplish with a little vector calculus. You can relate the time derivate of a vector **v** in a fixed system with its derivative in a rotating coordinate system with this formula, which results from the definition of the derivative in such a situation:

$$\left(\frac{d\mathbf{v}}{dt}\right)_{\text{fixed}} = \left(\frac{d\mathbf{v}}{dt}\right)_{\text{rotating}} + (\boldsymbol{\omega} \times \mathbf{v})$$

Applying this formula to the equation of motion yields the following:

$$\tau = I\alpha + (\omega \times I\omega)$$

In this coordinate system, the moment of inertia tensor is constant, so we only have to calculate it once. This equation isn't quite as pretty as the original, but it's easier to use.

The Parallel Axis Theorem in Three Dimensions

The components of the moment of inertia tensor across the diagonal (I_{xx}, I_{yy}, I_{zz}) are called the *moments of inertia*. The parallel axis theorem for them is the same as the parallel axis theorem for the scalar moment of inertia:

$$I_{xx} = I_{cm(yz)} + Mh^2$$
$$I_{yy} = I_{cm(zx)} + Mh^2$$
$$I_{zz} = I_{cm(xy)} + Mh^2$$

where the distance h and the center of mass are measured in the plane perpendicular to the moment of inertia. For example, everything for I_{xx} component is measured in the yz plane.

There is also a parallel axis theorem for the off-diagonal components of the moment inertia tensor. These components are called the *products of inertia*:

$$I_{xy} = I_{cm(xy)} + Mh_x h_y$$
$$I_{xz} = I_{cm(xz)} + Mh_x h_z$$
$$I_{yz} = I_{cm(yz)} + Mh_y h_z$$

Here, h_x is the x component of the separation between the two axes, h_y is the y component, and h_z is the z component.

The Principal Axes

I mentioned in passing earlier that the matrix is not the moment of inertia tensor, but rather is just its components in some coordinate system. There's nothing unique about the coordinate system. Choosing different definitions for x, y, and z gives you entirely different components, but it yields the same moment of inertia tensor.

As it turns out, you can always choose a set of coordinates so that the products of inertia disappear. These coordinates are called the *principal axes*.

The principal axes are important if you're figuring these things by hand, but for a numerical model, they're not nearly so important. I just thought you might like to know.

Orientation

We've discussed every aspect of 3D rigid bodies except one. We can apply torques and calculate the new angular velocity for any shape for which we can calculate the moment of inertia tensor. The piece we're missing was the simplest piece in two dimensions: figuring the orientation from the angular velocity.

In two dimensions, the orientation was given by a scalar, θ, and you could figure it from ω using a finite difference method:

$$\omega = \frac{\Delta\theta}{\Delta t}$$

You might hope for something similar in three dimensions, but it just isn't true. In fact, ω isn't the derivative of any vector, which is a bit of a snag. What are we going to do about it?

Because we can't go easily from the angular velocity to the orientation, let's try working backward. Orientation is more complicated in three dimensions. Game programmers use two major methods to code the orientation: rotation matrices and quaternions. Each has its advantages and disadvantages. Rotation matrices are the most common and most straightforward way of approaching this problem. Direct3D, as well as systems such as OpenGL, have used them for years. However, quaternions can be more efficient. The drawback to quaternions is that most people have a difficult time using them.

note

If you're feeling brave, I encourage you to dive into quaternions. Direct3D now has support for them.

Because rotation matrices are easier to understand and implement, I'll stick with them for the rest of this book. We've already covered rotation matrices pretty extensively. You know how to figure rotation matrices for rotations about the x, y, and z axes. Here they are:

$$R_x = \begin{bmatrix} 1 & 0 & 0 & 0 \\ 0 & \cos(\varphi) & \sin(\varphi) & 0 \\ 0 & -\sin(\varphi) & \cos(\varphi) & 0 \\ 0 & 0 & 0 & 1 \end{bmatrix}$$

$$R_y = \begin{bmatrix} \cos(\alpha) & 0 & -\sin(\alpha) & 0 \\ 0 & 1 & 0 & 0 \\ \sin(\alpha) & 0 & \cos(\alpha) & 0 \\ 0 & 0 & 0 & 1 \end{bmatrix}$$

$$R_z = \begin{bmatrix} \cos(\theta) & \sin(\theta) & 0 & 0 \\ -\sin(\theta) & \cos(\theta) & 0 & 0 \\ 0 & 0 & 1 & 0 \\ 0 & 0 & 0 & 1 \end{bmatrix}$$

What we need to do is figure out how these rotation matrices change with time. To start, we'll make each of these three angles a function of time. For small periods of time, they will be linear functions:

$$\varphi = \omega_x t$$
$$\rho = \omega_y t$$
$$\theta = \omega_z t$$

Substitute in these linear functions, and multiply the three rotation matrices to get the total rotation matrix. Use a computer that is running a math program such as Maple from MapleSoft. The algebra is not worth your time.

$$R = R_x R_y R_z$$

Now differentiate R with respect to time. What you'll find is that

$$\frac{dR}{dt} = \omega R$$

where ω is this matrix:

$$\omega = \begin{bmatrix} 0 & -\omega_z & \omega_y \\ \omega_z & 0 & -\omega_x \\ -\omega_y & \omega_x & 0 \end{bmatrix}$$

What's nifty about this is that you only have to calculate the rotation matrix once using those expensive trig functions. After you have it, you can calculate your new angular velocity ω for each frame and then just perform a matrix multiply.

To implement this method, you have to deal with round-off error. Small errors in the computations due to finite precision grow large quickly. To keep your rotation matrix from degenerating into a total mess, enforce the orthogonality condition fairly often:

$$R^T R = I$$

With that caveat, this is a good system for dealing with rotations in games. It's easy to understand, and it uses the same old matrix multiplications that we've been using all along, which can be optimized for speed. It's not a bad choice.

tip

As I mentioned previously, quaternions have recently become very popular as a method of representing the orientation of objects in 3-D. After you complete this book, I strongly suggest you look into quaternions further. Although the math behind them is rather rigorous, they can be quite useful.

Implementing Rigid Bodies in 3-D

Finally, we're to the point where we can build the rigid body class in 3-D. It might seem awfully simple at this point after all the work put into it.

note

The code for this chapter's sample program is on the CD-ROM in the folder `Source\Chapter09\RigidBody`.

The d3d_rigid_body Class

The rigid body is going to need the variables of a point particle to take care of its translation dynamics, such as mass, position, velocity, and total force. It's also going to need the analogous quantities for the rotational dynamics.

In addition, the rigid body has a mesh associated with it. The center of mass is assumed to be at the origin of the mesh. That assumption is okay for now, but it's not something you want to use in your games. Complex rigid bodies almost never have their centers of mass at the origins of their meshes. Later chapters demonstrate a fix for this.

The class uses a bounding sphere for collision testing. Therefore, its definition contains a member for the bounding sphere's radius.

note

The definition of the rigid body class is in the file `PMRigidBody.h` in the folder `Source\Chapter09\RigidBody`.

Listing 9.1 gives the definition of the rigid body class.

Listing 9.1
The d3d_rigid_body Class

```
1     class d3d_rigid_body
2     {
3     private:
4         d3d_mesh objectMesh;
5
6         // Physical and linear motion properties
7         scalar mass;
8         vector_3d centerOfMassLocation;
9         vector_3d linearVelocity;
10        vector_3d linearAcceleration;
11        force sumForces;
12
13        // Rotational motion properties
14        angle_set_3d currentOrientation;
15        vector_3d angularVelocity;
16        vector_3d angularAcceleration;
17        vector_3d rotationalInertia;
18        vector_3d torque;
19
20        D3DXMATRIX worldMatrix;
21
22    public:
23        d3d_rigid_body(void);
24
25        bool LoadMesh(
26            std::string meshFileName);
27
28        void Mass(
29            scalar massValue);
30        scalar Mass(void);
31
32        void Location(
33            vector_3d locationCenterOfMass);
34        vector_3d Location(void);
```

```
35
36          void LinearVelocity(
37              vector_3d newVelocity);
38          vector_3d LinearVelocity(void);
39
40          void LinearAcceleration(
41              vector_3d newAcceleration);
42          vector_3d LinearAcceleration(void);
43
44          void Force(
45              force sumExternalForces);
46          force Force(void);
47
48          void CurrentOrientation(
49              angle_set_3d newOrientation);
50          angle_set_3d CurrentOrientation(void);
51
52          void AngularVelocity(
53              vector_3d newAngularVelocity);
54          vector_3d AngularVelocity(void);
55
56          void AngularAcceleration(
57              vector_3d newAngularAcceleration);
58          vector_3d AngularAcceleration(void);
59
60          void RotationalInertia(vector_3d inertiaValue);
61          vector_3d RotationalInertia(void);
62
63          void Torque(vector_3d torqueValue);
64          vector_3d Torque(void);
65
66          bool Update(
67              scalar changeInTime);
68          bool Render(void);
69      };
```

Like the d3d_point_mass class from previous chapters, the d3d_rigid_body class contains a d3d_mesh object, as shown in Listing 9.1. It also has members that it uses to keep track of its linear dynamics on lines 7–11. The data members on lines 14–18 store the corresponding information for the rigid body's rotational dynamics.

The d3d_rigid_body class defines member functions for setting and getting its data. It also has Update() and Render() functions that do exactly what you think they do.

Things are pretty straightforward so far. Let's move on and see how this class is used.

Initializing a d3d_rigid_body Object

This chapter's sample program demonstrates the use of the d3d_rigid_body class. The file that implements the logic that is specific to this program is called RigidBodyTest.cpp. It contains the functions that the physics modeling framework requires.

As required by the framework, the function that initializes Direct3D is OnAppLoad(). The only thing to note about this version of OnAppLoad() is that it disables Direct3D's lighting functionality. The early triangle sample programs didn't use it, but the bowling ball samples did. Because of the way this program uses materials and textures, it doesn't need Direct3D's lighting.

note

> To see how this sample works, copy the files tiger.x and tiger.bmp from the DirectX SDK. After you install the SDK, go to the drive where it's installed. You'll see a folder called DXSDK\Samples\Media. Copy the tiger.x and tiger.bmp files from that folder into your project folder.

The function that initializes the rigid body is GameInitialization(). Listing 9.2 presents the code for the GameInitialization() function.

Listing 9.2
Initializing the Rigid Body

```
1     bool GameInitialization()
2     {
3         // Set up the view matrix, as in previous examples.
4         D3DXVECTOR3 eyePoint(0.0f,3.0f,-10.0f);
5         D3DXVECTOR3 lookatPoint(0.0f,0.0f,0.0f);
6         D3DXVECTOR3 upDirection(0.0f,1.0f,0.0f);
7         D3DXMATRIXA16 tempViewMatrix;
8         D3DXMatrixLookAtLH(
9             &tempViewMatrix,&eyePoint,&lookatPoint,&upDirection);
10        theApp.ViewMatrix(tempViewMatrix);
11        // Set up the projection matrix, as in previous examples.
12        D3DXMATRIXA16 projectionMatrix;
13        D3DXMatrixPerspectiveFovLH(
14            &projectionMatrix,D3DX_PI/4,1.0f,1.0f,100.0f);
15        theApp.ProjectionMatrix(projectionMatrix);
16
17        // Load the object's mesh.
18        theObject.LoadMesh("tiger.x");
```

```
19
20          theObject.AngularVelocity(vector_3d(0.0,0.0,0.0));
21          theObject.AngularAcceleration(vector_3d(0.0,0.0,0.0));
22          theObject.RotationalInertia(vector_3d(39.6f,39.6f,12.5f));
23          theObject.Torque(vector_3d(0.0,0.0,0.0));
24
25          // Set the object in motion.
26          force theForce;
27          theForce.Force(vector_3d(1.0,0.0,0.0f));
28          theForce.ApplicationPoint(vector_3d(0.0,0.0,-1.0f));
29          theObject.Force(theForce);
30
31          theObject.Mass(100);
32
33          return (true);
34      }
```

In this sample program, the GameInitialization() function sets the view matrix on lines 4–9 of Listing 9.2. On lines 12–15, it sets the projection matrix. Because the viewpoint and perspective don't change from frame to frame, you don't need to recalculate them, as is commonly done in sample programs in the DirectX SDK. Your program can just set them once and not worry about them further.

On line 18 of Listing 9.2, the GameInitialization() function loads the mesh to use for the rigid body. In this case, it's a mesh of a tiger from the DirectX SDK.

The initialization of the d3d_rigid_body object starts on line 20. Lines 20–23 set the tiger's rotational properties. You might wonder how I got the values for setting the rotational inertia on line 22. The answer is that I treated the tiger as a cylinder and used the formulas from Table 9.1. Note that, when the tiger is loaded, it is looking down the z axis directly at you. If you're treating the tiger as a cylinder, rotating around the z axis uses the formula $I=MR^2/2$. On the other hand, rotation around the x or y axis uses the formula $I=MR^2/2+ ML^2/12$. For these calculations, I used a length of 2 meters (discounting the tail) and a mass of 100 kg.

The GameInitialization() function in Listing 9.2 also sets the tiger in motion by exerting a force on it. Lines 26–29 demonstrate how this is done. There's something important to notice here. I've created a new class for this sample program called force. Instead of the force acting on an object and being just a vector, it's now an entity in itself. I did this because forces have more information associated with them in rotational dynamics than they do in linear dynamics. In linear dynamics, forces are always applied at the center of mass. That just isn't the case in rotational dynamics. When you're dealing with rotating rigid bodies, you need to account for forces that are applied at random points on the surface of the body.

Why do rigid bodies have forces acting on them at random locations?

Well, think about a multiplayer bumper car game. Players run the bumper cars into each other at random times. They don't always crash along the cars' primary axes. Players are not very considerate that way. As a result, the software has to handle collisions on any point on the surface of the car.

All of this is a rather long way of saying that a force object has to store both its force vector and a vector indicating where the force is applied. Listing 9.3 gives the definition of the force class.

Listing 9.3
The force Class

```
1      class force
2      {
3      private:
4          vector_3d forceVector;
5          vector_3d forceLocation;
6
7      public:
8
9          // This is the actual force.
10         void Force(
11             vector_3d theForce);
12         vector_3d Force(void);
13
14         // This indicates where the force is applied.
15         void ApplicationPoint(
16             vector_3d forceApplicationPoint);
17         vector_3d ApplicationPoint(void);
18     };
```

This class is simple. It contains just two vectors, as well as the member functions needed to set and get their values. If you look back at Listing 9.1, you'll see that the d3d_rigid_body class has a data member of type force. It also defines member functions for getting and setting the force. The GameInitialization() function in Listing 9.2 calls the Force() function on line 29 to set the force acting on the tiger. The force does not act through the center of mass, so in addition to moving the tiger linearly, it makes the tiger spin. When you run the program, the tiger spins slowly as it moves off the right edge of the program's window.

Updating a d3d_rigid_body Object

During each frame, the framework calls the UpdateFrame() function, which is shown in Listing 9.4.

Listing 9.4
The UpdateFrame() Function

```
1    bool UpdateFrame()
2    {
3        static bool forceApplied = false;
4
5        // If the initial force was applied...
6        if (forceApplied)
7        {
8            // Set the object's force to 0.
9            force offCenterForce;
10           offCenterForce.Force(vector_3d(0.0,0.0,0.0f));
11           offCenterForce.ApplicationPoint(vector_3d(0.0,0.0,0.0));
12           theObject.Force(offCenterForce);
13       }
14       // Else the initial force has not yet been applied...
15       else
16       {
17           // Apply it.
18           forceApplied=true;
19       }
20
21       theObject.Update(1);
22       return (true);
23   }
```

This function tests to see if the initial force set in the GameInitialization() function has already been applied to the tiger. During the first frame of animation, it hasn't, so the UpdateFrame() function applies the force by calling the d3d_rigid_body::Update() function. After the first frame, the force is applied. We don't want the force applied again, or the tiger will continue to accelerate. UpdateFrame() sets the force to 0 on lines 9–12.

Let's take a quick look at the d3d_rigid_body::Update() function. After all, that's where the physics happens.

Listing 9.5
The d3d_rigid_body::Update() Function

```
1    bool d3d_rigid_body::Update(
2        scalar changeInTime)
3    {
4        //
5        // Begin calculating linear dynamics.
6        //
7
```

```
8        // Find the linear acceleration.
9        // a = F/m
10       assert(mass!=0);
11       linearAcceleration = sumForces.Force()/mass;
12
13       // Find the linear velocity.
14       linearVelocity += linearAcceleration * changeInTime;
15
16       // Find the new location of the center of mass.
17       centerOfMassLocation += linearVelocity * changeInTime;
18
19       //
20       // End calculating linear dynamics.
21       //
22
23       // Create the translation matrix.
24       D3DXMATRIX totalTranslation;
25       D3DXMatrixTranslation(
26           &totalTranslation,
27           centerOfMassLocation.X(),
28           centerOfMassLocation.Y(),
29           centerOfMassLocation.Z());
30
31       //
32       // Begin calculating rotational dynamics.
33       //
34
35       // Use the force to calculate the torque.
36       torque =
37           sumForces.ApplicationPoint().Cross(sumForces.Force());
38
39       /* Use the torque and inertia to calculate the angular
40       acceleration.*/
41       angularAcceleration.X(
42           torque.X()/rotationalInertia.X());
43       angularAcceleration.Y(
44           torque.Y()/rotationalInertia.Y());
45       angularAcceleration.Z(
46           torque.Z()/rotationalInertia.Z());
47
48       /* Change the angular velocity according to the angular
49       acceleration. */
```

```
50        angularVelocity += angularAcceleration * changeInTime;
51
52        //
53        // Use angular acceleration to calculate the angles of rotation.
54        //
55        currentOrientation.XAngle(
56            currentOrientation.XAngle() +
57            angularVelocity.X() * changeInTime);
58        currentOrientation.YAngle(
59            currentOrientation.YAngle() +
60            angularVelocity.Y() * changeInTime);
61        currentOrientation.ZAngle(
62            currentOrientation.ZAngle() +
63            angularVelocity.Z() * changeInTime);
64
65        //
66        // End calculating rotational dynamics.
67        //
68
69        // Build a rotation matrix for each axis.
70        D3DXMATRIX rotationX, rotationY, rotationZ;
71        D3DXMatrixRotationX(&rotationX,currentOrientation.XAngle());
72        D3DXMatrixRotationY(&rotationY,currentOrientation.YAngle());
73        D3DXMatrixRotationZ(&rotationZ,currentOrientation.ZAngle());
74
75        D3DXMATRIX totalRotations;
76
77        // Multiply them into the world matrix.
78        D3DXMatrixMultiply(
79            &totalRotations,
80            &rotationX,
81            &rotationY);
82        D3DXMatrixMultiply(
83            &totalRotations,
84            &totalRotations,
85            &rotationZ);
86
87        /* Combine the rotation and translation matrices into the world
88        matrix. */
89        D3DXMatrixMultiply(
90            &worldMatrix,
91            &totalRotations,
```

```
92              &totalTranslation);
93
94          return(true);
95      }
```

As you can see, this is a real workhorse function. Its first task is to use the force on the object to calculate the object's linear displacement. Using the force and the mass, the Update() function finds the acceleration. On line 14 of Listing 9.5, the function obtains the change in velocity. From that, it can find the displacement vector for the object's center of mass. The displacement vector gets built into a translation matrix on lines 24–29.

So far, a rigid body looks just like a point mass. Starting on line 36, the Update() function demonstrates how rigid bodies differ from point masses. Lines 36–37 use the formula $\tau = \mathbf{r} \times \mathbf{F}$ to calculate the torque on the object. With the torque and the rotational inertia, the Update() function calculates the angular acceleration on lines 41–46. Next, it uses the angular velocity to find the angles of rotation in the x, y, and z directions. After it has those angles, it builds rotation matrices on lines 70–73.

The Update() function is nearly done. But before it returns, it combines all the rotation matrices into one on lines 78–85. It also combines the rotation and translation matrices on lines 89–92 and stores the result as the object's world matrix. With that, Update() is done.

Rendering a d3d_rigid_body Object

As with updating a rigid body, two functions render a rigid body. First is the RenderFrame() function called by the framework, shown in Listing 9.6.

Listing 9.6
The RenderFrame() Function

```
1       bool RenderFrame()
2       {
3           // Set the view matrix.
4           theApp.D3DRenderingDevice()->SetTransform(
5               D3DTS_VIEW,
6               &theApp.ViewMatrix());
7
8           // Set the projection matrix.
9           theApp.D3DRenderingDevice()->SetTransform(
10              D3DTS_PROJECTION,
11              &theApp.ProjectionMatrix());
12
13          // Render the object.
14          theObject.Render();
```

```
15        return (true);
16    }
```

As you can see from Listing 9.6, the RenderFrame() function sets the view and projection matrices every time it renders a frame. You might ask whether this is necessary.

Given the fact that neither the viewpoint nor the view volume changes from frame to frame, the answer is no. For this example, you could move the function calls on lines 4–11 into the GameInitialization() function.

Why did I put them there? To illustrate a point. In most games, the view matrix needs to be updated and set on a frame-by-frame basis because the camera moves constantly. The projection matrix might change as well. If that's the case with your game, you need to set one or both of these matrices each time you render a frame. You could set them in the UpdateFrame() function, but you would have to be sure to do it last. If your program needs to set them, it's better to set them here in the RenderFrame() function.

To render the tiger, the RenderFrame() function calls the d3d_rigid_body::Render() function, which appears in Listing 9.7.

Listing 9.7
Rendering a rigid_body Object

```
1     bool d3d_rigid_body::Render(void)
2     {
3         // Save the world transformation matrix.
4         D3DXMATRIX saveWorldMatrix;
5         theApp.D3DRenderingDevice()->GetTransform(
6             D3DTS_WORLD,
7             &saveWorldMatrix);
8
9         // Apply the world transformation matrix for this object.
10        theApp.D3DRenderingDevice()->SetTransform(
11            D3DTS_WORLD,&worldMatrix);
12
13        // Now render the object with its transformations.
14        bool renderedOK=objectMesh.Render();
15
16        // Restore the world transformation matrix.
17        theApp.D3DRenderingDevice()->SetTransform(
18            D3DTS_WORLD,
19            &saveWorldMatrix);
20
21        return (renderedOK);
22    }
```

As with point masses, the Render() function for rigid bodies is much simpler than the Update() function. Render() saves the current world matrix and then sets its own world matrix. Next, it renders its mesh at the location and orientation specified by its world matrix. Finally, it restores the original world matrix.

Summary

That was a healthy amount of math and programming. But what you got for it was a rigid body class that you can use to simulate the complex physics presented in the previous few chapters of this book. You can simulate almost anything in a game as a point mass, a rigid body, a collection of point masses, or a collection of rigid bodies. As you'll see soon, the tools you have to work with are becoming very powerful indeed.

But before you can use these classes in games, you need to deal with collisions of rigid bodies. That's presented in the next chapter.

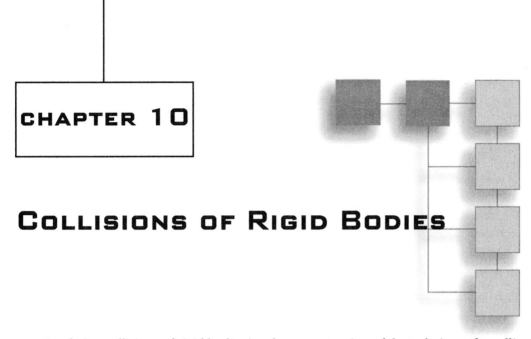

CHAPTER 10

COLLISIONS OF RIGID BODIES

Simulating collisions of rigid bodies involves an extension of the techniques for collisions of point particles. As with point particles, collisions involve two main tasks: collision detection and collision response. Let's look at some ways of handling both of these tasks.

Collision Detection

The techniques you use for collision detection depend on the type of game you're writing. For many games, rough approximations are fine. This is particularly true of arcade-style games. However, if you're simulating something complex, such as the human form, rough approximations just won't cut it. Therefore, to write 3-D games, you need to be familiar with a wide variety of techniques that range from simple to complex.

Rough Approximations

The primary advantage of using rough approximations for collision detection is that they are fast. Another is that they are generally easy to code. Common techniques for rough approximations include bounding spheres, bounding boxes, and bounding cylinders, presented in Chapter 8, "Collisions of Point Particles." Chapter 8 also illustrated the methods for collision detection using spheres, boxes, or cylinders.

If you use bounding spheres, boxes, or cylinders for collision detection in your game, it generally means you're approximating rigid bodies as point particles for linear motion. This is a good working assumption. Almost all 3-D games can process linear forces on rigid bodies just as if they were point particles without any loss of realism. If this is true for your game, the game's rigid bodies are candidates for using bounding spheres, boxes, or cylinders for collision detection.

235

In the final analysis, the determining factor of whether you use bounding spheres, boxes, or cylinders is the shape of the object you're trying to simulate. Suppose, for example that you're writing a game in which the player uses rockets to destroy bombs being dropped. For linear motion, you can treat all these objects as point masses. Also, rockets and bombs are simple shapes. They tend to fit snugly in bounding cylinders or spheres.

More complex shapes preclude the use of simple bounding shapes. For example, Figure 10.1 shows the tiger that was used in the examples in previous chapters. As noted in Chapter 9, "Rigid Body Dynamics," tigers are not usually considered rigid bodies, so we'll again imagine that this is a tiger statue. As the sample program in this chapter will demonstrate, tigers don't fit well into spheres. A cylinder or box would be a better approximation, but even those aren't very good.

Figure 10.1
A tiger in a rectangular bounding box.

Imagine two tigers spinning through space. Forget for a moment that the tigers would die. Using simple bounding volumes, such as the rectangle shown in Figure 10.1, would result in false positives when the game tests for collisions. Figure 10.2 illustrates how that might happen.

Figure 10.2
The limitations of bounding rectangles.

As you can see in Figure 10.2, the bounding boxes just barely overlap. However, there is no collision between these two tigers. A tiger is just too complex a shape to be accurately contained in a bounding sphere, box, or cylinder.

Improved Collision Detection

How can we improve over simple bounding volumes without significantly increasing the processing overhead of the game?

Many attempts have been made to answer that question, with varying degrees of success. It's important to remember that collision detection is not a question of physics, but of geometry and programming. Because the focus of this book is physics, I'll only be able to give a brief overview of the most common methods of advanced collision detection.

Bounding Volume Trees

One of the most efficient and flexible methods of advanced collision detection is to use a collection of bounding volumes stored in an array or tree. Let's take another look at the tiger to see how this works.

Figure 10.3 shows the tiger once again. This time, several rectangles, rather than just one, bound the tiger.

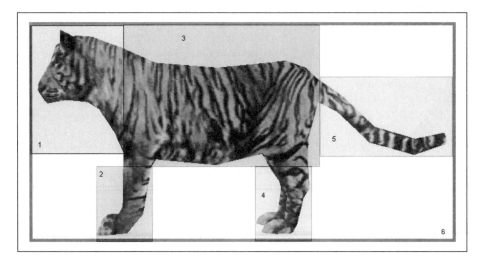

Figure 10.3
A better set of bounding volumes for the tiger.

There are six bounding rectangles in Figure 10.3. First, the entire tiger is enclosed in the same bounding rectangle shown in Figure 10.1. I've given this rectangle a heavy outline and labeled it rectangle 6. A collision with this rectangle indicates that an object might have collided with the tiger. Maybe not. It might be a case similar to that shown in Figure 10.2.

A program finds out whether a collision has really occurred by testing the other bounding boxes. Figure 10.3 shows bounding boxes for the tiger's head, body, legs, and tail. I've shaded and numbered the boxes to make them easier to see.

When a collision occurs with the outer bounding box (box 6 in Figure 10.3), the program must check the bounding boxes around the head, body, legs, and tail. If there is a collision with one of them, the program should apply the appropriate forces to the tiger to make it bounce.

If a collision occurs with the outer bounding box but none of the inner bounding boxes, the collision point is somewhere in the empty space between the inner and outer boxes. That is not considered a true collision, so the program should not react.

You might ask why the outer bounding box is needed at all. The only reason for having it is efficiency. If there's no collision with the outer bounding box, there's no need to check any of the inner boxes. Having both the inner and outer boxes provides efficiency when objects aren't colliding and accuracy when they are.

note

It might be tempting to throw away the outer bounding box in this example to save some memory. I highly recommend against it. I wouldn't have said that 20 years ago when 256KB was a lot of memory. However, today's computers have enough memory so that you don't have to scrimp and save every byte you can. The biggest limiting factor in games usually is not memory. Today, it's more likely to be limited by the speed of the microprocessor than memory. So, in general, it's okay to sacrifice a little memory to increase microprocessor efficiency.

Do all the bounding volumes have to be of the same type? In other words, could we have used a bounding sphere for the head, cylinders for the legs, and rectangles for the tail and body?

Absolutely. It's just a matter of taking advantage of inheritance in C++. To have many different types of bounding volumes, you would create a base class that all your bounding volumes are derived from. You could call it bounding_volume. You would then create classes called bounding_rectangle, bounding_sphere, and bounding_cylinder. All three of these classes would be derived from bounding_volume. That way, you could store all of them together in the same data structure.

Speaking of data structures, what's the best way to store your bounding volumes? The answer: Any way you want. Bounding volumes can be stored with an array or an array of pointers to dynamically allocated objects. It's common to store them in trees so that they're in a rapidly searchable order.

For example, if a possible collision occurs near the front of the tiger in the previous examples, your program can test the collision point's x and y values. Assuming that the coordinate system is at the center of the tiger's mass, an x value less than 0 means that the possible collision point is near the head. So the program would start by testing rectangle 1, then 2, and then 3. The program wouldn't even need to bother with rectangles 4 and 5. If x is less than 0 and a collision didn't occur in rectangles 1, 2, or 3, then there is no collision.

warning

This technique works only if you translate the possible collision point from world coordinates into local coordinates.

Axis-Aligned Bounding Boxes and Oriented Bounding Boxes

If bounding boxes provide enough accuracy for your game, they can be very fast. Games typically implement one of two types of bounding boxes. The first is axis-aligned bounding boxes (AABBs).

You typically store AABBs in a special type of tree structure called an *octree*. The advantage of AABBs is that they are defined in world coordinates and aligned with the x, y, and z axes of the world coordinate system. So for any possible collision point, your program simply compares the x, y, and z values of the coordinate to the top, bottom, left, right, front, and back values of each box. These comparisons are fast.

What Are Octrees?

In discussions of collision detection, invariably the subject of octrees comes up. Octrees are different from other common tree structures. For example, binary trees have left and right branches at each tree node. Essentially, they're 2-D data structures. The same is not true of octrees. They're 3-D.

Suppose that you use a laser to cut a 3-D shape into small boxes. Imagine also that all the pieces of the object are still in their original places. Basically, you're partitioning the object's volume into boxes. Next, you index the boxes with a tree structure. The tree has a pointer to each box. The tree structure essentially provides a way of indexing the 3-D volume. That's what octrees do.

The disadvantage of AABBs is that the bounding boxes in the tree must stay aligned with the world coordinate axes even if the object changes alignment. This can cause the accuracy of the bounding boxes to vary, resulting in false positives when the game tests for collisions. Therefore, AABBs work best for objects that naturally stay aligned with the world coordinate axes, such as buildings.

Another approach is to use oriented bounding boxes (OBBs). Like AABBs, OBBs contain each of the parts of the rigid object. They fit tightly around the individual parts to provide the best accuracy possible. However, unlike AABBs, OBBs are defined in the rigid object's local coordinate space. As the object rotates, translates, or skews, so do the bounding boxes.

Because OBBs are defined in the object's local space, your program must convert the point to be tested into the object's local coordinates. The conversion results in some additional overhead when compared to AABBs, but not much. And OBBs are much better suited to objects that do not stay aligned with the world coordinate system.

Like AABBs, programmers usually implement OBBs in octrees because octrees lend themselves well to searching for a collision point. However, don't feel obligated to implement octrees into your program. For rigid objects that are not overly complex, octrees can be overkill. If you find that's the case for your game, use a simpler type of tree.

Collision Response

Collision response is about modeling physics in software. To produce an accurate model of complex physical objects in software, your program must model both linear and angular dynamics. In addition, each rigid body must contain information that enables it to respond properly to collisions. This includes the rigid body's bounding volume and its coefficient of restitution.

note

Recall that the coefficient of restitution, which was presented in Chapter 8, is a measure of the elasticity of an object.

Games also need to model the forces that act on rigid bodies in collisions. They must use these forces to calculate both the linear and angular collision responses.

Linear Collision Response

The linear collision response of a rigid body is governed by the same equations used for the linear collision response of a point mass. Why? Because for any rigid body, we can substitute a point mass at its center of mass. That means that no matter what rigid body your game works with, you can pretend it's just a point mass that exists at the rigid body's center of mass. As a result, you already know how to deal with linear collision response. You saw how it's done in Chapter 8. All of the formulas presented there apply here.

Chapter 8 showed that when collisions occur, a force is generated. The force comes from the motion of the rigid bodies involved in the collision. It is an intense force that acts over a short time. Recall that physicists call this the *impulse force*.

Collisions of point masses cause the impulse force to occur at the object's center of mass. But rigid bodies can have multiple points of contact, as shown in Figure 10.4.

When rigid bodies 1 and 2 in Figure 10.4 collide, the two objects exert forces at the points of impact. The points of impact are labeled P and Q. In the figure, only rigid body 1 is in motion. Therefore, only rigid body 1 contributes forces to the collision. However, the forces affect both rigid bodies. The effects depend on the masses according to the now-familiar equation **F=ma.**

The question is this: How do you simulate these linear forces at all of these points of impact?

The answer is this: You needn't bother. For linear motion, you can pretend that these two rigid bodies are point masses.

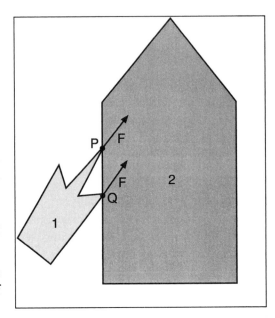

Figure 10.4
Two rigid bodies colliding.

Therefore, the collision exerts all of its forces at the centers of mass. Rather than deal with each force at each contact point, game programmers simply sum the forces and apply the result to the centers of mass for each rigid body in the collision.

It's important to remember that the total linear force generated by the collision is the same on both rigid bodies. However, if the force on rigid body 1 is F_I, the force on rigid body 2 is $-F_I$.

Angular Collision Response

Chapter 9 presented the equations for the angular motion of a rigid body. Those same equations apply to collisions. However, when dealing with angular forces, we can't assume that the rigid body is a point mass. The force must be applied at the point of contact.

If you look back at Figure 10.4, you'll see two rigid bodies colliding. However, there are two points of contact. How do you handle that?

Answer: Cheat.

For the most part, objects in games have fairly regular and symmetrical shapes. Of course, that is changing as games become more realistic. However, it generally doesn't matter. We can usually make our collisions look right by using only one point of contact in the collision. And if it looks right, it *is* right.

For the collision depicted in Figure 10.4, you can cheat using the technique shown in Figure 10.5.

The simple trick demonstrated in Figure 10.5 is to cheat collisions by finding a point that indicates the center of the collision. Point R is halfway between points P and Q. To calculate the angular collision response, you can apply the appropriate force at point R on *both* rigid bodies. Even though point R isn't physically on rigid body 1, you can pretend that it is and apply the impulse force there. It gives results that are correct enough for virtually every game, and this technique is computationally inexpensive.

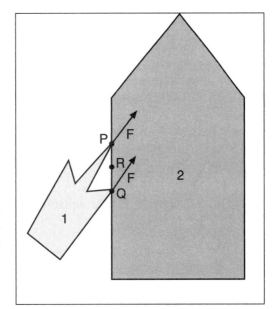

Figure 10.5
Cheating on a collision.

You can apply this same technique to collisions that involve many more points of collision. Suppose, for instance, that a car hits the right front fender of another car at a 90° angle. The entire front end of the first car and most of the right front fender of the second car are involved in the collision. To get a quick and reasonably accurate angular collision response, use the point where the center of the front end of the first car meets the right front fender of the second car, as shown in Figure 10.6.

The point P_{Center} in Figure 10.6 indicates the center of the collision. If you apply the angular response at P_{Center}, the results will look right.

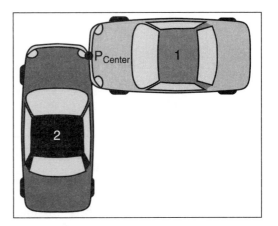

Figure 10.6
Finding the point at the center of the collision.

Combining Linear and Angular Collision Response

Collisions that do not occur along a line that passes through the center of mass require both a linear and angular response. So we need an equation that gives us the collision's impulse force in terms of both its linear and angular components. To find that equation, start with Newton's second law.

If we apply this to the impulse force, we get this:

$$\mathbf{F_I} = m\mathbf{a_I}$$

where F_I is the impulse force, m is the mass, and a_I is the acceleration during the collision. The acceleration is going to be as follows:

$$\mathbf{a_I} = \mathbf{v_f} - \mathbf{v_i}$$

In this equation, v_f and v_i are the final and initial velocities of the rigid body during the collision. Unfortunately, we don't know v_f. We need another equation to help solve this.

Recall from Chapter 8 that the equation for the coefficient of restitution is this:

$$e = \frac{-\left(v_{1f} - v_{2f}\right)}{\left(v_{1i} - v_{2i}\right)}$$

We now have three questions to help us find the answer. Why three? Because the impulse force is equal in magnitude for both bodies. As a result, we get the following three equations:

$$\mathbf{F_I} = m_1\left(\mathbf{v_{1f}} - \mathbf{v_{1i}}\right)$$

$$-\mathbf{F_I} = m_2\left(\mathbf{v_{2f}} - \mathbf{v_{2i}}\right)$$

$$e = \frac{-\left(v_{1f} - v_{2f}\right)}{\left(v_{1i} - v_{2i}\right)}$$

note

As I mentioned in Chapter 8, I'm using the symbol F_I to indicate the impulse force. Most physics books use the letter J instead.

Now we have equations and three unknowns (F_I, v_{1f}, and v_{2f}), so we can solve for v_{1f} and v_{2f} and substitute the results into the equation for e. That gives us this:

$$e = \frac{-\left(\left(\dfrac{F_I}{m_1} + v_{1i}\right) - \left(\dfrac{F_I}{m_2} + v_{2i}\right)\right)}{\left(v_{1i} - v_{2i}\right)}$$

Part of this equation is $v_{1i}-v_{2i}$. This expression represents the relative velocities of the rigid bodies right before the impact. We can make the rest of the equations easier by letting

$$v_r = v_{1i} - v_{2i}$$

That gives us this:

$$e = \frac{-\left(\left(\dfrac{F_I}{m_1} + v_{1i}\right) - \left(\dfrac{F_I}{m_2} + v_{2i}\right)\right)}{v_r}$$

Now we have the linear impulse force in terms of the masses, the initial velocities just before the impact, and the coefficient of restitution. The next step is to add in the angular collision response.

Chapter 9 stated that the velocity of a point P at position **r** away from the center of mass is given by the following equation:

$$\mathbf{v}_p = \boldsymbol{\omega} \times \mathbf{r}$$

You can apply this equation before or after a collision. If we make the point P the collision point, we can get its total velocity after the collision:

$$\mathbf{v}_p = \mathbf{v}_{cm} + (\ldots \times \mathbf{r})$$

In this equation, you add the rotational velocity plus the linear velocity of the center of mass to get the final velocity of the collision point P. Applying this equation to each rigid body in the collision gives this:

$$\mathbf{v}_{fcm1} = \left(\frac{F_I}{m_1} + \mathbf{v}_{1i}\right) + (\ldots_1 \times \mathbf{r}_1)$$

$$\mathbf{v}_{fcm2} = \left(\frac{F_I}{m_2} + \mathbf{v}_{2i}\right) + (\ldots_2 \times \mathbf{r}_2)$$

Now we have two more unknowns, v_{fcm1} and v_{fcm2}. These represent the final velocity of the centers of mass of rigid bodies 1 and 2, respectively. Because we have two more unknowns, we need two more equations. We can get them from the equations for finding torque:

$$\tilde{} = \mathbf{r} \times \mathbf{F}$$

$$\tilde{} = \mathrm{I}{-} = \mathrm{I}(\ldots_f - \ldots_i)$$

If we set these two torque equations equal to each other, we get this:

$$\mathbf{r} \times \mathbf{F} = \mathrm{I}(\ldots_f - \ldots_i)$$

We can now apply this equation to each body in the collision:

$$\mathbf{r}_1 \times \mathbf{F}_I = \mathrm{I}_1(\ldots_{1f} - \ldots_{1i})$$

$$\mathbf{r}_2 \times (-\mathbf{F}_I) = \mathrm{I}_2(\ldots_{2f} - \ldots_{2i})$$

Then we just substitute and rearrange. Here's the result:

$$\mathbf{F}_I = \frac{-v_r(e+1)}{\dfrac{1}{m_1} + \dfrac{1}{m_2} + \mathbf{n} \bullet \left[\left(\dfrac{(\mathbf{r}_1 \times \mathbf{n})}{\mathrm{I}_1} \right) \times \mathbf{r}_1 \right] + \mathbf{n} \bullet \left[\left(\dfrac{(\mathbf{r}_2 \times \mathbf{n})}{\mathrm{I}_2} \right) \times \mathbf{r}_2 \right]}$$

Wow! It took a while to get here, but we have a formula for the impulse force that accounts for both the linear and angular components of the problem. Note that the vector $\mathbf{n}$ in this equation is the unit normal vector at point P.

This gives us everything we need. If we can specify the impulse force and the point at which it occurs, we can pass that information to the d3d_rigid_body class presented in Chapter 9. It can then calculate how each rigid body in the collision behaves. So let's jump into code.

Updating the Physics Modeling Framework

In Chapter 9, I introduced the d3d_rigid_body class that models both types of rigid body dynamics. In this chapter, I've enhanced the class and modified the physics modeling framework that it's a part of. Beginning with this chapter, both the d3d_mesh class and the d3d_rigid_body class are much more about modeling physics than about Direct3D. Therefore, I've renamed them to just mesh and rigid_body.

In addition, the physics modeling framework now contains three libraries. The first is the math library developed in Chapters 2, "Simulating 3-D with Direct X," and 3, "Mathematical Tools for Physics and 3-D Programming." The second is the graphics library that gets Direct3D up and running. As of this chapter, the graphics library will contain only the d3d_app class.

The third library that the framework now contains is a physics library that contains objects modeling forces, meshes, rigid bodies, and collisions. This chapter will demonstrate the use of the physics library shortly.

note

Sometimes it helps to know why software designers make the decisions they do. In this case, it came down to opinion and convenience. Specifically, you could argue that the mesh class should not have been renamed and that it belongs in the graphics library. That point of view is equally logical in my mind with what I've done in this chapter. In the end, putting the mesh class in the physics library was both more convenient and as logical as having it in the graphics library, so I moved it.

I've continued the trend from Chapter 9 of moving the definition for each object into its own header file. For example, the force class is now in the file force.h. If you look on the CD-ROM in the Source\Chapter 10 folder, you'll see that it contains a lot of new header files. Fortunately, you don't have to worry about which ones to include or what order they need to be included in. Just include the file PMFramework.h in all your .cpp files.

Setting Things in Motion

In the sample program for this chapter, we'll write a program called Tiger Toss. This program creates three rigid bodies, each in the shape of a tiger. It launches the tigers at each other in such a way as to cause both linear and angular motion. They move toward each other until they collide. The simulation models both the angular and linear results of the collision.

note

No actual tigers were harmed in this simulation.

To see all of this work, let's look at some of the functions in the file TigerToss.cpp. It's in the folder Source\Chapter 10 on the CD-ROM that comes with this book.

Listing 10.1
Initializing Tiger Toss

```
1     bool GameInitialization()
2     {
3         D3DXVECTOR3 eyePoint(0.0f,3.0f,-10.0f);
4         D3DXVECTOR3 lookatPoint(0.0f,0.0f,0.0f);
5         D3DXVECTOR3 upDirection(0.0f,1.0f,0.0f);
6         D3DXMATRIXA16 tempViewMatrix;
7         D3DXMatrixLookAtLH(
8             &tempViewMatrix,&eyePoint,&lookatPoint,&upDirection);
9         theApp.ViewMatrix(tempViewMatrix);
10
11        D3DXMATRIXA16 projectionMatrix;
12        D3DXMatrixPerspectiveFovLH(
```

```
13              &projectionMatrix,D3DX_PI/4,1.0f,1.0f,100.0f);
14         theApp.ProjectionMatrix(projectionMatrix);
15
16         vector_3d tempVector(0.0,0.0,0.0);
17         force theForce;
18
19         allTigers[0].LoadMesh("tiger.x");
20
21         tempVector.SetXYZ(-3.0f,0.0,0.0);
22         allTigers[0].Location(tempVector);
23         tempVector.SetXYZ(39.6f,39.6f,12.5f);
24         allTigers[0].RotationalInertia(tempVector);
25         tempVector.SetXYZ(1.0,0.0,0.0f);
26         theForce.Force(tempVector);
27         tempVector.SetXYZ(0.0,0.0,-1.0f);
28         theForce.ApplicationPoint(tempVector);
29         allTigers[0].Force(theForce);
30         allTigers[0].Mass(100);
31         allTigers[0].BoundingSphereRadius(0.75f);
32         allTigers[0].CoefficientOfRestitution(0.9f);
33
34         allTigers[2]=allTigers[1]=allTigers[0];
35
36         tempVector.SetXYZ(0.0,3.0f,0.0);
37         allTigers[1].Location(tempVector);
38         tempVector.SetXYZ(-1.0f,-1.0f,0.0);
39         theForce.Force(tempVector);
40         tempVector.SetXYZ(0.0,-1.0f,-1.0f);
41         theForce.ApplicationPoint(tempVector);
42         allTigers[1].Force(theForce);
43         allTigers[1].CoefficientOfRestitution(1.0f);
44
45         tempVector.SetXYZ(0.0,-3.0f,0.0);
46         allTigers[2].Location(tempVector);
47         tempVector.SetXYZ(0.0,2.0,0.0);
48         theForce.Force(tempVector);
49         tempVector.SetXYZ(1.0f,-1.0f,0.0);
50         theForce.ApplicationPoint(tempVector);
51         allTigers[2].Force(theForce);
52         allTigers[2].CoefficientOfRestitution(0.5f);
53
54         return (true);
55    }
```

The GameInitialization() function begins as it did in Chapter 9. It sets the view matrix on lines 3–9 and the projection matrix on lines 11–14. On lines 16–17, it declares a couple of variables needed later. The function then loads the mesh for the tiger on line 19.

It's generally the case that if a game has multiple objects that use the same mesh, the game loads the mesh only once. If none of the objects that use the mesh change it in any way, this is a great way to save memory and microprocessor time. Tiger Toss loads the tiger mesh once and uses it for all three tigers.

On lines 21–22 of Listing 10.1, the GameInitialization() function sets the starting position of the first of three tigers. The tigers are stored in an array declared near the top of the file TigerToss.cpp. Here's what the array declaration looks like:

```
#define TOTAL_TIGERS 3
rigid_body  allTigers[TOTAL_TIGERS];
```

The allTigers variable is just an array of rigid_body objects. I've defined the constant TOTAL_TIGERS to make it easy to loop through the array.

Back in the GameInitialization() function in Listing 10.1, lines 23–24 set the rotational inertia in the x, y, and z directions. I used the formulas in Table 9.1 (in Chapter 9) to calculate these inertias. To do this, I treated the tiger as a cylinder with a mass of 100 Kg (220 lbs.) and a length of 2 meters (6 feet 6 inches).

note

In reality, this is probably a bit small for a grown tiger, but these assumptions made the math easy.

In your games, you'll have to analyze each rigid body and make these kinds of generalizations to calculate the rotational inertia. The basic technique is to look at the body and determine which portions of it contribute significantly to the mass. Find a shape from Table 9.1 that generalizes the shape of each portion. Use the formulas for those shapes and the parallel axis theorem to add up the rotational inertia for the entire rigid body.

After it sets the rotational inertia, the GameInitialization() function sets the force being applied to the first tiger. This is shown in lines 25–29 of Listing 10.1. The function next sets the tiger's mass, bounding sphere radius, and coefficient of restitution. This tiger has a coefficient of restitution of 0.9, making it pretty bouncy.

Line 34 of Listing 10.1 copies all the information in the first tiger into the other two tigers. This saves the program from having to reinitialize information that doesn't change from tiger to tiger, such as the mass.

Lines 36–43 set the location, force, and coefficient of restitution for the second tiger. Note that collisions with the second tiger are completely elastic.

The information for the final tiger is set on lines 45–52. This tiger has a coefficient of restitution of 0.5. It's not nearly as bouncy as the other two.

Finding and Handling Collisions

Collisions for the Tiger Toss program are handled in the functions UpdateFrame() and HandleOverlapping(), which are in the file TigerToss.cpp. But before we look at those functions, we need to look at some of the code these functions depend on (see Listing 10.2).

Listing 10.2
A New Version of the rigid_body Class

```
1      class rigid_body
2      {
3      private:
4          mesh objectMesh;
5
6          // Physical and linear motion properties
7          scalar mass;
8          vector_3d centerOfMassLocation;
9          vector_3d linearVelocity;
10         vector_3d linearAcceleration;
11         force sumForces;
12
13         // Rotational motion properties
14         angle_set_3d currentOrientation;
15         vector_3d angularVelocity;
16         vector_3d angularAcceleration;
17         vector_3d rotationalInertia;
18         vector_3d torque;
19
20         // Collision properties
21         scalar coefficientOfRestitution;
22         scalar boundingSphereRadius;
23
24         D3DXMATRIX worldMatrix;
25
26     public:
27         rigid_body(void);
28
29         bool LoadMesh(
30             std::string meshFileName);
31
32         void Mass(
```

```
33              scalar massValue);
34          scalar Mass(void);
35
36          void Location(
37              vector_3d locationCenterOfMass);
38          vector_3d Location(void);
39
40          void LinearVelocity(
41              vector_3d newVelocity);
42          vector_3d LinearVelocity(void);
43
44          void LinearAcceleration(
45              vector_3d newAcceleration);
46          vector_3d LinearAcceleration(void);
47
48          void Force(
49              force sumExternalForces);
50          force Force(void);
51
52          void CurrentOrientation(
53              angle_set_3d newOrientation);
54          angle_set_3d CurrentOrientation(void);
55
56          void AngularVelocity(
57              vector_3d newAngularVelocity);
58          vector_3d AngularVelocity(void);
59
60          void AngularAcceleration(
61              vector_3d newAngularAcceleration);
62          vector_3d AngularAcceleration(void);
63
64          void RotationalInertia(vector_3d inertiaValue);
65          vector_3d RotationalInertia(void);
66
67          void Torque(vector_3d torqueValue);
68          vector_3d Torque(void);
69
70          void CoefficientOfRestitution(
71              scalar elasticity);
72          scalar CoefficientOfRestitution(void);
73
74          void BoundingSphereRadius(scalar radius);
```

```
75          scalar BoundingSphereRadius(void);
76
77          bool Update(
78              scalar changeInTime);
79          bool Render(void);
80      };
```

Listing 10.2 shows an updated definition of the rigid_body class. It has some changes from
the version presented in Chapter 9. First, the d3d_mesh object in line 4 is now a mesh object.
On lines 21–22, the class declares data members that are specifically for handling collisions. These are the coefficient of restitution and the radius of the bounding sphere.

Earlier in this chapter, I pointed out that a bounding sphere was probably not the best
type of bounding volume for a tiger. This program proves it. When you run the Tiger Toss
program, you'll see the tigers bounce off of each other without actually touching.

note

> The primary reason I used bounding spheres in this program was to keep the code simple. For the
> same reason, I'll continue to use them throughout this book. However, I strongly encourage you
> to experiment with other types of bounding volumes.

Lines 70–75 show that member functions were added to the rigid_body class for the new
data members.

If the physics modeling framework is going to be any good for complex simulations, it
needs a way to detect when a collision occurs and calculate its effects. Therefore, the
framework provides the collision class, which appears in Listing 10.3.

Listing 10.3
The Contents of PMCollision.h

```
1       #ifndef _PMCOLLISION_H
2       #define _PMCOLLISION_H
3
4       namespace pmframework
5       {
6
7       enum collision_status
8       {
9           COLLISION_NONE,
10          COLLISION_TOUCHING,
11          COLLISION_OVERLAPPING
12      };
13
```

```
14    class collision
15    {
16    private:
17        rigid_body *object1;
18        rigid_body *object2;
19
20    public:
21        collision();
22        collision(
23            rigid_body *firstObject,
24            rigid_body *secondObject);
25
26        void FirstObject(
27            rigid_body *firstObject);
28        rigid_body *FirstObject(void);
29
30        void SecondObject(
31            rigid_body *firstObject);
32        rigid_body *SecondObject(void);
33
34        collision_status CollisionOccurred(void);
35        bool CalculateReactions(void);
36    };
37
38    inline collision::collision()
39    {
40        object1=object2=NULL;
41    }
42
43    inline collision::collision(
44        rigid_body *firstObject,
45        rigid_body *secondObject)
46    {
47        assert(firstObject!=NULL);
48        assert(secondObject!=NULL);
49
50        object1=firstObject;
51        object2=secondObject;
52    }
53
54    inline void collision::FirstObject(
55        rigid_body *firstObject)
```

```
56    {
57        assert(firstObject!=NULL);
58
59        object1=firstObject;
60    }
61
62    inline rigid_body *collision::FirstObject(void)
63    {
64        return (object1);
65    }
66
67    inline void collision::SecondObject(
68        rigid_body *secondObject)
69    {
70        assert(secondObject!=NULL);
71
72        object2=secondObject;
73    }
74
75    inline rigid_body *collision::SecondObject(void)
76    {
77        return (object2);
78    }
79
80    }
81
82    #endif
```

The first definition in Listing 10.3 is the `collision_status` enumerated type. The purpose of this type is to differentiate between the various kinds of collisions that can occur. Figure 10.7 illustrates these collisions.

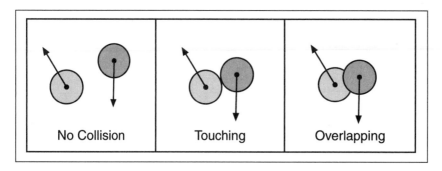

Figure 10.7
Possible collision conditions.

At any given moment, two rigid bodies, shown in Figure 10.7 as spheres, might be in one of three states. They might not be colliding at all, which requires no response. Alternatively, they might be touching; if so, a reaction needs to be calculated. If the two bodies are moving quickly, it is possible that they can move from a noncolliding state to an overlapping state in a single frame. Overlapping collisions look very unrealistic if they are displayed on the screen. The user sees objects inside one another when they should not be. You need to take additional action when an overlapping collision occurs. The collision_status type defines constants that differentiate among all three of these collision states.

The class definition for the collision object begins on line 14 of Listing 10.3. The class contains pointers to two rigid bodies as its private member data. Pointers are used because this class needs to update the actual objects involved in the collision.

On lines 21–32, the collision class gives the prototypes for the functions that construct the object and set its data members. The code for these functions appears on lines 43–80. The only member functions whose code does not appear in PMCollision.h are CollisionOccurred() and CalculateReactions(). These two functions are given in PMCollision.cpp, which is presented in Listing 10.4.

Listing 10.4
The CollisionOccurred() and CalculateReactions() Functions

```
1       collision_status collision::CollisionOccurred(void)
2       {
3           scalar distance;
4           vector_3d distanceVector;
5           collision_status collisionStatus = COLLISION_NONE;
6
7           //
8           // Find the distance between the two bounding spheres.
9           //
10          distanceVector = object1->Location() - object2->Location();
11          distance = AbsValue(distanceVector.Norm()) -
12              object1->BoundingSphereRadius() -
13              object2->BoundingSphereRadius();
14
15          // If the distance is essentially zero...
16          if (CloseToZero(distance))
17          {
18              // The bounding spheres are touching.
19              collisionStatus = COLLISION_TOUCHING;
20
21          }
22          // Else if the bounding spheres are overlapping...
```

```
23          else if (distance < 0.0)
24          {
25              collisionStatus = COLLISION_OVERLAPPING;
26          }
27
28          return (collisionStatus);
29      }
30
31      bool collision::CalculateReactions(void)
32      {
33          /* First, calculate the average coefficient of restitution, which
34          is a measure of the elasticity of the objects involved. */
35          scalar averageElasticity =
36              (object1->CoefficientOfRestitution()+
37              object2->CoefficientOfRestitution())/2;
38
39          //
40          // Now find the numerator.
41          //
42          vector_3d relativeVelocity =
43              object1->AngularVelocity() - object2->AngularVelocity();
44          vector_3d numerator =
45              -1 * relativeVelocity * (averageElasticity+1);
46
47          //
48          // Find the denominator. This is complex, so do it in steps.
49          //
50          /* First, find the unit normal, which is the normalized vector
51          from the center of mass of object 1 to the center of mass of
52          object 2. */
53          vector_3d unitNormal = object1->Location()-object2->Location();
54          unitNormal = unitNormal.Normalize(SCALAR_TOLERANCE);
55
56          // Now find the point at which the force acts on object 2.
57          vector_3d forceLocation2 =
58              unitNormal * object2->BoundingSphereRadius();
59
60          vector_3d tempVector = forceLocation2.Cross(unitNormal);
61
62          // Divide by the rotational inertia.
63          tempVector.X(tempVector.X()/object2->RotationalInertia().X());
64          tempVector.Y(tempVector.Y()/object2->RotationalInertia().Y());
```

```
65          tempVector.Z(tempVector.Z()/object2->RotationalInertia().Z());
66
67          // Cross the answer with the vector r for object 2.
68          tempVector = tempVector.Cross(forceLocation2);
69
70          // Now dot that with the unit normal.
71          scalar part1 = unitNormal.Dot(tempVector);
72
73          // Now find the point at which the force acts on object 1.
74          unitNormal *= -1;
75          vector_3d forceLocation1 =
76              unitNormal * object1->BoundingSphereRadius();
77
78          tempVector = forceLocation1.Cross(unitNormal);
79
80          // Divide by the rotational inertia.
81          tempVector.X(tempVector.X()/object1->RotationalInertia().X());
82          tempVector.Y(tempVector.Y()/object1->RotationalInertia().Y());
83          tempVector.Z(tempVector.Z()/object1->RotationalInertia().Z());
84
85          // Cross the answer with the vector r for object 1.
86          tempVector = tempVector.Cross(forceLocation1);
87
88          // Now dot that with the unit normal.
89          scalar part2 = unitNormal.Dot(tempVector);
90
91          scalar denominator =
92              1/object1->Mass() + 1/object2->Mass() + part2 + part1;
93
94          force impulseForce;
95          impulseForce.Force(numerator/denominator);
96          impulseForce.ApplicationPoint(forceLocation1);
97
98          vector_3d existingForce = object1->Force().Force();
99
100         force totalForce;
101         totalForce.Force(existingForce + impulseForce.Force());
102         object1->Force(totalForce);
103
104         existingForce = object2->Force().Force();
105         totalForce.Force(existingForce - impulseForce.Force());
106         object2->Force(totalForce);
```

```
107
108         return (true);
109    }
```

The `CollisionOccurred()` function in Listing 10.4 starts by assuming there is no collision. Next, it calculates the distance between the colliding objects. To find that distance, it uses the inaccurate method of finding the distance between the two bounding spheres. This is a decent working method for now, and it helps keep the code simple.

On line 16, the `CollisionOccurred()` function tests to see if the distance is essentially 0. The function `CloseToZero()` appears in `PMMathFunctions.h`. Due to floating-point errors, it's best not to test for equality to 0.0. If the distance is close enough to 0 to look like a collision is occurring, it's close enough to respond to the collision. So if `CloseToZero()` returns `true`, the edges of the bounding spheres are touching.

warning

Floating-point errors are something you have to be constantly on guard against as you write your games. They can cause a world of headaches. One of the easiest ways you can solve floating-point errors before they happen is to remember that you should not test whether a value is exactly 0.0. The answer is almost never right. Test to see if it's close enough to 0.0 to be considered 0.0. As my father used to say, if it's within spitting distance, that's good enough.

If the distance is not essentially 0, line 23 tests to see if the bounding spheres are overlapping. It does this by seeing if the distance is less than 0. If it is, the `CollisionOccurred()` function sets the `collisionStatus` variable to indicate an overlapping collision.

If neither condition evaluates to `true`, then the original assumption was correct and there is no collision.

The `CalculateReactions()` function begins on line 31 of Listing 10.4. It starts by calculating a coefficient of restitution for the collision on lines 35–37. To do this, it averages the coefficients of restitution for the two objects involved. Using this average enables each object to contribute its elasticity (or lack thereof) to the collision.

The rest of the function uses the formula that calculates an impulse force with both linear and angular components. Here it is again:

$$F_I = \frac{-v_r\left(e+1\right)}{\dfrac{1}{m_1}+\dfrac{1}{m_2}+\mathbf{n}\bullet\left[\left(\dfrac{(\mathbf{r}_1\times\mathbf{n})}{I_1}\right)\times\mathbf{r}_1\right]+\mathbf{n}\bullet\left[\left(\dfrac{(\mathbf{r}_2\times\mathbf{n})}{I_2}\right)\times\mathbf{r}_2\right]}$$

This is a complex calculation, so I broke it down into several steps in the CalculateReactions() function. First, the function calculates the numerator on lines 42–45. Finding the denominator is harder. I split the task into parts and worked from the right end of the equation to the left.

First, CalculateReactions() finds the unit normal vector by subtracting the location vectors for the centers of mass. It then normalizes the result of the subtraction so that it is a unit vector. This gives $\mathbf{n}$ in the previous equation.

On lines 57–58, the CalculateReactions() function finds a vector to the point of contact. As stated previously, we're using the contact point between the bounding spheres for now. This calculation gives us the term $\mathbf{r_2}$ in the impulse force equation.

In line 60, the CalculateReactions() function crosses $\mathbf{r_2}$ with $\mathbf{n}$. Lines 63–65 divide the result by the rotational inertia of rigid body 2. CalculateReactions() then crosses that answer with $\mathbf{r_2}$. At this point, the function has completed one term in the denominator. It has to repeat the entire process for rigid body 1, which it does on lines 73–89.

On lines 91–92, the CalculateReactions() function finishes the calculation for the denominator. It uses that denominator to set the impulse force vector for rigid body 1 on line 95. After setting the point on body 1 on which the force acts, it adds the impulse force to any existing force that might be acting on rigid body 1. This can include gravity, a force from a previous collision, or anything else. The point is that these forces are cumulative. The impulse force can't be taken as the only force acting on the body if you want your game to look good.

The CalculateReactions() function ends by adding the negative impulse force to object 2 to any existing force that might be acting on object 2. Because the force is the negative impulse, the calculation ends up being a subtraction.

Understanding how collisions are detected and reacted to makes it a lot easier to see how they can be handled.

What? There's more to handling collisions than detecting and reacting to them?

You bet. Just look at Listing 10.5.

Listing 10.5
Functions for Handling Collisions

```
1       bool UpdateFrame()
2       {
3               static bool forceApplied = false;
4               int i;
5
6               scalar timeIncrement = 1;
7
```

```
8          DWORD currentTime = ::timeGetTime();
9          if (!TimeToUpdateFrame(currentTime))
10             return (true);
11
12         // For each object...
13         for (i=0;i<TOTAL_TIGERS-1;i++)
14         {
15             // Find collisions with other objects.
16             for (int j=i+1;j<TOTAL_TIGERS;j++)
17             {
18                 // If a collision occurred...
19                 collision theCollision(
20                     &allTigers[i],
21                     &allTigers[j]);
22                 collision_status collisionOccurred =
23                     theCollision.CollisionOccurred();
24                 switch (collisionOccurred)
25                 {
26                     case COLLISION_TOUCHING:
27                         // Bounce the objects.
28                         theCollision.CalculateReactions();
29                         // The bounce force has not been applied.
30                         forceApplied=false;
31                     break;
32
33                     case COLLISION_OVERLAPPING:
34                         HandleOverlapping(
35                             timeIncrement,i,j,theCollision);
36                         forceApplied=false;
37                     break;
38
39                     case COLLISION_NONE:
40
41                     break;
42                 }
43             }
44         }
45
46         if (forceApplied)
47         {
48             // Set the forces to 0.
49             for (i=0;i<TOTAL_TIGERS;i++)
```

```
50              {
51                  force theForce;
52                  theForce.Force(vector_3d(0.0,0.0,0.0f));
53                  theForce.ApplicationPoint(vector_3d(0.0,0.0,0.0));
54                  allTigers[i].Force(theForce);
55              }
56          }
57          else
58          {
59              forceApplied=true;
60          }
61
62          for (i=0;i<TOTAL_TIGERS;i++)
63          {
64              allTigers[i].Update(timeIncrement);
65          }
66
67          return (true);
68      }
69
70
71      bool TimeToUpdateFrame(DWORD currentTime)
72      {
73          static DWORD lastTime=0;
74          bool updateFrame=false;
75
76          if (currentTime-lastTime >= MILLISECONDS_PER_FRAME)
77          {
78              updateFrame=true;
79              lastTime=currentTime;
80          }
81          return (updateFrame);
82      }
83
84
85      void HandleOverlapping(
86          scalar timeIncrement,
87          int tiger1,
88          int tiger2,
89          collision &theCollision)
90      {
91          scalar changeInTime = timeIncrement;
```

```
92        collision_status collisionOccured =
93            COLLISION_OVERLAPPING;
94
95      for (bool done=false;
96            (!done) && (!CloseToZero(changeInTime));
97            /* No increment or decrement*/)
98      {
99          switch (collisionOccured)
100         {
101             case COLLISION_OVERLAPPING:
102             {
103                 rigid_body object1 = allTigers[tiger1];
104                 rigid_body object2 = allTigers[tiger2];
105
106                 vector_3d tempVector =
107                     object1.AngularVelocity();
108                 tempVector *= -1;
109                 object1.AngularVelocity(tempVector);
110                 tempVector = object1.LinearVelocity();
111                 tempVector *= -1;
112                 object1.LinearVelocity(tempVector);
113                 object1.Force().Force(
114                     object1.Force().Force() * -1);
115
116                 // Reverse the velocities and force.
117                 tempVector =
118                     object2.AngularVelocity();
119                 tempVector *= -1;
120                 object2.AngularVelocity(tempVector);
121                 tempVector = object2.LinearVelocity();
122                 tempVector *= -1;
123                 object2.LinearVelocity(tempVector);
124                 object2.Force().Force(
125                     object2.Force().Force() * -1);
126
127                 object1.Update(changeInTime);
128                 object2.Update(changeInTime);
129
130                 changeInTime/=2;
131
132                 tempVector =
133                     object1.AngularVelocity();
```

```
134                    tempVector *= -1;
135                    object1.AngularVelocity(tempVector);
136                    tempVector = object1.LinearVelocity();
137                    tempVector *= -1;
138                    object1.LinearVelocity(tempVector);
139                    object1.Force().Force(
140                        object1.Force().Force() * -1);
141
142                    tempVector =
143                        object2.AngularVelocity();
144                    tempVector *= -1;
145                    object2.AngularVelocity(tempVector);
146                    tempVector = object2.LinearVelocity();
147                    tempVector *= -1;
148                    object2.LinearVelocity(tempVector);
149                    object2.Force().Force(
150                        object2.Force().Force() * -1);
151
152                    object1.Update(changeInTime);
153                    object2.Update(changeInTime);
154
155                    allTigers[tiger1] = object1;
156                    allTigers[tiger2] = object2;
157
158                    collisionOccured =
159                        theCollision.CollisionOccurred();
160
161                }
162            break;
163
164            case COLLISION_TOUCHING:
165                theCollision.CalculateReactions();
166                done=true;
167            break;
168
169
170            case COLLISION_NONE:
171                allTigers[tiger1].Update(changeInTime);
172                allTigers[tiger2].Update(changeInTime);
173            break;
174        }
175    }
176 }
```

The function that makes all this work is UpdateFrame(). The physics modeling framework calls UpdateFrame() on each iteration through the game's main loop. UpdateFrame() has to update all objects in the scene, which in this case is three tigers. It must use the collision class to detect collisions and calculate the resulting forces. After the forces have been applied for one frame, UpdateFrame() must cancel them out. Remember that these are impulse forces that act over a short period of time.

UpdateFrame() begins by setting the status variable forceApplied to false. This means that any forces currently acting on the rigid bodies in the scene have not yet been applied. The rigid bodies have not yet been animated to reflect the forces that are currently acting on them.

On line 6, the UpdateFrame() function sets the time increment to 1. Remember that the GameInitialization() function sets the mass of the tigers to 100 kg. The units of the forces acting on the tigers are in kg m/sec^2. Therefore, this time increment is 1 second.

note

> I set the time increment to accommodate those who do not have video cards that support the latest DirectX 9 features. This sample program uses hardware vertex processing, if it's available. If it's not available, the program uses a software simulator instead. As of this writing, people who have video cards more than 2–3 years old do not have hardware vertex processing. For them, the time increment must be about 1 second to produce reasonably paced motion on the screen. If you find that this program runs quickly and produces choppy animation, change the time increment to MILLISECONDS_PER_FRAME/1000. This sets the time increment to match a frame rate of 30 frames per second. It produces nice animation for those who have the right video cards.

Next, UpdateFrame() gets the current time and calls the TimeToUpdateFrame() function. The code for TimeToUpdateFrame() is on lines 71–82 of Listing 10.5. It checks to see if 33 milliseconds have gone by. If so, it returns true. Otherwise, it returns false. The purpose of calling TimeToUpdateFrame() is to limit the animation to a constant frame rate of 30 frames per second. Users who have faster computers won't see your animation speed up to unreasonable frame rates. If less than 33 milliseconds have gone by since the last frame was updated, lines 9–10 cause the UpdateFrame() function to return.

If it's time to update the frame, the UpdateFrame() function loops through the list of tigers with a pair of for loops. Each tiger in the list is compared to all the remaining tigers in the list. Lines 19–23 create a collision variable and test for a collision between the two tigers in question. UpdateFrame() processes the results with the switch statement that begins on line 24. If the bounding spheres are touching, UpdateFrame() calls the collision::CalculateReactions() function to apply the resulting forces to the colliding tigers. If there is no collision, the UpdateFrame() function doesn't react.

note

It's obvious that the COLLISION_NONE case does not need to be in the switch statement. I just put it in as a form of documentation. It demonstrates that nothing happens if there is no collision.

The most complex case is when the bounding spheres overlap. In that event, UpdateFrame() calls the HandleOverlapping() function. The code for the HandleOverlapping() function appears on lines 85–176.

The HandleOverlapping() function fixes the problem of overlapping objects by backing up time in the game. On lines 106–128 of Listing 10.5, HandleOverlapping() reverses the forces, linear velocities, and angular velocities of both bodies involved in the collision. It then updates the rigid bodies. This has the effect of backing time up to before the collision.

On line 130, HandleOverlapping() cuts the time increment in half. Lines 132–153 restore the directions of the forces, linear velocities, and angular velocities of both bodies. HandleOverlapping() does another update to move the bodies forward in time. It tests for a collision on lines 158–159. Execution then jumps to the beginning of the for loop on line 95. The switch statement beginning on line 101 reacts to the type of collision again. If backing up the rigid bodies results in them just touching, HandleOverlapping() calculates the resulting forces and ends the loop. If the bodies are still overlapping, HandleOverlapping() backs them up again, cuts the time increment in half, and tries it all one more time. This continues until the bodies are just touching and not overlapping.

It's possible to back up the bodies too far. In that event, a collision is no longer occurring. The fix for this is to update the movement of the rigid bodies one more time with the current time increment. This moves the bodies forward until they collide again. The code for this eventuality appears on lines 170–173.

After the HandleOverlapping() function backs up the rigid bodies until they're touching and applies the impulse force to them, it exits back to UpdateFrame(). Specifically, it returns to line 35 of Listing 10.5.

Because new forces have been applied to the rigid bodies, UpdateFrame() sets the forceApplied variable to false. When UpdateFrame() gets down to line 46, it tests forceApplied. If it is true (meaning the forces were applied to the bodies and do not need to be applied again), UpdateFrame() sets the force on each tiger to 0. If the forces have not been applied, the function sets the forceApplied variable to true on line 59. This causes the forces to be zeroed out the next time UpdateFrame() is called.

Just before UpdateFrame() ends, it loops through the list of tigers again to update them. At this point, they are in the proper position and are ready to be drawn on the screen by the RenderFrame() function. I didn't include the code for the RenderFrame() function because it's so trivial. You can look at it in the TigerToss.cpp file on the CD-ROM.

Summary

You can now model both the linear and angular motion of a rigid body. You can also detect and respond to collisions between rigid bodies. When you run the sample program for this chapter, a lot of processing is occurring. And it all models the actual physics of rigid bodies in the real world. If you think about it, that's pretty impressive. But it's not the end by any means. Now you need to know how to add gravity to your simulations. That's the subject of the next chapter.

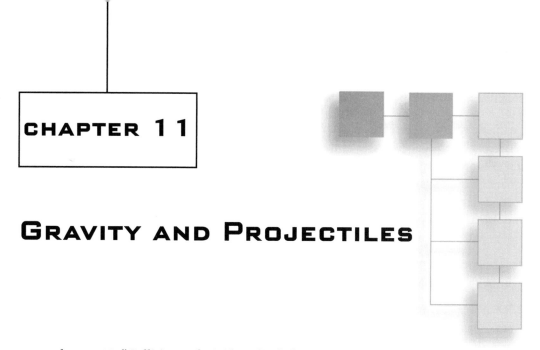

CHAPTER 11

GRAVITY AND PROJECTILES

C hapter 10, "Collisions of Rigid Bodies," demonstrated how to simulate rigid bodies crashing together in an environment that is free of gravity and friction. Most of us, however, do not live in such an environment. To increase the realism of our games, we have to at least do something about gravity. Adding the force of gravity to games is not hard. It flows naturally from the ideas presented in previous chapters.

Newton's Law of Gravitation

Gravity. It's all around you. You can't get away from it, even in space. Everything on the surface of the Earth stays close to the Earth because of gravity. The Earth orbits the sun because of gravity, and the sun orbits the galaxy because of gravity. No matter where you go, gravity is something you can't get away from.

Sir Isaac Newton is credited with working out the universal law of gravity when he was just 23. In 1665, he moved from Cambridge, where he was attending college, to Lincolnshire, a rural area of England. During that year, the college was closed due to the rapid spread of the bubonic plague. Anyone who could got out of the cities, where the infection rate was at its highest.

note

People sometimes say that Newton "discovered" gravity. This is not an accurate statement. To discover something, you have to be the first to find it. Newton was definitely not the first person to figure out that if you drop something, it falls.

Newton's great achievement during his stay in Lincolnshire was the realization that the same force that makes things fall to the ground also keeps the moon in orbit around the Earth. Making that connection enabled him to work out the fact that the force of gravity between two objects decreases as the objects get farther apart. In fact, he was able to calculate that gravity is directly proportional to mass and inversely proportional to the square of the distance between objects. This means that objects that have large masses exert strong gravitational pull. Objects that have little mass exert so little gravity that it's unnoticeable in everyday life. In addition, Newton's conclusions show that, as objects move apart, the gravitational pull between them drops off rapidly.

An Apple Did NOT Hit Newton on the Head!

There's a popular myth that Newton "discovered" gravity when an apple fell from an apple tree and hit him on the head. However, this is nothing more than a myth.

This story stems from a conversation Newton had with a friend of his about 50 years after Newton stayed in Lincolnshire. At that time, William Stukeley was having tea with Newton under some apple trees. Newton told Stukeley that the setting was the same as when he got the idea of gravitation. Newton then related that during 1665, he had been sitting under an apple tree in a contemplative mood when he noticed an apple fall. It did not hit his head. This incident generated the first of a series of ideas that led Newton to the universal law of gravitation.

You can calculate the gravitational attraction between two objects by starting with the same formula we've used as the starting point for almost all the physics presented so far: **F = ma.**

Calculating gravitational attraction between two objects must take into account the mass of both objects. As Newton discovered, the acceleration experienced by the objects is inversely proportional to the square of the distance between them. However, the distance alone is not the only factor. There is also a universal constant that is the same for all particles of any size above the atomic level. The value of the constant, called G, is shown here:

$$G = 6.673 \times 10^{-11} \frac{m^3}{kg \bullet s^2}$$

Including G and both objects' masses, our **F=ma** formula becomes this:

$$F = G \frac{m_1 m_2}{r^2}$$

Note that the force on both objects is the same. If I drop a baseball from a tall building (not recommended), the ball begins to drop. The gravitational force exerted on the ball is the same as the force exerted on the Earth. However, the Earth doesn't appear to move. That's because even though the force on both objects is the same, the mass of the Earth is huge compared to the mass of the ball. Therefore, the resulting acceleration of the ball is *much* larger than any acceleration the force might cause on the Earth. This makes the ball move toward the Earth without moving the Earth to a measurable degree.

The acceleration of objects near the surface of the Earth is essentially constant. When I say "essentially" constant, I mean the acceleration doesn't vary enough to be noticeable. It's true that there is a slightly lower gravitational attraction when you're high in the mountains than when you're at sea level. However, the variation is so slight that we don't notice it. So if we call the gravitational acceleration of objects near the Earth's surface g, then g = –9.8 m/s².

Physicists often express g as a vector. The direction of g is toward the center of the Earth. Typically, that's in the negative direction along the y axis of a 3-D coordinate system. Of course, it doesn't have to be. However, that's often the way Cartesian coordinate systems are set up in both physics and computer graphics, so that's what we'll use. Therefore, the value of the vector **g** is –9.8 m/s². The minus sign indicates that g points downward.

It's important to remember that G is not the same as **g**. G is the universal gravitational constant, whereas **g** is the acceleration of an object near the Earth's surface.

Projectile Trajectories

Because of the constant acceleration near the Earth's surface due to gravity, all projectiles move in predictable ways. We normally think of a projectile as a missile or a rocket. However, for the purposes of this discussion, a projectile is anything you drop or throw.

Think about the forces on a projectile, such as a ball, that's dropped. For now, ignore things like wind and air resistance. If you just release the ball from your hand, you're not exerting forces on it. However, the Earth is. Therefore, gravity is the force that governs the motion of the ball in this case. Figure 11.1 shows the force on the ball.

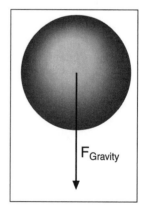

Figure 11.1
Gravity acting on a dropped ball.

You can see from Figure 11.1 that the path of the ball is going to be straight down. We know from experience that gravity always pulls toward the center of the Earth. In games, as in real life, that means that gravity exerts a vertical force on everything.

What if you give the ball a push in the horizontal direction when you release it? For example, suppose you dropped the ball from an airplane, as shown in Figure 11.2.

The horizontal motion of the airplane causes a horizontal force on the ball. Of course, gravity continues to act on both the plane and the ball. When the ball is released, the airplane no longer exerts a force on it. However, if we discount air resistance, the ball continues to move at the same horizontal velocity. In addition, the ball acquires a downward vertical velocity because gravity still exerts a vertical force on it. To get the resulting veloci-

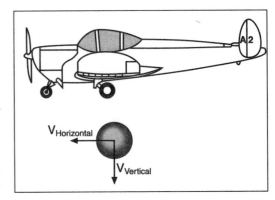

Figure 11.2
A projectile that is acted on by a horizontal force and gravity.

ty, you add the horizontal and vertical velocity vectors. Figure 11.3 shows the ball's path after it's released from the plane as seen from the ground.

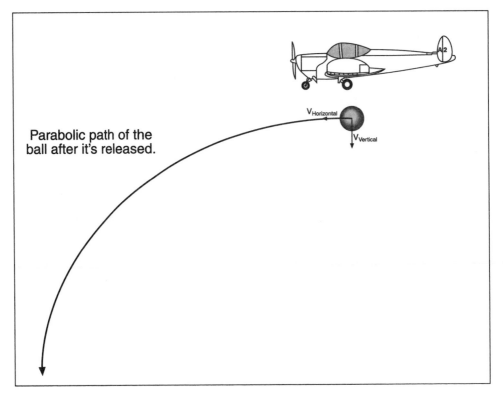

Parabolic path of the ball after it's released.

Figure 11.3
The path of a projectile with horizontal velocity.

The path of a dropped projectile that has horizontal velocity is a portion of a parabola. Any projectile that is released with horizontal velocity in a gravity field follows a parabolic path. It might not traverse the whole parabola. The ball in Figure 11.3 traverses only half of the parabola.

Bullets act just like this. When you shoot a gun in the real world, the bullet has a huge horizontal motion caused by the force of the exploding gunpowder. If the bullet doesn't hit anything, it traverses a large horizontal distance. However, as the bullet moves, it also drops due to the force of gravity. The path is one half of a flat parabola. That's why sharpshooters aim just a bit higher if the target is far away. Aiming higher accounts for the effect of gravity.

Thrown projectiles act the same way. Thrown projectiles in games usually include anything your character throws, such as balls or grenades. Thrown projectiles follow a parabolic path, as shown in Figure 11.4.

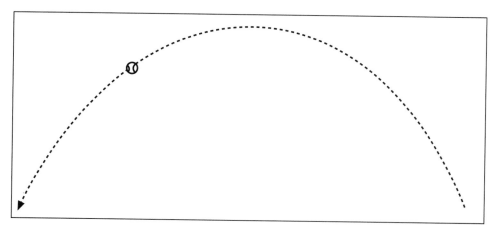

Figure 11.4
Thrown projectiles follow a full parabolic path.

Projectiles fired from a device such as a cannon follow the same full parabolic path as thrown objects. If a projectile's destination is at the same vertical height as the starting point, the projectile traverses the entire parabola. If the ending point is lower, the projectile just continues on the parabolic path. It it's higher, the projectile doesn't traverse the entire parabola.

All of this assumes that no other forces are acting on the projectile. If the projectile hits something, it encounters an impulse force that deflects it from its path. If the projectile is a rocket, the force of the burning fuel acts on it. That force can deflect the rocket into a nonparabolic path. For now, we'll ignore the case of the rocket.

Everything in your game that gets thrown must follow a parabolic path. So must everything that is shot from any kind of cannon or gun. Fortunately, this is easy to implement. You do not have to know anything at all about parabolic equations.

Modeling Projectile Motion

Think about objects in the real world. No one calculates the parabolas of projectiles that they throw. Projectiles move the way they move because of the forces that act on them. Simulations are the same. If the simulation handles the forces acting on projectiles in a way that mimics conditions in the real world, then simulated projectiles will behave as they do in the real world.

note

You'll find the code for the version of the rigid body simulator that handles gravity on the CD-ROM that comes with this book. It's in the folder `Source\Chapter11\Launcher`.

As in the real world, launched projectiles in your games don't need to have their paths calculated. All they need to do is mimic how forces act in the real world. The natural result of that will be a nice parabolic path.

Differentiating Between Impulse and Constant Forces

Recall from Chapter 10 that the `rigid_body` class simulates the way real objects move and rotate as a result of forces acting on them. To add gravity to the simulation, all that's needed is to differentiate between constant and impulse forces.

As Chapter 10 showed, impulse forces occur when objects collide. They can also occur when an object is launched, as in the cases of guns and cannons. Impulse forces occur over a short period of time. For games, that usually means just one frame of animation. After that one frame, the game should not continue exerting the impulse force on the object. Of course, constant forces such as gravity always apply.

To add gravity to the simulation from Chapter 10, the program must treat impulse and constant forces differently. That requires that the software keep track of them separately. As a result, we need to modify the `rigid_body` class to handle that (see Listing 11.1).

Listing 11.1
The Updated rigid_body Class

```
1      class rigid_body
2      {
3      private:
4          mesh objectMesh;
```

```
5
6          // Physical and linear motion properties
7          scalar mass;
8          vector_3d centerOfMassLocation;
9          vector_3d linearVelocity;
10         vector_3d linearAcceleration;
11         force constantForce;
12         force impulseForce;
13
14         // Rotational motion properties
15         angle_set_3d currentOrientation;
16         vector_3d angularVelocity;
17         vector_3d angularAcceleration;
18         vector_3d rotationalInertia;
19         vector_3d torque;
20
21         // Collision properties
22         scalar coefficientOfRestitution;
23         scalar boundingSphereRadius;
24
25         D3DXMATRIX worldMatrix;
26
27     public:
28         rigid_body(void);
29
30         bool LoadMesh(
31             std::string meshFileName);
32
33         void Mass(
34             scalar massValue);
35         scalar Mass(void);
36
37         void Location(
38             vector_3d locationCenterOfMass);
39         vector_3d Location(void);
40
41         void LinearVelocity(
42             vector_3d newVelocity);
43         vector_3d LinearVelocity(void);
44
45         void LinearAcceleration(
46             vector_3d newAcceleration);
```

```
47          vector_3d LinearAcceleration(void);
48
49          void ConstantForce(
50              force sumConstantForces);
51          force ConstantForce(void);
52
53          void ImpulseForce(
54              force sumImpulseForces);
55          force ImpulseForce(void);
56
57          void CurrentOrientation(
58              angle_set_3d newOrientation);
59          angle_set_3d CurrentOrientation(void);
60
61          void AngularVelocity(
62              vector_3d newAngularVelocity);
63          vector_3d AngularVelocity(void);
64
65          void AngularAcceleration(
66              vector_3d newAngularAcceleration);
67          vector_3d AngularAcceleration(void);
68
69          void RotationalInertia(vector_3d inertiaValue);
70          vector_3d RotationalInertia(void);
71
72          void Torque(vector_3d torqueValue);
73          vector_3d Torque(void);
74
75          void CoefficientOfRestitution(
76              scalar elasticity);
77          scalar CoefficientOfRestitution(void);
78
79          void BoundingSphereRadius(scalar radius);
80          scalar BoundingSphereRadius(void);
81
82          bool Update(
83              scalar changeInTime);
84          bool Render(void);
85      };
```

The rigid_body class needs only minor modifications to handle gravity and other constant forces. In particular, it now has data members for two forces instead of one. Lines 11–12 of Listing 11.1 contain the definitions of two members of type force. The first stores the sum of all constant forces that are acting on the rigid_body object. The second stores the sum of all impulse forces.

The constant force in this version of the rigid_body class must act through the center of mass. Gravity does exactly that. Also, if you're simulating a rocket during launch, the rocket's thrust acts along the long axis of the rocket. This axis passes through the center of mass, so the rigid_body class can be used for a rocket or missile.

It's possible for so-called "off axis" constant forces to occur. An example would be a spacecraft firing one of its attitude jets. The purpose of attitude jets is to adjust the direction the spacecraft is pointing, so they do not act through the center of gravity. An attitude jet can exert a constant force if it is left running. This version of the rigid_body class does not accommodate such situations.

Lines 49–51 of Listing 11.1 show the prototypes for two member functions. These functions set and get, respectively, the constant force exerted on the rigid_body object. Lines 53–55 show the prototypes for functions that set and get the impulse force.

With the rigid_body class able to accommodate both impulse and constant forces, we must also make some adjustments to the Update() function. The new version is shown in Listing 11.2.

Listing 11.2
rigid_body::Update() Now Handles Both Impulse and Constant Forces

```
1     bool rigid_body::Update(
2         scalar changeInTime)
3     {
4         //
5         /* Begin calculating linear dynamics. These act at the center of
6         mass. */
7         //
8
9         // Sum the forces acting on the rigid_body.
10        force sumForces;
11        sumForces.Force(
12            constantForce.Force() + impulseForce.Force());
13
14        // Find the linear acceleration.
15        // a = F/m
16        assert(mass!=0);
17        linearAcceleration = sumForces.Force()/mass;
18
19        // Find the linear velocity.
20        linearVelocity += linearAcceleration * changeInTime;
```

```
21
22          // Find the new location of the center of mass.
23          centerOfMassLocation += linearVelocity * changeInTime;
24
25          //
26          // End calculating linear dynamics.
27          //
28
29          // Create the translation matrix.
30          D3DXMATRIX totalTranslation;
31          D3DXMatrixTranslation(
32              &totalTranslation,
33              centerOfMassLocation.X(),
34              centerOfMassLocation.Y(),
35              centerOfMassLocation.Z());
36
37          //
38          // Begin calculating rotational dynamics.
39          //
40
41          // Use the impulse force to calculate the torque.
42          torque =
43              impulseForce.ApplicationPoint().Cross(impulseForce.Force());
44
45          /* Use the torque and inertia to calculate the angular
46          acceleration.*/
47          angularAcceleration.X(
48              torque.X()/rotationalInertia.X());
49          angularAcceleration.Y(
50              torque.Y()/rotationalInertia.Y());
51          angularAcceleration.Z(
52              torque.Z()/rotationalInertia.Z());
53
54          /* Change the angular velocity according to the angular
55          acceleration. */
56          angularVelocity += angularAcceleration * changeInTime;
57
58          //
59          // Use angular acceleration to calculate the angles of rotation.
60          //
61          currentOrientation.XAngle(
62              currentOrientation.XAngle() +
```

```
63                  angularVelocity.X() * changeInTime);
64          currentOrientation.YAngle(
65              currentOrientation.YAngle() +
66              angularVelocity.Y() * changeInTime);
67          currentOrientation.ZAngle(
68              currentOrientation.ZAngle() +
69              angularVelocity.Z() * changeInTime);
70
71          //
72          // End calculating rotational dynamics.
73          //
74
75          // Build a rotation matrix for each axis.
76          D3DXMATRIX rotationX, rotationY, rotationZ;
77          D3DXMatrixRotationX(&rotationX,currentOrientation.XAngle());
78          D3DXMatrixRotationY(&rotationY,currentOrientation.YAngle());
79          D3DXMatrixRotationZ(&rotationZ,currentOrientation.ZAngle());
80
81          D3DXMATRIX totalRotations;
82
83          // Multiply them into the world matrix.
84          D3DXMatrixMultiply(
85              &totalRotations,
86              &rotationX,
87              &rotationY);
88          D3DXMatrixMultiply(
89              &totalRotations,
90              &totalRotations,
91              &rotationZ);
92
93          /* Combine the rotation and translation matrices into the world
94          matrix. */
95          D3DXMatrixMultiply(
96              &worldMatrix,
97              &totalRotations,
98              &totalTranslation);
99
100         //
101         // The impulse force has now been applied. Reset it to zero.
102         //
103         vector_3d tempVector(0.0,0.0,0.0);
104         impulseForce.Force(tempVector);
```

```
105        impulseForce.ApplicationPoint(tempVector);
106
107        return(true);
108    }
109
110
111    bool rigid_body::Render(void)
112    {
113        // Save the world transformation matrix.
114        D3DXMATRIX saveWorldMatrix;
115        theApp.D3DRenderingDevice()->GetTransform(
116            D3DTS_WORLD,
117            &saveWorldMatrix);
118
119        // Apply the world transformation matrix for this object.
120        theApp.D3DRenderingDevice()->SetTransform(
121            D3DTS_WORLD,&worldMatrix);
122
123        // Now render the object with its transformations.
124        bool renderedOK=objectMesh.Render();
125
126        // Restore the world transformation matrix.
127        theApp.D3DRenderingDevice()->SetTransform(
128            D3DTS_WORLD,
129            &saveWorldMatrix);
130
131        return (renderedOK);
132    }
```

The rigid_body::Update() function in Listing 11.2 begins by declaring a variable called sumForces. Because the rigid_body class now handles impulse and constant forces separately, the Update() function must add them when it needs the sum of all forces acting on the rigid_body object. It does this when it calculates the linear forces acting on the rigid_body object.

When the Update() function calculates the rotational dynamics, it does not use the constant force. As I stated previously, this is because this version of the rigid_body class does not handle off-angle constant force. It assumes that all constant forces act through the center of mass.

Line 43 of Listing 11.2 shows the calculation of torque using the impulse force. Just before this function ends, it sets the impulse force to 0 on lines 103–105. This used to be handled by the UpdateFrame() function, which is not a member of the rigid_body class. Dealing with it here is both better software design and easier to code.

Another function that needs modification is `collision::CalculateReactions()`. Recall from Chapter 10 that `CalculateReactions()` calculates the forces exerted on `rigid_body` objects as a result of a collision. Of course, forces in collisions are impulse forces. And now that the `rigid_body` keeps track of impulse forces separately from constant forces, we must adjust the `CalculateReactions()` function to use only impulse forces. Listing 11.3 shows the code for `CalculateReactions()`.

Listing 11.3
CalculateReactions() Now Uses Impulse Forces

```
1    bool collision::CalculateReactions(void)
2    {
3        /* First, calculate the average coefficient of restitution, which
4        is a measure of the elasticity of the objects involved. */
5        scalar averageElasticity =
6            (object1->CoefficientOfRestitution()+
7            object2->CoefficientOfRestitution())/2;
8
9        //
10       // Now find the numerator.
11       //
12       vector_3d relativeVelocity =
13           object1->AngularVelocity() - object2->AngularVelocity();
14       vector_3d numerator =
15           -1 * relativeVelocity * (averageElasticity+1);
16
17       //
18       // Find the denominator. This is complex, so do it in steps.
19       //
20       /* First, find the unit normal, which is the normalized vector
21       from the center of mass of object 1 to the center of mass of
22       object 2. */
23       vector_3d unitNormal = object1->Location()-object2->Location();
24       unitNormal = unitNormal.Normalize(SCALAR_TOLERANCE);
25
26       // Now find the point at which the force acts on object 2.
27       vector_3d forceLocation2 =
28           unitNormal * object2->BoundingSphereRadius();
29
30       vector_3d tempVector = forceLocation2.Cross(unitNormal);
31
32       // Divide by the rotational inertia.
33       tempVector.X(tempVector.X()/object2->RotationalInertia().X());
34       tempVector.Y(tempVector.Y()/object2->RotationalInertia().Y());
```

```
35      tempVector.Z(tempVector.Z()/object2->RotationalInertia().Z());
36
37      // Cross the answer with the vector r for object 2.
38      tempVector = tempVector.Cross(forceLocation2);
39
40      // Now dot that with the unit normal.
41      scalar part1 = unitNormal.Dot(tempVector);
42
43      // Now find the point at which the force acts on object 1.
44      unitNormal *= -1;
45      vector_3d forceLocation1 =
46          unitNormal * object1->BoundingSphereRadius();
47
48      tempVector = forceLocation1.Cross(unitNormal);
49
50      // Divide by the rotational inertia.
51      tempVector.X(tempVector.X()/object1->RotationalInertia().X());
52      tempVector.Y(tempVector.Y()/object1->RotationalInertia().Y());
53      tempVector.Z(tempVector.Z()/object1->RotationalInertia().Z());
54
55      // Cross the answer with the vector r for object 1.
56      tempVector = tempVector.Cross(forceLocation1);
57
58      // Now dot that with the unit normal.
59      scalar part2 = unitNormal.Dot(tempVector);
60
61      scalar denominator =
62          1/object1->Mass() + 1/object2->Mass() + part2 + part1;
63
64      //
65      // Apply the impulse force to rigid body 1.
66      //
67      force impulseForce;
68      impulseForce.Force(numerator/denominator);
69      impulseForce.ApplicationPoint(forceLocation1);
70      object1->ImpulseForce(impulseForce);
71
72      //
73      // Apply the inverse impulse force to rigid body 2.
74      //
75      impulseForce.Force(
76          -1*impulseForce.Force());
```

```
77          object2->ImpulseForce(impulseForce);
78
79          return (true);
80     }
```

The version of collision::CalculateReactions() shown in Listing 11.3 uses the impulse force to model the reactions of the rigid bodies to a collision. It applies the impulse force to both rigid bodies. You can see this on lines 67–77.

At this point, the framework is ready to handle gravity. However, before the sample program can display projectiles hitting the ground, it has to have a ground to hit. For that, we can use the framework to create an object of type ground. We can then add both the ground object and gravity to the sample program. Listing 11.4 gives the code for the ground class.

Listing 11.4
The File Ground.h
```
1      #include "PMFramework.h"
2
3      using namespace pmframework;
4
5      class ground
6      {
7      private:
8          vector_3d location;
9          mesh groundMesh;
10
11     public:
12         ground();
13
14         void Location(vector_3d newLocation);
15         vector_3d Location();
16
17         bool LoadMesh(std::string meshFileName);
18
19         bool Render(void);
20     };
21
22     inline ground::ground()
23     {
24     }
25
26
27     inline void ground::Location(vector_3d newLocation)
```

```
28    {
29         location = newLocation;
30    }
31
32    inline vector_3d ground::Location()
33    {
34         return (location);
35    }
36
37    inline bool ground::LoadMesh(std::string meshFileName)
38    {
39         return (groundMesh.Load(meshFileName));
40    }
41
42    inline bool ground::Render(void)
43    {
44         return (groundMesh.Render());
45    }
```

In this listing, I've shown the entire file to emphasize that this object is not part of the framework; it's part of the simulation. The ground class is implemented using the framework, so it includes the file PMFramework.h. It uses the pmframework namespace on line 3.

The ground class declares some private member data on lines 8–9. The first data member keeps track of the ground's location, which enables a program to position the ground higher or lower than the origin of the world coordinate system. In this program, the ground is assumed to be essentially flat. Therefore, the program currently uses only the y component of the location vector.

The groundMesh member enables the program to load a mesh and bitmap for the ground's appearance.

All the member functions of this class are extremely simple. The constructor does nothing. The other member functions get or set the member data.

In Listing 11.5, we write a simulation that uses gravity.

Listing 11.5
The File Launcher.cpp

```
1    #include "PMFramework.h"
2    #include "Ground.h"
3
4    using namespace pmframework;
5
6    #define MILLISECONDS_PER_FRAME 33
```

```
7    #define TOTAL_BALLS 5
8
9    rigid_body allBalls[TOTAL_BALLS];
10   ground theGround;
11
12   bool TimeToUpdateFrame(
13       DWORD currentTime);
14   void HandleOverlapping(
15       scalar timeIncrement,
16       int object1,
17       int object2,
18       collision &theCollision);
19
20   bool OnAppLoad()
21   {
22       window_init_params windowParams;
23       windowParams.appWindowTitle = "Gravity Test";
24       windowParams.defaultX=100;
25       windowParams.defaultY=100;
26       windowParams.defaultHeight=400;
27       windowParams.defaultWidth=400;
28
29       d3d_init_params d3dParams;
30       d3dParams.renderingDeviceClearFlags =
31               D3DCLEAR_TARGET | D3DCLEAR_ZBUFFER;
32       d3dParams.surfaceBackgroundColor = D3DCOLOR_XRGB(0,0,255);
33       d3dParams.enableAutoDepthStencil = true;
34       d3dParams.autoDepthStencilFormat = D3DFMT_D16;
35       // This call must appear in this function.
36       theApp.InitApp(windowParams,d3dParams);
37
38       return (true);
39   }
40
41
42   bool PreD3DInitialization()
43   {
44       return (true);
45   }
46
47
48   bool PostD3DInitialization()
```

```
49    {
50        return (true);
51    }
52
53    bool GameInitialization()
54    {
55        // Set up the view matrix as in previous examples.
56        D3DXVECTOR3 eyePoint(0.0f,3.0f,-10.0f);
57        D3DXVECTOR3 lookatPoint(0.0f,0.0f,0.0f);
58        D3DXVECTOR3 upDirection(0.0f,1.0f,0.0f);
59        D3DXMATRIXA16 tempViewMatrix;
60        D3DXMatrixLookAtLH(
61            &tempViewMatrix,&eyePoint,&lookatPoint,&upDirection);
62        theApp.ViewMatrix(tempViewMatrix);
63
64        // Set up the projection matrix.
65        D3DXMATRIXA16 projectionMatrix;
66        D3DXMatrixPerspectiveFovLH(
67            &projectionMatrix,D3DX_PI/4,1.0f,1.0f,100.0f);
68        theApp.ProjectionMatrix(projectionMatrix);
69
70        vector_3d tempVector(0.0,0.0,0.0);
71        force theForce;
72
73        /* Load the mesh for the "ball".
74        Reminder: The ball's mesh comes with the DirectX SDK. You must
75        copy it from the folder
76        <SDKDIR>\Samples\C++\Direct3D\Tutorials\Tut06_Meshes
77        where <SDKDIR> is the drive letter and full path to the folder
78        that you installed the DirectX SDK into. Copy the files tiger.x
79        and tiger.bmp into the folder for this program.*/
80        allBalls[0].LoadMesh("tiger.x");
81
82        // Set the initial position of the first ball.
83        tempVector.SetXYZ(-3.0f,5.0,5.0);
84        allBalls[0].Location(tempVector);
85
86        theForce.Force(vector_3d(0.0,-9.8f,0.0));
87        theForce.ApplicationPoint(tempVector);
88        allBalls[0].ConstantForce(theForce);
89
90        // Set the ball's rotational inertia.
```

```
91       tempVector.SetXYZ(39.6f,39.6f,12.5f);
92       allBalls[0].RotationalInertia(tempVector);
93
94       // Set the force vector to make the ball move linearly.
95       tempVector.SetXYZ(1.0,-1.0,0.0f);
96       theForce.Force(tempVector);
97
98       // Set the point at which the force is applied.
99       tempVector.SetXYZ(0.0,0.0,-1.0f);
100      theForce.ApplicationPoint(tempVector);
101
102      // Store the force in the rigid_body object.
103      allBalls[0].ImpulseForce(theForce);
104
105      // Set the ball's mass.
106      allBalls[0].Mass(100);
107
108      // Set the ball's bounding sphere.
109      allBalls[0].BoundingSphereRadius(0.75f);
110
111      // Set the ball's elasticity.
112      allBalls[0].CoefficientOfRestitution(0.5f);
113
114      // Copy the info from the first ball into the others.
115      allBalls[4]=allBalls[3]=allBalls[2]=allBalls[1]=allBalls[0];
116
117      /* Give the second ball a different starting location than the
118      first ball. */
119      tempVector.SetXYZ(0.0,3.0f,5.0);
120      allBalls[1].Location(tempVector);
121
122      theForce.Force(vector_3d(0.0,-9.8f,0.0));
123      theForce.ApplicationPoint(tempVector);
124      allBalls[1].ConstantForce(theForce);
125
126      // Apply a different force.
127      tempVector.SetXYZ(-1.0f,-1.0f,0.0);
128      theForce.Force(tempVector);
129      tempVector.SetXYZ(0.0,-1.0f,-1.0f);
130      theForce.ApplicationPoint(tempVector);
131      allBalls[1].ImpulseForce(theForce);
132
```

```
133        // Set the ball's elasticity.
134        allBalls[1].CoefficientOfRestitution(0.001f);
135
136        /* Give the third ball a different starting location than the
137        first and second balls. */
138        tempVector.SetXYZ(4.0,4.0f,7.0);
139        allBalls[2].Location(tempVector);
140
141        theForce.Force(vector_3d(0.0,-9.8f,0.0));
142        theForce.ApplicationPoint(tempVector);
143        allBalls[2].ConstantForce(theForce);
144
145        // Apply a different force.
146        tempVector.SetXYZ(-3.0,20.0,0.0);
147        theForce.Force(tempVector);
148        tempVector.SetXYZ(1.0f,-1.0f,0.0);
149        theForce.ApplicationPoint(tempVector);
150        allBalls[2].ImpulseForce(theForce);
151
152        // Set the ball's elasticity.
153        allBalls[2].CoefficientOfRestitution(0.17f);
154
155        // Set the starting location.
156        tempVector.SetXYZ(0.0,4.0f,-15.0f);
157        allBalls[3].Location(tempVector);
158
159        // Apply gravity.
160        theForce.Force(vector_3d(0.0,-9.8f,0.0));
161        theForce.ApplicationPoint(tempVector);
162        allBalls[3].ConstantForce(theForce);
163
164        // Apply an impulse forcce.
165        tempVector.SetXYZ(0.0,30.0,50.0);
166        theForce.Force(tempVector);
167        tempVector.SetXYZ(0.0,-1.0f,0.0);
168        theForce.ApplicationPoint(tempVector);
169        allBalls[3].ImpulseForce(theForce);
170
171        // Set the ball's elasticity.
172        allBalls[3].CoefficientOfRestitution(0.3f);
173
174        // Set the starting location.
```

```
175        tempVector.SetXYZ(-10.0f,4.0f,5.0f);
176        allBalls[4].Location(tempVector);
177
178        // Apply gravity.
179        theForce.Force(vector_3d(0.0,-9.8f,0.0));
180        theForce.ApplicationPoint(tempVector);
181        allBalls[4].ConstantForce(theForce);
182
183        // Apply an impulse force.
184        tempVector.SetXYZ(10.0,50.0,0.0);
185        theForce.Force(tempVector);
186        tempVector.SetXYZ(0.0,0.0f,1.0);
187        theForce.ApplicationPoint(tempVector);
188        allBalls[4].ImpulseForce(theForce);
189
190        // Set the ball's elasticity.
191        allBalls[4].CoefficientOfRestitution(0.6f);
192
193        theGround.LoadMesh("seafloor.x");
194
195
196
197        return (true);
198    }
199
200
201    bool HandleMessage(
202        HWND hWnd,
203        UINT msg,
204        WPARAM wParam,
205        LPARAM lParam)
206    {
207        return (false);
208    }
209
210
211    bool UpdateFrame()
212    {
213        int i;
214
215        scalar timeIncrement = 1;
216
```

```
217          DWORD currentTime = ::timeGetTime();
218          if (!TimeToUpdateFrame(currentTime))
219              return (true);
220
221          // For each object...
222          for (i=0;i<TOTAL_BALLS-1;i++)
223          {
224              // Find collisions with other objects.
225              for (int j=i+1;j<TOTAL_BALLS;j++)
226              {
227                  // If a collision occurred...
228                  collision theCollision(
229                      &allBalls[i],
230                      &allBalls[j]);
231                  collision_status collisionOccurred =
232                      theCollision.CollisionOccurred();
233                  switch (collisionOccurred)
234                  {
235                      case COLLISION_TOUCHING:
236                          // Bounce the objects.
237                          theCollision.CalculateReactions();
238                      break;
239
240                      case COLLISION_OVERLAPPING:
241                          // The balls are overlapping. Back them off.
242                          HandleOverlapping(
243                              timeIncrement,i,j,theCollision);
244                      break;
245
246                      case COLLISION_NONE:
247                          // Do nothing here. Just added for completeness.
248                      break;
249                  }
250              }
251          }
252
253          //
254          // Test for a collision with the ground.
255          //
256          // For each "ball"...
257          for (i=0;i<TOTAL_BALLS;i++)
258          {
```

```
259          /* Find the distance from the lower edge of the bounding
260          sphere to the ground. */
261          scalar distance =
262              allBalls[i].Location().Y() -
263              allBalls[i].BoundingSphereRadius() -
264              theGround.Location().Y();
265
266          /* If the distance is less than the radius of the bounding
267          sphere... */
268          if ((CloseToZero(distance)) || (distance < 0.0))
269          {
270              /* Bounce the object by reflecting the y component of
271              its linear velocity. Account for the object's elasticity
272              using its coefficient of restitution.*/
273              vector_3d tempVector = allBalls[i].LinearVelocity();
274              tempVector.Y(
275                  -tempVector.Y() * allBalls[i].CoefficientOfRestitution());
276              allBalls[i].LinearVelocity(tempVector);
277
278              // Make sure that the object is just touching the ground.
279              scalar verticalDistance =
280                  allBalls[i].BoundingSphereRadius() +
281                  theGround.Location().Y();
282              /* Move it up slightly so it's no longer in contact with
283              the ground. */
284              verticalDistance +=
285                  allBalls[i].BoundingSphereRadius() * 0.01f;
286              allBalls[i].Location().Y(verticalDistance);
287          }
288      }
289
290      // Update each ball.
291      for (i=0;i<TOTAL_BALLS;i++)
292      {
293          allBalls[i].Update(timeIncrement);
294      }
295
296      return (true);
297  }
298
299
300  bool RenderFrame()
```

```
301    {
302        // Set the view matrix in case it's changed.
303        theApp.D3DRenderingDevice()->SetTransform(
304            D3DTS_VIEW,
305            &theApp.ViewMatrix());
306
307        // Set the projection matrix in case it's changed.
308        theApp.D3DRenderingDevice()->SetTransform(
309            D3DTS_PROJECTION,
310            &theApp.ProjectionMatrix());
311
312        // Render each ball.
313        for (int i=0;i<TOTAL_BALLS;i++)
314        {
315            allBalls[i].Render();
316        }
317
318        theGround.Render();
319        return (true);
320    }
321
322
323    bool GameCleanup()
324    {
325        return (true);
326    }
327
328
329    bool TimeToUpdateFrame(
330        DWORD currentTime)
331    {
332        // This initialization is done only once.
333        static DWORD lastTime=0;
334
335        // This initialization happens each time the function is called.
336        bool updateFrame=false;
337
338        // If enough milliseconds have elapsed...
339        if (currentTime-lastTime >= MILLISECONDS_PER_FRAME)
340        {
341            // It's time to update the frame.
342            updateFrame=true;
```

```
343
344              // Save the time that the frame was updated.
345              lastTime=currentTime;
346          }
347      return (updateFrame);
348  }
349
350
351  void HandleOverlapping(
352      scalar timeIncrement,
353      int ball1,
354      int ball2,
355      collision &theCollision)
356  {
357      scalar changeInTime = timeIncrement;
358
359      // We know that an overlapping collision has already happened.
360      collision_status collisionOccurred =
361          COLLISION_OVERLAPPING;
362
363      // While not done and the time increment has not gone to zero...
364      for (bool done=false;
365           (!done) && (!CloseToZero(changeInTime));
366           /* No increment or decrement*/)
367      {
368          // Check which type of collision occurred.
369          switch (collisionOccurred)
370          {
371              // If the bounding spheres are still overlapping...
372              case COLLISION_OVERLAPPING:
373              {
374                  rigid_body object1 = allBalls[ball1];
375                  rigid_body object2 = allBalls[ball2];
376
377                  // Reverse the velocities and force.
378                  vector_3d tempVector =
379                      object1.AngularVelocity();
380                  tempVector *= -1;
381                  object1.AngularVelocity(tempVector);
382                  tempVector = object1.LinearVelocity();
383                  tempVector *= -1;
384                  object1.LinearVelocity(tempVector);
```

```
385          object1.ImpulseForce().Force(
386              object1.ImpulseForce().Force() * -1);
387
388          // Reverse the velocities and force.
389          tempVector =
390              object2.AngularVelocity();
391          tempVector *= -1;
392          object2.AngularVelocity(tempVector);
393          tempVector = object2.LinearVelocity();
394          tempVector *= -1;
395          object2.LinearVelocity(tempVector);
396          object2.ImpulseForce().Force(
397              object2.ImpulseForce().Force() * -1);
398
399          // Move back in time.
400          object1.Update(changeInTime);
401          object2.Update(changeInTime);
402
403          // Set a smaller time increment.
404          changeInTime/=2;
405
406          //
407          // Get ready to move forward again.
408          //
409
410          /* Set the velocities and force to move
411          forward. */
412          tempVector =
413              object1.AngularVelocity();
414          tempVector *= -1;
415          object1.AngularVelocity(tempVector);
416          tempVector = object1.LinearVelocity();
417          tempVector *= -1;
418          object1.LinearVelocity(tempVector);
419          object1.ImpulseForce().Force(
420              object1.ImpulseForce().Force() * -1);
421
422          /* Set the velocities and force to move
423          forward. */
424          tempVector =
425              object2.AngularVelocity();
426          tempVector *= -1;
```

```
427                         object2.AngularVelocity(tempVector);
428                         tempVector = object2.LinearVelocity();
429                         tempVector *= -1;
430                         object2.LinearVelocity(tempVector);
431                         object2.ImpulseForce().Force(
432                             object2.ImpulseForce().Force() * -1);
433
434                         // Move forward by a smaller amount.
435                         object1.Update(changeInTime);
436                         object2.Update(changeInTime);
437
438                         allBalls[ball1] = object1;
439                         allBalls[ball2] = object2;
440
441                         // Check the collision status again.
442                         collisionOccurred =
443                             theCollision.CollisionOccurred();
444                     }
445                 break;
446
447                 // If the bounding spheres are now touching...
448                 case COLLISION_TOUCHING:
449                     // Bounce the objects.
450                     theCollision.CalculateReactions();
451                     done=true;
452                 break;
453
454                 // If there is no longer a collision occurring...
455                 case COLLISION_NONE:
456                     // Back up too far. Move forward.
457                     allBalls[ball1].Update(changeInTime);
458                     allBalls[ball2].Update(changeInTime);
459
460                     // Check the collision status again.
461                     collisionOccurred =
462                         theCollision.CollisionOccurred();
463                 break;
464             }
465         }
466     /* If the loop exited because the time increment is
467     essentially 0... */
468     if (CloseToZero(changeInTime))
```

```
469          {
470              // Bounce the objects.
471              theCollision.CalculateReactions();
472              allBalls[ball1].Update(changeInTime);
473              allBalls[ball1].Update(changeInTime);
474          }
475      }
```

Listing 11.5 contains the code in the file `Launcher.cpp`. In some ways, it's similar to `TigerToss.cpp` from Chapter 10. In other ways, it's quite different. Let's take a closer look at it.

note

To save space in this book, I've removed a lot of the comments from this listing. If you look at the file `Launcher.cpp` on the CD-ROM, you'll find that it is much better commented than the listing shown here.

`Launcher.cpp` treats all of its moving objects as balls. However, just because I like the absurdity of it, I'm continuing to use the tiger mesh from previous chapters. In any case, `Launcher.cpp` declares an array of five "balls" on lines 7–9.

On line 10, the program declares an object of type `ground`. If you skip down to the `GameInitialization()` function, which begins on line 53, you see the code that loads the meshes for both the balls and the ground. This function gives each ball a different starting location and initial impulse force.

In addition, the `GameInitialization()` function sets the constant force acting on each ball to –9.8 along the y axis of the world. Recall that the acceleration due to gravity, which is represented as the vector **g**, is equal to –9.8 meters/sec^2. It acts downward toward the ground, so the vector must point in the –y direction in this coordinate system.

The only initialization needed for the `ground` object is to load its mesh. The `GameInitialization()` function does this on line 193.

The `UpdateFrame()` function, which begins on line 211, does much of the work for this program. Like the Tiger Toss simulation, the `UpdateFrame()` function for the Launcher uses a pair of loops to iterate through the list of balls and check for collisions.

Beginning on line 257, the `UpdateFrame()` function also tests for collisions with the ground. `UpdateFrame()` examines each ball and tests to see if its bounding sphere is touching or has penetrated the ground. If so, it sets the position of the ball such that its bounding sphere just touches the ground on lines 279–281. If the program leaves the ball touching the ground, it detects another collision on the next frame. This is not what we want. So on lines 284–286, `UpdateFrame()` moves the ball so that it is just slightly above the ground. The distance above the ground is 1% of the radius of the bounding sphere. Typically, this is a good fudge factor to use in games. The player can't see it, but the software can detect it.

note

Notice that the UpdateFrame() function no longer zeros the impulse forces on the rigid_body objects as it did in Chapter 10. That is now handled in the rigid_body::Update() function.

The version of the RenderFrame() function for this program requires only one change from the RenderFrame() function that appeared in Chapter 10. After RenderFrame() renders the balls, it renders the ground.

When you run this program, you'll see that the balls (the tigers) fly around and bounce off each other as they did in Chapter 10. However, because the tigers now have the constant force of gravity acting on them, they fall to the ground. When they hit, they bounce according to their coefficients of restitution. Unless you set the tigers' coefficients of restitution, gravity makes them bounce less and less each time they hit. Eventually, they roll out of the simulation's field of view.

Rolling

Speaking of rolling, objects in this simulation do not really roll. Recall that the program checks to see if the balls are in contact with the ground. If they are, the program shifts them up a tiny bit so that the software won't detect another bounce on the next frame. In other words, the program assumes that if something is touching the ground, it's bouncing. However, the height that the object is bouncing from is just barely above the surface of the ground. In fact, the player can't see the bounce. The balls look as if they're rolling. This isn't a problem, right?

Well, it depends on your point of view. For objects that are rolling on the ground, this simulation detects a collision in every single frame and reacts to it. The reaction requires minimal computational overhead. You might just want to ignore it.

If you're not happy with ignoring this problem, there are a few different ways to solve it. The first is a programmatic solution.

If your object is rolling along a flat ground, you can test whether its linear velocity in the y direction is essentially 0. If it is, don't bounce. However, this solution won't work if the object is rolling up or down a hill because that causes the y component of the linear velocity to be non-zero.

Another way to solve the problem involves a fair amount of programming and a bit of physics. Add a data member to the rigid_body class that keeps track of the object's location during the previous frame. (Or just back up the object a frame, as is done in the

HandleOverlapping() function.) Use the previous location, the height of the ground, and the formula **F=mg** to calculate the force of impact. If the force is essentially 0, the object is rolling. Don't bounce. Just move the object forward as indicated by the linear velocity.

A third way to roll objects without bouncing is to use more physics with just a bit of programming. Add an acceleration of 9.8 meters/sec² in a direction that is perpendicular to the ground. You'll be adding that force to the existing force of gravity and any existing impulse force. The rigid_body class causes the object to react accordingly.

But if you want my advice, ignore this entire issue. As the simulation is written, gravity causes the y component of the linear velocity to eventually go to 0. After that, the program always keeps the object the same distance above the ground. It looks right. And, in this case, that's good enough for me.

warning

These solutions work only if the ground is flat. Chapter 15, "Cars, Hovercraft, Ships, and Boats," demonstrates how to handle uneven terrain.

Summary

This chapter demonstrated that understanding basic physics enables you to easily add greater degrees of realism to your games. If your software correctly simulates how forces act on objects, adding new forces like gravity is not hard to program.

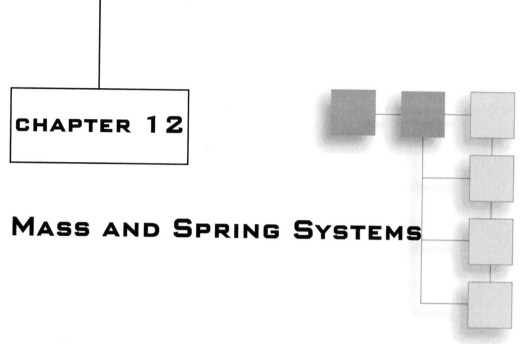

CHAPTER 12

MASS AND SPRING SYSTEMS

Significant advances have been made in recent years toward increasing the realism of computer-generated graphics. Some of the most interesting of these advances have to do with simulations built from masses and springs. The physics behind these systems is deceptively simple; that is, the equations that make it all work are not complex. However, mass and spring systems are notoriously difficult to simulate. The primary problem with them is numerical stability.

This chapter presents an overview of mass and spring systems. It shows how to use them to simulate common objects in the real world and make your games much more pleasing to the eye. It also points out where some of the problem areas are in implementing mass and spring systems.

What Can I Do with Springs?

Springs are a surprisingly useful tool in computer graphics and games. However, for many years, springs were ignored. Most game developers thought of springs only as a way of simulating specific situations, such as bungee jumpers. Some very insightful developers realized that springs have much broader applications than was previously thought.

For example, one of the great limitations in computer graphics and games was simulating flexible materials such as hair and cloth. Breakthroughs were made when developers realized that both hair and cloth can be simulated with springs.

Hair and Ponytails

Until recently, most characters in games had stiff hair. If you watch the hair in games that simulate people, such as role-playing games, the hair does not move, flow, and flex the way that real hair does. A good example of this is in the popular game *The Sims*. In *The Sims*, long hair is as stiff as a board.

If you want characters in your games to have hair and ponytails that move realistically, you must implement their hair and ponytails as collections of masses and springs. Figure 12.1 illustrates how this works.

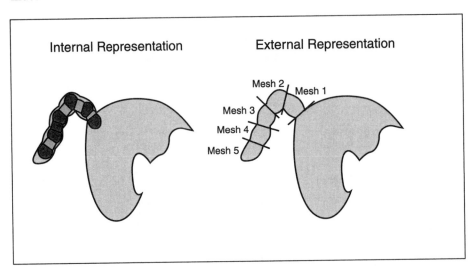

Figure 12.1
A ponytail made of masses and springs.

Figure 12.1 shows two views of the ponytail. The first, shown on the left, is an internal representation of the ponytail. The player never sees this representation. The representation on the right is what the player actually sees.

Why use two representations?

Internally, your game represents the ponytail as a series of masses connected by springs. The spring at the top end of the ponytail must be much stiffer than the springs near the bottom of the ponytail if you want realistic movement. As the character's head moves back and forth, it exerts linear forces on the point mass at the top of the ponytail. The point mass, in turn, transmits those forces to the first spring. The transmitted forces cause the spring to be stretched or compressed. The spring then exerts a force on the next point mass and causes it to move. This sequence continues down the system of masses and springs. Using this technique enables your game to track the position of each segment of the ponytail.

When it comes time to draw the ponytail, your game draws it one segment at a time. The external representation of each segment is simply a sausage-shaped mesh with a texture applied to it. The program must match the position of each segment's mesh to the position of the corresponding point mass. As the masses move and bounce, the ponytail's segments also move and bounce. How realistically they move depends on the weights of the masses and the characteristics of the springs.

If you have the processing power, you can apply this technique to every strand of hair on a character's head. However, if you have that kind of processing power, you are probably not using a computer manufactured on this planet. Typically, if you want to simulate the movement of long hair, you need to treat it as if it were one or more sheets of cloth.

Cloth

Simulating cloth is much like simulating a collection of interconnected ponytails. Figure 12.2 illustrates how this is done.

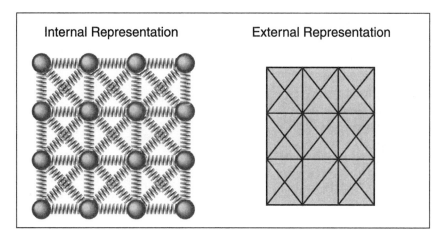

Figure 12.2
The internal and external representations of cloth.

As you can see from Figure 12.2, the internal representation of a piece of cloth is a grid of point masses. Each mass is connected horizontally, vertically, and diagonally to its neighbors in the grid by springs. The springs enable the cloth to move realistically. The external representation of the cloth is simply a flat mesh with textures applied to both sides. The position of every vertex in the mesh must be matched to the position of a point mass in the grid.

When you implement cloth, you need to make the point masses much smaller than those shown in Figure 12.2. The springs will be much looser than the springs in a ponytail.

One of the great advantages of using this technique for simulating cloth is that the point masses in the cloth can interact with any other object in your game. You use the same collision detection and response techniques shown in earlier chapters. With these techniques, the cloth can drape over other objects, flutter in the wind, and generally act like cloth is supposed to act.

It All Starts with Harmonic Motion

Think for a moment about a point mass suspended from the ceiling by a spring, as shown in Figure 12.3. Suppose that the spring does not initially have the mass connected to it. If you can connect the mass and let go, gravity pulls on the point mass and causes the spring to stretch. Next, the spring exerts an upward force on the mass. The result is that the mass bounces back up. Gravity pulls the mass back down again, so it continues to bounce. In the real world, the bouncing would come to a stop due to the natural dampening characteristics of the spring. However, let's ignore that for now and say that the mass keeps bouncing. This is an example of simple harmonic motion.

A pendulum, like the one shown in Figure 12.4, is an even more straightforward example of simple harmonic motion. Examining the behavior of a pendulum helps us understand the physics behind simple harmonic motion. This in turn makes it easy to learn about springs.

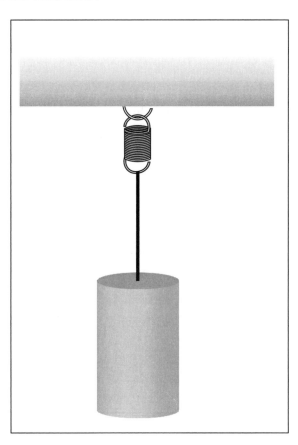

Figure 12.3
A mass and a spring hanging from the ceiling.

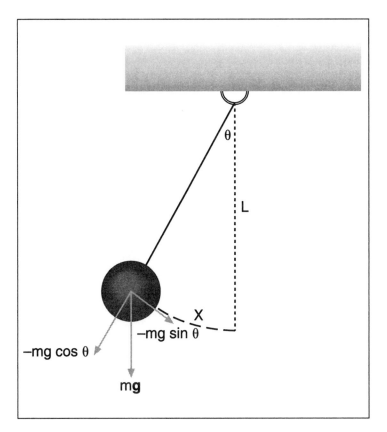

Figure 12.4
A simple pendulum.

If you start a pendulum swinging, the mass on the end is displaced. Gravity pulls the pendulum back toward its initial vertical position. The restoring force of gravity is given by the following equation:

$$F = -mg \sin \theta$$

In this formula, m and g are, respectively, the mass of the particle and the acceleration of gravity. The angle θ is the angle of displacement from vertical. For simple harmonic motion, the length of the arc through which the mass moves to get back to the vertical position is represented as the value x. You can calculate x with the following formula:

$$x = \theta \cdot L$$

Here, L is the length of the cord that suspends the mass from the ceiling, as we saw in Figure 12.4. For small displacements, sin θ nearly equals θ, so you can solve for θ and substitute this equation into the previous one:

$$F = -mg \; \frac{x}{L}$$

We can rearrange this to read as follows:

$$F = -\frac{mg}{L}x$$

If we keep the length of the string constant, then (mg/L) is also constant. Let's assign the letter k to represent (mg/L). That gives us the formula shown here:

$$F = -kx$$

Hooke's Law

Hooke's law is a simple formula for calculating the restoring force of a mass connected to a spring. Here it is:

$$F = -kx$$

Hey! That's the formula for the harmonic motion of a pendulum!

We use the same formula because springs produce harmonic motion. For springs, the value of k is not necessarily equal to (mg/L). The value of k depends entirely on the strength of the spring. Stiff springs produce a stronger restoring force, so their k values are higher. Loose springs have a low k value, so they produce a weaker restoring force.

Dampened Harmonic Motion

In the real world, masses that are suspended from springs don't continue bouncing forever. That's because the spring has the natural dampening force of friction built in. Also, the system might have air resistance or even water resistance. Figure 12.5 displays a system that demonstrates the effects of dampening on harmonic motion.

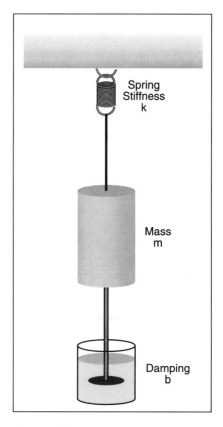

Figure 12.5
Dampened harmonic motion.

The mass in Figure 12.5 is suspended by a spring. In addition, a damper hangs from the weight into a thick liquid. The liquid provides a dampening force that is proportional to the velocity of the mass but in the opposite direction. Therefore, the formula for calculating the dampening force is as follows:

$$\mathbf{F} = -\mathbf{bv}$$

Here, b is a constant that is a measure of the strength of the dampening force, and $\mathbf{v}$ is the velocity of the mass at the end of the spring. Following is the total force on the mass:

$$\mathbf{F} = -\mathbf{kx} - \mathbf{bv}$$

This nifty formula is ideally all you need to implement systems of particles and springs. Unfortunately, reality is somewhat different. Let's implement some cloth so that you can see why.

Implementing Cloth

A piece of cloth is a rather complex system to implement in software. It involves all the physics of point masses plus all the physics and springs. In addition, you must know how to warp or deform a mesh in Direct3D so that you can match the positions of the mesh vertices to the positions of the point masses. This takes an advanced knowledge of Direct3D that is beyond the scope of this book. We'll approximate the appearance of cloth using oversized meshes for point masses. Although this technique produces cloth that is not completely realistic looking, it helps us to stay focused on physics rather than DirectX.

note

> To find out more about mesh warping, I highly recommend the book *Special Effects Game Programming with DirectX* (Premier Press). The book has an entire chapter dedicated to the subject of image warping. After you read that chapter, improving the appearance of your cloth should be fairly straightforward.

Upgrading Point Masses

Before we get too far into implementing cloth, we need to think about some of the characteristics of cloth. For instance, we can fasten cloth to other objects in a 3-D scene. A tapestry on a castle wall is a good example of this. The corners of the tapestry should remain fixed while the rest of the tapestry moves and flutters. Recall that the position of every vertex in the cloth's mesh is calculated using a point mass. Therefore, we need a way to tell a point mass not to move.

In addition, the real implementation of cloth requires that the point masses be invisible.

What gets displayed on the screen is the cloth's mesh. Therefore, to implement cloth, our games also need a type of point mass that has no mesh. Even though we're not fully implementing the appearance of cloth, I've upgraded the point_mass class to meet these needs.

In the cloth simulation program, the point_mass class is now derived from a base class using C++ inheritance. Listing 12.1 provides the code for the base class.

note

You can find the code for the sample program for this chapter on the CD-ROM in the folder Source\Chapter12\Cloth. If you want to see the sample program in action, you'll find an executable version of it in the Source\Chapter12\Bin folder.

Listing 12.1
The point_mass_base Class

```
1      class point_mass_base
2      {
3      private:
4          scalar mass;
5          vector_3d centerOfMassLocation;
6          vector_3d linearVelocity;
7          vector_3d linearAcceleration;
8          vector_3d constantForce;
9          vector_3d impulseForce;
10
11         scalar radius;
12         scalar coefficientOfRestitution;
13
14         bool isImmovable;
15
16     public:
17         point_mass_base();
18
19         void Mass(
20             scalar massValue);
21         scalar Mass(void);
22
23         void Location(
24             vector_3d locationCenterOfMass);
25         vector_3d Location(void);
26
27         void LinearVelocity(
28             vector_3d newVelocity);
```

```
29          vector_3d LinearVelocity(void);
30
31          void LinearAcceleration(
32              vector_3d newAcceleration);
33          vector_3d LinearAcceleration(void);
34
35          void ConstantForce(
36              vector_3d sumConstantForces);
37          vector_3d ConstantForce(void);
38
39          void ImpulseForce(
40              vector_3d sumImpulseForces);
41          vector_3d ImpulseForce(void);
42
43          void BoundingSphereRadius(
44              scalar sphereRadius);
45          scalar BoundingSphereRadius(void);
46
47          void Elasticity(scalar elasticity);
48          scalar Elasticity(void);
49
50          void IsImmovable(
51              bool isMassImmovable);
52          bool IsImmovable(void);
53
54          virtual bool Update(
55              scalar changeInTime);
56      };
```

The class in Listing 12.1, called point_mass_base, contains almost all the functionality that the point_mass class had. However, it does not have a data member of type mesh. In addition, it lacks a data member in which to store a world matrix. Finally, it does not have a Render() function. All three of these changes reflect the fact that the point_mass_base class cannot be rendered to the screen.

Notice also that the Update() function is now virtual so that it can be overridden easily in derived classes. Also, programs are now able to get and set the impulse force acting on a point mass separately from the constant force.

The point_mass_base class has a new data member called isImmovable. If this value is true, the point mass cannot be moved. There are member functions for getting and setting the value of the isImmovable data member. The other member functions in the point_mass_base class use the isImmovable data member to ensure that the point mass cannot move. Listing

12.2 shows the code for some of the point_mass_base class's member functions that use the isImmovable data member.

Listing 12.2
Using the isImmovable Data Member

```
1     inline void point_mass_base::LinearVelocity(
2         vector_3d newVelocity)
3     {
4         if (!isImmovable)
5         {
6             linearVelocity = newVelocity;
7         }
8         else
9         {
10            linearVelocity = vector_3d(0.0,0.0,0.0);
11        }
12    }
13
14
15    inline vector_3d point_mass_base::LinearVelocity(void)
16    {
17        return (linearVelocity);
18    }
19
20
21    inline void point_mass_base::LinearAcceleration(
22        vector_3d newAcceleration)
23    {
24        if (!isImmovable)
25        {
26            linearAcceleration = newAcceleration;
27        }
28        else
29        {
30            linearAcceleration = vector_3d(0.0,0.0,0.0);
31        }
32    }
33
34
35    inline vector_3d point_mass_base::LinearAcceleration(void)
36    {
37        return (linearAcceleration);
38    }
```

```
39
40
41    inline void point_mass_base::ConstantForce(
42        vector_3d sumConstantForces)
43    {
44        if (!isImmovable)
45        {
46            constantForce = sumConstantForces;
47        }
48        else
49        {
50            constantForce = vector_3d(0.0,0.0,0.0);
51        };
52    }
53
54
55    inline vector_3d point_mass_base::ConstantForce(void)
56    {
57        return (constantForce);
58    }
59
60
61    inline void point_mass_base::ImpulseForce(
62        vector_3d sumImpulseForces)
63    {
64        if (!isImmovable)
65        {
66            impulseForce = sumImpulseForces;
67        }
68        else
69        {
70            impulseForce = vector_3d(0.0,0.0,0.0);
71        };
72    }
73
74
75    inline vector_3d point_mass_base::ImpulseForce(void)
76    {
77        return (impulseForce);
78    }
```

All the set functions in Listing 12.2 check the isImmovable data member to see whether the point mass is immovable. If it is immovable, these functions set the linear velocity, linear acceleration, constant force, or impulse force to 0. Otherwise, the functions set their respective point mass characteristics to the values passed in through their parameter lists. If a point mass is immovable, it can never have any velocity, acceleration, or forces acting on it. As a result, the point mass will not move unless the program specifically sets its location.

If you want your program to display a point mass on the screen, do not use the point_mass_base class. Instead, use the point_mass class, which is now derived from point_mass_base. Listing 12.3 presents the new definition for the point_mass class.

Listing 12.3
The New point_mass Class

```
1     class point_mass : public point_mass_base
2     {
3     private:
4         mesh objectMesh;
5
6         D3DXMATRIX worldMatrix;
7
8     public:
9         bool LoadMesh(
10            std::string meshFileName);
11
12        void ShareMesh(
13            point_mass &sourceMass);
14
15        bool Update(
16            scalar changeInTime);
17        bool Render(void);
18    };
```

The point_mass class is now very short. Listing 12.3 shows that the point_mass class inherits most of its functionality from the point_mass_base class. The point_mass class now has only two data members. The first member contains the point mass's mesh. The second contains its world matrix. This class has these two data members because it can be displayed on the screen.

Because the point_mass class has a mesh that can be displayed on the screen, it provides a LoadMesh() function. It also provides a special function, called ShareMesh(), that enables multiple point mass objects to use the same mesh. The Update() function for the point_mass class overrides the Update() function in the point_mass_base class. And unlike the point_mass_base class, the point_mass class provides a Render() function. The code for the Update() and Render() functions appears in Listing 12.4.

Listing 12.4
The Update() and Render() Functions for the point_mass Class

```
1     bool point_mass::Update(
2         scalar changeInTime)
3     {
4         point_mass_base::Update(changeInTime);
5
6         // Create the translation matrix.
7         D3DXMatrixTranslation(
8             &worldMatrix,
9             Location().X(),
10            Location().Y(),
11            Location().Z());
12
13        return(true);
14    }
15
16    bool point_mass::Render(void)
17    {
18        // Save the world transformation matrix.
19        D3DXMATRIX saveWorldMatrix;
20        theApp.D3DRenderingDevice()->GetTransform(
21            D3DTS_WORLD,
22            &saveWorldMatrix);
23
24        // Apply the world transformation matrix for this object.
25        theApp.D3DRenderingDevice()->SetTransform(
26            D3DTS_WORLD,&worldMatrix);
27
28        // Now render the object with its transformations.
29        bool renderedOK=objectMesh.Render();
30
31        // Restore the world transformation matrix.
32        theApp.D3DRenderingDevice()->SetTransform(
33            D3DTS_WORLD,
34            &saveWorldMatrix);
35
36        return (renderedOK);
37    }
```

The Update() function for the point_mass class doesn't do nearly as much work as it did before. Instead, point_mass::Update() calls point_mass_base::Update() on line 4 of Listing 12.4. The point_mass_base::Update() function performs all the linear motion calculations.

After those calculations are complete, the point_mass:: Update() function creates a world matrix for the point_mass object using the x, y, and z coordinates calculated by the point_mass_base::Update() function.

As with previous versions of the point_mass class, the Render() function saves the current world matrix. It then gives Direct3D the world matrix contained in the current point_mass object. Next, it renders the point_mass object's mesh. Finally, it restores the original world matrix.

Having the point_mass and point_mass_base classes enables us to create point masses that are visible on the screen and point masses that are invisible. When you create invisible point masses in your programs, it would be nice to use a more descriptive name in your variable declarations than point_mass_base. Therefore, I've provided a type definition that renames the point_mass_base class to invisible_point_mass. The invisible_point_mass type adds no functionality to the point_mass_base class. It just provides a more descriptive name.

Springs

To implement objects such as cloth and hair, your game needs to simulate springs. Ideally, simulated springs should work just like real springs. Your program should be able to set the spring force constant (k) and the dampening factor (b) and use the spring equations shown earlier in this chapter to get simulated springs to perform exactly like real springs. Unfortunately, simulating springs isn't that easy.

One reason that simulating springs is not easy is that the spring equations do not fully describe what happens with real springs. The spring force equations assume that springs are never compressed or stretched beyond the physical limits. If they are, the spring equations break down. They cause point masses that are attached to the springs to move in wild and often unpredictable ways. When this problem occurs, your piece of cloth often moves in insane ways, usually either growing or shrinking in the process.

One of the ways you can solve this problem is to enforce the compression and expansion limits of your simulated springs. This sounds simple, but it's a rather complex programming task. If a spring is stretched or compressed beyond its limits, it must adjust the positions of the particles to which it is attached, which can cause repercussions throughout the particle-spring system. Adjusting the position of any particle in the system can cause a wave of adjustments throughout the system. This is another way to end up with insane cloth.

You can enforce spring compression and expansion limits, but not in the spring class. You have to do this at the level of the particle-spring system. In other words, you must put that code into the cloth class. The adjustments that the cloth class must make are complex and often situation dependent. The result is that the cloth class is often not generic enough to be useful. Finding a simpler approach would be better.

Rather than enforce spring compression and expansion limits, you can stabilize particle-spring systems by applying additional dampening forces. This helps prevent the particles in the system from moving wildly. It also helps settle them down quickly when they do. Applying extra dampening is a programmatically easy solution that does not involve a lot of calculation overhead. As a result, it's a solution that programmers use a lot. The extra dampening is added at the level of the particle-spring system. That means that it's in the cloth class and not the spring class. The reason for this is that different types of particle-spring systems use different types of dampening.

The long and short of this is that the spring class ends up being fairly simple. Listing 12.5 presents the definition of the spring class.

Listing 12.5
A Simple spring Class

```
1    class spring
2    {
3    private:
4        scalar restLength;
5        scalar forceConstant;
6        scalar dampeningFactor;
7
8        point_mass_base *pointMass1;
9        point_mass_base *pointMass2;
10
11   public:
12       spring();
13
14       void Length(
15           scalar springLength);
16       scalar Length(void);
17
18       void ForceConstant(
19           scalar springForceConstant);
20       scalar ForceConstant(void);
21
22       void DampeningFactor(
23           scalar dampeningConstant);
24       scalar DampeningFactor(void);
25
26       void EndpointMass1(
27           point_mass_base *particle1);
28       point_mass_base *EndpointMass1(void);
29
```

```
30          void EndpointMass2(
31              point_mass_base *particle2);
32          point_mass_base *EndpointMass2(void);
33
34          bool IsDisplaced(void);
35
36          void CalculateReactions(
37              scalar changeInTime);
38      };
```

The spring class in Listing 12.5 contains five data members. The first holds the spring's rest length, which is the length of the spring when it is neither compressed nor stretched. On lines 5–6 of Listing 12.5, the spring class defines data members that hold the spring's k and b values, respectively.

The spring class also keeps pointers to the point masses to which it is attached. Notice that the type of the pointer is point_mass_base. This enables you to attach a spring to either visible or invisible point masses. That is, you can set the pointers defined on lines 8–9 to point to objects of type point_mass or objects of type invisible_point_mass.

Lines 14–32 define member functions for getting and setting the member data. The IsDisplaced() function determines whether the spring is stretched or compressed. The CalculateReactions() function calculates the force that the spring exerts on the point masses to which it is attached. Let's look at the code for these two functions in Listing 12.6.

Listing 12.6
The Workhorse Functions of the spring Class

```
1       bool spring::IsDisplaced(void)
2       {
3           assert(pointMass1!=NULL);
4           assert(pointMass2!=NULL);
5
6           bool isDisplaced = false;
7
8           vector_3d currentLength;
9
10          /* Find the distance between the particles to which the spring is
11          connected. */
12          currentLength =
13              pointMass1->Location() - pointMass2->Location();
14
15          /* Find the difference between the rest length and the current
16          length. */
17          scalar lengthDifference =
```

```
18              currentLength.NormSquared() - (restLength*restLength);
19
20          // If the difference is not essentially zero...
21          if (!CloseToZero(lengthDifference))
22          {
23              isDisplaced=true;
24          }
25
26          return (isDisplaced);
27      }
28
29
30      void spring::CalculateReactions(
31          scalar changeInTime)
32      {
33          assert(pointMass1!=NULL);
34          assert(pointMass2!=NULL);
35
36          vector_3d currentLength;
37
38          // Get the current length of the spring.
39          currentLength =
40              pointMass1->Location() - pointMass2->Location();
41
42          // Change it to a scalar.
43          scalar currentLengthMagnitude = currentLength.Norm();
44
45          /* Find the difference between the current length and the rest
46          length. */
47          scalar changeInLength = currentLengthMagnitude-restLength;
48
49          // If the change in length is close to zero...
50          if (CloseToZero(changeInLength))
51          {
52              // Set it to zero.
53              changeInLength=0.0;
54          }
55
56          // Find the magnitude of the force the spring exerts.
57          scalar springForceMagnitude =
58              forceConstant * changeInLength;
59
```

```
60          // Find the magnitude of the dampening force on the spring.
61          scalar dampeningForceMagnitude;
62          if (changeInTime<1.0f)
63          {
64              dampeningForceMagnitude =
65                  dampeningFactor * changeInLength * changeInTime;
66          }
67          else
68          {
69              dampeningForceMagnitude =
70                  dampeningFactor * changeInLength / changeInTime;
71          }
72
73          // The dampening force can't be greater than the spring force.
74          if (dampeningForceMagnitude > springForceMagnitude)
75          {
76              dampeningForceMagnitude = springForceMagnitude;
77          }
78
79          //Dampen the spring force.
80          scalar responseForceMagnitude =
81              springForceMagnitude - dampeningForceMagnitude;
82
83          // Change the response force to a vector.
84          vector_3d responseForce =
85              responseForceMagnitude *
86              currentLength.Normalize(SCALAR_TOLERANCE);
87
88          // Apply the response force to the particles.
89          pointMass1->ImpulseForce(
90              pointMass1->ImpulseForce() + -1*responseForce);
91          pointMass2->ImpulseForce(
92              pointMass2->ImpulseForce() + responseForce);
93      }
```

The IsDisplaced() function finds the current length of the spring by subtracting the locations of the centers of mass of the two particles to which it is attached. This gives a vector whose magnitude is the distance between the centers of the two particles. It is assumed that the spring is attached to the centers of mass. Therefore, the distance between the centers of mass is the length of the spring.

On lines 17–18, the IsDisplaced() function finds the vector's magnitude, or norm. Calculating the norm involves calculating a square root. To avoid that, the IsDisplaced()

function uses the norm squared. It subtracts the square of the rest length from the square of the norm. This is okay because this function doesn't really need the distance between the two particles. It just needs to know if the spring is stretched or compressed. Using the squares rather than the actual distances tells us that.

The `CalculateReactions()` function, which begins on line 30 of Listing 12.6, calculates the force that the spring exerts on the point masses to which it is attached. The first step in doing this is to find the current length of the spring on lines 39–40. Unlike the `IsDisplaced()` function, the `CalculateReactions()` function must have the exact length of the spring. Using the square of the length will not do.

note

> You might wonder why I did not name the `CalculateReactions()` function `Update()`, as I did with most of the other classes in the physics modeling framework. This was a design decision based on my opinions. Because a spring is never displayed on the screen, and because the only thing a spring does is exert forces on other objects, it seemed to me that springs are conceptually different enough from the other objects in the framework to warrant a function with a different name.

Next, the `CalculateReactions()` function finds the magnitude of the vector that specifies the spring's current length. On line 47, it finds the difference between that magnitude and the rest length of the spring. That difference is multiplied by the spring's force constant in accordance with the formula $F=-kx$, where x is the displacement of the spring.

The dampening force is calculated on lines 61–71. The calculated magnitude of the spring force can be less than the magnitude of the dampening force. Whether or not this is true depends on the values that your program sets for the spring force constant (k) and the dampening force constant (b). If the dampening force constant is large compared to the spring force constant, the spring produces a huge dampening force that overwhelms the spring force. This, however, is physically impossible. So the `if` statement on lines 74–77 makes sure that the dampening force is never greater than the spring force. That goes a long way toward keeping your particle-spring systems stable.

On lines 80–81, the `CalculateReactions()` function combines the spring and dampening forces to obtain the overall force that the spring exerts on the two point masses to which it is attached. Lines 84–86 convert the magnitude of that force into a vector. The `CalculateReactions()` function ends by assigning that force, in opposite directions, to the two point masses as an impulse force.

That's really all there is to simulating springs in software. As stated previously, however, it takes some additional work to keep springs stable.

The cloth Class

With the point masses and springs we've defined in this chapter, we can begin to build particle-spring systems such as cloth. Figure 12.2, near the beginning of this chapter, depicted conceptually how particle-spring systems such as cloth are implemented. As you might expect, the implementation in code is significantly more complex. Listing 12.7 gives the definition of the cloth class.

Listing 12.7
The cloth Class

```
1     class cloth
2     {
3     // Private types
4     private:
5         enum cloth_constants
6         {
7             PARTICLES_PER_SQUARE=4,
8             TOP_LEFT_PARTICLE=0,
9             TOP_RIGHT_PARTICLE,
10            BOTTOM_LEFT_PARTICLE,
11            BOTTOM_RIGHT_PARTICLE,
12            TOP_SPRING = 0,
13            BOTTOM_SPRING,
14            RIGHT_SPRING,
15            LEFT_SPRING,
16            TOP_RIGHT_TO_BOTTOM_LEFT_SPRING,
17            TOP_LEFT_TO_BOTTOM_RIGHT_SPRING,
18            SPRINGS_PER_SQUARE=6,
19        };
20
21        struct index_pair
22        {
23            int row,col;
24        };
25
26        struct cloth_square
27        {
28            index_pair particleIndex[PARTICLES_PER_SQUARE];
29            int springIndex[SPRINGS_PER_SQUARE];
30        };
31
32    // Private data
33    private:
```

```
34        int totalRows;
35        int totalCols;
36        int totalSprings;
37        point_mass **allParticles;
38        spring *allSprings;
39        cloth_square **allSquares;
40        scalar linearDampeningCoefficient;
41
42   // Private functions
43   private:
44   void cloth::HandleCollision(
45        vector_3d separationDistance,
46        scalar changeInTime,
47        index_pair firstParticle,
48        index_pair secondParticle);
49
50   // Public functions
51   public:
52        cloth(
53            int particleRows,
54            int particleCols,
55            scalar particleMass,
56            scalar particleRadius,
57            scalar particleElasticity,
58            scalar spaceBetweenParticles,
59            scalar clothStiffness,
60            scalar dampeningFactor,
61            scalar linearDampeningFactor,
62            vector_3d upLeftCorner);
63
64        void ParticleImpulseForce(
65            int row,int col,vector_3d impulseForce);
66        vector_3d ParticleImpulseForce(
67            int row,int col);
68
69        void ParticleConstantForce(
70            int row,int col,vector_3d constantForce);
71        vector_3d ParticleConstantForce(
72            int row,int col);
73
74        void IsParticleImmovable(
75            int row,int col,bool isMassImmovable);
```

```
76        bool IsParticleImmovable(
77            int row,int col);
78
79        bool LoadMesh(std::string meshFileName);
80        bool Update(scalar changeInTime);
81        bool Render(void);
82    };
```

The cloth class provides a wider range of functionality that is actually used in the sample program for this chapter. Specifically, it divides the cloth into squares whose corners are defined by four of the point masses in the particle-spring system. This gives you a number of advantages in working with cloth. First, it enables you to add custom code to the cloth class member functions that perform special processing on individual squares. You'll find that handy in advanced cloth simulations. Second, dividing the cloth into squares enables you to add a mesh for each square rather than defining a single mesh for the entire piece of cloth. This gives you a lot of options for controlling the appearance of the cloth.

To make the process of dividing the cloth into squares easier, the cloth class defines some private types and constants. All the constants appear in the cloth_constants enumerated type, which is shown on lines 5–19 of Listing 12.7. The constants specify the number of particles per square, which is 4, of course, as well as the position of each particle in the square. The constants also specify the number and positions of the springs that connect the particles.

The index_pair type provides an easy way to specify the row and column of particles and squares. It is used in the cloth_square type, which appears on lines 26–30 of Listing 12.7. Each cloth_square object contains an array of index pairs, as shown on line 28. This array contains the row and column number of each particle in a square. The cloth_square type also specifies an array of integers. These integers hold the index numbers of the springs in the square.

If you look back at Figure 12.2, it's pretty easy to see the squares that make up the cloth. It's also readily apparent that both springs and particles are shared between squares. Therefore, it makes sense not to store the springs and particles in the cloth_square type. If we did, many springs and particles would be duplicated, wasting memory.

The private member data for the cloth class appears on lines 34–40 of Listing 12.7. These data members store the number of rows and columns of particles in the particle-spring system, as well as the total number of springs in the system.

The cloth class contains a pointer to pointers to point_mass objects on line 37. Using a pointer to pointers enables the cloth class to dynamically allocate any number of particles for the cloth. As you'll see soon, the constructor uses this pointer to pointers to dynamically allocate a two-dimensional array.

note

Reminder: The cloth class contains point_mass objects rather than invisible_point_mass objects because we're not going to get into mesh warping. Instead, we'll use a collection of oversized point mass meshes to create the approximate appearance of cloth. If you want to use the cloth class in your games, you must learn to do mesh warping and then change the point_mass objects in the cloth class to invisible_point_mass objects.

In addition, the cloth class holds a pointer to springs. The class uses this pointer as a dynamically allocated, one-dimensional array of springs. Because the squares in the cloth are conceptually in rows and columns, the cloth class also defines a pointer to pointers to cloth_square structures on line 39. The cloth class uses this pointer to pointers as a dynamically allocated two-dimensional array of squares.

The cloth class also defines several member functions, some of which are private and some public. Let's start by looking at the constructor.

Initializing a Piece of Cloth

Initializing a cloth object is not particularly straightforward. You can see how it's done in Listing 12.8.

Listing 12.8
The cloth Class Constructor

```
1     cloth::cloth(
2           int particleRows,
3           int particleCols,
4           scalar particleMass,
5           scalar particleRadius,
6           scalar particleElasticity,
7           scalar spaceBetweenParticles,
8           scalar clothStiffness,
9           scalar dampeningFactor,
10          scalar linearDampeningFactor,
11          vector_3d upLeftCorner)
12    {
13          assert(particleRows>=2);
14          assert(particleCols>=2);
15
16          linearDampeningCoefficient = linearDampeningFactor;
17
18          // Allocate memory for one dimension of the array of particles.
19          allParticles = new point_mass * [particleRows];
20
```

```
21          // If the memory was not allocated...
22          if (allParticles==NULL)
23          {
24              // Throw an exception.
25              pmlib_error outOfMemory("Can't allocate memory for cloth.");
26              throw outOfMemory;
27          }
28
29          //
30          // Allocate memory for the second dimension of the array.
31          //
32          int i,j;
33          // For each row...
34          for (i=0;i<particleRows;i++)
35          {
36              // Allocate a particle for each column in the row.
37              allParticles[i] = new point_mass [particleCols];
38
39              // If the particle couldn't be allocated...
40              if (allParticles[i]==NULL)
41              {
42                  // Throw an exception.
43                  pmlib_error outOfMemory(
44                      "Can't allocate memory for cloth.");
45                  throw outOfMemory;
46              }
47          }
48
49          // Set the total number of springs needed for the grid.
50          totalSprings =
51              (particleRows * (particleCols-1)) +
52              ((particleRows-1) * particleCols) +
53              ((particleRows-1) * (particleCols-1) * 2);
54
55          // Allocate the springs.
56          allSprings = new spring [totalSprings];
57
58          // If the springs weren't allocated...
59          if (allSprings==NULL)
60          {
61              // Throw an exception.
62              pmlib_error outOfMemory("Can't allocate memory for cloth.");
```

```
63          throw outOfMemory;
64      }
65
66      // Allocate the rows for the array of squares.
67      allSquares = new cloth_square *[particleRows-1];
68
69      // If the array wasn't allocated...
70      if (allSquares==NULL)
71      {
72          // Throw an exception.
73          pmlib_error outOfMemory("Can't allocate memory for cloth.");
74          throw outOfMemory;
75      }
76      // Else the array was allocated...
77      else
78      {
79          // For each row in the array.
80          for (i=0; i<particleRows-1; i++)
81          {
82              // Allocate the squares for each column in the row.
83              allSquares[i] = new cloth_square[particleCols-1];
84
85              // If the squares weren't allocated...
86              if (allSquares[i]==NULL)
87              {
88                  // Throw an exception.
89                  pmlib_error outOfMemory(
90                      "Can't allocate memory for cloth.");
91                  throw outOfMemory;
92              }
93          }
94      }
95
96      vector_3d location=upLeftCorner;
97
98      // Set the properties of each particle.
99      for (i=0; i<particleRows; i++)
100     {
101         for (j=0; j<particleCols; j++)
102         {
103             allParticles[i][j].Mass(particleMass);
104             allParticles[i][j].BoundingSphereRadius(particleRadius);
```

```
105              allParticles[i][j].Elasticity(particleElasticity);
106              allParticles[i][j].Location(location);
107              location.X(
108                  location.X() + spaceBetweenParticles);
109          }
110      location.X(
111          upLeftCorner.X());
112      location.Y(
113          location.Y() - spaceBetweenParticles);
114      }
115
116      //
117      /* For each square, connect the horizontal springs for the top
118      and bottom of each square. */
119      //
120      index_pair tempIndex;
121      int currentSpring;
122      for (i=0,currentSpring=0; i<particleRows ;i++)
123      {
124          for (j=0; j<particleCols-1; j++,currentSpring++)
125          {
126              // Connect the top.
127              allSprings[currentSpring].EndpointMass1(
128                  &allParticles[i][j]);
129              allSprings[currentSpring].EndpointMass2(
130                  &allParticles[i][j+1]);
131
132              // If this is not the last row of particles...
133              if (i<particleRows-1)
134              {
135                  // Store the index of the top spring.
136                  allSquares[i][j].springIndex[TOP_SPRING] =
137                      currentSpring;
138
139                  // Store the indices of the two particles it connects.
140                  tempIndex.row = i;
141                  tempIndex.col = j;
142                  allSquares[i][j].particleIndex[TOP_LEFT_PARTICLE] =
143                      tempIndex;
144                  tempIndex.col = j+1;
145                  allSquares[i][j].particleIndex[TOP_RIGHT_PARTICLE] =
146                      tempIndex;
```

```
147                     }
148
149                     // If this is not the first row of particles...
150                     if (i>0)
151                     {
152                         /* This spring is already connected, store it as the
153                         index of the bottom spring. */
154                         allSquares[i-1][j].springIndex[BOTTOM_SPRING] =
155                             currentSpring;
156
157                         // Store the indices of the two particles it connects.
158                         tempIndex.row = i;
159                         tempIndex.col = j;
160                         allSquares[i-1][j].particleIndex[BOTTOM_LEFT_PARTICLE] =
161                             tempIndex;
162                         tempIndex.col = j+1;
163                         allSquares[i-1][j].particleIndex[BOTTOM_RIGHT_PARTICLE] =
164                             tempIndex;
165                     }
166                 }
167             }
168
169         //
170         /* For each square, connect the vertical springs for the left
171         and right of each square. */
172         //
173         for (i=0; i<particleRows-1 ;i++)
174         {
175             for (j=0; j<particleCols; j++,currentSpring++)
176             {
177                 // Connect the left.
178                 allSprings[currentSpring].EndpointMass1(
179                     &allParticles[i][j]);
180                 allSprings[currentSpring].EndpointMass2(
181                     &allParticles[i+1][j]);
182
183                 //If this is not the last column of particles...
184                 if (j<particleCols-1)
185                 {
186                     // Store the index of the left spring.
187                     allSquares[i][j].springIndex[LEFT_SPRING] =
188                         currentSpring;
```

```
189
190                        // Store the indices of the two particles it connects.
191                        tempIndex.row = i;
192                        tempIndex.col = j;
193                        allSquares[i][j].particleIndex[TOP_LEFT_PARTICLE] =
194                            tempIndex;
195                        tempIndex.row = i+1;
196                        allSquares[i][j].particleIndex[BOTTOM_LEFT_PARTICLE] =
197                            tempIndex;
198                    }
199
200                    // If this is not the first column of particles...
201                    if (j>0)
202                    {
203                        // Store the index of the bottom spring.
204                        allSquares[i][j-1].springIndex[RIGHT_SPRING]=
205                            currentSpring;
206                        // Store the indices of the two particles it connects.
207                        tempIndex.row = i;
208                        tempIndex.col = j;
209                        allSquares[i][j-1].particleIndex[TOP_RIGHT_PARTICLE] =
210                            tempIndex;
211                        tempIndex.row = i+1;
212                        allSquares[i][j-1].particleIndex[BOTTOM_RIGHT_PARTICLE] =
213                            tempIndex;
214                    }
215                }
216            }
217
218        //
219        // For each square, connect the diagonal springs.
220        //
221        for (i=0; i<particleRows-1 ;i++)
222        {
223            for (j=0; j<particleCols-1; j++)
224            {
225                /* Connect the spring from the top left to the bottom
226                right. */
227                allSprings[currentSpring].EndpointMass1(
228                    &allParticles[i][j]);
229                allSprings[currentSpring].EndpointMass2(
230                    &allParticles[i+1][j+1]);
```

```
231          allSquares[i][j].springIndex[TOP_RIGHT_TO_BOTTOM_LEFT_SPRING] =
232              currentSpring++;
233
234          /* Connect the spring from the top right to the bottom
235          left. */
236          allSprings[currentSpring].EndpointMass1(
237              &allParticles[i][j+1]);
238          allSprings[currentSpring].EndpointMass2(
239              &allParticles[i+1][j]);
240          allSquares[i][j].springIndex[TOP_LEFT_TO_BOTTOM_RIGHT_SPRING] =
241              currentSpring++;
242        }
243     }
244
245     // Now set the common properties of all springs.
246     for (i=0; i<totalSprings; i++)
247     {
248        allSprings[i].DampeningFactor(dampeningFactor);
249        allSprings[i].ForceConstant(clothStiffness);
250        vector_3d tempVector =
251            allSprings[i].EndpointMass1()->Location() -
252            allSprings[i].EndpointMass2()->Location();
253        allSprings[i].Length(tempVector.Norm());
254     }
255
256     totalRows = particleRows;
257     totalCols = particleCols;
258  }
```

That's one *long* constructor! It starts by storing the linear dampening coefficient in the object on line 16. Recall that earlier in this chapter I talked about putting additional dampening into the cloth class to make it more stable. That is what the linear dampening coefficient is for.

Next, the constructor allocates an array of pointers to point_mass objects. If the array of pointers is not allocated, the function throws an exception on lines 22–27. Otherwise, the constructor continues and allocates point masses for each row in the way. If the row is not allocated properly, the constructor throws an exception on lines 40–46.

warning

This constructor should delete the array of pointers that was allocated on line 19 before it throws the exception on line 45. If it does not, there might be a memory leak. I omitted it from this implementation because the constructor is huge enough as it is.

On lines 50–53, the constructor calculates the total number of springs needed for the particle-spring system. It then allocates those springs on line 56. Again, the constructor throws an exception if the springs were not allocated. It should delete all previously allocated arrays before throwing the exception on line 63.

The `cloth` constructor next allocates an array of pointers to squares. If the array was allocated, the constructor allocates each row of squares on lines 80–94.

Beginning on line 96, the constructor initializes the characteristics of each particle, spring, and square in the cloth. On lines 99–114, `cloth` uses a pair of nested `for` loops to set the common properties that all particles share. The loops also set the position of each particle in the grid. The constructor takes a simple approach to initializing the particle locations. It assumes that the sheet of cloth is in a vertical position. If you want the cloth in any other position, your program must set the location of each particle after it calls the constructor.

At this point, the constructor is ready to begin connecting the springs. Because this process is somewhat complex, I've broken it into a series of tasks. First, the constructor uses a pair of `for` loops that begin on line 122 to connect the top spring for each square. It also stores the index numbers of the spring and particles being connected in the appropriate spot in each square. If the spring is not in the first row of particles, it serves as both the top spring in the current square and the bottom spring in the square above it. So lines 150–165 connect the current spring as the bottom spring in the appropriate square. After these loops complete, the top and bottom springs in all the squares are connected properly.

Starting on line 173, the constructor uses a similar algorithm to connect the left and right springs in each square. The pair of loops that began on line 221 connects the diagonal springs. If it exits, the constructor loops through the array of springs and sets their common properties. It also saves the total number of rows and columns of particles in the system.

Now we're ready to see `cloth` in action.

Updating and Rendering a Piece of Cloth

To behave like cloth, all the particles and springs in a `cloth` object must react to the forces exerted on them. The particles have to bounce off each other when they collide. Although the particles cannot be very springy, they cannot have a coefficient of restitution of 0.0. If they do, they'll stick together, and that's not how cloth acts.

When the particles in the cloth do collide with each other, they must transmit the collision forces through the springs. The springs in turn transmit those forces to other particles.

There's really a lot that goes on in cloth. It's easy to see why a particle-spring system can quickly become unstable. To help prevent that, the `cloth::Update()` function must not only process all the forces due to the springs and collisions, but it also must appropriately dampen the motion of the particles in the system. Listing 12.9 shows how this can be done.

Listing 12.9
The cloth::Update() Function

```
1     bool cloth::Update(
2         scalar changeInTime)
3     {
4         int i,j;
5
6         // Calculate the force exerted by each spring.
7         for (i=0;i<totalSprings;i++)
8         {
9             if (allSprings[i].IsDisplaced())
10            {
11                allSprings[i].CalculateReactions(changeInTime);
12            }
13        }
14
15        // Update the position of every particle in the grid.
16        for (i=0;i<totalRows;i++)
17        {
18            for (j=0;j<totalCols;j++)
19            {
20                //
21                /* Test for a collision between the current particle and
22                the remaining particles. Don't bother to test against
23                previous particles in the array. */
24                //
25
26                for (int k=i;k<totalCols;k++)
27                {
28                    for (int m=j+1;m<totalCols;m++)
29                    {
30                        // Find the distance vector between the particles.
31                        vector_3d distance =
32                            allParticles[i][j].Location() -
33                            allParticles[k][m].Location();
34                        scalar distanceSquared = distance.NormSquared();
35
36                        // Find the square of the sum of the radii of the balls.
37                        scalar minDistanceSquared =
38                            allParticles[i][j].BoundingSphereRadius() +
39                            allParticles[k][m].BoundingSphereRadius();
40                        minDistanceSquared *= minDistanceSquared;
```

```
41
42                        // If there is a collision...
43                        if (distanceSquared < minDistanceSquared)
44                        {
45                            index_pair firstParticle,secondParticle;
46                            firstParticle.row=i;
47                            firstParticle.col=j;
48                            secondParticle.row=k;
49                            secondParticle.col=m;
50
51                            // Handle the collision.
52                            HandleCollision(
53                                distance,changeInTime,
54                                firstParticle,secondParticle);
55                        }
56                    }
57                }
58            }
59        }
60
61        //
62        /* This is cheating. Spring-particle systems are notoriously
63        unstable. To make this behave more like cloth, dampen the
64        movement of the particles in the system.*/
65        //
66        vector_3d dampening;
67        for (i=0;i<totalRows;i++)
68        {
69            for (j=0;j<totalCols;j++)
70            {
71                dampening =
72                    -linearDampeningCoefficient *
73                    allParticles[i][j].LinearVelocity();
74                allParticles[i][j].LinearVelocity(
75                    allParticles[i][j].LinearVelocity() +
76                    dampening);
77            }
78        }
79
80        // Update each ball.
81        for (i=0;i<totalRows;i++)
82        {
```

```
83              for (j=0;j<totalCols;j++)
84              {
85                      allParticles[i][j].Update(changeInTime);
86              }
87          }
88
89          return (true);
90      }
```

Listing 12.9 shows that the Update() function begins by calculating the reactions of the springs in the system to the displacements of the individual particles. The loop that does this is on lines 7–13. Next, the Update() function enters a pair of nested for loops that test for collisions between particles. This is essentially the same code that was used for collision detection and response in previous chapters. If it looks unfamiliar to you, I suggest that you review Chapter 8, "Collisions of Point Particles."

The comment on lines 62–64 says that the next bit of code is cheating. I wrote that because the code doesn't exactly model the internal physics of a spring. As mentioned earlier in this chapter, we'd have to enforce compression and expansion limits to do that. However, the code on lines 67–78 *is* modeling physics. It decreases the linear velocity of all particles in the grid by a linear dampening coefficient. The coefficient must be between 0.0 and 1.0 inclusive.

What's really happening here is that we're loosely modeling a type of friction. By tossing a bit of friction into the system and calling it "linear dampening," we make sure that the movement of the particles in the grid can't get too wild.

tip

Dampening the velocity of particles in a particle-spring system works well for cloth. However, this technique is not universally applicable. Depending on what you're trying to model with the particle-spring system, it might be better to dampen the linear acceleration instead. You generally should not dampen the forces that act on the particles. It doesn't stabilize them; rather, it causes them to move in slow motion.

After all the forces have been calculated and the velocities of the particles adjusted, the Update() function calls the point_mass::Update() function to update the position of every particle in the system.

As you probably expect by now, the cloth object is updated every time the framework calls the UpdateFrame() function. Before going on, let's take a quick look at it in Listing 12.10.

Listing 12.10
The UpdateFrame() Function

```
1    bool UpdateFrame()
2    {
3        // Is it time to update the frame?
4        DWORD currentTime = ::timeGetTime();
5        if (!TimeToUpdateFrame(currentTime))
6            return (true);
7
8        // After a certain number of frames go by...
9        static scalar frameCount = 0;
10       static int currentRow=0;
11       if (frameCount>=CLOTH_PARTICLE_ROWS*10)
12       {
13           //
14           // Apply a force to a row of particles.
15           //
16           vector_3d impulse;
17
18           // Set random x, y, and z values.
19           impulse.X(RandomScalar(20));
20           impulse.Y(RandomScalar(20));
21           impulse.Z(RandomScalar(20));
22
23           // Apply the force vector to every particle in the row.
24           for (int i=0;i<CLOTH_PARTICLE_COLS;i++)
25           {
26               theCloth.ParticleImpulseForce(
27                   currentRow++,
28                   i,
29                   impulse);
30           }
31
32           /* If the current row is greater than or equal to the last
33           row... */
34           if (currentRow>=CLOTH_PARTICLE_ROWS)
35           {
36               // Reset the current row to zero.
37               currentRow=0;
38           }
39           frameCount=0;
40       }
```

```
41        else
42        {
43            frameCount++;
44        }
45
46        theCloth.Update(STEP_SIZE);
47        return (true);
48    }
```

This function is rather straightforward. Every 50 frames, it creates a random impulse force. It then applies that force to every particle in the row. The result looks a bit like cloth waving in the wind.

Rendering the cloth is even easier. The cloth::Render() function appears in Listing 12.11.

Listing 12.11
The cloth::Render() Function

```
1     bool cloth::Render(void)
2     {
3         bool renderOK=true;
4
5         for (int i=0;(renderOK) && (i<totalRows);i++)
6         {
7             for (int j=0;(renderOK) && (j<totalCols);j++)
8             {
9                 renderOK = allParticles[i][j].Render();
10            }
11        }
12        return (renderOK);
13    }
```

As you can see, Render() just calls the point_mass::Render() function for each particle.

Tuning Cloth

Getting a cloth object to act like real cloth takes some tuning. You have to give each particle in the grid a small mass and radius. The coefficient of restitution should be less than or equal to 0.01. The springs need to be pretty stiff, so set the k value rather high. Dampening also helps. I set the b value to 1,000 for the sample program. You might not want to set yours that high, but I suspect you won't be able to use a value less than 500 unless your masses are very light.

To get the right linear dampening coefficient, you need to experiment. Generally, however, it will be the same order of magnitude as the mass.

Suggested Enhancements for Cloth

You can make lots of improvements to the cloth class if you want to use it in games. First, of course, is to add mesh warping. You'll also add a data member of type mesh to the cloth class. The cloth::Update() function needs to use mesh warping techniques to match the position of each vertex in the mesh to the position of a particle in the particle-spring system. The cloth::Render() function has to call the mesh::Render() function on the cloth class's private mesh data member that you add. That makes the cloth::Render() function even simpler. Finally, you must go through the files PMCloth.h and PMCloth.cpp and change all occurrences of point_mass to invisible_point_mass.

Another enhancement to the cloth class that I encourage you to add is collision detection and response between the cloth particles and other objects. Currently, the cloth class only detects and responds to collisions between the particles in the cloth. If the particles in the cloth object collide with something else in the 3-D scene, they pass right through it. That's not good. Adding collision detection and response should not be difficult at this point. It's just a matter of copying and adapting code from Chapter 8.

The grid in the sample program for this chapter contains five rows and five columns of particles. In your games, you will undoubtedly need to use a much finer grid. You'll have to add many more rows and columns of small particles.

An advanced enhancement you could add to the cloth class is square-by-square dampening. To be specific, you could add more dampening in squares when one or more of its particles are immoveable or in contact with another object. I've already done the hard work of building the squares for you.

Summary

Systems that are made up of particles and springs have a surprisingly wide variety of applications. Now that you know the basics of springs and have seen a sample particle-spring system, you have almost everything you need to simulate ponytails, hair, cloth, and other flexible materials.

CHAPTER 13

WATER AND WAVES

This chapter builds on the techniques you learned in Chapter 12, "Mass and Spring Systems," for building particle-spring systems. It presents the physics of water and explains several methods for simulating water.

Why, you might ask, are there several methods of simulating water?

Simply put, simulating water can be one of the hardest things to do in games. The physics of water is surprisingly complex. Fear not. There are some extremely straightforward techniques of simulating water and the behavior of objects in water that vastly simplify both the physics and your program code. This chapter presents these techniques.

tip
_____

By the way, a lot of the material presented here also applies to air. In fact, you could say that air is just a fluid with a very low density. So if you're simulating hot air or helium balloons moving in air, you can use most of the material given in this chapter.

_____

Water and Buoyancy

To get this discussion started, let's first look at the basic properties of water. This helps us understand the physics of buoyancy.

note
_____

Water is a surprising substance. By rights, it shouldn't exist in the form that it does. If you look in a periodic table of elements, all of the elements below oxygen are very toxic. The formula for water, of course, is H_2O. The element below oxygen is S, for sulfur. H_2S is an acid. So are H_2Se, H_2Te, and H_2Po. Common sense says that H_2O should be an acid. But it isn't because of the 105° angle between the hydrogen molecules. That unusual angle makes ordinary water a rather miraculous substance.

The Properties of Water

Water is made up of lots of little molecules all swishing around together in some kind of container. The ocean is, after all, just a big container of water.

Think about a molecule of water 1,000 feet (or 1,000 meters if you prefer) below the surface of the ocean. It has a lot of other water molecules piled on top of it. All of those molecules are pulled down by gravity, so they put pressure on the molecule in question.

Although this might seem obvious, please bear with me. There's a reason for going through this. And here it is.

Water is considered an incompressible fluid. You can squish a gas like oxygen into a small container, but the same can't be said of water. If you do compress oxygen into a container, you're increasing the density of the gas. That is, you're putting more and more oxygen molecules into the container.

Water keeps pretty much the same density. It's nearly impossible to force an increasing number of water molecules into an enclosed space after that space is filled with water.

If you put water into a container, it exerts pressure on that container. That pressure exerts a force. Figure 13.1 shows a square container of water. The force on any side of the container is equal to the pressure times the surface area. So the formula is as follows:

$$\mathbf{F} = p\mathbf{S}$$

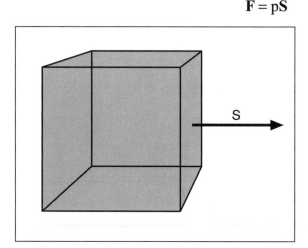

Figure 13.1
A square container of water.

In this formula, both **F** and **S** are vectors. Figure 13.1 shows that **S** represents the normal vector for the surface. All six sides of the container have a surface normal that points perpendicular to each surface. Figure 13.1 only shows the surface normal for the right side.

The magnitude of **S** is equal to the area of the surface. For a simple cubic container, each side is a square, which makes it easy to calculate the surface area and normal vector of the side. Just multiply the edge length of the cube by itself for the area. The surface normal points straight out from the surface. However, what about curved containers, like the one shown in Figure 13.2?

When you're calculating the force on a curved container of water, you approximate the curve with lots of tiny squares. For each square, use the surface normal and area of that square to calculate the force. Sum the forces for the individual squares, and you have the total force exerted on the container by the water pressure. This is a handy technique when you're programming a computer because we approximate curved containers with meshes divided into lots of little squares anyway. Getting the surface normal of a square in the mesh is simply a matter of adding the normals at the four vertices.

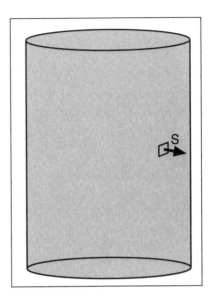

Figure 13.2
A curved container of water.

Okay, so we know how to find the force water exerts on its container. So what? How does that help us in games?

Well, water doesn't just exert forces on its container. If you put an object in water, the water exerts the same force on the object that it does on the container. That brings us to the physics of why things float.

Why Things Float

Most people know the answer to the question, "Why do things float?" Something floats if the water it displaces weighs more than the object itself. But let's take a close look at why that is so.

To figure out whether something is going to float in water, we first have to determine what total force the water exerts on it. To do that, let's begin by looking at Figure 13.3.

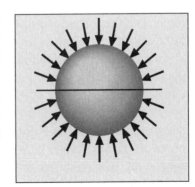

Figure 13.3
A spherical object in water.

In Figure 13.3, we've submerged a spherical object in water. As you can see in the figure, I've drawn a line through the sphere to differentiate the upper and lower halves. The arrows represent the forces the water exerts on the sphere due to pressure. We know that pressure increases the deeper we go. That means that the forces on the bottom are larger than the forces on the top. If I were to sum up all the forces on the upper and lower halves of the sphere, there would be a net force pushing upward. This is buoyancy.

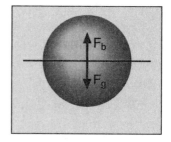

Figure 13.4
Yes, but will it float?

Suppose that we know the magnitude of the buoyant force on the sphere in Figure 13.3. Is that enough to determine whether the sphere floats?

Nope. There's another force acting on the sphere. As you probably have figured out, that force is gravity. Figure 13.4 gives a more complete picture of the forces acting on a sphere in water.

In Figure 13.4, I've summed up all the forces shown on the sphere in Figure 13.3 and represented them as F_b, which is the total force due to buoyancy. F_g in Figure 13.4 is the force due to gravity. If the downward force due to gravity is greater than the upward force on the sphere due to buoyancy, the sphere sinks. If the forces are equal, the sphere neither rises nor sinks. If F_b is greater, the sphere floats.

At this point, let's imagine that the sphere in Figure 13.4 is solid steel. We all know from experience that the sphere will sink. Well then, how do they make boats out of steel?

Figure 13.5 shows the steel sphere from Figure 13.4 plus a cutaway view of another steel sphere. The sphere on the left has the same mass as the sphere on the right. Both spheres have the same amount of steel in them, but the one on the left is hollow. Because we've spread out the steel into a hollow shell, the sphere on the left has much more surface area than the sphere on the right. And remember, the formula for the buoyancy force is $F=pS$. If you increase the surface area of the sphere, you increase S in the buoyancy formula. That increases the buoyancy force. In Figure 13.5, F_g for both spheres is the same because they have the same mass. But F_b for the sphere on the left is much larger than it is for the sphere on the right. As a result, the sphere on the left floats.

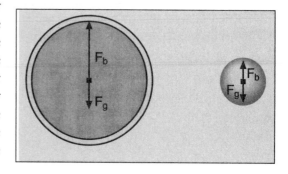

Figure 13.5
Two spheres with the same mass.

Finding Pressure and Density

At this point, we have a low-overhead formula, $F=pS$, that we can use to calculate whether the point masses and rigid bodies in our games should float. Nice. One problem, though. The formula depends on our ability to find the pressure at any given depth of water. Let's see how that's done.

In Figure 13.6, we have a container of water. In the water floats yet another sphere. This time, the forces of buoyancy and gravity acting on the sphere are equal. The sphere neither rises nor sinks. The total depth of the water is indicated by the term y_1. Let y_2 be the distance from the bottom. So the height of the water above the sphere is y_1-y_2. At the top of the water, the pressure is indicated by the term p_0. The pressure at the depth h, where the sphere floats, is p_h. With these terms, we can use the following formula to calculate the pressure at a given depth.

$$p_h = p_0 + \rho gh$$

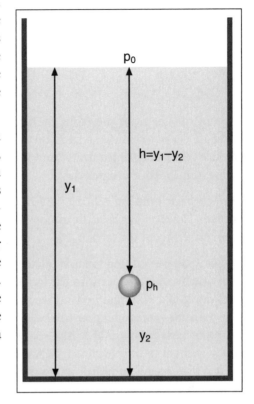

Figure 13.6
Pressure on a floating sphere.

This formula says that the pressure p_h at any given depth h is equal to the pressure on the top of the fluid plus the density of the fluid ρ multiplied by the acceleration of gravity g and the depth h.

For games, we can assume that the pressure at the top of the water is atmospheric pressure (1.0 atm). So let's rename the term p_0 to p_A. Now we can substitute the formula for pressure into the formula for the buoyancy force.

$$F_b = (p_A + \rho gh)S$$

The next question is this: What is the fluid density of water? For the answer, see Table 13.1.

Table 13.1 Water Densities in kg/m^3

Condition	Density
0° C at 1.0 atm	1000
100° C at 1.0 atm	958
0° C at 50 atm	1002

At you can see from the table, the density of water does not vary to any great degree. Because seawater contains such things as salts and minerals, its density is 1.03 g/cm^3. Notice that I've changed units from kg/m^3 to g/cm^3. That's because you often work with these units in your programs.

Atmospheric pressure is 1.013×10^5 N/m^2 in (SI) units, which is 14.7 lb/in^2 in the English system. However, because the atmosphere and the water are in a state of equilibrium, you can just drop out the term p_A.

What we've been doing so far is calculating the buoyancy of a point mass. However, that's not usually what you want to use in your games. But it gives us a basis for calculating the buoyancy of a 3-D rigid body. If we think about a rigid body of say, 1 meter in diameter, the pressure at the top is going to be slightly different from the pressure at the bottom. We saw that back in Figure 13.3. As a result, the total upward force due to buoyancy of a rigid body is equal to the weight of the volume of water it displaces. The weight of the water that is displaced is proportional to the density of the water times the gravitational acceleration. In other words, the final formula for the force of buoyancy that you can use in your games is as follows:

$$F_b = \rho g V$$

In this equation, V is the volume of water that is displaced. You have to calculate the volume of the rigid body when you write the game. You don't have to be exact for most games. The total volume of a real ship's hull is quite hard to calculate. Instead, estimate it with simpler shapes. For example, you can use a rectangular solid. Estimate the volume of the pointy bow of a ship using a pyramid with a square base. The shape of the volume you're calculating with this technique doesn't look exactly like a ship's hull, but it gives close enough results for games.

Resistance to Movement

Experience tells us that anything that moves through water moves slower than it does when moving through air. This is caused by water's viscosity. Viscosity is a measurement of the "thickness" of a fluid. Some fluids, like most motor oils, have higher viscosity than water.

The slowdown that objects experience as they move through viscous fluids is actually caused by friction. As the object moves through the fluid, the fluid moves around the object. Friction occurs between the object and the fluid that dissipates some of the energy of movement. This causes the object to move slower.

Back in Chapter 12, we dealt with particle-spring systems. To make them more stable, I threw in an additional dampening force I called linear dampening. That was actually friction.

A Quick Look at Friction

To understand friction in fluids, let's first look at how it works in general. Imagine a car driving down the street. Occasionally, the driver speeds the car up. Sometimes (when he sees a cop), the driver slows the car down. Friction is essential to all of this. Figure 13.7 clarifies how friction works in this case.

In this freeze-frame view of a tire in motion, the point P is the point at which the tire is in contact with the road. As the tire turns, it pushes on the road with the force F_t. The road pushes on the tire with the force F_r. The reason the road is able to push back on the tire is because of friction. If the road is covered with ice, the friction between the road and the tire, and consequently the force F_r, might be close to zero. The tire spins, but the car goes nowhere.

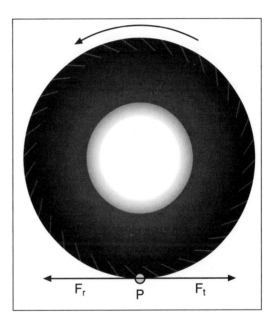

Figure 13.7
A freeze-frame of a rolling tire.

If an object is rolling across a surface, like tires do, the object and the surface are said to have *static friction* between them. Static friction occurs when the point of contact between an object and a surface is not sliding across the surface. So if point P in Figure 13.7 is rolling and not sliding relative to the ground, static friction exists between the ground and the tire. Here's the formula for static friction.

$$\mathbf{F}_s \leq \mu_s \mathbf{N}$$

In this formula, μ_s is the *static coefficient of friction*, and $\mathbf{N}$ is the normal force. The normal force for objects rolling across a surface is generally given by this equation:

$$N = -mg$$

The static coefficient of friction is a constant that is unique to the two objects involved in the interaction. So, for instance, the static coefficient of friction for a tire and the road is different from the static coefficient of friction for a tire and a sheet of ice.

If the driver slams on the brakes, the tires lock up. This causes them to slide across the road. At this point, there is no longer static friction between the tire and the road. Because the tire is now sliding, *dynamic friction* is involved. Dynamic friction occurs when an object is sliding across a surface. The formula for dynamic friction is this:

$$\mathbf{F_D} = \mu_D \mathbf{N}$$

As you can see, there is a *dynamic coefficient of friction* that determines the magnitude of the friction between sliding objects. The dynamic coefficient of friction for any two objects is generally less than the static coefficient of friction. This is why driving instructors the world over tell us to pump our brakes in emergencies so that we don't lock them up. As long as the tires are still spinning, the static coefficient of friction applies between the tires and the road. This results in more friction than if the tires lock up and the car slides. The car actually stops sooner if the tires are not sliding.

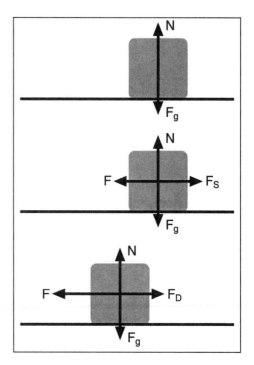

To see how all of these forces work together, look at Figure 13.8.

Figure 13.8 illustrates the forces acting on a square block as it is pushed across a surface. In the top panel of the figure, the block is at rest. Gravity pulls the block down with the force $\mathbf{F_g}$, which equals m**g**. The ground pushes up on the block with the normal force **N** whose magnitude and direction are −m**g**.

In the middle panel in Figure 13.8, a force **F** begins to push on the block. Because of the properties of the block and the surface, the force of static friction $\mathbf{F_S}$ opposes the force **F**. As long as $\mathbf{F_S}$ is greater than or equal to **F**, the block does not move. **F** must overcome static friction before it can move the block.

Figure 13.8
Forces on a moving block.

The bottom panel in Figure 13.8 shows the block in motion. **F** is now greater than **F**$_S$, so the block is sliding. The result is that static friction no longer applies. The force of dynamic friction **F**$_D$ now opposes the movement of the block.

Those are the basics of friction. Now let's get back to movement through water.

Viscous Drag

The friction caused by a viscous fluid is a form of dynamic friction. Figure 13.9 shows why.

The lines that bend around the sphere in Figure 13.9 are a simplified view of how fluid flows around the sphere as the sphere moves through the fluid. You can see that the sphere and the fluid slide past each other. Sliding means dynamic friction, not static friction.

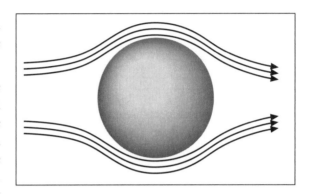

Figure 13.9
An object moving through a fluid.

Because the sphere in Figure 13.9 is not moving very fast, the flow lines of the fluid are smooth. That's another way of saying that the fluid does not become turbulent as the sphere moves through it. As long as the flow lines are not turbulent, the frictional force of viscous drag is given by the following formula:

$$\mathbf{F}_{FD} = -C_{FD}\mathbf{v}$$

Here **F**$_{FD}$ is the force due to frictional (or viscous) drag. C_{FD} is the coefficient of frictional drag, which is similar to the dynamic coefficient of friction in the previous formula. **v** is the velocity of the object. The negative sign indicates that the force of viscous frictional drag acts in a direction opposite to the velocity.

You can use this formula in most games to determine the force of viscous frictional drag on anything moving through water. This includes boats, ships, subs, and so forth. However, if the object moves fast enough through the water, the flow lines around it become turbulent. In that case, you need to use this formula:

$$\mathbf{F}_{FD} = -C_{FD}\mathbf{v}^2$$

When water becomes turbulent because the object is moving rapidly through it, friction goes up dramatically. The force of viscous frictional drag becomes a function of the velocity squared, rather than just the velocity. So this formula would be appropriate for a game that has speedboats racing or characters chasing each other on jet skis.

Currents in Water

It's often the case in our games that we want water to move. This results in currents, tides, riptides, and whirlpools. All of these have a few basic principles in common.

Consider a pipe, such as the one that appears in Figure 13.10. The diameter of this pipe is constant across its length. Therefore, for any cross-sectional area A of the pipe, you can determine the mass of the water that flows through it using this formula:

$$\Delta m_w = \rho A v \Delta t$$

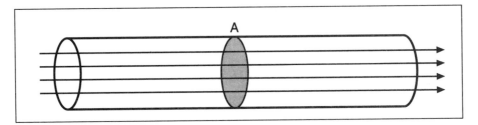

Figure 13.10
Water moving through a pipe of constant diameter.

This formula says that the mass, Δm, of the water that moves through the pipe during any time interval Δt is determined by the cross-sectional area of the pipe, the density of the fluid, and its velocity. This assumes that there are no sources or sinks in the pipe. That is, there's no place in the pipe other than the left end where water can enter. There is also no place other than the right end of the pipe where water can get out.

You can use this formula even if the pipe widens or narrows, as Figure 13.11 illustrates.

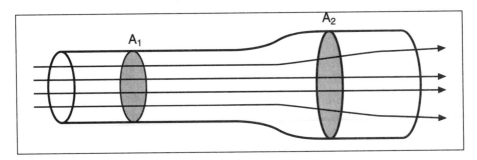

Figure 13.11
Water moving through a pipe of varying diameter.

Again, this assumes that there are no sources or sinks between the ends of the pipe. If that's the case, the mass of the water that flows through the cross-sectional area A_1 during the time interval Δt *has* to be the same as the mass of the water that flows through A_2 in the same amount of time. If a smaller mass of water flowed through A_2, that would mean that water was bunching up in the pipe. Water is not compressible, so that's impossible. If more water flows through A_2 than A_1, the pipe would soon empty out no matter how much water went in. That's also impossible. These physical facts give us the relationship shown here:

$$\rho A_1 v_1 \Delta t = \rho A_2 v_2 \Delta t$$

The density of water doesn't change at a constant temperature, so we can eliminate that from the equation. The time intervals on both sides of the equation are the same, so we can eliminate them. What we're left with is this:

$$A_1 v_1 = A_2 v_2$$

This relationship tells us that if A_2 is larger than A_1, v_2 must be smaller than v_1. In other words, the fluid slows down as the pipe gets larger. We generally know that from experience in the real world, but now we have mathematical proof.

How can you and I use these formulas in our games?

Suppose that you are writing a game in which the main character crosses a riverbed that is dammed off just upriver. Imagine further that there is a large keg of gunpowder on the dam. Just as the main character gets to the other side of the riverbed, the villain (boo, hiss) enters the riverbed in pursuit. Oh, look. The main character is getting out her bow and arrows. She has magic flaming arrows. Isn't that handy? She shoots an arrow at the powder keg. Boom! The dam is gone. Mr. Bad Guy has a huge wall of water coming at him. Will he be killed? Or will he simply be swept away and pursue the main character another day? Did Ms. Heroine fill the reservoir with enough water before she blew the dam?

The way to answer these questions is to calculate the force that Mr. Bad Guy gets hit with. How do we do that? I'll give you one guess. Yes, it's **F=ma** again. We need to combine that with our formula for calculating the mass of the water. The result looks like this:

$$\mathbf{F}_w = \rho A v \Delta t \mathbf{a}_w$$

The force that the water exerts on Mr. Bad Guy is equal to the mass of the water ($\rho A v \Delta t$) times the acceleration. The acceleration of what? Mr. Bad Guy's acceleration, that's what. Let's assume that Mr. Bad Guy goes from zero to the velocity of the water during the time interval. This formula then becomes as follows:

$$\mathbf{F}_W = \rho A \mathbf{v}_W \Delta t \left(\frac{\mathbf{v}_{MBG} - 0}{\Delta t} \right)$$

Because Mr. Bad Guy goes from zero to the velocity of the water during the time interval, his final velocity ($\mathbf{v}_{MBG}$) equals that of the water. Also, the Δt's in the formula cancel. Here's the final formula:

$$\mathbf{F}_W = \rho A \mathbf{v}^2$$

For the cross-sectional area A, we can use the area of a half-circle or a half-ellipse that is as wide as the riverbed. If the reservoir was full enough, or if there was some way of making the water move fast, Mr. Bad Guy would be toast. Otherwise, Ms. Heroine will have to deal with him again.

Waves

Another way that water moves is by wave propagation. The waves that travel through water are called *transverse waves*. In a transverse wave, the stuff that gets moved by the wave moves in a direction that is perpendicular to the direction of the wave. Figure 13.12 illustrates a transverse wave.

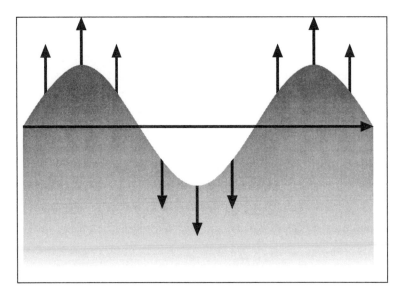

Figure 13.12
A transverse wave in water.

As the waves move from left to right through the water in Figure 13.12, the water itself moves up and down. That's perpendicular to the direction of the wave.

In reality, wave movement through water is not completely transverse. If you put a ping-pong ball (or other light object) into water and repeatedly make waves, the ball does move slightly in the direction of the wave. The same is true of the water in which the ball floats. However, the vast majority of the water's movement is vertical rather than horizontal.

When waves travel across the surface of water, we see them as circular. This is evident when you through a rock into a pond, lake, or even the ocean on a calm day. However, the waves only look like circles because we don't normally see what happens below the water. In reality, waves travel in spheres.

The example in Figure 13.13 shows a shock wave that results from an underwater explosion. The wave expands out spherically in all directions away from the source of the blast. Interestingly enough, the wave can never have a larger force than it had at the time of the initial blast. We can also say that the total power of the wave is constant over time. (Power and force are not quite the same thing.) The wave's power is spread out over the entire spherical surface of the wave front. As the wave front expands, the power gets spread out over a larger and larger sphere. So the intensity of the wave decreases as it moves away from its initial source. The intensity at any given moment can be found using the following formula:

$$I = \frac{P}{4\pi r^2}$$

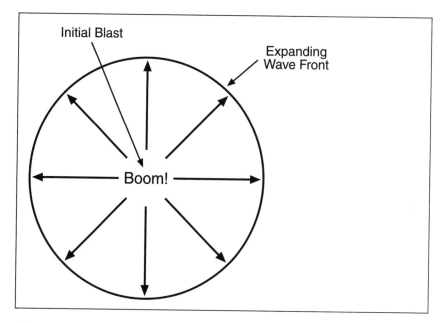

Figure 13.13
A spherical underwater wave.

This formula is extremely useful when you want to model the physics of a shock wave from a blast in a 3-D game. The shock wave starts out with an initial force, power, and intensity. Let's call them F_1, P_1, and I_1. After a time t, the wave has a force of F_2, P_2, and I_2. In games, we model physics by modeling forces. The thing you'll most need to calculate after the blast is F_2.

For example, suppose that you're writing a game in which an explosion occurs underwater. The main character is driving his minisub away from the source of the explosion as fast as he can. After the explosion occurs, you want to know if the force of the shock wave crushes his sub.

A simple way to answer this question is to model the shock wave as an object that contains two forces: a velocity and an initial position. One of the forces, called the longitudinal force, points directly away from the source of the blast. The other is the transverse force. As the shock wave moves away, it needs to decrease in strength.

The velocity in the shock wave object stores the velocity of the wave front. In reality, this depends on both the characteristics of the blast and the medium through which it moves. For games, however, it's straightforward to just set this and leave it as a constant until the wave dissipates.

To find the magnitude of the forces that a shock wave exerts as it moves away from its source, we can use the relationships of the intensities over time. Recall that we're calling the initial force, power, and intensity F_1, P_1, and I_1. We've said that the force, power, and intensity after a time t are F_2, P_2, and I_2. We know that the following relationships hold in this situation:

$$F_2 \leq F_1$$
$$P_2 = P_1$$
$$I_2 \leq I_1$$

We also can say that the ratio of F_1 to F_2 is the same as the ratio of I_1 to I_2. Writing that as a formula, we get this:

$$\frac{F_2}{F_1} = \frac{I_2}{I_1}$$

Now we can solve for F_2:

$$F_2 = F_1 \frac{I_2}{I_1}$$

If we substitute in the equations for power, we get the following:

$$F_2 = F_1 \frac{\dfrac{P_2}{4\pi r_2^2}}{\dfrac{P_1}{4\pi r_1^2}}$$

In this equation, r_1 is the radius of the initial shock wave. r_2 is the radius of the shock wave after time t.

This is beginning to look quite complex. However, P_1 equals P_2, so those terms just drop out. Because 4π is in both the numerator and the denominator, that drops out as well. The result is this:

$$F_2 = F_1 \frac{r_1^2}{r_2^2}$$

This is much easier to work with because F_1 and r_1 are known. You set them when you write your game. You simply decide that when the blast goes off, the initial shock wave has a given force and radius. You also set its initial position and velocity. After time t passes, your program uses the initial position and velocity to calculate the radius of the wave front. It can then use the preceding formula to calculate the forces exerted by the shock wave at a given point. The same formula can be applied to both the longitudinal and transverse forces. That is:

$$F_{2T} = F_{1T} \frac{r_1^2}{r_2^2}$$

$$F_{2L} = F_{1L} \frac{r_1^2}{r_2^2}$$

where F_{1T} and F_{1L} are the initial transverse and longitudinal forces, and F_{2T} and F_{2L} are the transverse and longitudinal forces after time t.

Implementing Water

Many approaches have been taken over the years to simulate water in games. I'll summarize the most common from easiest to hardest.

Low-Overhead Ways to Cheat

Most games simulate water by cheating. They find ways to make it look like there's water in the scene without dedicating a lot of CPU time. There are a few different ways to do this.

The easiest way to simulate water in a game is to just ignore it. You really can get away with that. For example, have you ever see a screen saver that showed fish swimming by? If you look closely, you'll see that the screen saver has a nice blue background to indicate that the fish are underwater. The bottom area of the screen might also show scenery from a coral reef. The person who wrote the screen saver is taking advantage of the fact that you know that fish and coral are underwater. Neither the water nor its effects, such as waves, ripples, and bubbles, are shown. The programmer just leaves it to you to understand that the animation is taking place under water.

Many games over the years have used this approach. Although it does work, it isn't as pleasing to the eye as the more advanced techniques.

Games that don't actually allow the player's character to go in the water often define the water as a polygon with a texture on it. Figure 13.14 illustrates how this is done.

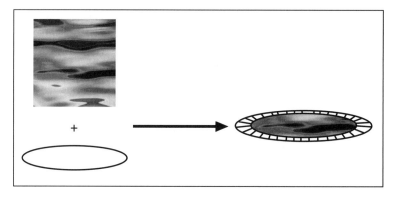

Figure 13.14
A pool of water as a polygon with a texture.

The basic technique is to start with a polygon that's the shape of the pool of water. You then add a texture to it. The texture does not have to be the same shape as the polygon. In fact, it's usually square, as shown in Figure 13.14. Combining the texture and the polygon gives you a nice pool of water. In the figure, I threw in some paving stones to make it look even more like a well. To make it look even more realistic, the game can put a new texture on the polygon every frame. This animates the water.

What can you do with simple pool like this? Almost anything. It might be just scenery. Or it might be the sacred well that the Water Nymph of Avalon lives in. And if your character has found the Sword of Laron to show that he's the true heir to the kingdom, she'll rise from the water and give him the Oracle of Souls that restores his health if he's collected enough manna.

3-D Water

The point of this chapter is to show how to use physics to put things in water and move them around. So how do we simulate water in 3-D and let game characters, boats, and so forth move around in it?

Here again, there are several approaches. A common one is to extend the method shown back in Figure 13.14 into 3-D. That is, instead of just applying a texture to a polygon, you apply it to the top of a 3-D volume.

Figure 13.15 shows the pool of water from Figure 13.14. However, instead of applying a texture to an ellipse, the figure applies it to the top of a cylinder. Now your game's character can jump into the water and swim to the bottom to retrieve the Oracle of Souls himself. While he's in the water, you apply the equations for buoyancy, gravity, viscous frictional drag, and so forth, as discussed earlier in this chapter.

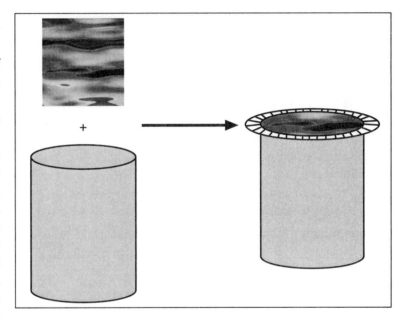

Figure 13.15
A pool of water in 3-D.

If you're dealing with a larger body of water, such as a lake or ocean, things get more complicated. You still need to use a 3-D volume as an external representation for the water.

note

Remember: As we saw in Chapter 12, you can have internal representations of objects that programs use for calculation purposes. You can also display an external representation, which is usually a mesh, to the player.

To get something that looks like a lake or ocean, you need to create the mesh for the 3-D volume in a 3-D modeling package such as MilkShape3D, which comes on the CD-ROM with this book. You'll find it in the folder Tools\MilkShape3D.

note

> The copy of MilkShape3D on the CD-ROM is a 30-day trial version of the program. To purchase a registered version, please contact chUmbaLum sOft at http://www.swissquake.ch/chumbalum-soft/.

After you have the 3-D mesh for your lake, you define a piece of cloth as an internal representation of the surface of the water. Cloth? Did I say cloth?

Yes, cloth. Because of the way I implemented cloth in Chapter 12, you can use it here for water.

The basic technique is to define a piece of cloth as an internal representation for the surface of the water. The way it's built, waves already propagate across it just like they do with water. It'll take some parameter tweaking to get the nice slow waves that appear on the surface of water. But when you get it working right, your program matches the position of each vertex on the surface of the lake/ocean mesh to the position of one of the particles of the cloth. You can apply all of the equations for buoyancy and so forth to any objects in the water. The result can be extremely realistic and satisfying.

There's just one drawback to this method. It's a very high-overhead way of doing water. However, with the constant increase in CPU speeds, that might not be an issue for you.

Putting Objects in Water

We've waded though enough of the background information. It's time to actually put some of this into practice. Let's start by adding the buoyancy and viscous drag equations to rigid bodies. Then we'll do a quick program to show them in action.

Adding Buoyancy to Rigid Bodies

Buoyancy is not hard to add to the physics modeling framework's rigid bodies. Probably the simplest approach is to use C++ inheritance. So, for this chapter, I created a class called immersible_rigid_body. This class is derived from the rigid_body class. When an immersible_rigid_body object is not in water, it behaves just like a rigid_body object. The code for the immersible_rigid_body class appears in Listing 13.1.

Listing 13.1
The immersible_rigid_body Class

```
1    class immersible_rigid_body : public rigid_body
2    {
```

```
3      private:
4          scalar volume;
5          bool isInWater;
6          bool buoyancyApplied;
7          scalar dragCoefficient;
8          bool constantForceChanged;
9          bool impulseForceChanged;
10
11     public:
12         immersible_rigid_body();
13
14         void Volume(
15             scalar shapeVolume);
16         scalar Volume(void);
17
18         void BuoyancyForce(force buoyancy);
19         force BuoyancyForce(void);
20
21         void IsImmersed(bool inWater);
22         bool IsImmersed(void);
23
24         void Mass(
25             scalar massValue);
26         scalar Mass(void);
27
28         void ConstantForce(
29             force sumConstantForces);
30         force ConstantForce(void);
31
32         void ImpulseForce(
33             force sumImpulseForces);
34         force ImpulseForce(void);
35
36         void DragCoefficient(
37             scalar resistance);
38         scalar DragCoefficient(void);
39
40         bool Update(
41             scalar changeInTime);
42     };
```

The immersible_rigid_body class inherits publicly from the rigid_body class. Its private data members add a variety of information to the information stored by the rigid_body class.

First, the `immersible_rigid_body` class must contain the object's volume. This is used to calculate the buoyancy, which is equal to the weight of the water the object displaces. The value of the `volume` data member must always be greater than 0.0.

note

> The value in the `rigid_body` class's `volume` member should be the portion of the object's total volume that is in the water. If the object is completely submerged, use its entire volume. Otherwise, use the part of the volume that's actually in the water.

In addition, the `immersible_rigid_body` class has a state variable, shown on line 5 of Listing 13.1, that keeps track of whether the object is in water. Any time the object enters the water, your game must call the function that sets this value. Set it to `true` when the object enters the water and `false` when it leaves the water.

Whenever an object enters the water, the `immersible_rigid_body` class must apply the force of buoyancy to the object. While the object is in the water, buoyancy is a constant force. Therefore, the `immersible_rigid_body` class stores the force of buoyancy in the `constantForce` member of the `rigid_body` class. After it's been stored in the `constantForce` member, it should not be applied again. So the `immersible_rigid_body` class has a data member called `buoyancyApplied` to keep track of that. The class automatically initializes `buoyancyApplied` to `false` when your program creates an `immersible_rigid_body` object. After the `immersible_rigid_body` class applies buoyancy to the object, it sets `buoyancyApplied` to `true`. The value of `buoyancyApplied` does not change unless the object comes up out of the water, changes its mass, or changes its volume. If any of those changes occur, `buoyancyApplied` is set to `false`.

The `dragCoefficient` member on line 7 stores the coefficient of frictional drag. Its value must be between 0.0 and 1.0 inclusive. The larger the value, the more drag there is. Larger values of drag occur when the object is in a thick fluid. In the sample program for this chapter, I set the drag coefficient to 0.5. That should be about right for most games. However, you might have to tweak that value to suit the needs of your game.

tip

> The value of the drag coefficient depends on what the object is made of, what its shape is, and what fluid it's moving through. Even if you say that all objects in your game move only through water, there is no one value that works for all of your objects. If you take time to tune the drag coefficient for all objects that go into the water, you'll find you get much more realistic movement. The time investment is worth the results.

Drag is a constant force while the object is in motion. However, it must be applied to all forces that might make the object move. Drag decreases the effects of both constant and impulse forces. The `immersible_rigid_body` class applies drag to the object's constant and impulse forces whenever they change. To keep track of when that happens, the `immersible_rigid_body` class defines the data members `constantForceChanged` and `impulseForceChanged`. A value of `true` in either one of these causes the `immersible_rigid_body` class to apply drag to their corresponding forces.

The `immersible_rigid_body` class contains public member functions that get and set the values of the member data. Note, however, that the `immersible_rigid_body` class overrides the overloaded `Mass()`, `ConstantForce()`, and `ImpulseForce()` functions. It also overrides the `Update()` function. To see why, look at Listing 13.2.

Listing 13.2
The Member Functions for the immersible_rigid_body Class

```
1      inline immersible_rigid_body::immersible_rigid_body() : rigid_body()
2      {
3          volume = 0.0;
4          isInWater = false;
5          buoyancyApplied = false;
6          dragCoefficient = 0.0;
7          constantForceChanged = false;
8          impulseForceChanged = false;
9      }
10
11     inline void immersible_rigid_body::Volume(
12         scalar shapeVolume)
13     {
14         assert(volume > 0.0);
15
16         volume = shapeVolume;
17         buoyancyApplied = false;
18     }
19
20     inline scalar immersible_rigid_body::Volume(void)
21     {
22         return (volume);
23     }
24
25     inline void immersible_rigid_body::IsImmersed(
26         bool inWater)
27     {
28         assert((isInWater!=true) && (inWater!=true));
29
30         isInWater = inWater;
```

```
31          if (inWater==false)
32          {
33              buoyancyApplied = false;
34          }
35      }
36
37      inline bool immersible_rigid_body::IsImmersed(void)
38      {
39          return (isInWater);
40      }
41
42      inline void immersible_rigid_body::Mass(
43              scalar massValue)
44      {
45          rigid_body::Mass(massValue);
46          buoyancyApplied = false;
47      }
48
49      inline scalar immersible_rigid_body::Mass(void)
50      {
51          return (rigid_body::Mass());
52      }
53
54      inline void immersible_rigid_body::ConstantForce(
55              force sumConstantForces)
56      {
57          rigid_body::ConstantForce(sumConstantForces);
58          constantForceChanged = true;
59      }
60
61      inline force immersible_rigid_body::ConstantForce(void)
62      {
63          return (rigid_body::ConstantForce());
64      }
65
66      inline void immersible_rigid_body::ImpulseForce(
67              force sumImpulseForces)
68      {
69          rigid_body::ImpulseForce(sumImpulseForces);
70          impulseForceChanged = true;
71      }
72
```

```
73    inline force immersible_rigid_body::ImpulseForce(void)
74    {
75        return (rigid_body::ImpulseForce());
76    }
77
78    inline void immersible_rigid_body::DragCoefficient(
79        scalar resistance)
80    {
81        assert((dragCoefficient>=0.0) && (dragCoefficient<=1.0));
82        dragCoefficient = resistance;
83    }
84
85    inline scalar immersible_rigid_body::DragCoefficient(void)
86    {
87        return (dragCoefficient);
88    }
89
90    bool immersible_rigid_body::Update(
91        scalar changeInTime)
92    {
93        // If the object is in water...
94        if (isInWater)
95        {
96            vector_3d tempVector;
97            force tempForce;
98
99            // If the buoyancy has not been applied (or recalculated)...
100           if (!buoyancyApplied)
101           {
102               // Calculate the buoyancy force.
103               tempVector.SetXYZ(0.0,1.0f,0.0);
104               tempForce.Force(
105                   9.8f*volume*tempVector);
106               tempVector = Location();
107               tempForce.ApplicationPoint(tempVector);
108               tempForce.Force(
109                   tempForce.Force() + rigid_body::ConstantForce().Force());
110               ConstantForce(tempForce);
111
112               buoyancyApplied=true;
113           }
114
```

```
115          // If the constant force has changed since the last frame...
116          if (constantForceChanged)
117          {
118              // Apply viscous water resistance (drag).
119              tempForce.Force(
120                  ConstantForce().Force() -
121                  (dragCoefficient * ConstantForce().Force()));
122              ConstantForce(tempForce);
123              constantForceChanged = false;
124          }
125
126          // If the impulse force has changed since the last frame...
127          if (impulseForceChanged)
128          {
129              // Apply viscous water resistance (drag).
130              tempForce.Force(
131                  ImpulseForce().Force() -
132                  (dragCoefficient * ImpulseForce().Force()));
133              ImpulseForce(tempForce);
134              impulseForceChanged = false;
135          }
136      }
137
138      /* Update the position and orientation of the immersible rigid
139      body based on the forces acting on it. */
140      return (rigid_body::Update(changeInTime));
141  }
```

warning

> Listing 13.2 contains the inline member functions from the file PMImmersibleRigidBody.h and the
> Update() function from the file PMImersibleRigidBody.cpp. I've put them all in the same code list-
> ing for convenience. The actual program is not laid out this way.

Most of the functions in Listing 13.2 are for getting and setting their associated member
data of immersible_rigid_body objects. However, it's important to note some of the additional work they do. For example, the Volume() function on lines 11–18 does more than
just set the volume of the immersible_rigid_body object. Whenever the volume changes, the
buoyancy needs to be recalculated. So the Volume() function also sets the buoyancyApplied
member to false.

Likewise, buoyancy needs to be recalculated whenever the `immersible_rigid_body` object enters or leaves the water. So the `IsImmersed()` function on lines 25–35 also sets `buoyancyApplied` to `false`.

The `immersible_rigid_body` class overrides the `Mass()` function for the same reason. If the mass of an object changes, it might no longer be buoyant. Or it might become more buoyant than it was before. Either way, the force of gravity needs to be recalculated, and so does buoyancy. The statement on line 46 of Listing 13.2 helps ensure that happens.

If the constant force does change, drag must be reapplied. So the `immersible_rigid_body` class overrides the `ConstantForce()` function of the `rigid_body` class. The version in the `immersible_rigid_body` class not only sets the constant force, but it also sets the data member `constantForceChanged` to `true`. This causes the `immersible_rigid_body::Update()` function to reapply drag.

As mentioned previously, drag occurs on both constant and impulse forces. So the `immersible_rigid_body` class overrides the overloaded `rigid_body::Impulse()` functions as well.

The `Update()` function, which begins on line 90, tests to see if the object is in the water. If it is, the function checks whether buoyancy has been applied. If that hasn't been done yet, `Update()` creates a unit vector that points straight up. It then calculates the magnitude of the buoyancy vector on lines 104–105. Notice that the calculation does not include the density of water. `Update()` uses the formula $F_b = \rho g V$ to calculate buoyancy. However, because of the units used in the code, ρ is 1 rather than 1,000. So the code on line 105 does not include it in the multiplication. After all, it's a waste of time to multiply a number by 1.

The `Update()` function adds buoyancy to the existing constant force on lines 108–109. It then saves the result as the constant force for the object on line 110. It also sets `buoyancyApplied` to `true`.

Lines 116–136 of Listing 13.2 handle drag forces. If drag has not been applied to the constant and impulse forces, the `Update()` function calculates it and subtracts it.

Will It Float?

The sample program for this chapter demonstrates buoyancy, frictional fluid drag, and simple currents. Listing 13.3 illustrates how the sample program is initialized.

Listing 13.3
Initializing the Sample Program

```
1    bool GameInitialization()
2    {
3        // Set up the view matrix as in previous examples.
4        D3DXVECTOR3 eyePoint(0.0f,0.0f,-20.0f);
```

```
5          D3DXVECTOR3 lookatPoint(0.0f,0.0f,0.0f);
6          D3DXVECTOR3 upDirection(0.0f,1.0f,0.0f);
7          D3DXMATRIXA16 tempViewMatrix;
8          D3DXMatrixLookAtLH(
9              &tempViewMatrix,&eyePoint,&lookatPoint,&upDirection);
10         theApp.ViewMatrix(tempViewMatrix);
11
12         // Set up the projection matrix.
13         D3DXMATRIXA16 projectionMatrix;
14         D3DXMatrixPerspectiveFovLH(
15             &projectionMatrix,D3DX_PI/4,1.0f,1.0f,100.0f);
16         theApp.ProjectionMatrix(projectionMatrix);
17
18         //
19         // Set the properties of the first ball.
20         //
21         vector_3d zeroVector(0.0,0.0,0.0);
22         allBalls[0].LinearVelocity(zeroVector);
23         allBalls[0].LinearAcceleration(zeroVector);
24         allBalls[0].BoundingSphereRadius(BOUNDING_SPHERE_RADIUS);
25         allBalls[0].CoefficientOfRestitution(COFFICIENT_OF_RESTITUTION);
26         allBalls[0].AngularAcceleration(zeroVector);
27         allBalls[0].AngularVelocity(zeroVector);
28         allBalls[0].CurrentOrientation(
29             angle_set_3d(0.0,0.0,0.0));
30         force tempForce;
31         tempForce.Force(zeroVector);
32         allBalls[0].ImpulseForce(tempForce);
33         allBalls[0].IsImmersed(true);
34         // Volume of a sphere is 4.3*pi*r^3.
35         allBalls[0].Volume(
36             4.0f/3.0f * D3DX_PI *
37             BOUNDING_SPHERE_RADIUS *
38             BOUNDING_SPHERE_RADIUS *
39             BOUNDING_SPHERE_RADIUS);
40         allBalls[0].LoadMesh("ball2.x");
41         allBalls[0].DragCoefficient(COEFFICIENT_OF_WATER_DRAG);
42
43         // Copy the settings to the other balls.
44         allBalls[2]=allBalls[1]=allBalls[0];
45
46         // Set the remaining properties of the first ball.
```

```
47          allBalls[0].Mass(BALL1_MASS);
48          allBalls[0].Location(BALL1_LOCATION);
49          scalar inertiaValue =
50              (2 * BALL1_MASS *
51              BOUNDING_SPHERE_RADIUS * BOUNDING_SPHERE_RADIUS)/5;
52          allBalls[0].RotationalInertia(
53              vector_3d(inertiaValue,inertiaValue,inertiaValue));
54
55          // Add gravity to the first ball.
56          tempForce.Force(
57              vector_3d(
58                  0.0f,
59                  GRAVITATIONAL_ACCELERATION*BALL1_MASS,
60                  0.0f));
61          tempForce.ApplicationPoint(BALL1_LOCATION);
62          allBalls[0].ConstantForce(tempForce);
63
64          // Set the remaining properties of the second ball.
65          allBalls[1].Mass(BALL2_MASS);
66          allBalls[1].Location(BALL2_LOCATION);
67          inertiaValue =
68              (2 * BALL2_MASS *
69              BOUNDING_SPHERE_RADIUS * BOUNDING_SPHERE_RADIUS)/5;
70          allBalls[1].RotationalInertia(
71              vector_3d(inertiaValue,inertiaValue,inertiaValue));
72
73          // Add gravity to the second ball.
74          tempForce.Force(
75              vector_3d(
76                  0.0f,
77                  GRAVITATIONAL_ACCELERATION*BALL2_MASS,
78                  0.0f));
79          tempForce.ApplicationPoint(BALL2_LOCATION);
80          allBalls[1].ConstantForce(tempForce);
81
82          // Set the remaining properties of the third ball.
83          allBalls[2].Mass(BALL3_MASS);
84          allBalls[2].Location(BALL3_LOCATION);
85          inertiaValue =
86              (2 * BALL3_MASS *
87              BOUNDING_SPHERE_RADIUS * BOUNDING_SPHERE_RADIUS)/5;
88          allBalls[2].RotationalInertia(
```

```
89            vector_3d(inertiaValue,inertiaValue,inertiaValue));
90
91        // Add gravity to the third ball.
92        tempForce.Force(
93            vector_3d(
94                0.0f,
95                GRAVITATIONAL_ACCELERATION*BALL3_MASS,
96                0.0f));
97        tempForce.ApplicationPoint(BALL3_LOCATION);
98        allBalls[2].ConstantForce(tempForce);
99
100       // Apply a current to the third ball.
101       tempForce.Force(
102           vector_3d(1.0f,0.0,0.0) + allBalls[2].ConstantForce().Force());
103       allBalls[2].ConstantForce(tempForce);
104
105       //
106       // Set up a diffuse directional light.
107       //
108       D3DLIGHT9 light;
109       ZeroMemory( &light, sizeof(light) );
110       light.Type = D3DLIGHT_DIRECTIONAL;
111
112       D3DXVECTOR3 vecDir;
113       vecDir = D3DXVECTOR3(0.0f, -1.0f, 1.0f);
114       D3DXVec3Normalize((D3DXVECTOR3*)&light.Direction,&vecDir);
115
116       // Set directional light diffuse color.
117       light.Diffuse.r = 1.0f;
118       light.Diffuse.g = 1.0f;
119       light.Diffuse.b = 1.0f;
120       light.Diffuse.a = 1.0f;
121       theApp.D3DRenderingDevice()->SetLight( 0, &light );
122       theApp.D3DRenderingDevice()->LightEnable( 0, TRUE );
123       theApp.D3DRenderingDevice()->SetRenderState(
124           D3DRS_DIFFUSEMATERIALSOURCE,
125           D3DMCS_MATERIAL);
126
127       return (true);
128   }
```

This program displays three balls in water. The leftmost balls floats up, the middle one sinks, and the rightmost ball floats in a state of equilibrium. It neither rises nor sinks. The program also applies a gentle current to the rightmost ball. The current carries it off the right edge of the program's window.

As with previous sample programs, the GameInitialization() function begins by setting up the view and projection matrices. It then initializes many of the properties of the first ball on lines 21–41. These are the properties that all the balls share. For example, they all share the same radius and drag coefficient. The program copies the shared properties to the other balls on line 44.

Next, the GameInitialization() function sets the properties that are unique to each ball. For instance, each ball has a different mass, location, and rotational inertia.

warning

Never set the rotational inertia of a rigid body to zero. It's physically impossible. While developing this sample program, I thoughtlessly made that mistake myself even though I know it's impossible. So I added some assertions to the rigid_body::RotationalInertia() function in PMRigidBody.h to help prevent that.

After initializing the unique properties of each ball, the program sets up a directional light on lines 108–125. It's now ready to start updating and rendering the balls. Listing 13.4 provides the code for the UpdateFrame() and RenderFrame() functions.

Listing 13.4
Updating and Rendering a Frame

```
1      bool UpdateFrame()
2      {
3          // Is it time to update the frame?
4          DWORD currentTime = ::timeGetTime();
5          if (!TimeToUpdateFrame(currentTime))
6              return (true);
7
8          // Update the positions of each of the balls.
9          for (int i=0; i<TOTAL_BALLS; i++)
10         {
11             allBalls[i].Update(STEP_SIZE);
12         }
13         return (true);
14     }
15
16
17     bool RenderFrame()
```

```
18    {
19        // Set the view matrix in case it has changed.
20        theApp.D3DRenderingDevice()->SetTransform(
21            D3DTS_VIEW,
22            &theApp.ViewMatrix());
23
24        // Set the projection matrix in case it has changed.
25        theApp.D3DRenderingDevice()->SetTransform(
26            D3DTS_PROJECTION,
27            &theApp.ProjectionMatrix());
28
29        // Render each ball.
30        for (int i=0; i<TOTAL_BALLS; i++)
31        {
32            allBalls[i].Render();
33        }
34
35        return (true);
36    }
```

The UpdateFrame() and RenderFrame() functions are straightforward. UpdateFrame() checks to see if it's time to render a frame. If it is, it enters a loop on line 9 of Listing 13.4 that calls the immersible_rigid_body::Update() function shown back in Listing 13.2. As we saw previously, the immersible_rigid_body::Update() function calculates the force of buoyancy and water resistance (drag) on an immersible_rigid_body object. It then calls the rigid_body::Update() function to update the location of the immersible_rigid_body object based on those forces and any others that might be acting on the object. These include the forces exerted by gravity and water currents.

The RenderFrame() function doesn't differ much from the RenderFrame() functions in previous programs. After setting the view and projection matrices, RenderFrame() simply calls the immersible_rigid_body::Render() function for each ball. That renders the balls to the back buffer, which is displayed on the screen by the physics modeling framework.

You'll notice when you run this program that I took the path of least resistance to simulating water. All I did was make the background a deep blue and add a touch of green to the color. That's often enough in games to get players to accept that the action is taking place underwater.

tip

Probably the best treatment I've seen of the various methods of simulating water can be found in the book *Special Effects Game Programming with DirectX* by Mason McCusky (Premier Press). I consider this book a must read for every game programmer.

Summary

Although water can be hard to simulate, simulating the behavior of objects in water is not a difficult task. Knowing the basic principles of buoyancy, pressure, viscous drag, currents, and waves enables you to model the way most objects behave in water. The formulas for these aspects of the physics of water are not difficult to master and can be widely applied.

PART THREE

HANDS-ON 3-D SIMULATION

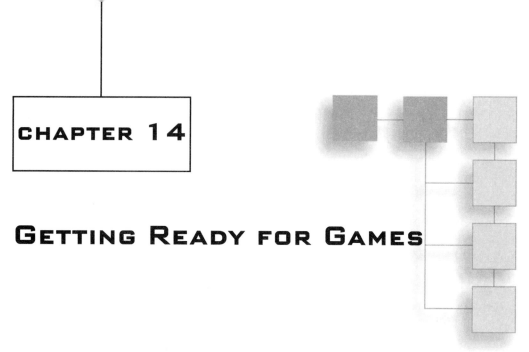

CHAPTER 14

GETTING READY FOR GAMES

L ike Chapter 6, "Meshes and X Files," this chapter contains no physics or math. At this point, we need a brief interlude in our discussion of physics modeling to cover some additional details about implementing games. Specifically, there are two essential tasks we need to take care of before moving on.

The first task is to upgrade the physics modeling framework. We want it to be usable for full-scale games rather than just the small simulations we've done so far. To do that, we have to upgrade its design. In addition, we have to add some processing that's required by DirectX.

The second task is to cover some of the additional capabilities of DirectX. Writing 3-D games requires that our programs process input from the user. So far, we've ignored that. Before we can go any further, we need to discuss getting user input with DirectInput. Also, the point of view has been stationary in the programs we've completed so far. In most 3-D games, the point of view moves around with the main character.

Redesigning the Physics Modeling Framework

The physics modeling framework that I've presented so far has been a helpful teaching tool. It demonstrates basic concepts of DirectX and graphics programming. It also implements the physics presented to this point. However, to write games with it, we need to upgrade some of its capabilities.

Simplifying Program Initialization

The first thing that we must improve in the framework is the method of initialization. Direct3D has a huge number of state variables that we can initialize. To keep our focus on physics, rather than Direct3D, I've just ignored most of them. This is safe because Direct3D initializes its state variables to reasonable defaults. That's a good way to design software. It helps reduce complexity.

As you gain proficiency with Direct3D and other DirectX components, it's likely that you'll want to use an increasing number of custom initializations. You might also want to use custom window initialization parameters.

The framework's initialization occurs in the files PMD3DApp.h and PMD3DApp.cpp. Suppose that you want to change back-face culling so that it's an initialization parameter. Here's what you have to do:

1. Add a new member to the d3d_init_params structure.

2. Add a new member to the d3d_app class.

3. Add code to the d3d_app constructor that initializes the new structure member.

4. Add code to the d3d_app::InitApp() function that copies the value of the new structure member to the new d3d_app class member.

5. Add code to the d3d_app::InitD3D() function that uses the new d3d_app class member.

This process can be simplified significantly. First, I'll rewrite the d3d_app class so that it does not contain an individual member for each Direct3D initialization parameter and each window initialization parameter. Listing 14.1 gives the new version of the d3d_app class.

Listing 14.1
The d3d_app Class with Simplified Initialization

```
1     class d3d_app
2     {
3     private:
4         // App properties
5         bool appInitialized;
6
7         // Window properties
8         std::string windowTitle;
9         int defaultX, defaultY;
10        int defaultHeight,defaultWidth;
11
12        // D3D properties
13        LPDIRECT3D9           direct3D; // Used to create the D3DDevice
14        LPDIRECT3DDEVICE9     d3dDevice; // Our rendering device
15        LPDIRECT3DVERTEXBUFFER9 vertexBuffer; // Buffer to hold vertices
16
```

```
17          window_init_params windowInitParams;
18          d3d_init_params d3dInitParams;
19
20          D3DXMATRIX viewMatrix;
21          D3DXMATRIX projectionMatrix;
22
23      public:
24          d3d_app();
25          bool InitApp(
26              window_init_params windowParams,
27              d3d_init_params d3dParams);
28
29          LPDIRECT3DDEVICE9 D3DRenderingDevice(void);
30
31          LPDIRECT3DVERTEXBUFFER9 D3DVertexBuffer(void);
32          void D3DVertexBuffer(
33              LPDIRECT3DVERTEXBUFFER9 vertexBufferPointer);
34
35          DWORD RenderingDeviceClearFlags(void);
36          D3DCOLOR BackgroundSurfaceColor(void);
37
38          void ViewMatrix(D3DMATRIX newViewMatrix);
39          D3DMATRIX ViewMatrix(void);
40
41          void ProjectionMatrix(
42              D3DMATRIX newProjectionMatrix);
43          D3DMATRIX ProjectionMatrix(void);
44
45          friend INT WINAPI AppMain(
46              HINSTANCE hInst,
47              HINSTANCE,
48              LPSTR,
49              INT);
50          friend HRESULT InitD3D(
51              HWND hWnd);
52          friend VOID CleanupD3D();
53      };
```

If you examine the private section of the d3d_app class in Listing 14.1, you'll see that it contains fewer data members. Rather than a data member for each window and Direct3D initialization parameter, the d3d_app class contains structure members. These appear on lines 17–18. One structure holds all the window initialization parameters, and the other holds the Direct3D initialization parameters. These small changes save a lot of work. You can add more initialization parameters to the framework by adding them to window_init_params and d3d_init_params. That automatically adds them to the d3d_app class as well.

The next step is to get the framework to initialize the window_init_params and d3d_init_params structures automatically. It would be nice if we didn't have to add a new initialization in the d3d_app class constructor every time a data member is added to window_init_params or d3d_init_params. Listing 14.2 demonstrates an easy way to handle that.

Listing 14.2
An Updated Constructor for the d3d_app Class

```
1       inline d3d_app::d3d_app()
2       {
3           direct3D = NULL;
4           d3dDevice = NULL;
5           vertexBuffer = NULL;
6
7           memset(&windowInitParams,0,sizeof(windowInitParams));
8           memset(&d3dInitParams,0,sizeof(d3dInitParams));
9
10          appInitialized=false;
11      }
```

The d3d_app class constructor in Listing 14.2 calls the C++ memset() function to initialize the window_init_params and d3d_init_params structures. The constructor uses the memset() function to set the contents of the window_init_params and d3d_init_params structures to zero. It determines the sizes of these structures at runtime. Therefore, it doesn't matter how many new members you add to these structures. The calls on lines 7–8 initialize all their members to zero.

Simplifying the transfer of initialization to the d3d_app class is just as easy. The InitApp() function in Listing 14.3 takes care of it.

Listing 14.3
The New d3d_app::InitApp() Function

```
1       inline bool d3d_app::InitApp(
2           window_init_params windowParams,
3           d3d_init_params d3dParams)
4       {
5           // Set the initial window parameters.
6           windowInitParams = windowParams;
7
8           // Set the initial D3D parameters.
9           d3dInitParams = d3dParams;
```

```
10
11          appInitialized=true;
12          return(appInitialized);
13      }
```

The InitApp() function in Listing 14.3 copies the initialization parameters into the d3d_app class with simple assignment statements. Using this method, you no longer have to add code every time to add a member to one of these structures.

I've modified the InitD3D() and WinMan() functions in the file PMD3DApp.cpp to use the members of the window_init_params and d3d_init_params structures. Now when you add an initialization parameter, you perform the following steps:

1. Add a new member to the d3d_init_params or window_init_params structure.
2. Add code to the d3d_app::InitD3D() or WinMain() function that uses the new structure member.

This process is a lot less trouble.

Adding a game Class

As you write games using the physics modeling framework, it's likely that you'll add hundreds—if not thousands—of functions. Also, you'll have large amounts of data that the functions will need access to. It would be nice to consolidate access to your data and functions. It would also be nice if that access were available from every file in your program.

The easiest way to make all of that happen is to create a game class. A game class enables you to access the game's data and functions from a single point that is available throughout every file in the program. Listing 14.4 presents the game class.

Listing 14.4
The game Class

```
1       class game
2       {
3       public:
4           virtual bool OnAppLoad() = 0;
5           virtual bool PreD3DInitialization() = 0;
6           virtual bool PostD3DInitialization() = 0;
7           virtual bool GameInitialization() = 0;
8           virtual bool HandleMessage(
9               HWND hWnd,
10              UINT msg,
11              WPARAM wParam,
12              LPARAM lParam) = 0;
13          virtual bool UpdateFrame() = 0;
```

```
14          virtual bool RenderFrame() = 0;
15          virtual bool GameCleanup() = 0;
16    };
```

The class in Listing 14.4 defines the prototypes for the framework's required functions. However, because they're pure virtual functions, no code for these functions is provided. I've added a pointer to the game class in the d3d_app class, as shown on line 23 of Listing 14.5.

Listing 14.5
Adding the game Class to the d3d_app Class

```
1     class d3d_app
2     {
3     private:
4         // App properties
5         bool appInitialized;
6
7         // Window properties
8         std::string windowTitle;
9         int defaultX, defaultY;
10        int defaultHeight,defaultWidth;
11
12        // D3D properties
13        LPDIRECT3D9              direct3D; // Used to create the D3DDevice
14        LPDIRECT3DDEVICE9       d3dDevice; // Our rendering device
15        LPDIRECT3DVERTEXBUFFER9 vertexBuffer; // Buffer to hold vertices
16
17        window_init_params windowInitParams;
18        d3d_init_params d3dInitParams;
19
20        D3DXMATRIX viewMatrix;
21        D3DXMATRIX projectionMatrix;
22
23        game *theGame;
24
25    private:
26        bool CreateGameObject(void);
27
28    public:
29        d3d_app();
30        bool InitApp(
31            window_init_params windowParams,
32            d3d_init_params d3dParams);
33
```

```
34          LPDIRECT3DDEVICE9 D3DRenderingDevice(void);
35
36          LPDIRECT3DVERTEXBUFFER9 D3DVertexBuffer(void);
37          void D3DVertexBuffer(
38              LPDIRECT3DVERTEXBUFFER9 vertexBufferPointer);
39
40          DWORD RenderingDeviceClearFlags(void);
41          D3DCOLOR BackgroundSurfaceColor(void);
42
43          void ViewMatrix(D3DMATRIX newViewMatrix);
44          D3DMATRIX ViewMatrix(void);
45
46          void ProjectionMatrix(
47              D3DMATRIX newProjectionMatrix);
48          D3DMATRIX ProjectionMatrix(void);
49
50          game *Game(void);
51
52          friend INT WINAPI AppMain(
53              HINSTANCE hInst,
54              HINSTANCE,
55              LPSTR,
56              INT);
57          friend HRESULT InitD3D(
58              HWND hWnd);
59          friend VOID CleanupD3D();
60      };
```

Notice on line 50 that there's a new member function. The Game() function returns a pointer to the game object. Recall that the framework automatically creates a global d3d_app variable called theApp. This variable is accessible to any file that includes the file PMFramework.h. So your program can get access to the game object through the theApp variable, like this:

```
theApp.Game();
```

However, for this to work, you have to create a class that is defined from the pmframework::game class. Also, your program must use the macro CREATE_GAME_OBJECT() and pass it the name of your game class. This is demonstrated in Listing 14.6.

Listing 14.6
Defining and Using a Game Class
```
1       class my_game : public game
2       {
```

```
3      private:
4          immersible_rigid_body allBalls[TOTAL_BALLS];
5
6      public:
7          bool OnAppLoad();
8          bool PreD3DInitialization();
9          bool PostD3DInitialization();
10         bool GameInitialization();
11         bool HandleMessage(
12             HWND hWnd,
13             UINT msg,
14             WPARAM wParam,
15             LPARAM lParam);
16         bool UpdateFrame();
17         bool RenderFrame();
18         bool GameCleanup();
19     };
20
21
22     CREATE_GAME_OBJECT(my_game);
```

The sample game class in Listing 14.6 is derived publicly from the framework's game class. If you want to see the implementations of the functions in the my_game class, I've provided them for you on the CD-ROM in the folder \Source\Chapter14\NewFloat. The program in the NewFloat folder is an implementation of the program from Chapter 13, "Water and Waves." However, this version uses the game class.

It's especially important to notice that line 22 of Listing 14.6 calls the CREATE_GAME_OBJECT() macro. The only parameter to the CREATE_GAME_OBJECT() macro is the name of the class that you derive from the framework game class. In this example, that is the my_game class.

The CREATE_GAME_OBJECT() macro actually creates a function in your program called CreateGameObject(). The framework automatically calls the CreateGameObject() function to allocate memory for an object of your class. In this example, it allocates memory for a my_game object. It also sets the pointer in the d3d_app class to point at the object it allocates.

warning

When you compile and link a game that uses the physics modeling framework, you might get an error indicating that the linker can't find the function CreateGameObject(). If you do, it means that you did not call the macro CREATE_GAME_OBJECT() in any of your program files.

The my_game class in Listing 14.6 holds the game's data. Because all of the workhorse functions in the game are now members of the my_game class, they have direct access to the game's private data.

All of this means that when you write games using the framework, you have to do the following:

1. Create a class that is derived from pmframework::game.

2. Write code in your class for the required functions.

3. Call the CREATE_GAME_OBJECT() macro.

Performing these three steps enables your program to access your custom game object and its member functions from anywhere in the program.

note

The three steps for creating a game are implemented in the file FloatTest.cpp in the folder \Source\Chapter14\NewFloat.

Setting Transformation Matrices Efficiently

A big source of overhead in the programs presented so far is that they update the view and projection matrices in every frame. Let's fix that and make it so that these two matrices are sent to Direct3D automatically by the framework whenever they change. To make this happen, the first thing we need to do is add some status variables to the d3d_app class. Listing 14.7 provides the updated version of the d3d_app class.

Listing 14.7
Adding Status Variables to the d3d_app Class

```
1       class d3d_app
2       {
3       private:
4           // App properties
5           bool appInitialized;
6
7           // Window properties
8           std::string windowTitle;
9           int defaultX, defaultY;
10          int defaultHeight,defaultWidth;
11
12          // D3D properties
13          LPDIRECT3D9              direct3D; // Used to create the D3DDevice
14          LPDIRECT3DDEVICE9        d3dDevice; // Our rendering device
```

```
15        LPDIRECT3DVERTEXBUFFER9 vertexBuffer; // Buffer to hold vertices
16
17        window_init_params windowInitParams;
18        d3d_init_params d3dInitParams;
19
20        D3DXMATRIX viewMatrix;
21        D3DXMATRIX projectionMatrix;
22
23        game *theGame;
24
25        bool viewMatrixDirty;
26        bool projectionMatrixDirty;
27
28    private:
29        bool CreateGameObject(void);
30
31    public:
32        d3d_app();
33        bool InitApp(
34            window_init_params windowParams,
35            d3d_init_params d3dParams);
36
37        LPDIRECT3DDEVICE9 D3DRenderingDevice(void);
38
39        LPDIRECT3DVERTEXBUFFER9 D3DVertexBuffer(void);
40        void D3DVertexBuffer(
41            LPDIRECT3DVERTEXBUFFER9 vertexBufferPointer);
42
43        DWORD RenderingDeviceClearFlags(void);
44        D3DCOLOR BackgroundSurfaceColor(void);
45
46        void ViewMatrix(D3DMATRIX newViewMatrix);
47        D3DMATRIX ViewMatrix(void);
48
49        void ProjectionMatrix(
50            D3DMATRIX newProjectionMatrix);
51        D3DMATRIX ProjectionMatrix(void);
52
53        game *Game(void);
54
55        friend INT WINAPI AppMain(
56            HINSTANCE hInst,
```

```
57                HINSTANCE,
58                LPSTR,
59                INT);
60        friend HRESULT InitD3D(
61                HWND hWnd);
62        friend VOID CleanupD3D();
63        friend VOID Render();
64    };
```

The version of the d3d_app class in Listing 14.7 contains two new variables, shown on lines 25–26. These Boolean variables are set to true any time the view or projection matrices change. If the matrices have changed since the last frame, they are said to be "dirty."

The framework's Render() function, found in the file PMD3DApp.cpp, is now a friend of the d3d_app class. This provides it direct access to the viewMatrixDirty and projectionMatrixDirty members and enables the Render() function to check whether the matrices are dirty and need to be sent to Direct3D. The framework performs this task automatically. With this new version of the d3d_app class, we can update the framework's Render() function, as shown in Listing 14.8.

Listing 14.8
The Framework's Render() Function

```
1     VOID Render()
2     {
3         // Clear the back buffer to a black color.
4         theApp.D3DRenderingDevice()->Clear(
5             0,NULL,
6             theApp.RenderingDeviceClearFlags(),
7             theApp.BackgroundSurfaceColor(),
8             1.0f,0);
9
10        // Begin the scene.
11        if(SUCCEEDED(theApp.D3DRenderingDevice()->BeginScene()))
12        {
13            if (theApp.viewMatrixDirty)
14            {
15                // Set the view matrix.
16                theApp.D3DRenderingDevice()->SetTransform(
17                    D3DTS_VIEW,
18                    &theApp.ViewMatrix());
19                theApp.viewMatrixDirty = false;
20            }
21
```

```
22                  if (theApp.projectionMatrixDirty)
23                  {
24                      // Set the projection matrix.
25                      theApp.D3DRenderingDevice()->SetTransform(
26                          D3DTS_PROJECTION,
27                          &theApp.ProjectionMatrix());
28                      theApp.projectionMatrixDirty = false;
29                  }
30
31                  theApp.Game()->RenderFrame();
32
33                  // End the scene.
34                  theApp.D3DRenderingDevice()->EndScene();
35              }
36
37              // Present the back buffer contents to the display.
38              theApp.D3DRenderingDevice()->Present(NULL,NULL,NULL,NULL);
39          }
```

On line 13 of Listing 14.8, the Render() function checks to see if the view matrix is dirty. If it is, the Render() function sends it to Direct3D on lines 16–18. On line 19, it sets viewMatrixDirty to false, which prevents the matrix from being sent to Direct3D again until it changes.

Similarly, the Render() function checks the projection matrix on line 22. If it's dirty, it's sent to Direct3D on lines 25–27. The Render() function sets projectionMatrixDirty to false on line 28.

To make all of this work, the view and projection matrices must be marked as dirty every time they change. That's done in the ViewMatrix() and ProjectionMatrix() functions, which appear in Listing 14.9.

Listing 14.9
Marking the View and Projection Matrices

```
1      inline void d3d_app::ViewMatrix(
2          D3DMATRIX newViewMatrix)
3      {
4          viewMatrix=newViewMatrix;
5          viewMatrixDirty = true;
6      }
7
8      inline void d3d_app::ProjectionMatrix(
9          D3DMATRIX newProjectionMatrix)
10     {
```

```
11        projectionMatrix=newProjectionMatrix;
12        projectionMatrixDirty = true;
13    }
```

Listing 14.9 displays new code for the `ViewMatrix()` and `ProjectionMatrix()` functions that are used to set the view and projection matrices, respectively. They set their associated status variables to `true` whenever their matrices change. That gives us everything we need to automate the updating of the view and projection matrices.

Restoring Lost Device Objects

As it stands, the framework contains a major omission that prevents it from being used in games. Sometimes Direct3D can lose control of graphics memory if the user resizes the program's window or switches to another graphics program. The sample programs presented so far are so small that it's unlikely to happen. However, in real games, losing device objects is a distinct possibility.

When your game loses its device objects, vertex buffers, textures, swap chains, target-rendering surfaces, and depth stencil resources get lost. However, they get lost only if they are allocated in graphics memory. Anything in `D3DPOOL_MANAGED` or `D3D_POOL_SYSTEMMEM` is safe.

Your program must use the following steps to regain control of the memory and restore the device objects.

1. Release all video memory that your program allocated in the `D3DPOOL_DEFAULT` memory class. This includes swap chains created with the `CreateAdditionalSwapChain()` function, target-rendering surfaces created with `CreateRenderTarget()`, and depth stencil resources allocated with `CreateDepthStencilSurface()`.
2. Query the device to determine whether your program can reset it.
3. When the device can be reset, call the `Reset()` function.
4. Set up the device again.
5. Re-create or reload anything that you deallocated in step 1.

I've modified the framework so that it takes care of most of this for you. The game class now has two new functions. The first is called `RestoreDeviceObjects()`. If your program needs to create device objects, put the code that creates it into the `RestoreDeviceObjects()` function. When your program first initializes, call the `RestoreDeviceObjects()` function from the `GameInitialization()` function. After that, the framework automatically calls `RestoreDeviceObjects()` whenever it needs to perform step 5.

The second new function in the game class is called `InvalidateDeviceObjects()`. Put any code that your game needs for cleaning up device objects in this function. When your game shuts down, it can call `InvalidateDeviceObjects()` from the `GameCleanup()` function. Also, the framework automatically calls `InvalidateDeviceObjects()` when it needs to perform step 1.

If you use the d3d_app class's vertex buffer, your game's InvalidateDeviceObjects() function does not need to invalidate it. The framework does that for you. However, your RestoreDeviceObjects() function must rebuild the vertex buffer from scratch.

That's all there is to it. And for the programs we're writing in this book, you don't even need to provide much code for the InvalidateDeviceObjects() and RestoreDeviceObjects() functions. The only class in the framework that uses textures is the mesh class. However, the mesh class keeps its textures and materials in system memory, which ensures they won't be lost. The only thing that the InvalidateDeviceObjects() and RestoreDeviceObjects() functions have to do in the sample programs is return the value true.

I've provided yet another version of the Float program from Chapter 13 that contains these modifications. You'll find it on the CD-ROM in the folder \Source\Chapter14\NewFloat2.

Redefining Rigid Bodies Using Point Masses

One thing you've probably noticed in the preceding chapters is that point masses and rigid bodies have a lot of common functionality. In fact, for linear dynamics, physicists generally treat rigid bodies as point masses. So for our purposes, we can say that a rigid body is everything a point mass is—plus some rotational dynamics.

The physics modeling framework should reflect this concept. The way to make it do that is to use C++ inheritance. Let's rewrite the rigid_body class so that it derives from the point_mass class. The advantage of doing this is that it eliminates a lot of redundant code in the rigid_body class. There's less to modify and maintain as you build your games with the framework.

This update requires some minor changes to the point_mass_base class. The new version is shown in Listing 14.10.

Listing 14.10
The Updated point_mass_base Class

```
1      class point_mass_base
2      {
3      private:
4          scalar mass;
5          vector_3d centerOfMassLocation;
6          vector_3d linearVelocity;
7          vector_3d linearAcceleration;
8          force constantForce;
9          force impulseForce;
10
11         scalar boundingSphereRadius;
12         scalar coefficientOfRestitution;
```

```
13
14        bool isImmovable;
15
16    public:
17        point_mass_base();
18
19        void Mass(
20            scalar massValue);
21        scalar Mass(void);
22
23        void Location(
24            vector_3d locationCenterOfMass);
25        vector_3d Location(void);
26
27        void LinearVelocity(
28            vector_3d newVelocity);
29        vector_3d LinearVelocity(void);
30
31        void LinearAcceleration(
32            vector_3d newAcceleration);
33        vector_3d LinearAcceleration(void);
34
35        void ConstantForce(
36            force sumConstantForces);
37        force ConstantForce(void);
38
39        void ImpulseForce(
40            force sumImpulseForces);
41        force ImpulseForce(void);
42
43        void BoundingSphereRadius(
44            scalar sphereRadius);
45        scalar BoundingSphereRadius(void);
46
47        void CoefficientOfRestitution(scalar elasticity);
48        scalar CoefficientOfRestitution(void);
49
50        void IsImmovable(
51            bool isMassImmovable);
52        bool IsImmovable(void);
53
54        virtual bool Update(
```

```
55              scalar changeInTime);
56      };
```

The most important change to note in the point_mass_base class is that it now uses force objects rather than vectors to store the constant and impulse forces. The member functions have been modified accordingly.

Another change is that the overloaded Elasticity() functions are now called CoefficientOfRestitution(). This gives a uniform way to set the elasticity of point masses and rigid bodies.

warning

These changes mean that this version of the physics modeling framework is not backward compatible with sample programs from previous chapters.

The new version of the rigid_body class is shown in Listing 14.11.

Listing 14.11
The rigid_body Class Now Derives from the point_mass Class

```
1       class rigid_body : public point_mass
2       {
3       private:
4           // Rotational motion properties
5           angle_set_3d currentOrientation;
6           vector_3d angularVelocity;
7           vector_3d angularAcceleration;
8           vector_3d rotationalInertia;
9           vector_3d torque;
10
11      public:
12          rigid_body(void);
13
14          virtual void CurrentOrientation(
15              angle_set_3d newOrientation);
16          virtual angle_set_3d CurrentOrientation(void);
17
18          virtual void AngularVelocity(
19              vector_3d newAngularVelocity);
20          virtual vector_3d AngularVelocity(void);
21
22          virtual void AngularAcceleration(
23              vector_3d newAngularAcceleration);
```

```
24          virtual vector_3d AngularAcceleration(void);
25
26          virtual void RotationalInertia(
27              vector_3d inertiaValue);
28          virtual vector_3d RotationalInertia(void);
29
30          virtual void Torque(
31              vector_3d torqueValue);
32          virtual vector_3d Torque(void);
33
34          virtual bool Update(
35              scalar changeInTime);
36      };
```

As Listing 14.11 shows, the rigid_body class is *much* shorter now. The member data and functions that dealt with linear dynamics are gone. So is the mesh and LoadMesh() function. They are all inherited from the point_mass class.

Notice also that there is no longer a Render() function in the rigid_body class. It's not needed. All it did was render the object's mesh using the current world matrix. The Render() function for the point_mass class does exactly that. So the rigid_body class now uses the Render() function in the point_mass class.

All of these changes have various impacts throughout the framework. Most of them are minor, and I've taken care of them for you. However, before we move on, let's take a quick look at the new version of the rigid_body::Update() function, shown in Listing 14.12.

Listing 14.12
The rigid_body::Update() Function

```
1     bool rigid_body::Update(
2         scalar changeInTime)
3     {
4         //
5         // Begin calculating rotational dynamics.
6         //
7
8         // Use the impulse force to calculate the torque.
9         torque =
10            ImpulseForce().ApplicationPoint().Cross(
11                ImpulseForce().Force());
12
13        /* Use the torque and inertia to calculate the angular
14        acceleration.*/
15        angularAcceleration.X(
```

```
16              torque.X()/rotationalInertia.X());
17          angularAcceleration.Y(
18              torque.Y()/rotationalInertia.Y());
19          angularAcceleration.Z(
20              torque.Z()/rotationalInertia.Z());
21
22          /* Change the angular velocity according to the angular
23          acceleration. */
24          angularVelocity += angularAcceleration * changeInTime;
25
26          //
27          // Use angular acceleration to calculate the angles of rotation.
28          //
29          currentOrientation.XAngle(
30              currentOrientation.XAngle() +
31              angularVelocity.X() * changeInTime);
32          currentOrientation.YAngle(
33              currentOrientation.YAngle() +
34              angularVelocity.Y() * changeInTime);
35          currentOrientation.ZAngle(
36              currentOrientation.ZAngle() +
37              angularVelocity.Z() * changeInTime);
38
39          //
40          // End calculating rotational dynamics.
41          //
42
43          // Build a rotation matrix for each axis.
44          D3DXMATRIX rotationX, rotationY, rotationZ;
45          D3DXMatrixRotationX(&rotationX,currentOrientation.XAngle());
46          D3DXMatrixRotationY(&rotationY,currentOrientation.YAngle());
47          D3DXMatrixRotationZ(&rotationZ,currentOrientation.ZAngle());
48
49          D3DXMATRIX totalRotations;
50
51          // Multiply them into the world matrix.
52          D3DXMatrixMultiply(
53              &totalRotations,
54              &rotationX,
55              &rotationY);
56          D3DXMatrixMultiply(
57              &totalRotations,
```

```
58              &totalRotations,
59              &rotationZ);
60
61      // Calculate the linear dynamics.
62      point_mass_base::Update(changeInTime);
63
64      // Create the translation matrix.
65      D3DXMATRIX totalTranslation;
66      D3DXMatrixTranslation(
67          &totalTranslation,
68          Location().X(),
69          Location().Y(),
70          Location().Z());
71
72      /* Combine the rotation and translation matrices into the world
73      matrix. */
74      D3DXMatrixMultiply(
75          &worldMatrix,
76          &totalRotations,
77          &totalTranslation);
78
79      /* The impulse force has now been applied. Reset it to zero.
80      Note that point_mass_base::Update() already set the magnitude and
81      direction of the force to zero. All we have to do here is to set
82      the application point to zero.*/
83      ImpulseForce().ApplicationPoint(vector_3d(0.0,0.0,0.0));
84
85      return(true);
86  }
```

This version of the Update() function looks really different from previous versions. For instance, it begins by calculating the rotational dynamics rather than the linear dynamics. You'll find the reason for that on line 62 of Listing 14.12. The rigid_body::Update() function calls the point_mass_base::Update() function. The point_mass_base::Update() function sets the magnitude and direction of the impulse force to zero. If the rigid_body::Update() function called point_mass_base::Update() before it calculated the rotational dynamics, point_mass_base::Update() would set the impulse force to zero and cause the rotational dynamics calculations to be wrong. Therefore, the rotational dynamics have to be calculated first.

It's also significant that the rigid_body::Update() function in Listing 14.12 calls the point_mass_base::Update() function rather than the point_mass::Update() function. The point_mass::Update() function calls the point_mass_base::Update() function and then puts the resulting translation into the point_mass object's world matrix. However, rigid_body objects must apply all rotations first and *then* put the translations in the world matrix. So rigid_body::Update() calls point_mass_base::Update() to calculate the translation on line 62. Next, it creates the translation matrix. It then combines the rotation and translation matrices on lines 74–77. This is done in a way that applies the rotations first and then the translations.

note

The CD-ROM has an updated version of the framework that contains these changes. You'll find it in the \Source\Chapter14\Framework folder.

The Center of Mass and the Origin of the Mesh

All of the programs in this book so far have been written with the assumption that the origin of the object's mesh is at the center of the object's mass. In real games, that's often not the case. The framework needs some minor modifications to enable your games to specify the origin of the mesh at a different location than the center of mass. Listing 14.13 shows a new version of the point_mass class that enables you to specify the mesh origin at a different point than the center of mass.

Listing 14.13
The point_mass Class with a Mesh Origin

```
1    class point_mass : public point_mass_base
2    {
3    private:
4        mesh objectMesh;
5        vector_3d meshOrigin;
6
7    protected:
8        D3DXMATRIX worldMatrix;
9
10   public:
11       bool LoadMesh(
12           std::string meshFileName);
13
14       void ShareMesh(
15           point_mass &sourceMass);
16
17       void MeshOriginOffset(
18           vector_3d offset);
19       vector_3d MeshOriginOffset(void);
```

```
20
21        bool Update(
22             scalar changeInTime);
23        bool Render(void);
24    };
```

To make the physics of your game's 3-D objects work out right, the position of every point mass and rigid body must be tracked by the position of the center of mass. The only thing that the mesh origin is used for is rendering a mesh.

The point_mass class in Listing 14.13 has a private data member called meshOrigin. It also provides functions for getting and setting the mesh's origin. The prototypes for these functions are on lines 17–19.

The vector in meshOrigin must be specified as an offset from the center of mass location. If your game sets meshOrigin to an absolute location in its 3-D space, the behavior is undefined.

The meshOrigin data member is used in the point_mass class's Render() function. Listing 14.14 shows how it's used.

Listing 14.14
The New point_mass::Render() Function

```
1     bool point_mass::Render(void)
2     {
3         // Save the world transformation matrix.
4         D3DXMATRIX saveWorldMatrix;
5         theApp.D3DRenderingDevice()->GetTransform(
6             D3DTS_WORLD,
7             &saveWorldMatrix);
8
9         // Add the mesh origin offset translation.
10        D3DXMATRIX meshOffsetTranslation;
11        D3DXMatrixTranslation(
12            &meshOffsetTranslation,
13            MeshOriginOffset().X(),
14            MeshOriginOffset().Y(),
15            MeshOriginOffset().Z());
16        D3DXMatrixMultiply(
17            &worldMatrix,
18            &worldMatrix,
19            &meshOffsetTranslation);
20
21        // Apply the world transformation matrix for this object.
```

```
22          theApp.D3DRenderingDevice()->SetTransform(
23              D3DTS_WORLD,&worldMatrix);
24
25          // Now render the object with its transformations.
26          bool renderedOK=objectMesh.Render();
27
28          // Restore the world transformation matrix.
29          theApp.D3DRenderingDevice()->SetTransform(
30              D3DTS_WORLD,
31              &saveWorldMatrix);
32
33          return (renderedOK);
34      }
```

The new version of the point_mass::Render() function shown in Listing 14.14 applies an additional translation after all translations and rotations have been applied to the world matrix. Lines 10–15 show that point_mass::Render() builds a translation matrix using the mesh origin offset. Lines 16–19 put the offset's translation into the world matrix. The Render() function then uses the world matrix to render the mesh.

By default, the vector_3d constructor initializes its data members to zero. Therefore, if a 3-D object in your game has its mesh origin at its center of mass, your program doesn't have to set the mesh origin. It's automatically initialized to zero. Because it's an offset, a vector of magnitude zero makes the code on lines 10–19 of Listing 14.14 do absolutely nothing.

Recall that the rigid_body class now inherits from the point_mass class. So because the mesh origin offset was added to the point_mass class, it also is applied to the rigid_body class.

note

The CD-ROM has an updated version of the framework that contains these changes. You'll find it in the \Source\Chapter14\Framework **folder.**

Introducing DirectInput

So far, the sample programs for this book have not accepted user input. That doesn't make for very fun games. The last few chapters of this book present game-like simulations that implement the physics we've been discussing. The simulations are interactive, so before we move on to them, we need to cover the basics of DirectInput.

DirectInput bypasses the normal Windows methods of getting user input. This is necessary because the normal Windows methods of getting user input are too slow for most games. DirectInput talks directly (no pun intended) with the device drivers for input devices. It can provide the real-time input that fast action games require.

Because DirectInput talks directly with the device drivers, it can provide two types of input. The first type, called *unbuffered input*, just reports the current state of the input device. It contains no information about transitions. That is, if a button was pressed before but isn't anymore, immediate input stores no information about that transition. It only reports that the button is not pressed now. If your program uses immediate input, it must keep past state information itself. That means you're getting very fast input at the expense of increased overhead in your program.

The other type of input that DirectInput provides is *buffered input*. This is rather similar to the way that Windows messages work. When something changes on a device, such as the user pressing a key on the keyboard, DirectInput generates an event for that and puts it in a buffer. Your program reads the buffer whenever it's ready.

DirectInput recognizes three types of devices: keyboards, mice, and joysticks. That doesn't mean your game can't support devices such as game pads and steering wheels. As far as DirectInput is concerned, anything that is not a keyboard or mouse is a joystick. Your games can support devices such as game pads and steering wheels by pretending they're joysticks.

DirectInput must acquire all input devices before your program can read input from them. The best times to do this are when the program becomes active and when getting input.

Compiling Programs That Use DirectInput

When you compile a program that calls DirectInput functions, Visual Studio requires that you add the library `dinput8.lib` to the Additional Dependencies. If you're using Visual Studio 6, select Project from the main menu and then Settings. Visual Studio displays the Project Settings dialog box. Click the Link tab. Look for the Object/Library Modules text box. In this box, enter the name of the library files you need. For most Direct3D applications, you'll just need to enter the following:

`dinput8.lib`

If you're using Visual Studio.NET, right-click the name of the project. Select Properties from the menu that appears. Click the Linker folder and then click Input. Type the list of libraries shown above into the Additional Dependencies box.

For your convenience, I've added `dinput8.lib` to the file `AdditionalDependencies.txt`. You'll find this file on the CD-ROM in the `Source` folder. You can save yourself some typing if you copy the text in `AdditionalDependencies.txt` and paste it into the Additional Dependencies box in Visual Studio.

Initializing DirectInput

To access input devices, your game must initialize both DirectInput and the devices themselves. Following are the basic steps for doing so:

1. Create a DirectInput interface by calling `DirectInput8Create()`.
2. Enumerate the devices that are attached using the `IDirectInput8::EnumDevices()` function.
3. Create interfaces for the individual devices by calling `IDirectInput8::CreateDevice()`.
4. Find out what sorts of controls (buttons, sliders, and so on) are on the device by calling `IDirectInputDevice8::EnumObjects`.
5. Set the data format of each device with the `IDirectInputDevice8::SetDataFormat()` function.
6. If the game supports buffered input, set the buffer size with the `IDirectInputDevice8::SetProperty()` function.

To make this easy, I've incorporated some of these steps into the physics modeling framework. The framework creates the DirectInput interface for you automatically. If you tell it to, it creates interfaces for the keyboard and mouse.

note

In case you're wondering, I did not suddenly switch from using DirectX 9 to using DirectX 8. DirectX 9 did not add functionality to DirectInput, so the interface number for DirectInput in DirectX 9 is still 8. Confused? You're not alone.

The way you tell the framework to initialize the keyboard and mouse is to use the game class's `OnAppLoad()` function, as shown in Listing 14.15.

Listing 14.15
Selecting Input Devices

```
1     bool my_game::OnAppLoad()
2     {
3         // Initialize the window parameters.
4         window_init_params windowParams;
5         windowParams.appWindowTitle = "DirectInput and Camera Test";
6         windowParams.defaultX=100;
7         windowParams.defaultY=100;
8         windowParams.defaultHeight=500;
9         windowParams.defaultWidth=500;
10
11        // Initialize Direct3D parameters.
12        d3d_init_params d3dParams;
13        d3dParams.renderingDeviceClearFlags = D3DCLEAR_TARGET | D3DCLEAR_ZBUFFER;
14        d3dParams.surfaceBackgroundColor = D3DCOLOR_XRGB(0,75,200);
15        d3dParams.enableAutoDepthStencil = true;
16        d3dParams.autoDepthStencilFormat = D3DFMT_D16;
```

```
17          d3dParams.enableD3DLighting = false;
18
19          // Initialize the DirectInput parameters.
20          direct_input_init_params diParams;
21          diParams.supportsKeyboard = true;
22          diParams.requiresKeyboard = true;
23          diParams.supportsMouse = true;
24          diParams.requiresMouse = false;
25
26          // This call MUST appear in this function.
27          theApp.InitApp(windowParams,d3dParams,diParams);
28
29          return (true);
30      }
```

Lines 20–24 of Listing 14.15 demonstrate the initialization of a new member of the d3d_app class. The d3d_app class now contains a structure of type direct_input_init_params. The definition of this new structure appears in Listing 14.16.

Listing 14.16
The direct_input_init_params Structure

```
1       struct direct_input_init_params
2       {
3           bool supportsKeyboard;
4           bool requiresKeyboard;
5           bool supportsMouse;
6           bool requiresMouse;
7       };
```

This simple structure enables your game to tell the framework that it supports the keyboard. It can also specify whether the keyboard is required. If you set requiresKeyboard to false, that says that your game uses the keyboard if it's there but doesn't require it.

Selecting the mouse works the same way. Your game can tell the framework that it supports the mouse by setting supportsMouse to true. If the mouse is required, set requiresMouse to true.

As Listing 14.15 showed, you set these structure members in the OnAppLoad() function. I've added a new parameter of type direct_input_init_params to the d3d_app:: InitApp() function. The d3d_app:: InitApp() function now copies the direct_input_init_params in its third parameter into a data member in the d3d_app class called directInputParams. The values in directInputParams are used in a new function called InitDirectInput(), which appears in Listing 14.17.

Listing 14.17
Initializing DirectInput

```
1     bool d3d_app::InitDirectInput()
2     {
3         bool noError = true;
4
5         // Create the DirectInput device.
6         HRESULT result =
7         DirectInput8Create(
8             GetModuleHandle(NULL),
9             DIRECTINPUT_VERSION,
10            IID_IDirectInput8,
11            (VOID**)&directInputDevice, NULL);
12
13        noError = (result==DI_OK);
14
15        // If the game supports the keyboard...
16        if ((noError) && (directInputParams.supportsKeyboard))
17        {
18            // Create the keyboard device.
19            result = directInputDevice->CreateDevice(
20                GUID_SysKeyboard,
21                &keyboardDevice,
22                NULL);
23
24            // If there was an error and the game requires a keyboard...
25            if ((result !=DI_OK) && (directInputParams.requiresKeyboard))
26            {
27                noError = false;
28            }
29        }
30
31        // If the game supports the mouse...
32        if ((noError) && (directInputParams.supportsMouse))
33        {
34            // Create the mouse device.
35            result = directInputDevice->CreateDevice(
36                GUID_SysMouse,
37                &mouseDevice,
38                NULL);
39
40            // If there was an error and the game requires a mouse...
```

```
41              if ((result !=DI_OK) && (directInputParams.requiresMouse))
42              {
43                  noError = false;
44              }
45          }
46
47          return (noError);
48      }
```

Listing 14.17 gives the code for a new function in the framework. You'll find this function in the file PMD3DApp.cpp. The InitDirectInput() function calls DirectInput8Create() to create an IDirectInput8 interface. Table 14.1 explains the parameters to DirectInput8Create().

Table 14.1 The Parameters for DirectInput8Create()

Parameter Name	Description
hinst	The handle of the current module. Just set this to the return value of GetModuleHandle(NULL).
dwVersion	Set this to DIRECTINPUT_VERSION.
riidltf	Interface identifier that lets you choose ANSI or Unicode. I recommend that you set this to IID_IDirectInput8 so that the choice will be based on your compiler settings. It makes life easier.
ppvOut	The address of the interface pointer. This is where DirectInput8Create() outputs the interface pointer to your program.
punkOuter	A pointer used for a real nasty COM technique called *aggregation*. If you don't know what that is, consider yourself lucky. Just set this to NULL and forget it. You won't use this because this kind of heavy-duty COM programming is waaaaaaaaay too slow for games.

The fourth parameter to DirectInput8Create() is the address of a pointer variable. That's where DirectInput8Create() stores the IDirectInput8 interface. The framework's d3d_app class now contains a pointer to the IDirectInput8 interface, so that's the variable you see named on line 11 of Listing 14.17. Your game can access the IDirectInput8 interface at any time by calling the d3d_app:: DirectInputDevice() function.

note

Now that the framework is incorporating functions that use additional DirectX components, such as DirectInput, I've redesigned it so that most of the functions in the file PMD3DApp.cpp are private members of the d3d_app class. That's why the InitDirectInput() function is a member of the d3d_app class. It provides a better structure that you can use to add initializations for more DirectX components.

If there is no error creating the IDirectInput8 interface, the framework's InitDirectInput() function checks the d3d_app class's directInputParams member to see if the keyboard is supported. If so, InitDirectInput() creates an IDirectInputDevice8 interface for the keyboard.

If there was an error while creating the keyboard's IDirectInputDevice8 interface and the game requires the keyboard, InitDirectInput() returns an error. If the keyboard is not required, InitDirectInput() just goes happily on. Creating an IDirectInputDevice8 interface for the mouse follows the same procedure.

At this point, your game has interface pointers to the input devices, but it still must set their data formats. In addition, if the game uses buffered input, it must set the sizes of the buffers. Both of these tasks are handled in the game class's GameInitialization() function or in a function called by GameInitialization(). Listing 14.18 gives the code for such a function.

Listing 14.18
Completing Input Device Initialization

```
1     void my_game::SetupInputDevices()
2     {
3         DIPROPDWORD dipdw;
4
5         if (theApp.Keyboard())
6         {
7             theApp.Keyboard()->SetDataFormat(&c_dfDIKeyboard);
8
9             dipdw.diph.dwSize = sizeof(DIPROPDWORD);
10            dipdw.diph.dwHeaderSize = sizeof(DIPROPHEADER);
11            dipdw.diph.dwObj = 0;
12            dipdw.diph.dwHow = DIPH_DEVICE;
13            dipdw.dwData = KEYBOARD_BUFFER_SIZE;
14
15            /* This sample does nothing to handle an error returned by
16            this function call. If there is an error, then something is
17            seriously wrong with the keyboard. Your game should let the
18            player know and exit gracefully. */
19            theApp.Keyboard()->SetProperty(
20                DIPROP_BUFFERSIZE,
21                &dipdw.diph);
22        }
23
24        if (theApp.Mouse())
25        {
26            theApp.Mouse()->SetDataFormat(&c_dfDIMouse);
27
```

```
28          dipdw.diph.dwSize = sizeof(DIPROPDWORD);
29          dipdw.diph.dwHeaderSize = sizeof(DIPROPHEADER);
30          dipdw.diph.dwObj = 0;
31          dipdw.diph.dwHow = DIPH_DEVICE;
32          dipdw.dwData = MOUSE_BUFFER_SIZE;
33
34          /* This sample does nothing to handle an error returned by
35          this function call. If there is an error, then something is
36          seriously wrong with the mouse. Your game should let the
37          player know and exit gracefully. */
38          theApp.Mouse()->SetProperty(
39              DIPROP_BUFFERSIZE,
40              &dipdw.diph);
41      }
42  }
```

Listing 14.18 gives the code for a function that finishes the initialization of the keyboard and mouse. This function would be called from GameInitialization(). The SetupInputDevices() function sets the data format of the keyboard by calling the IDirectInputDevice8::SetDataFormat() function. It passes SetDataFormat() a global variable that DirectInput defines. This global variable is one of a set of global variables that DirectInput defines for setting input device data formats. The entire group is explained in Table 14.2.

Table 14.2 The Global Variables for Setting Input Device Data Formats

Variable Name	Description
c_dfDIKeyboard	Standard data format for the keyboard. Creates an array of 256 bytes—one byte for each key on the keyboard, plus a few more.
c_dfDIMouse	Standard data format for the mouse. When your program gets input from the mouse, it sends your program a DIMOUSESTATE structure containing 4 bytes for button states.
c_dfDIMouse2	Extended data format for the mouse. When your program gets input from the mouse, it sends your program a DIMOUSESTATE2 structure containing 8 bytes for button states.
c_dfDIJoystick	Standard data format for joysticks. When your program gets input from the joystick, it sends your program a DIJOYSTATE structure.
c_dfDIJoystick2	Extended data format for the joysticks. When your program gets input from the joystick, it sends your program a DIJOYSTATE2 structure containing many more members that enable your game to support advanced joysticks, steering wheels, and so on.

After the SetupInputDevices() function sets the data formats of the keyboard on line 7 of Listing 14.18, it sets the buffer size for buffered input on lines 9–21. If your game uses immediate input, it can skip this step. The SetupInputDevices() function also shows how to set the buffer size for buffered mouse input on lines 28–40.

tip

Initializing joysticks and other devices follows essentially the same pattern as shown in the InitDirectInput() and SetupInputDevices() functions. The primary difference is that your game should also enumerate the buttons, sliders, and axes that the device supports.

The framework also provides you with a function that gives you an opportunity to poll the input devices for input. Let's take a look at how that's done.

Getting Keyboard and Mouse Input

When your program needs to get immediate (unbuffered) input data, it calls the IDirectInputDevice8::GetDeviceState() function. For buffered input, it must call IDirectInputDevice8::GetDeviceData(). Listing 14.19 illustrates how to get buffered input.

Listing 14.19
The ProcessInput() Function

```
1      bool my_game::ProcessInput()
2      {
3          DIDEVICEOBJECTDATA keyboardData[KEYBOARD_BUFFER_SIZE];
4          DIDEVICEOBJECTDATA mouseData[MOUSE_BUFFER_SIZE];
5          HRESULT result;
6          DWORD totalElements;
7          DWORD i;
8
9          totalElements = KEYBOARD_BUFFER_SIZE;
10         result = theApp.Keyboard()->GetDeviceData(
11             sizeof(DIDEVICEOBJECTDATA),
12             keyboardData,
13             &totalElements,
14             0);
15
16         if (result != DI_OK)
17         {
18             result = theApp.Keyboard()->Acquire();
19             while (result == DIERR_INPUTLOST)
20             {
21                 result = theApp.Keyboard()->Acquire();
```

```
22              }
23
24              /* If another app has priority or some other error has
25              occurred... */
26              if ((result == DIERR_OTHERAPPHASPRIO) ||
27                  (result == DIERR_NOTACQUIRED))
28              {
29                  // Just try again later.
30                  return (true);
31              }
32          }
33      else
34      {
35          for (i=0; i<totalElements; i++)
36          {
37              switch (keyboardData[i].dwOfs)
38              {
39                  // Up arrow
40                  case DIK_UP:
41                      // Insert code that handles the up arrow.
42                  break;
43
44                  // Down arrow
45                  case DIK_DOWN:
46                      // Insert code that handles the down arrow.
47                  break;
48
49                  // Left arrow
50                  case DIK_LEFT:
51                      // Insert code that handles the left arrow.
52                  break;
53
54                  // Right arrow
55                  case DIK_RIGHT:
56                      // Insert code that handles the right arrow.
57                  break;
58              }
59          }
60
61      }
62
63      totalElements = MOUSE_BUFFER_SIZE;
```

```
64        result = theApp.Mouse()->GetDeviceData(
65              sizeof(DIDEVICEOBJECTDATA),
66              mouseData,
67              &totalElements,
68              0);
69
70        /* Nothing is done with the mouse input; the code is just here for
71        demo purposes. */
72        if (result != DI_OK)
73        {
74              result = theApp.Mouse()->Acquire();
75              while (result == DIERR_INPUTLOST)
76              {
77                    result = theApp.Mouse()->Acquire();
78              }
79
80              /* If another app has priority or some other error has
81              occurred... */
82              if ((result == DIERR_OTHERAPPHASPRIO) ||
83                    (result == DIERR_NOTACQUIRED))
84              {
85                    // Just try again later.
86                    return (true);
87              }
88        }
89
90        return (true);
91    }
```

The function in Listing 14.19 is a new required function in the framework's game class. Before it calls the game class's UpdateFrame() function, the framework calls ProcessInput(). This enables your game to react to any user input it receives before it updates the frame based on the physics being simulated.

Every buffered input device needs its own input buffer. The ProcessInput() function declares input buffers for the keyboard and mouse on lines 3–4 of Listing 14.19. The sizes of these buffers must be at least as large as the sizes that your game passes to DirectInput's SetProperty() function. Recall that the SetProperty() function appeared back in Listing 14.18. The arrays created on lines 3–4 are arrays of DIDEVICEOBJECTDATA structures.

The ProcessInput() function invokes IDirectInputDevice8::GetDeviceData() to retrieve buffered keyboard input on lines 10–14. The GetDeviceData() function's first parameter is the number of bytes in a DIDEVICEOBJECTDATA structure. Its second parameter is the starting address of the keyboard buffer created on line 3.

The GetDeviceData() function's third parameter is the total number of structures in the buffer. When the GetDeviceData() function returns, the third parameter contains the actual number of input events in the buffer.

The final parameter is a set of flags. The only flag currently recognized is DIGDD_PEEK, which lets your program look at the data in the buffer without removing it. Subsequent calls to GetDeviceData() retrieve the same input. Usually, games set this parameter to zero, which means that the input should be removed from the buffer when it's read.

If the GetDeviceData() function can't read data from the keyboard, it usually means that access to the keyboard has been lost. This is similar to losing graphics surfaces. Fortunately, restoring access to the input device is easier than restoring lost graphics surfaces. All your program needs to do is call the IDirectInputDevice8::Acquire() function, as shown in line 18 of Listing 14.19.

It is possible that Acquire() might not be able to regain access to the input device. It might have to wait a while. If that's the case, the ProcessInput() function enters a while loop on line 19 that waits until the device can be reacquired. If another error prevents your game from gaining access to the input device, the ProcessInput() function returns true and waits for the next frame. It can try again to get access to the input device.

When the ProcessInput() function can get buffered keyboard input, it enters a for loop that begins on line 35 of Listing 14.19. The for loop iterates through every input event that GetDeviceData() passed to ProcessInput(). The identifier of each keystroke is contained in the DIDEVICEOBJECTDATA structure's dwOfs member. The example in Listing 14.19 demonstrates how to respond to the up, down, left, and right arrows.

tip

The identifiers that your program receives in the input buffer are different for keyboards, mice, and joysticks. You can find the list of keyboard identifiers in the DirectX documentation under the topic "Keyboard Device Enumerated Type." For a list of mouse input identifiers, see the topic "Mouse Device Enumerated Type." See "Joystick Device Constants" for the list of joystick input identifiers.

Buffered mouse and joystick input is processed in essentially the same manner as buffered keyboard input.

The only other thing to note is that devices are often lost when the player presses Alt+Tab and switches to another program. You might find that it increases efficiency if your program tries to reacquire input devices every time the player switches back to the game. Listing 14.20 gives a version of the game class's HandleMessage() function, which reacquires the keyboard and mouse when the game is reactivated.

Listing 14.20
Reacquiring Control of the Keyboard and Mouse After a Context Switch

```
1     bool my_game::HandleMessage(
2         HWND hWnd,
3         UINT msg,
4         WPARAM wParam,
5         LPARAM lParam)
6     {
7         switch (msg)
8         {
9             case WM_ACTIVATE:
10                // If we are gaining focus...
11                if (WA_INACTIVE != wParam)
12                {
13                    // If the keyboard was set up...
14                    if (theApp.Keyboard())
15                    {
16                        // Make sure the device is acquired,
17                        theApp.Keyboard()->Acquire();
18                    }
19
20                    // If the mouse was set up...
21                    if (theApp.Mouse())
22                    {
23                        // Make sure the device is acquired,
24                        theApp.Mouse()->Acquire();
25                    }
26                }
27            break;
28        }
29
30        return (false);
31    }
```

Closing Down DirectInput

Before your game exists, it should release all DirectInput interfaces that it creates. Take care of this in the GameCleanup() function. You don't have to release the mouse and keyboard interfaces. That's handled automatically in the framework.

Camera Movement in DirectX

The final topic we need to address before we can write some game-like physics simulations is camera movement. DirectX makes moving the camera, which is the player's point of view in the 3-D scene, easy. In fact, you already know how to do it. You can prove it by reading Listing 14.21.

Listing 14.21
Moving the Camera in Response to Player Input

```
1     bool my_game::ProcessInput()
2     {
3         DIDEVICEOBJECTDATA keyboardData[KEYBOARD_BUFFER_SIZE];
4         DIDEVICEOBJECTDATA mouseData[MOUSE_BUFFER_SIZE];
5         HRESULT result;
6         DWORD totalElements;
7         DWORD i;
8
9         totalElements = KEYBOARD_BUFFER_SIZE;
10        result = theApp.Keyboard()->GetDeviceData(
11            sizeof(DIDEVICEOBJECTDATA),
12            keyboardData,
13            &totalElements,
14            0);
15
16        if (result != DI_OK)
17        {
18            result = theApp.Keyboard()->Acquire();
19            while (result == DIERR_INPUTLOST)
20            {
21                result = theApp.Keyboard()->Acquire();
22            }
23
24            /* If another app has priority or some other error has
25            occurred... */
26            if ((result == DIERR_OTHERAPPHASPRIO) ||
27                (result == DIERR_NOTACQUIRED))
28            {
29                // Just try again later.
30                return (true);
31            }
32        }
```

```
33      else
34      {
35          bool cameraMoved = false;
36
37          for (i=0; i<totalElements; i++)
38          {
39              switch (keyboardData[i].dwOfs)
40              {
41                  // Up arrow
42                  case DIK_UP:
43                      // If the key was pressed...
44                      if (DirectInputKeyDown(keyboardData[i].dwData))
45                      {
46                          // Move the camera forward.
47                          lookatPoint.z += 1.0;
48                          eyePoint.z += 1.0;
49                          cameraMoved = true;
50                      }
51                  break;
52
53                  // Down arrow
54                  case DIK_DOWN:
55                      // If the key was pressed...
56                      if (DirectInputKeyDown(keyboardData[i].dwData))
57                      {
58                          // Move the camera back.
59                          lookatPoint.z -= 1.0;
60                          eyePoint.z -= 1.0;
61                          cameraMoved = true;
62                      }
63                  break;
64
65                  // Left arrow
66                  case DIK_LEFT:
67                      // If the key was pressed...
68                      if (DirectInputKeyDown(keyboardData[i].dwData))
69                      {
70                          // Move the camera left.
71                          lookatPoint.x -= 1.0;
72                          eyePoint.x -= 1.0;
73                          cameraMoved = true;
74                      }
```

```
75                      break;
76
77                      // Right arrow
78                      case DIK_RIGHT:
79                          // If the key was pressed...
80                          if (DirectInputKeyDown(keyboardData[i].dwData))
81                          {
82                              // Move the camera right.
83                              lookatPoint.x += 1.0;
84                              eyePoint.x += 1.0;
85                              cameraMoved = true;
86                          }
87                      break;
88                  }
89          }
90
91          // If the camera moved...
92          if (cameraMoved)
93          {
94              // Update the view matrix.
95              D3DXMATRIX tempViewMatrix;
96              D3DXMatrixLookAtLH(
97                  &tempViewMatrix,&eyePoint,&lookatPoint,&upDirection);
98              theApp.ViewMatrix(tempViewMatrix);
99          }
100     }
101
102     totalElements = MOUSE_BUFFER_SIZE;
103     result = theApp.Mouse()->GetDeviceData(
104         sizeof(DIDEVICEOBJECTDATA),
105         mouseData,
106         &totalElements,
107         0);
108
109     /* Nothing is done with the mouse input; the code is just here for
110     demo purposes. */
111     if (result != DI_OK)
112     {
113         result = theApp.Mouse()->Acquire();
114         while (result == DIERR_INPUTLOST)
115         {
116             result = theApp.Mouse()->Acquire();
```

```
117              }
118
119              /* If another app has priority or some other error has
120              occurred... */
121              if ((result == DIERR_OTHERAPPHASPRIO) ||
122                  (result == DIERR_NOTACQUIRED))
123              {
124                  // Just try again later.
125                  return (true);
126              }
127          }
128
129      return (true);
130  }
```

Listing 14.21 provides a fuller implementation of the game class's ProcessInput() function. This version sets the lookat point and the eye point in response to user input. You can see how that's done on lines 47–49, 59–61, 71–73, and 83–85. The variables lookatPoint, eyePoint, and cameraMoved are private data members in the game class, as shown in Listing 14.22.

Listing 14.22
A Game Class with a Movable Viewpoint

```
1    class my_game : public game
2    {
3    private:
4        // Geometry and scenery go here.
5        D3DXVECTOR3 eyePoint;
6        D3DXVECTOR3 lookatPoint;
7        D3DXVECTOR3 upDirection;
8
9        ground theGround;
10
11   public:
12       // These functions are required by the framework.
13       bool OnAppLoad();
14       bool PreD3DInitialization();
15       bool PostD3DInitialization();
16       bool GameInitialization();
17       bool HandleMessage(
18           HWND hWnd,
19           UINT msg,
20           WPARAM wParam,
21           LPARAM lParam);
```

```
22          bool ProcessInput();
23          bool InvalidateDeviceObjects();
24          bool RestoreDeviceObjects();
25          bool UpdateFrame();
26          bool RenderFrame();
27          bool GameCleanup();
28
29          // Initialization functions
30          void SetupInputDevices();
31          void SetupViewMatrix();
32          void SetupProjectionMatrix();
33          void SetupGeometry();
34     };
```

Because the variables that control the point of view are now data members in the game class, the game can change the point of view at any time. That's exactly what happens in the ProcessInput() function in Listing 14.21. When the player presses the up, down, left, or right arrow key, the ProcessInput() function updates the variables that track the player's point of view. On lines 92–99 of Listing 14.21, ProcessInput() passes the new viewpoint to Direct3D. It invokes the D3DXMatrixLookAtLH() function to build a view matrix and passes that view matrix to the d3d_app class. When the next frame update occurs, the framework automatically recognizes that the view matrix is now dirty (meaning it has changed) and sends the new view matrix to Direct3D. This is exactly the same process we've been using to set up your initial view matrices for the example programs.

If you want to see all of the code for the movable camera program, it's provided for you on the CD-ROM. Look in the folder \Source\Chapter14\Camera.

Summary

This chapter presented a considerable number of changes to the framework. These changes were necessary to prepare the framework for more realistic games. The CD-ROM has an updated version of the framework that contains all the changes described in this chapter. You can find it in the \Source\Chapter14\Framework folder.

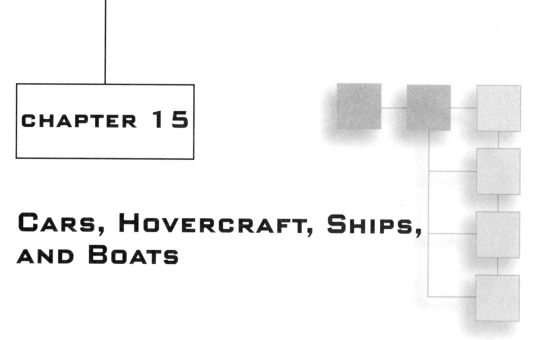

CHAPTER 15

CARS, HOVERCRAFT, SHIPS, AND BOATS

I t's time to apply the physics presented so far to complex, game-style 3-D simulations. This chapter explains the physics of cars, hovercraft, ships, and boats. Although it might not seem like it on first reflection, these vehicles have similar implementations.

Cars

When you first approach the problem, simulating a car driving down the road seems deceptively simple. In its most basic form, it *is* a fairly simple task. However, increasing the realism of your game quickly increases the complexity of the physics.

Power, Force, Acceleration, and Friction

For historical reasons, we normally measure the power output of a car's engine in horsepower. One horsepower is equal to 550 ft-lbs/sec. This is not a particularly useful unit of measure when you're doing physics. You'll find it much easier if you ignore power and focus on force instead.

Power and force are not the same thing. Power measures the total amount of work done by a force or a torque per unit of time. If you work directly with forces and torques rather than power, you'll generally simplify your simulations.

The pistons of engines turn a crankshaft, which turns a car's drive shaft. In other words, the engine produces a torque that is transmitted through a series of shafts to the drive wheel (or drive wheels, if you have 4-wheel drive). Of course, a tire is mounted on each wheel. As the wheel turns, the torque of the tire exerts a force on the road. This is illustrated in Figure 15.1.

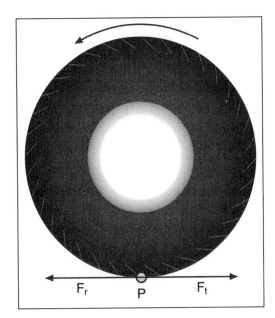

Figure 15.1
The forces acting on a drive wheel.

You've actually seen this diagram before. It's a repeat of Figure 13.7 in Chapter 13, "Water and Waves." As the figure shows, the tire exerts a force on the road, and the road pushes back on the tire. This is Newton's third law. Every action produces an equal and opposite reaction.

The force between the tire and the road depends on friction. As mentioned in Chapter 13, a tire that is not sliding is subject to static friction. As long as the force of the drive wheel is not large enough to overcome static friction, the drive wheel exerts a force that pushes backward on the road and forward on the car. The magnitude of the force depends on the torque from the engine. You calculate it using the following formula:

$$F = \frac{T}{r}$$

If, for instance, the car hits a patch of ice on the road, the coefficient of static friction goes down, and the force exerted by the tire might be greater than the force of static friction. In that case, the tire is subject to dynamic friction. It spins in place. Even though the car doesn't move, the surface of the tire slides across the surface of the road. Because the coefficient of dynamic friction is less than the coefficient of static friction, the force that the spinning tire is able to exert on the road is less than the force exerted under normal conditions. The tire spins without pushing the car forward very much.

Recall that the formula for calculating static friction is this:

$$F_s \leq \mu_s N$$

where F_s is the force of static friction, μ_s is the coefficient of static friction, and N is the normal force. In the case of a car, the normal force is the force of gravity, $F=mg$. So we can combine these two formulas to get the following:

$$F_s \leq \mu_s mg$$

This is something you can code directly into your program. If your game simulates a car on the road, your program can use the input techniques discussed in Chapter 14, "Getting Ready for Games," to poll the keyboard or joystick. When the user presses the up arrow on the keyboard or moves the joystick forward, your program can increase the force of the drive wheel. As soon as the force of the drive wheel becomes greater than $\mu_s mg$, the wheel should spin in place. The friction between the ground and the tire should be calculated using the formula for dynamic friction:

$$F_D \leq \mu_D N$$

note

Some physics books use the name *kinetic friction* rather than dynamic friction. They are the same thing.

This brings us back to drive wheels. Even if the car you're simulating has one drive wheel (it's not, for example, 4-wheel drive), you can usually apply the force of the drive wheel at the car's center of mass. This enables you to treat the car as a point mass for linear movement. However, if you want greater accuracy, you're going to have to apply the force at the location that the drive wheel makes contact with the road. Doing this enables you to simulate such situations as the car on ice.

Even on the slickest ice, the drive wheel exerts a force on the road at the point it makes contact with the road. Because that point is not the car's center of mass, the drive wheel force causes an imbalance of forces that exerts a torque on the car. The torque causes the car to spin. If you live in a snowy climate, you've probably experienced this yourself. It's never pleasant when you do.

Even under dry conditions, the torque is still there. However, the spinning force that the torque creates is much less than the force of static friction. As a result, the car goes forward. It doesn't spin around. Under icy conditions, static friction goes down. The torque exerted by the drive wheel can be greater than static friction. If it is, the car spins end for end.

If you want to simulate this situation in your game, your program has to keep track of the position of the point of contact between the drive wheel's tire and the ground. There are several ways of doing that. One is to define a vector that points to the contact location. Your program has to rotate and translate the vector as the car moves.

More advanced Direct3D programs use another way to keep track of the drive wheel's contact point with the ground. The program rotates and translates the car's mesh cumulatively. That is, it stores the results of translations and rotations in a vertex buffer. Whenever the program needs the contact point, it simply reads it from the vertex buffer.

If you drive a car with a stick shift, you might sometimes take the car out of gear and let it roll down the road. On a level road, the car eventually rolls to a stop. There are two reasons for this. One is air resistance, which we'll discuss next. The second is friction between the car's wheels and its other components. An accurate simulation of a car in a game should simulate this kind of friction as well. However, it's generally too complex of a calculation for games.

So how do we simulate the slowing friction between a car's moving parts without calculating the actual friction?

We cheat, that's how. When you implement a car class in your code, add an extra coefficient of friction, especially for this calculation. Let's call it μ_{CF}, which stands for the coefficient of car friction. Use that coefficient in the following formula:

$$v_{Final} = (1 - \mu_{CF})v_{Current}$$

where v_{Final} is the velocity at the end of a given time interval. The value $v_{Current}$ is the car's velocity at the start of the time interval. The value of μ_{CF} must be greater than 0.0 and less than 1.0. Using this formula, the velocity of the car gets smaller with each frame. Although this isn't true physics because it doesn't calculate the real frictional forces, the result is the same.

Air Resistance on Cars

Simulating air resistance is done in a couple of different ways in games. If you want your simulation to be physically accurate, you calculate the force of air resistance using the formulas for viscous drag that were presented in Chapter 13. Table 15.1 repeats them here for your convenience.

Table 15.1 Calculating Air Resistance

Formula	Description
$\mathbf{F}_{FD} = -C_{FD}\mathbf{v}$	Use this formula when the car is not moving fast enough to make the air turbulent.
$\mathbf{F}_{FD} = -C_{FD}\mathbf{v}^2$	Use this formula for fast-moving cars that cause lots of air turbulence, such as racecars.

The direction of the force $\mathbf{F}_{FD}$ points opposite to that of the velocity. Your game adds $\mathbf{F}_{FD}$ to the force that the drive wheel exerts.

For simpler, more basic cars, you can simulate air resistance without calculating its force. The approach you use is exactly like that of cheating on the friction of a car's moving parts. You simply add another coefficient of friction to your car class and use it in the following formula:

$$v_{Final} = (1 - \mu_{AF})v_{Current}$$

In this formula, μ_{AF} is the coefficient of friction due to air resistance. Like μ_{CF}, it must be greater than 0.0 and less than 1.0.

warning

You should not use this method of cheating the air resistance calculations if you're writing a racing game. It will not give accurate results at high speeds. Instead, use the formulas shown in Table 15.1.

Braking

Applying the brakes on a car is just the reverse of accelerating. The same forces apply. The brakes cause the wheels to spin more slowly. This results in a reverse force on the wheels, which is transmitted through the tires to the road, as shown in Figure 15.2.

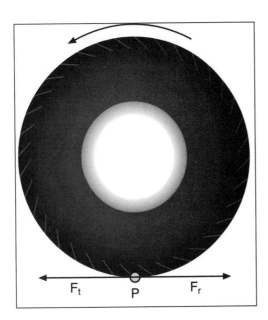

Figure 15.2
Forces on a tire during braking.

As long as the braking force that the tire exerts on the road is less than the force of static friction, the car slows nicely to a stop. If the driver locks the tires, they begin to slide over the surface of the road. In that case, dynamic friction applies. The stopping distance is always greater when the car is sliding.

You can calculate the stopping distance in multiple ways. You can find the stopping distance with this formula:

$$d = \frac{v^2}{2g(\mu \cos(\theta) + \sin(\theta))}$$

In this formula, d is the distance required to stop the car. The variable v represents the car's initial velocity. g is the acceleration due to gravity. The value μ is the static or dynamic coefficient of friction. Which you use depends on whether the car is sliding. The angle θ is in the formula in case the car is going up or down a hill. θ represents the angle that the slope of the hill is displaced from horizontal.

When you write your game correctly, you should not have to use this formula. If you simply apply the braking force to the car, the car will automatically slow down in the correct distance. The only thing you'll really need to keep track of is whether the braking force exceeds static friction. Of course, the same is true of acceleration. Basically, you use the same formulas for slowing down as you do for speeding up. The only real difference is that the direction of the force is reversed.

note

Unlike drive wheel forces, braking forces are always applied at the center of mass. This is because all four wheels have brakes. All of the brakes are equidistant from the center of mass. Therefore, the displacement vectors of the braking forces total 0.

Turning Cars

Turning a car can be simple or extremely complex. It depends on how realistic you want to be. The most basic implementations of cars move in a plane. So turning the cars is just a matter of applying a rotation to them. This is not physics, but it works for many games.

Games that show more realism need to model the actual forces on the car as it turns. Figure 15.3 shows some of those forces.

As the car in Figure 15.3 goes around the curve, several forces act on it. First, the car's front tires exert a turning force on the car. If this force is less than the static friction, the car turns nicely. Otherwise, the car slides out.

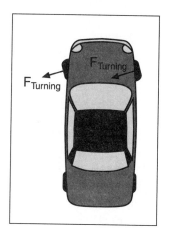

Figure 15.3
Forces on a turning car.

The turning force of the front tires is a centripetal force. Centripetal force was first presented in Chapter 9, "Rigid Body Dynamics." The centripetal force of the tires makes the front of the car turn. This centripetal force is actually two forces, one for each front tire. Your game can apply one-half of the total centripetal force at the point where the tires contact the road. This is the most accurate way to model the car. You can also apply the entire force at a point one-half of the distance between the two tires. Either way works, but if you use the latter method, you cannot model tire blowouts in the front tires.

note

The static friction between the front tires and the road causes the centripetal turning force.

All roadways are banked if the cars on them take curves at a high speed. Figure 15.4 shows a car on a banked roadway.

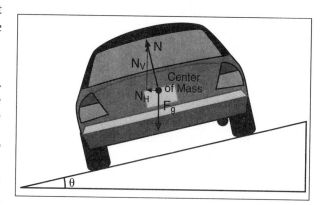

Figure 15.4
A car on a banked road.

The banked roadway exerts an additional centripetal force on the car. This is helpful to cars that are going fast around curves. If the roadway is not banked, the static friction between the tires and the road might not be enough to hold the car in place as it turns. The car can start to slide. The additional centripetal force caused by the banked road helps keep the car from sliding.

note

When you're riding in a car, you feel a centrifugal force that pushes you out away from the center of the turn. This is not a real force. It's caused by inertia. Your body has a tendency to keep going in the same direction it was before the turn. This is Newton's first law. That is, objects in motion tend to keep moving with the same speed and direction. It takes a force or group of forces to get them to change speed or direction.

What causes the centripetal force of banked roadways? Gravity. As you can see in Figure 15.4, gravity pulls straight down on the car. Because the roadway is at an angle, so is the normal force. The normal force has a component that pushes the car straight up in opposition to gravity. It also has a component that pushes the car down the slope of the road.

So to model the turning forces on a car, you can use the following formula:

$$\mathbf{F}_{\text{Turning}} = \mathbf{F}_{\text{CT}} + \mathbf{F}_{\text{CR}}$$
$$= \mu \mathbf{N} + \mathbf{N}_{\text{H}}$$

Here, $\mathbf{F}_{\text{Turning}}$ is the total turning force. $\mathbf{F}_{\text{CT}}$ represents the centripetal frictional force between the car's tires and the road, and $\mathbf{F}_{\text{CR}}$ is the centripetal force caused by the banking of the road. $\mathbf{F}_{\text{CT}}$ equals $\mu \mathbf{N} \cos\theta$, where μ is the static or dynamic coefficient of friction, depending on whether the car is sliding. $\mathbf{N}$ is the normal force, which equals $\mathbf{mg}$. In the previous formula, $\mathbf{N}_{\text{H}}$ is the horizontal component of the normal force. It points in toward the center of the turn.

You can calculate the velocity at which the car will begin to slide out as it turns. Use this formula:

$$v_{\text{T}} = \sqrt{rg(\tan\theta + \mu)}$$

Here, g is the acceleration due to gravity. The value r represents the radius of the curve, and θ is the banking angle of the roadway. μ is the coefficient of static friction between the tires and the road. The value v_{T} is the car's maximum tangential velocity before it starts to slide out.

note

Your game should decrease μ when conditions on the road are less than ideal.

If the velocity of a car in your game exceeds v_T, the game should start the car sliding and apply dynamic friction to it rather than static friction.

Implementing a Basic Car

In its most basic form, a car is not much more than a specialized rigid body. Listing 15.1 gives an implementation of a simple car class.

Listing 15.1
A Rudimentary Car Class

```
1    class basic_car : public rigid_body
2    {
3    private:
4        vector_3d initialForwardDirection;
5        vector_3d initialUpDirection;
6
7        force driveWheelForce;
8
9        scalar turnAngle;
10
11       scalar dragCoefficient;
12
13   public:
14       basic_car();
15
16       void InitialForwardDirection(
17           vector_3d forward);
18       vector_3d CurrentCarDirection(void);
19
20       void InitialUpDirection(
21           vector_3d up);
22
23       void DriveWheelForce(
24           force driveForce);
25       force DriveWheelForce(void);
26
27       void TurningAngle(
28           scalar theAngle);
29       scalar TurningAngle(void);
```

```
30
31          void DragCoefficient(scalar drag);
32          scalar DragCoefficient(void);
33
34          void WheelsLocked(bool areLocked);
35          bool WheelsLocked();
36
37          bool Update(
38              scalar changeInTime);
39      };
```

The car class in Listing 15.1 declares a pair of vectors that keep track of the car's orientation. As your program rotates the car, it has to rotate these two vectors as well. The car class also has a vector that contains the drive wheel force. If this force is positive, it's pushing the car forward. If it's negative, it's pushing the car backward or braking.

Line 9 of Listing 15.1 shows a private data member called turnAngle. This member holds the angle of rotation for a turn. A positive angle turns the car left, and a negative angle turns it right. Note that this angle is a rotation around the positive y axis. The car turns only in the xz plane. This implementation cannot show a car banking.

The last private data member in the class is the drag coefficient for wind resistance.

The member function in the basic_car class mostly just gets and sets its member data. However, two functions have implementations that are important to examine. These are shown in Listing 15.2.

Listing 15.2
The Workhorse Functions of the basic_car Class

```
1      vector_3d basic_car::CurrentCarDirection(void)
2      {
3          vector_3d currentDirection;
4
5          // First build a 2-D rotation matrix.
6          matrix2x2 carRotationMatrix;
7          carRotationMatrix.Element(
8              0,
9              0,
10             cosf(rigid_body::CurrentOrientation().YAngle()));
11         if (CloseToZero(
12             carRotationMatrix.Element(0,0)))
13         {
14             carRotationMatrix.Element(0,0,0.0);
15         }
```

```
16
17          carRotationMatrix.Element(
18              0,
19              1,
20              sinf(rigid_body::CurrentOrientation().YAngle()));
21          if (CloseToZero(
22              carRotationMatrix.Element(0,1)))
23          {
24              carRotationMatrix.Element(0,1,0.0);
25          }
26
27          carRotationMatrix.Element(
28              1,
29              0,
30              -sinf(rigid_body::CurrentOrientation().YAngle()));
31          if (CloseToZero(
32              carRotationMatrix.Element(1,0)))
33          {
34              carRotationMatrix.Element(1,0,0.0);
35          }
36
37          carRotationMatrix.Element(
38              1,
39              1,
40              cosf(rigid_body::CurrentOrientation().YAngle()));
41          if (CloseToZero(
42              carRotationMatrix.Element(1,1)))
43          {
44              carRotationMatrix.Element(1,1,0.0);
45          }
46
47          // Put the initial direction into a 2-D vector.
48          vector_2d temp2DVector;
49          temp2DVector.X(
50              initialForwardDirection.X());
51          temp2DVector.Y(
52              initialForwardDirection.Z());
53
54          // Now multiply the point by the rotation matrix.
55          temp2DVector =
56              carRotationMatrix * temp2DVector;
57
```

```
58        // Build the final 3-D vector.
59        currentDirection.X(
60            temp2DVector.X());
61        currentDirection.Y(0.0);
62        currentDirection.Z(
63            temp2DVector.Y());
64
65        return (currentDirection);
66    }
67
68
69    bool basic_car::Update(scalar changeInTime)
70    {
71
72        /* Determine the car direction by finding a unit vector pointing
73        from the center of mass to a point midway between the two front
74        wheels. */
75        vector_3d carDirection;
76        carDirection = CurrentCarDirection();
77        carDirection = carDirection.Normalize(SCALAR_TOLERANCE);
78
79        //
80        // Apply any existing turning force to the car.
81        //
82        force wheelTurningForce;
83        vector_3d turnDirection;
84
85        // If the car is moving and turning...
86        if ((!CloseToZero(point_mass::LinearVelocity().Norm())) &&
87            (!CloseToZero(turnAngle)))
88        {
89            // Convert to radians.
90            turnAngle = DegreesToRadians(turnAngle);
91
92            // The positive turn angle is a left turn. The negative is right.
93            angle_set_3d changeInAngle;
94            changeInAngle.SetXYZ(
95                0.0,
96                rigid_body::CurrentOrientation().YAngle() + turnAngle,
97                0.0);
98            rigid_body::CurrentOrientation(changeInAngle);
99        }
```

```
100
101
102        //
103        // Apply any drive wheel force to the car.
104        //
105
106        if (!CloseToZero(driveWheelForce.Force().Z()))
107        {
108            /* Point the force in the direction the car is moving when
109            accelerating or exactly opposite that direction when
110            braking. */
111            force engineForce;
112            engineForce.Force(
113                driveWheelForce.Force().Z() * carDirection);
114            engineForce.ApplicationPoint(vector_3d(0.0,0.0,0.0));
115
116
117            engineForce.Force(
118                engineForce.Force() +
119                point_mass::ImpulseForce().Force());
120            engineForce.ApplicationPoint(
121                point_mass::ImpulseForce().ApplicationPoint());
122            point_mass::ImpulseForce(engineForce);
123        }
124        else
125        {
126            driveWheelForce.Force(vector_3d(0.0,0.0,0.0));
127        }
128
129        //
130        // Apply wind resistance.
131        //
132        vector_3d windResistance;
133        windResistance =
134            point_mass::LinearVelocity() * dragCoefficient;
135        point_mass::LinearVelocity(
136            point_mass::LinearVelocity() - windResistance);
137        if (CloseToZero(point_mass::LinearVelocity().Norm()))
138        {
139            point_mass::LinearVelocity(vector_3d(0.0,0.0,0.0));
140        }
141
```

```
142        rigid_body::Update(changeInTime);
143
144        return (true);
145    }
```

The first of the two functions in Listing 15.2 is called CurrentCarDirection(). This function calculates and returns the direction that the car is pointed in the 3-D world. It must do this because the car class stores only the initial rotation it had when the scene started. If the class stored the current rotation, it would rotate the car by that amount each frame. The result would be a car that flip-flopped back and forth each frame. Instead, the class stores the initial setting and the turn angle, which is an offset from the initial position. Each frame, the program calculates the current position using the CurrentCarDirection() function.

To calculate the car's current direction, the CurrentCarDirection() function builds a 2-D rotation matrix. It only needs to be 2-D because the basic_car class moves the car only in the xz plane. The car cannot bank, which is fine for many games.

tip

If you want your game to show cars that bank as they go around turns, you need to override the CurrentCarDirection() and Update() functions in your derived car class. The CurrentCarDirection() and Update() functions must handle rotations in 3-D rather than 2-D.

After the CurrentCarDirection() function finishes building the 2-D rotation matrix, it creates a 2-D vector on lines 48–52. It sets this vector to the initial direction of the car. Notice that because the car moves in the xz plane, the x and z components of the 3-D directional vector are stored in the x and y components of the 2-D vector.

On lines 55–56 of Listing 15.2, the CurrentCarDirection() function multiplies the 2-D vector by the 2-D rotation matrix. It stores the results in a 3-D vector on lines 59–63. It ends by returning the 3-D vector.

Next, Listing 15.2 shows the Update() function. The first task that the Update() function performs is to call CurrentCarDirection() to get the car's current orientation. Next, it normalizes the vector. Recall that the drive wheel force always points in the +z direction. Braking or reverse force points in the –z direction. This enables the programmer who is using the class to accelerate and decelerate the car in a way that is conceptually similar to an actual car. However, it means that the Update() function must point the drive wheel force in the direction that the car is traveling. Also, the Update() function must know the car's current orientation so that it can turn the car properly. To accommodate both of these tasks, the Update() function calculates the car's direction first.

If the car is moving and turning, the Update() function rotates the car by the proper amount on lines 90–98 of Listing 15.2. To do this, it adds the turn angle to the current orientation. Because there is no banking, the rotation is around the y axis only.

Update() applies the drive wheel force beginning on line 106. It points the drive wheel force in the direction of the car's travel on lines 111–114. Because this is a simple implementation, it does not apply the drive wheel force at the point that the drive wheel contacts the ground. Instead, it simply applies the drive wheel force through the center of mass. This works well for the vast majority of games involving cars.

The drive wheel force is an impulse force. It is not constant because the player might accelerate or decelerate from one moment to the next. Update() stores the drive wheel force as an impulse force on lines 117–122.

Update() demonstrates the easy method of calculating wind resistance on lines 132–136 of Listing 15.2. On line 142, the Update() function calls the rigid_body::Update() function. This applies the constant and impulse forces to the car, moving it nicely through the 3-D world.

There's one important thing to notice about the implementation of the basic_car class: It does nothing about gravity. Does that mean the car floats off the ground? Absolutely not. The reason is that gravity is an external force. It pulls the car down to the ground, but the ground pushes back up with equal force. The sum of the external forces is 0. You only have to apply gravity to the car when it loses contact with the ground. In that situation, the sum of the external forces is no longer 0.

Hovercraft and Antigravity Vehicles

Hovercraft and cars are closely related. From a programming point of view, hovercraft are just specialized cars with different turning characteristics. Hovercraft are also a good basis for futuristic vehicles such as antigravity cars.

note

The technical name for hovercraft is Air Cushion Vehicles (ACVs) or Ground Effect Vehicles (GEVs).

How Hovercraft Work

Hovercraft use a kind of "skirt" to hold the air blowing downward from a fan. This creates a cushion of air on which the hovercraft rides. Figure 15.5 illustrates this effect.

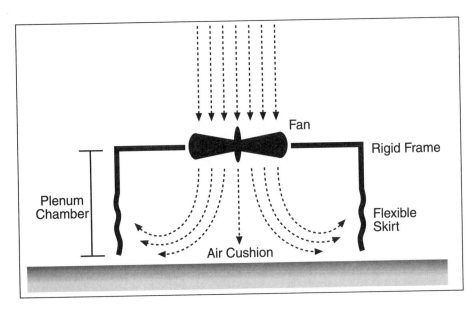

Figure 15.5
A hovercraft's air cushion.

The volume inside the hovercraft's skirt is called its plenum chamber. As the hovercraft moves, its air cushion enables it to float right over rough surfaces or even water. The skirt is flexible, so if the hovercraft encounters an obstacle such as a large rock or a moderately sized wave, the skirt bends. This protects the inflexible structure of the vehicle from being damaged.

Because hovercraft do not touch the surface over which they move, there is no real friction to slow them down. Hovercraft go much farther than cars on the same amount of forward thrust. Also, they have a stronger tendency than cars to keep going in the same direction they're moving, which can make them difficult to steer.

There are two ways to stop a hovercraft. The first is to let air resistance, which we'll talk about next, bring it to a stop. This generally does not work well because air resistance isn't strong enough for the fast decelerations that are common in games.

The other way to stop a hovercraft is to blow some air forward. This creates a force that acts just like the brakes on a car. Be aware, however, that air jets do not provide the same crisp deceleration response that brakes do. If your game uses this method of slowing hovercraft, you must balance your deceleration forces in such a way as to make a rather "mushy" braking effect.

Air Resistance on Hovercraft

Your game calculates air resistance for hovercraft in exactly the same way it is calculated for cars. The calculation for both cars and hovercraft is the same as was done for objects in water in Chapter 13.

Turning Hovercraft

Turning hovercraft is not like turning cars. Hovercraft generally move across mostly flat surfaces. When they turn, they do not bank. Instead, they do one of two things: They either use tail rudders (like an airplane's) to rotate the craft in the right direction and then apply thrust or they use air jets mounted on the front of the craft. Air jets on the bow can also be used as a braking system.

Turning the hovercraft with tail rudders means that your game has to simulate the forces of air pressure on the rudders. This is essentially the same as applying an air current to the tail rudders. Applying an air current works just like the water currents presented in the section titled "Currents in Water" in Chapter 13.

The forces on tail rudders cause a torque on the hovercraft that rotates it around its center of mass. The angle of rotation is always around the vertical axis. After the hovercraft rotates, the driver can apply a forward thrust with the rear fans to move the hovercraft in the right direction.

Like tail rudders, bow jets cause a torque that makes the craft rotate around its center of mass. With bow jets, hovercraft tend to handle a bit more like a car.

Ships and Boats

When you're writing games, implementing ships and boats seems very much like implementing a complex car or hovercraft. There is a variety of additional issues, but the basic principles are closely related.

Buoyancy of Ships and Boats

In Chapter 13, we took an in-depth look at why things float. We saw that the formula for calculating buoyancy is as follows:

$$F_b = \rho g V$$

where F_b is the upward force of buoyancy, ρ is the density of water, and V is the volume of water displaced by the hull of the boat or ship.

note

Never ask someone in the navy or merchant marine, "What kind of boat do you ride on?" They're likely to look at you in a sour way and explain that boats are something you row or ski behind. They tell you they sail on ships, not boats. I know this from experience.

That's all well and good. But the volume of a hull can be extremely complex to calculate. Let's take a quick look at how that's done in games.

Calculating Hull Volume

It would be nice if there were a simple way to calculate the volume of a hull. There isn't. The hulls of boats and ships can be very complicated. They have lots of curvature in them. They can have recesses in or appendages on the hull. Finding the volume of a hull is a task that even engineers struggle with.

Does that mean that you and I have to struggle with complex formulas and advanced calculus to write our games?

By now, you've probably guessed that I'm about to present some good ways to cheat that are perfectly acceptable for games. You're right. You know me so well.

Even in high-speed boat racing games, estimations of the volumes of hulls are just fine. If the calculations are a bit off, it doesn't generally matter. Why? Because the calculations are consistently off for all the boats in the game. All the calculations have essentially the same errors in them, so almost all hull configurations in your games will be correct in relation to each other.

The easiest way to approximate the volume of a hull is to use rectangular solids and pyramids. Yes, pyramids. Figure 15.6 shows how the technique works.

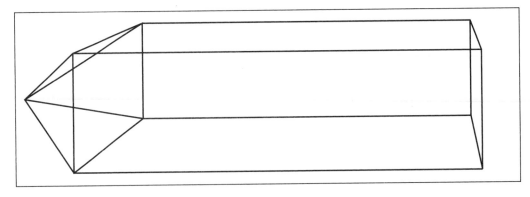

Figure 15.6
Estimating the volume of a hull.

Figure 15.6 shows a rectangular solid with a pyramid stuck on the front. It doesn't look much like the hull of a ship. The bottom isn't curved like a hull, the sides don't taper outward, and the front certainly doesn't look like the front of a boat. How can this work?

The answer: It's good enough for games.

A rectangular solid can often be used to approximate most of a hull's volume. If you're finding the volume of a complex hull, such as a hydroplane, you'll probably have to use more than one rectangular solid. Even so, your calculations are usually just fine.

tip

The volume of a rectangular solid is length×width×height.

The front of the boat is a bit tricky. It tapers up and forward so that it cuts through the water with minimal resistance. The deeper the V of the hull, the more complicated finding its volume gets.

A simple way to estimate the volume of the forward part of the hull is to approximate it with a pyramid. They have similar volumes. Following is the formula for calculating the volume of a pyramid:

$$\frac{1}{3} \times \text{length} \times \text{width}$$

where length and width are the length and width of the base, respectively.

A better approximation is to use a three-sided pyramid. This is actually called a tetrahedron. It is made up of four equilateral triangles. Equilateral triangles are triangles whose sides are all the same length and whose corners all have the same angle. Following is the formula for calculating the volume of a tetrahedron:

$$\frac{1}{3} \times \text{Area}_{\text{Base}} \times \text{Height}$$

where $\text{Area}_{\text{Base}}$ is the area of the base triangle and Height is the height of the tetrahedron. You can find the area of the base triangle with this formula:

$$\frac{1}{2} \times s \times h$$

where s is the length of the one side of the triangle and h is the triangle's height.

You can find the height of a tetrahedron with this formula:

$$s\sqrt{\frac{3}{2}}$$

where s is the length of one of the sides.

As you can see, using a tetrahedron is slightly more complex, but not much. And it gives you a much closer approximation of the front of a ship's hull.

Stability of Ships and Boats

Ships can be stable or unstable. Stability is determined by the position of the ship's *center of gravity* (center of mass), its center of buoyancy, and its metacenter. These are illustrated in Figure 15.7.

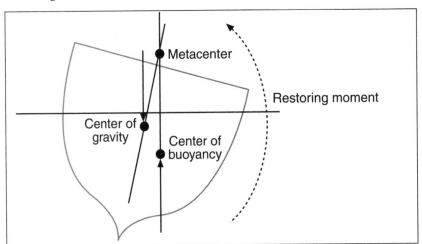

Figure 15.7
Stability in ships.

In Figure 15.7, the ship's center of mass is fairly low in the hull. This helps make the ship stable. The *center of buoyancy* is the point through which the total buoyancy force acts. When this ship is in its full upright position, the center of buoyancy should be below the center of gravity. As the ship tips toward starboard (right) or port (left), the center of buoyancy moves in the direction that the ship is tipped. The line of action for the buoyancy force remains vertical at all times. If you extend a vector from the ship's lengthwise centerline through its center of gravity, the vector eventually crosses the line of action of the buoyancy force. The point at which those two vectors cross is called the *metacenter*.

To keep a ship from capsizing, the metacenter must remain above the center of gravity. If a ship tips too far, the metacenter moves below the center of gravity. When that happens, the ship capsizes.

When a ship tips, the center of gravity and the center of buoyancy are offset from one another. That's because the center of buoyancy moves to starboard or port. Remember that the force of gravity works downward through the center of gravity, and the force of buoyancy works upward through the center of buoyancy. When these two centers are not aligned, their respective forces create a torque that acts in the opposite direction that the ship is tipped. That torque is called the *restoring moment*.

Applying this to games can get very complex, depending on the approach you take. Calculating centers of mass, centers of buoyancy, and metacenters is another job for people with advanced mechanical and nautical engineering experience. The best thing you and I can do when we're modeling the physics of a ship is to just arbitrarily set the center of gravity and metacenter. You might have to use experimentation to get the best values.

After you've set the center of gravity and the metacenter, you're ready. As the ship tips, the metacenter moves in a circle around the center of gravity. Get the restoring moment (which is a torque) by applying the force of buoyancy at the metacenter rather than at the center of buoyancy. It's actually cheating to apply it at the metacenter, but it saves you from having to find the center of buoyancy.

Mass and Virtual Mass

The mass of a moving ship can actually be higher than the mass of the ship and its cargo. As a ship moves through water, friction accelerates some of the water around the ship.

Essentially, some of the fluid "sticks" to the surface of the hull because of friction. The result is that particles of fluid right next to the hull have the same velocity as the hull. As you move away from the hull, the fluid particles have a velocity that is closer and closer to that of the surrounding water. After a certain distance, the hull has no effect on the velocity of the water particles.

Taken together, the mass of the ship plus the mass of the water that moves with the ship is called *virtual mass*. For large ships, the layer of accelerated water can be several feet thick. This adds a significant mass to all of the force and resistance calculations. To be accurate, your ship should simulate a large ship's virtual mass.

note

Virtual mass is not significant with small ships and boats. Games should not bother calculating virtual mass unless they are simulating large ships such as tankers and aircraft carriers.

Accurately calculating virtual mass is another task we'll leave to engineers who design boats. It's far too complex to be done in a single frame of a game. However, we can estimate the virtual mass pretty easily. Most methods of estimation use an ellipsoid that is the same length as the ship. I'll jump straight to the result without going into exactly how these methods actually work.

Virtual mass estimation methods need a coefficient that we can multiply by the mass to get a reasonable result. To get the coefficient, imagine that we can make a ship that has an infinitely thin beam (width). We can't do that, but imagine we can. At this width, the added mass is essentially 0. Ellipsoid estimation methods show that the coefficient of virtual mass is 0.0 when the beam is 0.

Now imagine that we have a ship whose beam is equal to its length. The ship is perfectly round. At that beam, ellipsoid estimation methods show that the coefficient of virtual mass is 0.5.

Using this range, we can express the ship's virtual mass as a percentage of its actual mass. For instance, a spherical ship has a virtual mass that is 1.0 + 0.5 times its actual mass, or 150% of its actual mass.

I can honestly say that I've never seen a spherical boat. In reality, most ships have an added mass that does not exceed 20% of their actual mass. Therefore, almost all ships have a virtual mass that is less than 120% of their actual mass. For most ships, the virtual mass is somewhere between 104% and 115% of the actual mass.

We can express all this in terms of a coefficient of virtual mass in the following formula:

$$m_v = m(1 + c_{vm})$$

In this equation, m_v is the virtual mass of the ship, and m represents the actual mass. c_{vm} is the coefficient of virtual mass. Its value should be as follows:

$$0.0 \le c_{vm} \le 0.5$$

This simple equation can be used to estimate virtual mass any time your ship is moving. You can then apply the virtual mass to all of the calculations of movement.

tip

Finding the best coefficient of virtual mass for the ships in your games requires some experimentation and parameter tweaking. Try it initially with a value of 0.10 and increase or decrease from there as needed.

Resistance and Ships

In Chapter 13, you saw that water exerts a resistance whenever objects move through it. This viscous drag is calculated with the formulas you saw earlier in this chapter. Recall that Table 15.1 gives the formulas for air resistance. Both air and water are fluids, so you use the same formulas for calculating resistance in both. The only difference is that for air resistance, you use a lower coefficient of frictional drag than you do in water.

However, when a ship moves through water, viscous drag isn't the only thing that can exert a resisting force on it. If you're ever on a boat, go to the stern (back) and look down at the water as the boat moves. Whether you're on a sailboat or a powerboat, there's always a place right at the back where the water swirls behind the boat. That swirling water sets up an area of low pressure behind the boat. The low pressure causes a force that pushes in a direction opposite to the movement of the ship. That means the total resistance is this:

$$R_{Total} = R_{Drag} + R_{Pressure}$$

Calculating the resistance due to pressure requires a detailed knowledge of computational fluid dynamics. But again, we can estimate it. Resistance from pressure is never more than 10% of resistance from drag. We can easily invent a formula that expresses the pressure resistance:

$$R_{Pressure} = R_{Drag}\left(1 + C_{Pressure}\right)$$

As you might expect, values $R_{Pressure}$ and R_{Drag} in this formula represent the resistance due to pressure and drag, respectively. $C_{Pressure}$ is a coefficient invented just for this formula. It represents the "coefficient of pressure," expressed as a number between 0.0 and 0.10 inclusive. The coefficient of pressure doesn't really exist in physics. I made it up simply for convenience.

Set the coefficient of pressure higher for larger ships. For all but supertankers and aircraft carriers, this coefficient should be less than 0.05.

tip

> If you want to be more detailed, you can also add resistance due to waves pushing on the ship's hull. However, unless your ship is in a storm, I recommend against it. If you decide to add it in, estimate it just like we did for pressure resistance. Make up a "coefficient of wave resistance" and use the formula $R_{Wave} = R_{Drag} (1 + C_{WR})$, where R_{Wave} is wave resistance and C_{WR} is the coefficient of wave resistance. The value of C_{WR} should vary between 0.0 and 1.0, depending on weather conditions.

Air Resistance

High-speed boats are subject to significant air resistance, just like racing cars. By now you know that you use the formulas in Table 15.1 to calculate air resistance.

It's possible for air resistance to impede even large, slow-moving ships. This occurs when the wind is blowing fast, as it sometimes does at sea. If your game has a large ship that's in a storm, the force of air resistance should be added to your calculations. However, if the wind speed is below 40 mph (64 kph), don't bother adding air resistance to the movement of large ships.

Currents and Waves

For greatest realism, your game can take water currents and waves into account. They are not as hard to deal with as you might expect.

Water currents have a significant effect on the navigation of ships and boats. Figure 15.8 shows why.

The figure shows an overhead view of a boat moving through the water. A current moves from left to right. The intent is for the boat to move straight forward. However, because of the force exerted by the current, the boat's actual destination is to the right of its intended destination.

To simulate a current in water, you basically imagine that there is a large pipe traveling next to your boat. The pipe contains a flow of water that comes out the end and pushes on the boat. With this image in our minds, we can use the same formula for currents that we used for water moving through pipes in Chapter 13. Here it is again:

$$\mathbf{F_W} = \rho A v^2$$

The cross-sectional area of the imaginary pipe is a half ellipse that is the same length as your ship. The velocity is the velocity of the water, not the velocity of the ship.

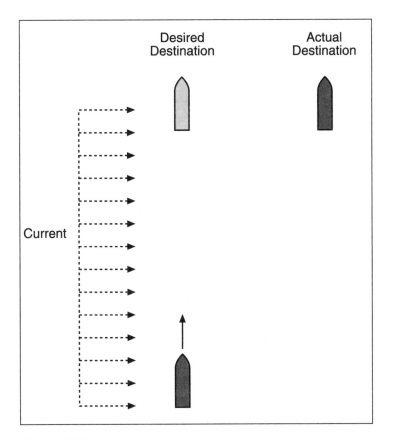

Figure 15.8
Currents in water.

note

In software, you can model complex currents as a series of connected point masses. For the vast majority of games, however, the "imaginary pipe" technique is sufficient.

Modeling the effects of waves is not as hard as modeling the waves themselves. A wave is essentially a pulsating current. You can use the same formula to calculate the force of a wave that we used for the "imaginary pipe" technique. However, that is not realistic.

The force of the wave can push the ship forward or backward, if it is strong enough. It can make the ship tip from side to side. In heavy weather, waves often make the bows of ships bob up and down. In a storm, the up and down motion can become a rather relentless pounding. To model all these effects of waves realistically, you need to use the wave formulas presented in the "Waves" section in Chapter 13. Here they are again for your convenience.

$$F_{2T} = F_{1T} \frac{r_1^2}{r_2^2}$$

$$F_{2L} = F_{1L} \frac{r_1^2}{r_2^2}$$

If you're modeling the bobbing motion caused by waves, use the first formula. It gives a wave's transverse force. To model the pushing effects of waves, use the second formula. It's for finding longitudinal forces exerted by waves.

Summary

Although games contain many different types of vehicles, the techniques you use for modeling their physics are similar for each vehicle type. The essential technique, which this chapter demonstrated, is to find the forces that the vehicle exerts on its environment and the forces that the environment exerts on the vehicle. In almost every circumstance, this gives you a good model of how a vehicle behaves in reality.

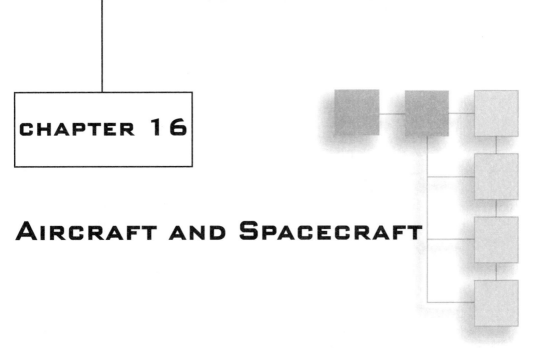

CHAPTER 16

AIRCRAFT AND SPACECRAFT

I took my first computer graphics class in college shortly before the dinosaurs went extinct. Well, sometimes it seems like it was that long ago. My project for the class was a flight simulator. That was one of the hardest programs I've ever written in my entire career.

Why?

Partly, it was because I really didn't know a lot about what I was attempting. I found out later that most people who took that class were much less ambitious in their projects.

Another reason that writing a flight simulator was such a daunting task was because I had to write the entire thing from scratch on a DOS computer with an EGA screen. When I needed a rasterizer, I had to write it. I wrote the routines that painted the entire landscape, including the buildings and trees. There was none of this loading-a-mesh stuff. And textures? Forget about textures.

Well, two or three ice ages have gone by since then. With the tools you have now, you can write a simple flight simulator with just a couple of hundred lines of code. This chapter shows how. In addition, it presents an overview of the physics involved in making planes fly, rockets launch, and spacecraft travel the universe.

Flight Simulators the Easy Way

To start our discussion of aircraft and spacecraft, we'll examine ways to cheat. It's okay. Game programmers cheated for years before they started using physics in their flight simulators.

To understand how to write a convincing flight simulator, it's necessary to know how planes move while in flight. Figure 16.1 illustrates the basic movements of an aircraft.

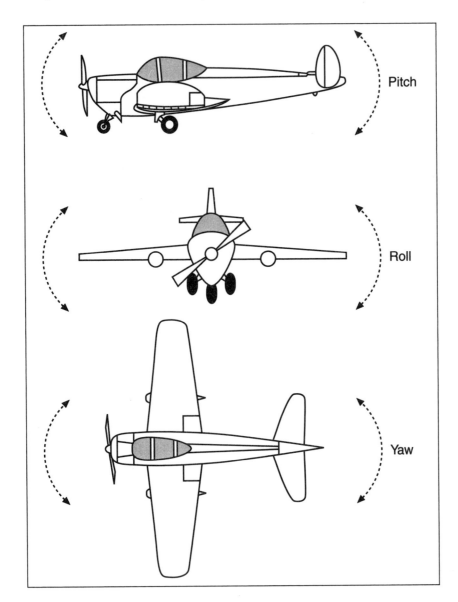

Figure 16.1
The movements of an aircraft in flight.

Figure 16.1 shows that the three basic movements of airplanes are rotations. When the plane rotates the nose upward or downward, it's called the *pitch*. Moving the nose of the plane left or right is called *yaw*. If the plane turns around its lengthwise axis, the wingtips move up or down. This movement is called *roll*. By mimicking these three basic movements, you can simulate the flight of an airplane.

Flight with Little or No Physics

In its simplest form, you do not need physics to write a flight simulator. All you need to do is write a program that rolls the point of view around in the same way an airplane moves. Add decent scenery and a convincing set of controls across the bottom of the screen, and you have a fun game. For years, this was exactly how flight simulators were written.

With Direct3D, this whole process is incredibly easy. That's especially true if you use the framework provided with this book. In Chapter 14, "Getting Ready for Games," I presented a program that demonstrated how to move the camera around. You can write a convincing flight simulator using that program as a basis. It does not require physics.

Implementing a Simple Flight Simulator

To provide a basis for the discussions of physics presented later, let's first implement a flight simulator that uses very little physics. In this flight simulator, we'll write the point of view in third person. In other words, the player will be able to see the airplane moving over the landscape.

The basic_flyer Class

The first thing that the flight simulator needs is a class to represent in the airplane. It must load the plane's mesh. Like the car simulation in the previous chapter, the airplane in this program will stay in the center of the screen. The scenery will move around in a way that gives the impression that the plane is turning, rolling, and so forth. Listing 16.1 gives the definition of the basic_flyer class.

note

You'll find the code for the basic_flyer class on the CD-ROM. It's in the folder Source\Chapter16\BasicFlyer. The files you're looking for are PMBasicFlyer.h and PMBasicFlyer.cpp.

Listing 16.1
The basic_flyer Class

```
1     class basic_flyer : public rigid_body
2     {
3     private:
4         angle_set_3d turnAngles;
5         vector_3d initialForwardDirection;
6         vector_3d initialUpDirection;
7
8     public:
```

```
9         basic_flyer();
10
11        void Pitch(scalar changeInPitch);
12        scalar Pitch(void);
13
14        void Yaw(scalar changeInYaw);
15        scalar Yaw(void);
16
17        void Roll(scalar changeInRoll);
18        scalar Roll(void);
19
20        void InitialForwardDirection(
21            vector_3d forward);
22
23        void InitialUpDirection(
24            vector_3d up);
25
26        vector_3d CurrentDirection(void);
27
28        vector_3d CurrentUpDirection(void);
29
30        virtual bool Update(
31            scalar changeInTime);
32    };
```

The basic_flyer class is derived from the rigid_body class. The data members that it adds are for maneuvering the vehicle. They specify the pitch, yaw, roll, and initial orientation.

warning

Your program must set the private data members initialForwardDirection and initialUpDirection immediately after it loads the vehicle's mesh and before it does any transformations on the mesh. The basic_flyer class must know the initial orientation of the mesh when it is loaded to be able to position it properly as the vehicle flies.

The member functions whose prototypes appear on lines 9–24 set or get the values of the private member data. In addition, the basic_flyer class provides functions to calculate the current orientation and to update the position of the vehicle. It does not provide a Render() function. Instead, it uses the Render() function it inherits.

The Design of the basic_flyer Class

The basic_flyer class is designed so that the vehicle it displays does not exactly mimic the movements of an airplane. This is done on purpose so that you can use this class as the basis for a large number of flying vehicles. If you run the sample program for this chapter on the CD-ROM, you'll see that the "airplane" does not bank as it turns. Real airplanes must bank as you turn them. You *can* bank and turn the vehicle that the sample program displays. But those actions require you to press two different controls.

You can make the classes that you derive from the basic_flyer class bank the aircraft as it turns. Or you can make those separate operations. It just depends on what kind of vehicle you're making. For instance, if you're writing an airplane simulator, your derived class needs to add banking.

Alternatively, if you're creating a fighter vehicle that flies through space, banking might not be something you want to add. You can even use the basic_flyer class as the basis of a game similar to the *Descent* series. In *Descent*, you worked your way through underground tunnels full of insane robots controlled by an alien computer virus. The fighter that you flew in had separate controls for pitch, yaw, and roll. Aliens could come from any direction. There was no real concept of up and down. For a while, *Descent* was a favorite of mine. I enjoyed the freedom of movement that the game simulated. As I commuted to and from work, I often wished I had a vehicle that could move as freely.

The CurrentDirection(), CurrentUpDirection(), and Update() functions all appear in the file PMBasicFlyer.cpp. Listing 16.2 displays their implementations.

Listing 16.2
The Implementations of the CurrentDirection(), CurrentUpDirection(), and Update() Functions

```
1     vector_3d basic_flyer::CurrentDirection(void)
2     {
3         matrix4x4 rotationMatrix;
4
5         return (
6             rotationMatrix.RotateXYZ(
7                 initialForwardDirection,
8                 rigid_body::CurrentOrientation()));
9     }
10
11
12    vector_3d basic_flyer::CurrentUpDirection(void)
13    {
14        matrix4x4 rotationMatrix;
15
```

```
16          return (
17              rotationMatrix.RotateXYZ(
18                  initialUpDirection,
19                  rigid_body::CurrentOrientation()));
20      }
21
22  bool basic_flyer::Update(
23      scalar changeInTime)
24  {
25      // If the craft is turning...
26      if ((!CloseToZero(turnAngles.XAngle())) ||
27          (!CloseToZero(turnAngles.YAngle())) ||
28          (!CloseToZero(turnAngles.ZAngle())))
29      {
30          //
31          // Rotate the aircraft.
32          //
33          angle_set_3d changeInAngle;
34          changeInAngle.SetXYZ(
35              rigid_body::CurrentOrientation().XAngle() + turnAngles.XAngle(),
36              rigid_body::CurrentOrientation().YAngle() + turnAngles.YAngle(),
37              rigid_body::CurrentOrientation().ZAngle() + turnAngles.ZAngle());
38
39          rigid_body::CurrentOrientation(changeInAngle);
40
41          //
42          // Rotate the velocity vector with the aircraft.
43          //
44          vector_3d newVelocity;
45          matrix4x4 rotationMatrix;
46
47          // Find the direction of the new velocity.
48          newVelocity =
49              rotationMatrix.RotateXYZ(
50                  initialForwardDirection,
51                  changeInAngle);
52
53          // Change it to a unit vector.
54          newVelocity = newVelocity.Normalize(SCALAR_TOLERANCE);
55
56          // Multiply in the current magnitude of the velocity.
57          newVelocity *= rigid_body::LinearVelocity().Norm();
```

```
58
59              // Set the velocity with the proper direction.
60              rigid_body::LinearVelocity(newVelocity);
61
62              /* Reset the turn angles to zero in preparation for the next
63              frame. */
64              turnAngles.SetXYZ(0.0,0.0,0.0);
65          }
66
67      return (rigid_body::Update(changeInTime));
68  }
```

To implement the CurrentDirection() function in Listing 16.2, I added matrix4x4 and vector_4d classes to the physics modeling framework's math library. These two classes are the 4-D equivalent of the matrix3x3 and vector_3d classes. You use them to do transformations in 3-D. Specifically, the CurrentDirection() function uses the matrix4x4 and vector_4d classes to rotate the vector that points forward. Recall that the basic_flyer class contains a vector called initialForwardDirection. The CurrentDirection() function passes the rotation angles stored in the rigid_body class, which is the parent of basic_flyer, to the matrix4x4 class's RotateXYZ() function. The RotateXYZ() function rotates the vector in initialForwardDirection to the angles specified by rigid_body::CurrentOrientation(). The result is a vector that points in the vehicle's current forward direction.

The CurrentUpDirection() function works in a manner that is almost the same as the CurrentDirection() function. The only real difference is that the CurrentUpDirection() function rotates the vector that points in the "up" direction. The "up" direction does not have to be pointing away from the surface of the Earth. It points whichever way the top of the pilot's head points. So if the pilot is doing a barrel roll and the vehicle is currently upside down, the "up" direction points straight at the ground.

The basic_flyer class's Update() function appears on lines 22–68 of Listing 16.2. It rotates the vehicle from the current orientation by the angles specified in the private data member turnAngles.

In addition, the Update() function rotates the vehicle's velocity vector. This keeps the vehicle moving in the same direction that it's pointing. To rotate the velocity vector, the Update() function first finds the current direction that the vehicle is pointing. Next, it converts the direction vector into a unit vector on line 54. Update() then gets the magnitude of the velocity vector and multiplies it by the unit direction vector. The result is a vector that points in the direction that the vehicle is facing and has the magnitude of the current velocity. On line 60, the Update() function sets this new vector as the linear velocity. It also sets the turn angles to zero on line 64. Before the Update() function exists, it updates the vehicle's position by invoking the rigid_body::Update() function.

Using the basic_flyer Class

Building a flight simulator with the basic_flyer class requires only a few hundred lines of code. The essential tasks you have to accomplish are as follows:

1. Initialize Direct3D.
2. Initialize the scene's geometry and the basic_flyer object.
3. Process the user's input.
4. Update the scene based on the user's input.
5. Update the camera position based on the movement of the vehicle.
6. Render the scene.

Steps 1, 4, and 6 should be fairly straightforward to you by now, so we'll focus on steps 2, 3, and 5. The code that accomplishes these tasks appears in Listing 16.3.

Listing 16.3
Important Functions from FlightSim.cpp

```
1      void my_game::SetupGeometry()
2      {
3          // Set up the ground.
4          theGround.LoadMesh("ground.x");
5
6          // Now add the plane.
7          thePlane.LoadMesh("plane.x");
8
9          //
10         // Set the plane's properties.
11         //
12         thePlane.InitialForwardDirection(
13             vector_3d(0.0,0.0,-1.0f));
14         thePlane.InitialUpDirection(
15             vector_3d(0.0,1.0f,0.0));
16         thePlane.Location(vector_3d(0.0,7.0,0.0));
17         thePlane.BoundingSphereRadius(2.0);
18         thePlane.Mass(1000.0f);
19         thePlane.RotationalInertia(
20             vector_3d(5000.0f,5000.0f,1000.0f));
21
22         /* Rotate the plane so that it's pointing away from the
23         viewer. */
24         thePlane.CurrentOrientation(
25             angle_set_3d(
```

```
26                    0.0,
27                    DegreesToRadians(180.0f),
28                    0.0));
29
30        // Set the velocity in the direction you want the plane to fly.
31        thePlane.LinearVelocity(
32            vector_3d(0.0,0.0,30.0f));
33    }
34
35    void my_game::SetViewPoint()
36    {
37        // Get a unit vector in the plane's direction of travel.
38        vector_3d planeDirection;
39        planeDirection = thePlane.CurrentDirection();
40        planeDirection = planeDirection.Normalize(SCALAR_TOLERANCE);
41
42        vector_3d planeUpDirection;
43        planeUpDirection = thePlane.CurrentUpDirection();
44        planeUpDirection = planeUpDirection.Normalize(SCALAR_TOLERANCE);
45
46        // Point to a specific location straight back behind the plane.
47        planeDirection *= 20;
48
49        // Set the camera slightly "above" that location.
50        eyePoint =
51            thePlane.Location() -
52            planeDirection +
53            (planeUpDirection * 5);
54
55        lookatPoint = thePlane.Location();
56        upDirection.x = planeUpDirection.X();
57        upDirection.y = planeUpDirection.Y();
58        upDirection.z = planeUpDirection.Z();
59
60        D3DXMATRIX tempViewMatrix;
61        D3DXMatrixLookAtLH(
62            &tempViewMatrix,&eyePoint,&lookatPoint,&upDirection);
63        theApp.ViewMatrix(tempViewMatrix);
64    }
65
66
67    bool my_game::ProcessInput()
```

```
68    {
69        const int KEYBOARD_DATA_ARRAY_SIZE = 256;
70        BYTE keys[KEYBOARD_DATA_ARRAY_SIZE];
71        static int accelMagnitude = 0;
72        static int decelMagnitude = 0;
73        static int leftMagnitude = 0;
74        static int rightMagnitude = 0;
75
76        vector_3d tempVector;
77        force tempForce;
78
79        HRESULT result =
80            theApp.Keyboard()->GetDeviceState(
81                KEYBOARD_DATA_ARRAY_SIZE,
82                keys);
83
84        // If the input could not be retrieved...
85        if (result != DI_OK)
86        {
87            result = theApp.Keyboard()->Acquire();
88            while (result == DIERR_INPUTLOST)
89            {
90                result = theApp.Keyboard()->Acquire();
91            }
92
93            /* If another app has priority or some other error has
94            occurred... */
95            if ((result == DIERR_OTHERAPPHASPRIO) ||
96                (result == DIERR_NOTACQUIRED))
97            {
98                // Just try again later.
99                return (true);
100           }
101       }
102       // Else the input was retrieved...
103       else
104       {
105           // If the up arrow is pressed...
106           if (DirectInputKeyDown(keys[DIK_UP]))
107           {
108               // The control stick is pushed forward.
109               thePlane.Pitch(
```

```
110                            thePlane.Pitch() + 5);
111                    }
112                    // Else if the down arrow is pressed...
113                    else if (DirectInputKeyDown(keys[DIK_DOWN]))
114                    {
115                        // The control stick is pulled backward.
116                        thePlane.Pitch(
117                            thePlane.Pitch() - 5);
118                    }
119
120                    // If the left arrow is pressed...
121                    if (DirectInputKeyDown(keys[DIK_LEFT]))
122                    {
123                        // The control stick is pushed left.
124                        thePlane.Yaw(
125                            thePlane.Yaw() - 5);
126                    }
127                    // Else if the right arrow is pressed...
128                    else if (DirectInputKeyDown(keys[DIK_RIGHT]))
129                    {
130                        // The control stick is pushed right.
131                        thePlane.Yaw(
132                            thePlane.Yaw() + 5);
133                    }
134
135                    // If A is pressed...
136                    if (DirectInputKeyDown(keys[DIK_A]))
137                    {
138                        // The left rudder pedal is pressed.
139                        thePlane.Roll(
140                            thePlane.Roll() + 5);
141                    }
142                    // Else if S is pressed...
143                    else if (DirectInputKeyDown(keys[DIK_S]))
144                    {
145                        // The right rudder pedal is pressed.
146                        thePlane.Roll(
147                            thePlane.Roll() - 5);
148                    }
149            }
150
151        return (true);
152    }
```

Listing 16.3 begins with the SetupGeometry() function. The SetupGeometry() function initializes the 3-D scene through which the airplane flies. It also loads the airplane. As in past chapters, I didn't put error checking into the code of the SetupGeometry() function for clarity and simplicity. Your programs obviously need to add error checking to be robust.

After the SetupGeometry() function loads the scene and the airplane, it sets the plane's properties. On lines 12–13, SetupGeometry() sets the direction that the plane's mesh points when it's loaded. It sets the plane's up direction on lines 14–15. These initializations must be performed for the basic_flyer class to function properly.

On lines 16–60 of Listing 16.3, SetupGeometry() initializes the basic physics parameters required for proper movement. It does not apply forces to the plane. The statements on lines 24–28 reorient the plane so that it points away from the player. On lines 31–32, SetupGeometry() sets the plane's velocity. That is the only bit of physics that this simulation employs.

The SetViewPoint() function begins on line 35 of Listing 16.3. This function uses the airplane's forward and up vectors to orient the camera. It sets the camera at a position that is behind and slightly above the plane. SetViewPoint() then points the camera at the plane's center of mass.

You might be wondering why the camera is positioned slightly above the plane. This camera position helps the player get a better view of the plane. If the camera were straight back, the player would see just the tail and wings. Most of the body would be obscured.

tip

When you're writing programs that are more complex than the examples in this book, it's wise to pay attention to small details such as camera angles. People's impressions and opinions of your game are built on such small details.

The last function in Listing 16.3 is ProcessInput(). For the purposes of this discussion, the interesting part begins on line 106. This is where the ProcessInput() function reacts to user input. The program uses the up and down arrow keys to simulate the control stick being pressed forward and pulled backward. This is the plane's pitch. Beginning on line 121, ProcessInput() uses the left and right arrow keys to control the plane's yaw. On lines 136–148, the function uses the A and S keys to control the plane's roll.

Using these control keys, you can ascend, descend, roll, and turn the plane. In real planes, pilots use both the control stick and the rudder pedals to bank the plane. In many flight simulators, however, the games perform both the yaw and roll functions using only the left and right arrows. This makes the plane bank realistically when it turns. It also simplifies the control of the airplane for the average player who might not have a strong background in flying aircraft.

The Physics of Aircraft

Flight simulators these days are much more sophisticated than the one we just implemented. They almost always use at least the basic physics of flight. Most use real engineering data collected from actual wing configurations. Some enable you to design your own airplane. You can put the wings of a 747 onto a Cessna and see what happens (*lots* of lift)!

To implement a flight simulator that actually uses physics, game programmers need a good grasp of the components of an aircraft and the forces that act on them.

Essential Parts of an Aircraft

An aircraft is more than just wings. It has a collection of parts that have to work together to keep the craft in the air. Figure 16.2 shows the most important components of an airplane.

Every aircraft needs a fuselage. That is the main part of the plane. Somewhere on the fuselage is the cockpit, where the pilot sits. On small aircraft, the cockpit is often over the wings. The center of the airplane's gravity (mass) is along the centerline of the fuselage. It is positioned somewhere between the wings.

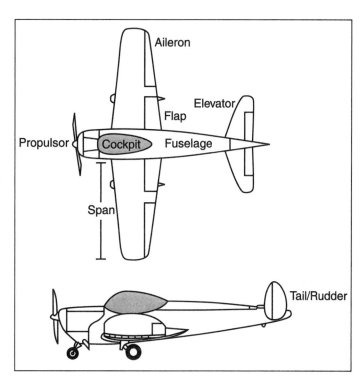

Figure 16.2
The primary components of an aircraft.

warning

It is possible (but dangerous) for the center of mass not to be between the wings. However, aircraft like that are *much* less stable. Most of the plane's weight should be between or on the wings.

Wings come in many shapes. Small planes have wings that are generally rectangular in shape when viewed from above. Faster planes use backward-swept wings because they decrease the turbulence that develops over the wings at high speeds. Some experimental aircraft use forward-swept wings. Forward-swept wings enable planes to be much more nimble in the air. However, they are inherently unstable, so planes that have them must be controlled partially by computer. The computer controls the plane in such a way as to compensate for the instability. The computer must do it because it's not possible for a human pilot to react fast enough when flying at supersonic speeds.

In Figure 16.2, you can see that a plane's control surfaces are attached to its wings. For takeoff and landing, planes extend their flaps. Flaps are control surfaces designed to provide additional lift. They also increase the drag on the plane. Additional drag is just what the occupants want when the plane is landing. It helps slow the plane down. In general, flaps are deflected downward 30 to 60°. During takeoff, they are not deflected as much—often less than 45° upward. Extending them less means less lift, but it also means less drag. Drag is not something that you want a lot of during takeoff.

Ailerons are also shown attached to the wings in Figure 16.2. The ailerons roll the plane around its lengthwise axis. When the left aileron goes up, the right one goes down and vice versa.

The propulsor drives the airplane forward. A propulsor can be a propeller, as shown in Figure 16.2, a jet engine, or even a rocket engine. In the case of small, propeller-driven planes, the propulsor is usually mounted on the front and pulls the plane forward. However, some models have the propeller mounted on the back, and it pushes the plane forward. Propulsors also can be mounted on the wings.

Pilots change the pitch of their aircraft with elevators. An elevator can be mounted on the front of the plane, but it's most common to mount them on the airplane's tail, as shown in Figure 16.2. In some cases, the entire tail wings rotate to form the elevator.

The final control surface is the rudder. Unlike other control surfaces, rudders are vertical. They control the plane's yaw. The rudder can be a surface mounted on the rear of the tail, or the entire vertical section of the tail can rotate as a rudder.

The Invention of Control Surfaces

In the early days of aviation, pilots flew unpowered gliders that needed no control surfaces. Hang gliders are the modern form of these vehicles. Orville and Wilbur Wright, inspired by these early attempts at flight, decided to try to build a powered aircraft.

During their early tests, the Wright brothers quickly realized that a steering rudder, much like that of a boat, would be needed. The need for an elevator to control pitch also became quickly obvious. However, no one had yet dealt with the idea of lateral control (roll).

As the Wrights approached their first powered flight, they discovered that lateral control (roll) was critical for two reasons. First, gusts of wind from the right or left can tip an airplane upside down if a pilot has no means of compensating. Second, turning an aircraft without banking results in a flat, skipping motion. This kind of turn is highly unstable.

While thinking about this problem one day, Wilbur Wright was looking at a small box he was holding in his hands. The box was long, narrow, and somewhat flat, rather like an airplane wing. As he looked at it, Wilbur flexed the box with a twisting motion. With that, the idea of wing warping was born.

By pulling cords that differentially twisted the wing, the Wrights were able to introduce lateral control into powered aircraft. Before their first powered flight, the Wrights patented the idea of wing warping.

Not long after the Wrights' historic flight, a group called the Aerial Experiment Association flew a powered aircraft called the Red Wing. It had no wing warping or lateral control. Those on the project were aware of the Wright brothers' patent and decided to try something different so as not to infringe on it. Their new approach was a set of small, hinged surfaces that the pilot could swivel up and down using cords. These surfaces became known as ailerons (French for "little wings") and were soon recognized as vastly superior to wing warping. The Aerial Experiment Association built an airplane called the White Wing that was the first to use ailerons. By World War I, flaps had also been added to airplane wings.

Although it's been more than 100 years since the first powered flight, rudders, elevators, ailerons, and flaps are still the basic control surfaces on all airplanes.

Basic Forces

The flight of aircraft is a product of the forces that the plane exerts on its environment and the forces that the environment exerts on the plane. The plane's propulsor exerts a driving force moving the plane forward. This force is called *thrust*.

As a plane accelerates, the air exerts both lift and drag forces on it. The lift must overcome gravity, which is another force exerted on the plane.

Lift and Gravity

Chapter 11, "Gravity and Projectiles," presented an overview of gravity and how it affects objects close to the Earth's surface. Applying gravity to airplanes is just like applying it to any other object. Simply apply this formula:

$$F=mg$$

through the plane's center of mass.

Lift, on the other hand, is not nearly so simple. Lift is created by a difference in air pressure between the upper and lower surfaces of a wing. Figure 16.3 illustrates how this works.

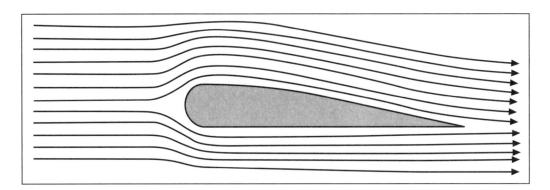

Figure 16.3
Creating lift.

Figure 16.3 shows a cross-section of a wing. As the wing moves through the air, air flows across its upper and lower surfaces. Because of the shape of the wing, the air moving across the top has farther to travel than the air moving across the bottom. The air above the wing must move across the wing in the same amount of time as the air below the wing. As a result, the air speeds up. This causes a low-pressure area above the wing. That low pressure is lift.

To calculate lift, your games can use the following formula:

$$L = 0.5C_L\rho v^2 S$$

In this equation, L is lift, S is the surface area of the wing, v is the velocity, and ρ is the density of air. The value C_L represents the coefficient of lift. This coefficient is different for every wing design. Engineers determine it from wind tunnel tests. The easiest way to come up with the lift coefficient is to make it up. Seriously. In general, you know from your experience with planes in the real world which wing configurations give better lift. As long as the lift equation for that configuration gives a higher value for lift than the equation for a less efficient wing, your results will be okay. Make a guess, do some experiments with your game, and then adjust the lift coefficient up or down as needed.

tip

Don't be afraid of approximate or relative results when they will save you a lot of work. For instance, it doesn't matter if you get exactly the same lift coefficients that airplane designers use in the real world. As long as the various aircraft in your game perform properly relative to each other and behave in a believable way, your game will be fine.

Thrust and Drag

The type of engine that your aircraft sports determines the thrust. You can either go to the Internet and get real-world data on various types of aircraft engines or just fake it. This is another one of those values that I suggest you try guessing at and then adjusting as needed.

Drag, on the other hand, is a calculated value. It is a function of both velocity and the surface area of the wing. The same phenomenon that causes lift also causes a drag force that acts in the opposite direction of the plane's velocity. Drag increases with the angle of attack. That is, the more tilted upward the plane is, the more drag it encounters. There comes a point at which the plane is tilted up so far that drag overcomes lift and causes the aircraft to stall. This is generally bad news for an airplane because it tends to result in a nearly vertical and high-speed landing. Passengers get agitated about things like that.

You calculate drag with nearly the same formula as lift. Here it is:

$$D = 0.5C_D \rho v^2 S$$

In this version of the formula, D is the force of drag and C_D is the coefficient of drag. Drag coefficients should never be more than half the value of the lift coefficient. Most likely, the drag coefficient should be less than a third of the value of the lift coefficient.

All parts of the aircraft can cause drag. Calculating drag is a job for aerodynamics engineers, not game programmers. Instead, you can approximate it with the formulas for air resistance presented in Chapter 15, "Cars, Hovercraft, Ships, and Boats." Table 16.1 repeats them here for your convenience.

Table 16.1 Calculating Air Resistance

Formula	Description
$\mathbf{F_{FD}} = -C_{FD}\mathbf{v}$	Use this formula when the plane is not moving fast enough to make the air very turbulent.
$\mathbf{F_{FD}} = -C_{FD}\mathbf{v}^2$	Use this formula for fast-moving planes that cause lots of air turbulence.

Modeling Aircraft: The Right Forces in the Right Places

Modeling an aircraft in software is mostly a matter of putting the right forces in the right places. Both the forward thrust of the engine and gravity should act through the plane's center of mass. This enables you to treat the plane as a typical rigid body.

What about lift? Should you place it at some point on the wings or at the center of mass?

The answer depends on your implementation. For simplicity, I generally recommend that you place the center of mass at the point where the centerline of the wingspan crosses the longitudinal (lengthwise) axis of the airplane. If you follow that advice, the answer is easy. Apply lift at the center of mass.

When the flaps are extended, they produce extra lift and extra drag. Most games just apply both at the center of mass. In extremely realistic simulations where you're simulating what happens when one flap fails to extend, you might want to apply the extra lift and drag at the center point of the flap. However, in the vast majority of flight simulators, you can apply these forces at the plane's center of mass.

When ailerons are tilted upward or downward, they deflect air. That deflection causes a force that acts downward or upward, respectively. The upward or downward force creates a torque around the lengthwise axis of the plane, so the plane rolls. To simulate these physics, your game needs to apply the ailerons' forces at their center point.

Because rudders are just vertical versions of ailerons, you must treat them the same way in your program. The rudder generates a left or right force when it is turned left or right. Apply the left or right force at the center point of the rudder.

The Physics of Spacecraft

Simulating the movements of a spacecraft can be very simple or very difficult, depending on what type of spacecraft you want to portray in your game. If the player is flying a fighter craft, things can be extremely simple. However, if he's blasting off of Earth in a rocket or landing on the moon in a Lunar Module (LM), you need to use much more physics to accurately portray the situation.

Dogfights in Space

I was a teenager when the movie *Star Wars* came out. It was like nothing that had ever come before it. I was so dazzled that I went to see it four times in the first month it was out. One of the best parts of the movie was when Luke Skywalker and friends attacked the Death Star in their space fighters.

It wasn't too many years later that games for personal computers portrayed similar situations to the attack on the Death Star. In fact, the *Wing Commander* series was built almost completely on that premise. It cast you as a space fighter pilot in a war with an alien race and gave you missions to fly.

I haven't seen many games like that lately. I guess it's because they're so easy to write now If you want to write one yourself, you can do it easily with the basic_flyer class shown earlier in this chapter. You don't really need any physics. In open space, there is no gravity pulling your fighter downward unless you get too near a planet. Most games don't portray such a situation. You just basically go at each other in the absence of any external forces. The `basic_flyer` class works perfectly for that.

Rockets

All the real spacecraft invented so far use rockets. Simulating a game that uses rocket-powered spacecraft is not as simple as doing a space-going fighter. You need to understand the basic operation of a rocket and the forces it produces. You also have to know the physics of getting into planetary orbit and flying between planets.

How Rockets Work

A rocket is just a big, three-chambered thermos. Really. Figure 16.4 shows the essential parts of a rocket.

There are three chambers inside the rocket in Figure 16.4. Each one is insulated like a regular lunchbox thermos. Insulation is required because the liquid oxygen and the liquid hydrogen are stored at extremely low temperatures. The cold makes them liquid. Normally, hydrogen and oxygen are gasses.

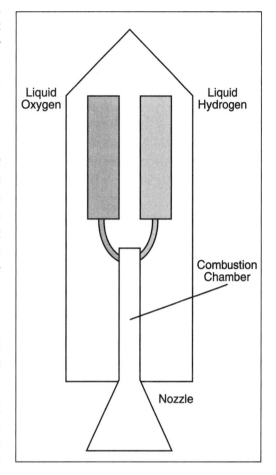

Figure 16.4
The basic components of a rocket.

One of the most important characteristics of hydrogen and oxygen is that they like each other. There's a strong chemical attraction between them. Given the chance, they'll combine to form water. That's what happens when you start the liquid oxygen and liquid hydrogen flowing into the rocket's combustion chamber. The little oxygens each find two hydrogens and form a very stable water molecule. When this happens, energy is released. All that energy and hot water come shooting out the nozzle of the rocket, and away the rocket flies.

The explosive reaction in a rocket's combustion chamber exerts a pressure force on all sides of the chamber. However, there is no bottom, so the gasses go rushing out. Now according to Newton's third law, for every action there is an equal and opposite reaction.

The escape of the hot water out the nozzle of the rocket pushes the rocket in the opposite direction. Voilà! Flight!

Getting into Orbit

The main reason for using rockets is to get people and stuff into orbit. The technical term for the "people and stuff" that rockets carry is *payload*. We use rockets to launch payloads into orbit. If I'm writing a game that simulates launching rockets into orbit, it's sensible to ask how rockets achieve orbits.

Chapter 11 presented an overview of gravity and projectiles. That overview was limited to projectiles near the surface of the Earth. Orbits can be understood as an extension of that overview.

Here's one way of looking at it. Imagine that you fire a cannon tilted at a 45° angle. The path of the cannonball is a parabola. What would happen if we stuffed the cannon with some *really* powerful gunpowder? I'm not talking regular gunpowder here. This is special super gunpowder. It packs a *huge* punch compared to regular gunpowder. We'll ignore the fact that the cannon itself would probably blow up. Instead, we'll say that the cannonball flies out of the cannon at a tremendous speed.

In this example, what would happen if the cannonball were shot so far that it went thousands of miles?

Over that kind of distance, we can't ignore the curvature of the Earth. In other words, the Earth curves away from the cannonball. If the cannon shoots the ball far enough, the ball falls toward the Earth as fast as the Earth curves away from it.

That's a simplistic example, I know. But it provides a simple way to conceptualize orbits. The more technical reason that objects orbit planets and stars is that gravity creates a centripetal force on the orbiting object. The object also has a tangential force moving it forward. The object achieves orbit when these two forces are balanced.

To get into orbit, a rocket must work. I do not mean work in the everyday sense of the word. Work in physics has a specific meaning. It refers to the energy required to cause change in a physical system. Here's an example to illustrate the idea of work.

Suppose that you're standing outside and you throw a ball straight up. There is a specific amount of energy or work that you expend in making the ball go up. As the ball rises, its potential energy increases. To understand potential energy, just stand there and look straight up at the ball. When the ball stops moving upward, it has its maximum potential energy to fall back down and hit you in the face.

That's essentially the way that gravitational systems work. Inside the gravity field, it takes work to move an object upward. The object gains potential energy as it moves up. The potential energy is released when the object falls. Specifically, the potential energy is converted to kinetic energy. The amount of kinetic energy you get when the object falls equals the amount of work required to push it up. These facts give us the following formulas:

$$W = -U$$

$$\Delta U + \Delta K = 0$$

These formulas tell us that the potential energy that an object gains when it's pushed upward is equal in magnitude to the work expended to get it there. The direction in which work increases is up, whereas the direction in which the potential energy increases is down. The formulas also tell us that the total change in energy in the system is exactly 0. That is, the kinetic energy decreases as the potential energy increases. People know this by experience. We've all seen a thrown ball slow down as it rises. That's evidence of lower kinetic energy and higher potential energy. As the ball falls, it gains kinetic energy and loses potential energy. When it strikes the ground, it has its maximum kinetic energy and no potential energy.

The formula for the work required to move an object, such as a rocket, upward is this:

$$W = \frac{GMm}{r}$$

where G is a universal gravitational constant that equals 6.67×10^{-11} (N m²)/kg², M is the mass of the Earth (or any other planet), m is the mass of the rocket, and r is the radial distance of the rocket away from the Earth. We can use the work equation to find the force that potential energy creates as the rocket goes up:

$$F = -\frac{\Delta U}{\Delta r} = -\frac{\Delta\left(-\dfrac{GMm}{r}\right)}{\Delta r} = -\frac{GMm}{r^2}$$

The potential energy of the system equals the work put into it, so the change in potential energy is the change in the work energy. Potential energy changes as the distance from the Earth increases or decreases. The long and short of it is that the attractive force that the Earth exerts on a rising rocket is inversely proportional to the square of the distance between them.

In reality, orbits can be circular or elliptical. To keep things easy to manage, let's deal only with circular orbits. Here's the formula for centripetal force in uniform circular motion:

$$F = mv_r^2 r$$

The value v_r in this formula is the radial velocity, or the velocity at which the satellite falls toward the Earth.

Staying in Orbit

The centripetal force of gravity for a rocket or satellite is also equal to the potential energy. We can set these two formulas equal to each other, like this:

$$\frac{-GMm}{r^2}=mv_r^2$$

If we solve for v_r, we get the radial velocity of the rocket or satellite.

$$v_r = \sqrt{\frac{GM}{r^3}}$$

The time that it takes for an orbiting object to complete its orbit is given by a closely related formula:

$$T=\sqrt{\frac{4\pi^2r^3}{GM}}$$

In this formula, T is the time or period of one orbit.

What about finding the tangential velocity? We need that to be able to move the object along its orbit. Here's the formula:

$$v_t = \sqrt{\frac{GM}{r}}$$

Both the radial and the tangential velocities are vectors. We can add vectors, so let's do that:

$$v_s = v_r + v_t$$

This formula shows what Figure 16.5 illustrates. The velocity of the satellite is the radial velocity plus the tangential velocity.

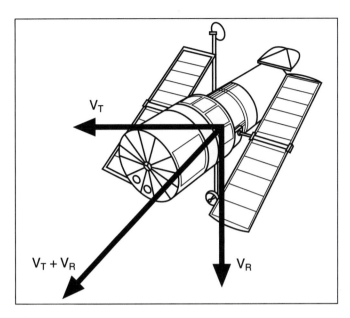

Figure 16.5
The velocity of a satellite.

With the ability to calculate the forces and velocities necessary to achieve orbit, you can extend the basic_flyer class to simulate the movements of space vehicles.

note

Orbital velocity used by NASA during the Apollo program was approximately 5,000 miles per hour (8,000 kph).

Toward Other Planets

To travel to other planets, your spacecraft must reach escape velocity. Escape velocity is the velocity at which a spacecraft overcomes the radial force of gravity that keeps it in orbit. You use essentially the same equations to calculate escape velocity that you use to calculate orbital velocities. First, you start with the fact that the work energy required to push an object up is the same as the kinetic energy that you get when the object falls back down.

$$W = K$$

If we substitute the formula we got for W, we get the following:

$$\frac{GMm}{r} = K$$

However, there is another formula that tells the kinetic energy of falling objects:

$$K = \frac{1}{2}mv^2$$

Now let's substitute this equation into the previous one:

$$\frac{GMm}{r} = \frac{1}{2}mv^2$$

Now we can solve for v:

$$v = \sqrt{\frac{2GM}{r}}$$

This comes out to about 25,000 mph or 40,200 kph when you launch from the surface of the Earth or low-Earth orbit.

Lunar Landers

Rockets carry payloads into orbit and beyond. Landing on other planets, however, requires specialized landing craft. The Apollo program used a Lunar Excursion Module (LEM), which was later renamed a Lunar Module (LM).

Some games have simulated LMs landing on the moon. The physics involved is simply that of a rigid body. From orbit, an LM must fire its rockets to exert a decelerating force. Your game can apply such a force to an object created from the physics modeling framework's rigid_body class.

As the tangential velocity of the LM decelerates, its angular (radial) velocity from gravity pulls it downward. As it does, the radial velocity increases. The player must keep the LM from crashing by firing the thrusters that orient the LM. He can then align the LM properly to provide downward thrust to oppose gravity as the LM approaches the ground.

note

The moon's gravity is about 1/6 that of Earth's. So your games can use the value 9.8/6 for the value of g in the rigid body formulas.

That's really all there is to it. Writing an LM simulator is just a special case of rigid body physics.

Getting to Other Planets with Known Physics

Many science fiction stories and movies have been written about traveling to planets other than our own moon. According to current physics, there are a few different ways that we could possibly get there.

Ion Drives

An ion drive is an extremely fuel-efficient way to get a spacecraft to another planet. It works by giving a gas an electrical charge, or ionizing it. The electricity comes from solar panels that collect the sun's energy. The gas used for fuel is xenon.

After it has a negative electrical charge, the xenon can be accelerated in a particular direction with electromagnets. The xenon stream exerts a force on the spacecraft that pushes it in the opposite direction as the xenon flow.

The total pressure from an ion drive is small—about the weight of a piece of paper. However, because it gets most of its energy from the sun, a spacecraft using an ion drive requires much less fuel than one powered by chemical rockets. The gentle push of the ion drive can eventually accelerate a ship to speeds high enough to move from planet to planet. It might even be possible to use ion drives to leave the solar system.

Simulating a spacecraft powered by an ion drive is another special application of rigid bodies. The engine provides a constant but gentle push on the craft. If it pushes long enough, the spacecraft accelerates beyond escape velocity and can make its way into deep space.

tip

Be sure that you slowly decrease the mass of your spacecraft as long as the ion drive is in operation. It does make a difference. You will not get an accurate simulation if you assume that your ship has a constant mass.

Nuclear Plasma Drives

It is speculated that we could travel to other planets with ships powered by nuclear plasma drives. The idea is pretty straightforward. You stick a long beam on the back of the crew's living module. On the far end of the beam, you put a nuclear reactor of the type that is commonly used on Earth. The fuel is ordinary water. The reactor superheats the water until it becomes plasma. Then the engine lets the plasma shoot out the back of the spacecraft. The plasma stream pushes the ship forward.

A spacecraft of this kind has several advantages and some disadvantages. One of the advantages is that the ship accelerates quickly like a chemical rocket. Another is that you can refuel anywhere you find water. The rings of Saturn are mostly water. That brings up one of the disadvantages. If you start moving much traffic around the solar system, you can kiss the rings of Saturn goodbye. Can you say "environmental impact?"

Another disadvantage is that the plasma stream that comes out the back of the ship is radioactive. In other words, don't get a ship like that near Earth. If we really used such a ship, we would have to build it in lunar orbit and launch from there.

note

> The *Discovery*, the ship in the movie *2001: A Space Odyssey*, was powered by a nuclear plasma engine.

Like simulating an ion drive spacecraft, simulating a spacecraft powered by a nuclear plasma engine is an application of rigid body physics.

Bussard Ramjets

A better possibility for interstellar travel is the Bussard ramjet. The Bussard ramjet does not carry much of its own fuel. Instead, a huge funnel-shaped scoop that is magnetized is mounted on the front of the spacecraft. The magnetism pushes hydrogen down the funnel.

Interstellar space has a thin haze of hydrogen. The ramjet's forward scoop collects the hydrogen. The engine is nuclear powered and uses some of the hydrogen as fuel. The nuclear engine provides electricity to huge electromagnets. The magnets accelerate the rest of the hydrogen to tremendous speeds. The fast-moving jet of hydrogen shoots out the back of the ship, propelling it forward.

Because space is mostly empty, a ramjet spacecraft won't even work unless it's going 6% of the speed of light. The speed of light is 186,000 miles per second. When the scoop starts working, however, the ramjet can provide constant thrust for the spacecraft. As long as it does not slow down too much, the spacecraft can keep working virtually indefinitely.

note

> The ship in the British comedy *Red Dwarf* is powered by a Bussard ramjet. That's why the *Red Dwarf* could keep going for 3 million years without running out of fuel.

Time Dilation

To cross interstellar distances, spaceships must accelerate close to the speed of light. As they do, time slows down for someone on the spaceship as seen by someone who is at rest. To understand why this is so, let's try a thought experiment similar to one proposed by Albert Einstein.

Imagine a clock that is made of a laser that sends out a short pulse of light every second. The light hits a mirror and bounces back to a detector mounted on the laser. Figure 16.6 shows such a clock.

Imagine that the laser clock is inside a spaceship. An observer on Earth also has a laser clock that is synchronized with the one on the ship. As the ship begins to move, the observer on the ground sees that the pulse of light from the spaceship's laser clock travels a greater distance than the pulse of light from the clock on the ground. Figure 16.7 depicts the path of the light pulse from the ship's clock as seen by someone on the ground.

The laser clock in Figure 16.7 is mounted on a spaceship moving from left to right. The clock is at position A when the light pulse is released. By the time the pulse bounces off the mirror, the laser clock has moved to position B. It reaches the detector when the clock is at position C.

A person on the ship sees the light pulse going straight out of the laser and bouncing straight back to the detector, as shown in Figure 16.6. Because the ship is moving from left to right, the observer on the ground sees that the light pulse moves from left to right with the ship as it also moves up and down from the laser to the mirror and back again. The Earth-based observer sees the zigzag path shown in Figure 16.7.

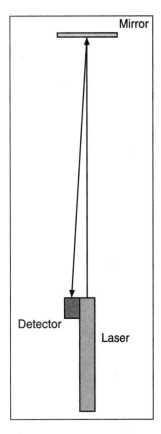

Figure 16.6
Light from the laser clock reflects in a nearly straight path.

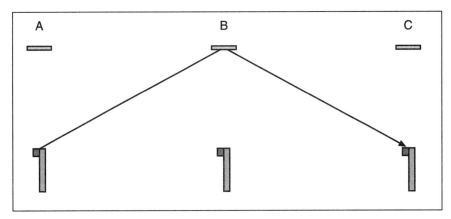

Figure 16.7
The path of the laser pulse on the ship.

Now here's the important bit. The light from both clocks travels at the same speed.

So what?

Look again at Figure 16.7. The light from the clock on the ship is zigzagging as seen by the observer on the Earth. As a result, the Earth observer sees the light travel farther in one second than the light from the clock on the ground. The light can't change its speed to cover the longer distance in the same amount of time, because light travels with the same velocity no matter where it is emitted or observed. It has a farther distance to go in the same amount of time, but it can't change its speed. The only way that the pulse can cover the increased distance in one second is if a second is longer on the ship than it is on the ground.

Say what?

It's true. Light can't change its speed, so the flow of time has to change. That means that people on a ship moving close to the speed of light age more slowly than those on the ground. Time goes more slowly on the spaceship relative to time on the Earth.

You can calculate the differences in the time intervals using the following formula:

$$\Delta t_{Ship} = \Delta t_{Earth}\sqrt{1 - \frac{v^2}{c^2}}$$

In this equation, the value Δt_{Earth} is the amount of time that passes for the observer on Earth. The value Δt_{Ship} is the amount of time that passes for the observer on the ship. The variable v represents the distance the ship travels in the time interval Δt_{Ship}. The constant c is the speed of light (186,000 miles per second).

Games that simulate interstellar space travel can use time dilation in their plots. The player can travel between widely separated spaces and times. It is perfectly reasonable for someone who travels close to the speed of light to make two visits to the same planet that are 3,000 years apart.

Getting to Other Planets with Speculative Physics

Many science fiction stories and movies have familiarized players with shortcuts through the universe that rapidly take characters to other planets. These shortcuts are based on very speculative physics. However, as long as they are consistent with themselves and known physics, players accept them without a problem.

The fictional methods of traveling to other worlds involve bypassing the speed limit imposed by the speed of light. The most common involve sending ships through higher dimensions or warping space.

Hyperspace

The four basic forces in the universe are electromagnetism, the strong nuclear force, the weak nuclear force, and gravity. Currently, no single theory explains and describes all of these forces. The one that comes the closest is called string theory.

In string theory, physicists say that the universe actually has more than three dimensions. After you get beyond three dimensions, you're dealing with hyperdimensional space, or hyperspace.

Speculative physics postulates that the speed limit in hyperspace is higher than the speed of light. Actually, if hyperspace exists at all, it might or might not be possible to move through it. Even if it is possible to traverse hyperspace, it is just as reasonable that the maximum speed you can go is slower than the speed of light. But we tend to ignore that when we write games.

Traveling through hyperspace is usually simulated by streaking the stars across the screen. Ships either "jump the lightspeed" (*Star Wars*), open some sort of "jump gate" (*Babylon 5*), or find a "jump point" (*Andromeda*). Players accept these methods of space travel without question.

Wormholes

Another method of getting around the cosmos involves wormholes. A wormhole is supposed to be a tunnel through higher-dimensional space that connects two points in the normal universe. There is actually a theoretical basis for the existence of wormholes. However, according to current theory, travelers through wormholes would be crushed by the extreme gravity that creates them. Travelers generally don't care for that.

If you're going to use wormholes as a method of getting around, fear not. It has been speculated that there is a kind of energy called *ghost radiation*. Some say that ghost radiation is predicted by quantum theory. According to some theories, ghost radiation can cancel the effects of normal energy such as gravity. So if your wormhole traveler has special shielding based on ghost radiation, he should be able to safely traverse wormholes.

Warp Drives, Infinite Improbability Drives, and Other Fun Stuff

Some forms of space travel have no real basis in physics at all. However, people accept them because they don't conflict with known physics and they sound reasonable. A case in point is the warp drives used in the various incarnations of *Star Trek*.

Supposedly, warp engines warp space so that the normal laws of physics don't apply. This also enables interstellar travelers to communicate faster than the speed of light. They simply send their signals through subspace, which seems to be similar to hyperspace.

If your game satirizes normal physics and science fiction, you can travel by methods that are nothing but sheer humor. A good example is the *Hitchhiker's Guide to the Galaxy* series. The main characters travel about the galaxy in a spaceship that generates improbability. The idea is that it becomes so improbable that the ship is in any given location that it isn't. When you restore probability to normal levels, you're somewhere else. In the meantime, anything can happen and often does.

The same series of books also describes a spaceship that is styled to simulate a bistro. You make it go by arguing with the waiter over the bill. This unbalances the numeric forces of the universe and moves you to another location. It's thoroughly ridiculous but thoroughly fun.

Players have a willingness to suspend their sense of disbelief of odd methods of space travel. However, to make that work for you, you have to be consistent. Speculative physics presented in later versions of your game cannot conflict with what you presented in earlier versions. Just make things reasonably sensible, and most people will play along and enjoy it.

Summary

This chapter presented techniques for flying through the sky and through space. It showed simple ways to implement these techniques and explained how to enhance them for your needs. Being able to fly, rocket into space, and travel to other planets opens up a lot of potential fun for your games.

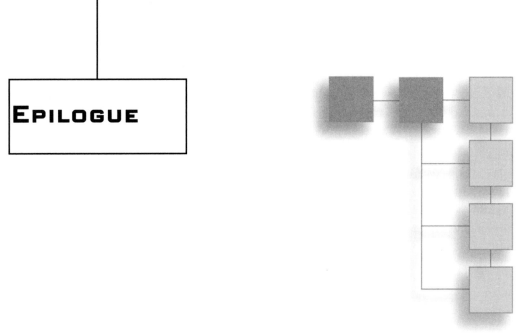

EPILOGUE

Through the course of this book, a lot of information was presented. It started with Windows and DirectX programming, essential math, and geometry. As you progressed through the book, you went from the physics of bouncing balls off of walls to the physics of space travel. With time dilation, you even pushed into the boundaries of Einstein's theory of relativity. That's a long way to come in one short book.

You should now be able to build games with the same physics that game programming professionals use. This type of physics will make your 3-D games simulate the real world with enough accuracy to satisfy even demanding players.

You should get good mileage out of this book's code. The physics modeling framework is built with the idea that you'll be writing your game engine from scratch. That's why I've provided code for getting Windows and DirectX up and running quickly. You can easily expand the framework so that you can initialize and control all aspects of Windows and DirectX.

If you don't want to write a game engine from scratch, don't worry. You can port the physics and math routines from my physics modeling framework into nearly any game engine. What's nice about that approach is that it lets you get to the fun of writing your game much more quickly.

I encourage you to keep studying physics. You now know most of the basic concepts of physics and the essential terms used in physics books. That gives you a good basis for moving on into more advanced physics concepts.

As computers acquire faster microprocessors and more memory, the ability of games to simulate real-world physics more accurately also increases. Knowing physics makes you more valuable to game programming companies.

Be aware, however, that all the physics in the world won't guarantee that your game is good. It all comes down to gameplay. Build physics into your games. It will help make them stand out and be more immersive. But don't be so concentrated on the physics that you lose sight of good gameplay.

Game programming lets you be a programmer, physicist, artist, musician, and maybe even storyteller. Have fun with it. That's what game programming is all about. If it's not fun, why do it? Lots of jobs are no fun, and most of them are a whole lot easier than game programming. So have fun. Be inventive and creative. You have the power to immerse an audience in a world that consists solely of your creativity. What could be more fun than that?

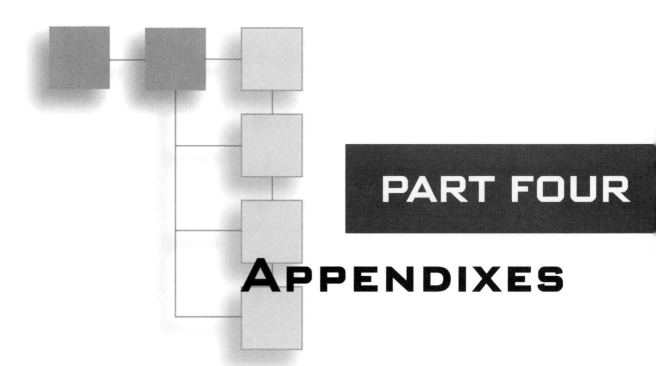

PART FOUR

APPENDIXES

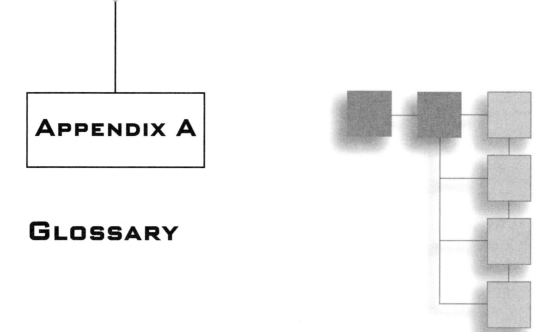

APPENDIX A

GLOSSARY

back buffer—A Direct3D surface that is drawn onto and then presented to the viewer using page flipping.

center of buoyancy—On a ship, the point through which the sum of the buoyancy forces acts.

center of gravity—The point through which the sum of the gravitational forces acts. This is the same as the center of mass.

Component Object Model (COM)—A model for building software objects that enables programmers to offer objects' functionality through interfaces of methods. COM objects are dynamically linked at runtime.

dynamic coefficient of friction—A constant indicating the magnitude of the dynamic frictional force between any two objects. The value of the coefficient depends on the properties of the two objects.

dynamic friction—Friction that occurs when objects slide across each other.

encapsulation—A technique used in object-oriented programming for controlling access to data in software objects.

function overloading—Multiple functions with the same name in a class.

Hardware Abstraction Layer (HAL)—A low-level API that translates DirectX commands into hardware commands.

Hardware Emulation Layer (HEL)—A low-level API that simulates hardware capabilities that are supported by the user's PC.

hypotenuse—The longest side of a right triangle.

identity matrix—A matrix that has ones as its element values along the upper-left to lower-right diagonal. All other elements are zeros.

interface—A collection of related functions. In COM, the functions are called methods and are accessed through a COM object.

local coordinates—The coordinate system in which a 3-D model is defined, usually with the origin at the center of the model.

metacenter—On a ship, the point at which the vector of the buoyancy force intersects a vector through the ship's centerline and its center of mass.

method—A function in a COM interface.

model coordinates—Another term for local coordinates.

normal vector—A vector that is perpendicular to a given plane.

orthogonal—Perpendicular.

orthogonal matrix—A matrix whose inverse is equal to its transpose.

page flipping—Exchanging the front and back buffers so that the back buffer becomes the front and the front buffer becomes the back.

payload—The passengers and cargo that a rocket or spaceship carries.

pitch—Moving the nose of an aircraft or spacecraft up or down relative to the pilot's orientation.

rasterization—Drawing a 3-D scene after it has been through the rendering pipeline.

ray tracing—Calculating the path of a ray of light from its source to the viewer's eye.

reference counting—A method of sharing data between objects by having multiple objects refer to the same data.

restoring moment—A torque that causes a ship to return to its full and upright position.

right triangle—A triangle containing one angle of exactly 90°.

roll—Rotating an aircraft or spacecraft around its longitudinal axis.

scalar—A number that has only magnitude and no directional information.

splash screen—A screen displayed by most games upon startup. Typically, the splash screen contains the name of the game and the company logo of the developer.

static coefficient of friction—A constant indicating the magnitude of the static frictional force between any two objects. The value of the coefficient depends on the properties of the two objects.

static friction—Friction that occurs when the point of contact between an object and the surface it is on is not sliding across the surface.

surface, Direct3D—A bitmap buffer in memory that Direct3D draws a frame of animation onto.

tearing—A condition that occurs if the front buffer changes while the screen is being updated. The monitor ends up displaying part of the original buffer and part of the updated buffer at the same time.

tensor—A geometric object whose components in some coordinate system are a square matrix.

texel—One dot of color from a texture. Analogous to a pixel.

transverse waves—Waves in which the motion of the matter particles is perpendicular to the direction of the wave propagation.

unit matrix—*See* identity matrix.

vector—A quantity with both a magnitude and a direction.

vertex buffer—A block of system or graphics memory that stores lists of vertices for batch processing.

virtual mass—The mass of a ship plus the water that moves with it.

world coordinates—The coordinate system of a 3-D scene.

yaw—Turning the nose of an aircraft or spacecraft left or right relative to the pilot's orientation.

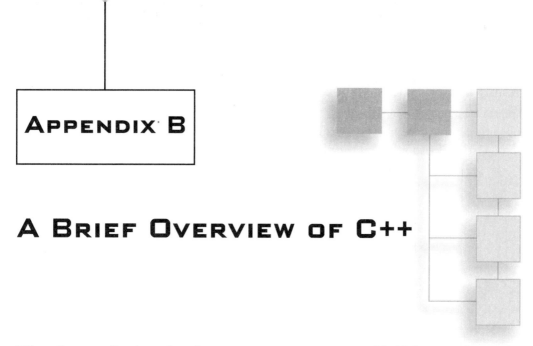

APPENDIX B

A BRIEF OVERVIEW OF C++

When C++ was first introduced, many game programmers avoided it because they said it slowed down their games. C++ compilers have come a long way since then. These days, C++ generates code that is fast and efficient. Most games are written in C++.

If you're unfamiliar with C++, I can't really teach it to you in the space available in this book. The only thing I can do in this appendix is give you a brief overview of C++. Although this overview does not cover many of the features of C++, it should help you become familiar enough with C++ to read the code samples.

The basis of C++ is formed by two basic concepts. These two concepts are *functions* and *objects*. In this appendix, we'll take a quick look at each. We'll also briefly examine some of the secondary supporting language features of C++.

It All Begins with Functions

In college, I majored in computer science. As all computer science students do, I learned basic skills of writing and designing software. Later in my career, the circumstances opened opportunities for writing about computers. One of the first things that I realized as a writer was that writing software and writing books require almost the same skills. The idea with both tasks is to learn a language to communicate a logical flow of ideas.

When you write computer programs, each statement is comparable to a sentence. Every sentence has some sort of verb. Statements in C++ programs are similar to sentences. In C++ statements, the verbs are functions. Functions in C++ programs perform actions, just like verbs do in sentences. A function is a block of code with a name that performs a particular task.

main() and Functions Called By main()

The C++ language defines a special function called `main()`. C++ programs begin executing with the first statement in `main()`. This makes `main()` the primary function in the program. Listing B.1 shows what the `main()` function looks like.

Listing B.1
An Empty main() Function

```
1     int main()
2     {
3          // C++ statements go here.
4
5          return (0);
6     }
```

The `main()` function in Listing B.1 contains the characteristics that all C++ functions share. The first is a name. Of course, the name of this function is `main()`. All functions also have parameter lists and return types, which we'll discuss shortly. The statements between the { and the } (opening and closing braces) are where the actions of the function are performed. All the statements in a function go between the opening and closing braces.

The `main()` function is called when the program starts. Other functions are called by `main()`. They can also be called by functions that are called by functions that are called by `main()`. Or they can be called by functions that are called by functions that are called by functions that are called by `main()`, and so on. There is a limit to the number of levels of functions that you can call, but programmers seldom approach that limit.

The `main()` function in Listing B.1 does nothing. The only statements it contains are a comment and a `return` statement. Comments are for humans. The compiler completely ignores them. We'll discuss `return` statements shortly.

Parameters

When a function calls another function, it can pass information through the parameter list. For example, suppose that I write a function called `UpdateAnimationFrame()` that animates an alien walking across the screen. Suppose further that `UpdateAnimationFrame()` calls another function named `CalculateNextPosition()`. The `UpdateAnimationFrame()` function can pass information to the `CalculateNextPosition()` function through the `CalculateNextPosition()` function's parameter list. The parameter list is everything inside the parentheses.

Parameter lists can be empty, or they can contain data. You must specify the type for each parameter. The most common types have names like `int` (for integer) and `float` (a floating-point number).

Return Values

Functions can pass information back to the function that called them. This is usually done with a `return` statement. You can get information back in other ways, but that's beyond the scope of this overview. To return a value, simply put the `return` statement in your function, followed by the value to be returned. `return` statements usually occur at the end of the function.

Inline Functions

Inline functions are critically important to game programmers. They make C++ programs faster.

With normal functions, the program jumps from the point the function is called to the function. When it finishes the function it called, it jumps back to the calling point. That's not the case with inline functions. The compiler substitutes the code for inline functions directly into the program. This makes the program larger but faster. There is no jumping around when you call inline functions.

Not all functions can or should be inline. Only short functions that do not call lots of other functions can be inline. In general, if a function is much more than 10 lines of code, I don't write it as an inline function.

Listing B.2 demonstrates how to define an inline function.

Listing B.2
An Inline Function

```
1      inline scalar DegreesToRadians(float degrees)
2      {
3          return (degrees*D3DX_PI/180);
4      }
```

Classes and Object-Oriented Programming

C++ enables you to define your own data types. You can also associate functions with those data types. The functions form the set of all valid operations that you can perform on data of that particular type. The principle way of defining your types, along with their set of valid operations, is with classes.

Classes contain collections of member data and member functions. Each data member holds one piece of data that describes the type. Typically, programmers define the member data so that only the member functions can get access to it. This technique is called *encapsulation*. By limiting the access of member data to member functions, you can prevent software from setting member data into invalid states. This helps control errors.

Listing B.3 demonstrates how to define a class.

Listing B.3
Defining a Class

```
1       class point
2       {
3       private:
4           int x,y;
5
6       public:
7           point();
8           point(int xValue,int yValue);
9
10          void X(int xValue);
11          int X(void);
12
13          void Y(int yValue);
14          int Y(void);
15      };
```

All class definitions in C++ begin with class. Next is the name of the class. The { and the } contain all the class's member data and the prototypes for the member functions. The prototypes describe the functions. They state the name, return type, and parameter list of each function.

The class in Listing B.3 is called point. The point class has two data members: x and y. These two data members are of type int, which is an integer. Because the class contains private before the declaration of the member data, only member functions can get access to x and y. And, of course, the member functions are the functions whose prototypes are listed on lines 7–14.

The point class has six member functions. Two of the member functions are called point(). They are special member functions called *constructors*. Programs use constructors to initialize software objects to known values.

Both member functions on lines 10–11 of Listing B.3 are called X(). It's allowable and even desirable to give the same name to multiple functions. This is called *function overloading*. Notice that the X() function on line 10 enables a program to pass an integer through the parameter list. The X() function on line 11 takes no parameters. Instead, it returns an integer. These two functions set and get, respectively, the value of the private data member called x. Listing B.4 shows what they look like.

Listing B.4
Two X() Functions for the point Class

```
1       inline void point::X(int xValue)
2       {
3             x = xValue;
4       }
5
6
7       inline int point::X(void)
8       {
9             return (x);
10      }
```

You might wonder how the program knows which of these two functions to invoke when it sees a call to a function named X(). The answer is that it can tell by the parameter lists and return values. If the call to the function named X() contains an integer in its parameter list, the program is calling the function on lines 1–4. If the parameter list is empty, it is calling the function on lines 7–10.

If we look at a sample main() function, we can see how objects are used. Listing B.5 demonstrates.

Listing B.5
Using the point Class

```
1       int main()
2       {
3             point p;
4
5             p.X(10);
6
7             int anXValue = p.X();
8
9             return (0);
10      }
```

The main() function in Listing B.5 declares a variable, called p, that is of type point. That variable contains the two integers on line 4 of Listing B.3. To set the private data member of p named x, the program calls the public member function named X(). When the member function is public, any other function in the program can call it.

The call to the X() function on line 5 passes the value 10 into the function through its parameter list. The function sets the private data member of p named x to 10. On line 7, the main() function calls the other X() function to retrieve the value of the private data member of p named x. It assigns the value it retrieves to an integer variable.

Namespaces

It's common when writing complex programs like games to use libraries provided by multiple companies. Sometimes those libraries have functions or classes with the same names. C++ provides a handy method, called *namespaces*, of grouping classes and functions logically together. Namespaces group all functions and classes in a particular library together under the same name. Use the scope resolution operator to distinguish which namespace you are accessing.

For example, throughout this book, you'll see the development of a physics modeling library. All the functions and classes in this library are accessed through the library's namespace, which is pmframework.

You define a namespace with the namespace statement. For instance, everything in the pmframework namespace is defined inside the following statement:

```
namespace pmframework
{
// Classes, functions, and so on go here.
}
```

All the classes, functions, and so forth that are included in the namespace are defined between the { and the }.

To tell your program that you're using items in the pmframework namespace, you put a using statement at the top of each .cpp file, like this:

```
using pmframekwork;
```

With this statement at the top of your .cpp file, your program can access anything in the physics modeling library by name.

Suppose that your program uses the physics modeling library and a graphics library. The physics modeling library contains a class called vector_3d. Imagine that the graphics library also contains a class with the same name. How do you tell your program which vector_3d class you're using?

Using the scope resolution operator, you can always distinguish between two classes or functions with the same name. As long as they reside in different namespaces, there's no problem. Here's an example:

```
pmframework::vector_3d vectorVariable;
a_graphics_lib::vector_3d anotherVectorVariable;
```

Both these statements declare a variable of type vector_3d. However, the first one uses the vector_3d class in the physics modeling framework. The second one uses a vector_3d class in a namespace called a_graphics_lib. Even though two classes are named vector_3d, they are two completely different classes in two completely different namespaces.

Inheritance

Inheritance is a feature that is common to object-oriented programming languages. It provides an easy way to reuse code. Through inheritance, you can enhance existing classes without having to rewrite or modify their existing code.

Classes from which other classes inherit are called *base* or *parent* classes. Classes that inherit from other classes are called *derived* or *child* classes. Child classes inherit all the member data and member functions of the parent classes. In fact, in most compiler implementations, child classes actually have a copy of the parent inside them.

To derive a class from another class, you must state the name of the parent in the definition of the child class. Listing B.6 demonstrates.

Listing B.6
Using Inheritance

```
1     class point_3d : public point
2     {
3     private:
4         int z;
5
6     public:
7         point_3d();
8         point_3d(int xValue,int yValue,int zValue);
9
10        void Z(int zValue);
11        int Z(void);
12    };
13
14    inline point_3d::point_3d() : point()
15    {
16        z=0;
17    }
18
19    inline point_3d::point_3d(
20        int xValue,
21        int yValue,
22        int zValue) : point(xValue,yValue)
23    {
24        z=zValue;
25    }
26
27    inline void point_3d::Z(int zValue)
28    {
```

```
29              z=zValue;
30      }
31
32      inline int point_3d::Z(void)
33      {
34              return (z);
35      }
```

Listing B.6 defines a class called point_3d. The point_3d class inherits from the point class shown previously. The inheritance is defined on line 1, after the colon. Notice that the point_3d class inherits from the point class publicly. This means that any program that declares a variable of type point_3d can use that variable to call the member functions from the point class. We'll see how that works momentarily.

The point_3d class defines only one data member. Because it inherits from the point class, the point_3d class also contains all the data members of the point class. Therefore, the point_3d class actually contains three data members.

Not only does the point_3d class inherit all the data members from its base class, but it also inherits all of the member functions. So the point_3d class has all the member functions shown in its definition. It also has all the member functions defined in the point class.

The constructors for the point_3d class work a little bit differently than normal constructors because of inheritance. Lines 14–17 of Listing B.6 present the constructor for the point_3d class that does not take parameters. Because parameters are often called arguments in C++ programming, this constructor is also called the no-arg constructor. The first thing that the no-arg constructor for the point_3d class does is call the no-arg constructor for the point class. This initializes the x and y data members in the point class. In between the { and the }, the point_3d constructor initializes its own data member, z.

The point_3d class also provides a constructor that takes three parameters, shown on lines 19–25. This constructor calls the two-argument constructor from the point class on line 22. It passes its first two arguments to the point constructor so that the point constructor can use those values to initialize the x and y data members. It uses the third argument to initialize its own data member.

You use the point_3d class just like you would any other. See the short program in Listing B.7 for a demonstration.

Listing B.7
Using the point_3d Class

```
1       int main()
2       {
3               point p;
4
```

```
5           p.X(10);
6
7           int anXValue = p.X();
8
9           point_3d p2;
10          p2.X(10);
11          p2.Y(20);
12          p2.Z(30);
13
14          return (0);
15      }
```

This program shows that you can use both the parent class and the child class in the same function. It declares variables of type point and point_3d. On lines 10–11, the program uses a point_3d variable to call the X() and Y() functions that the point_3d class inherits from the point class. On line 12, it calls the Z() function defined in its own class definition.

Overriding Functions

It's possible for a function in a child class to have the same name as a function in the parent class. When we write functions like this, we say that we are overriding the function in the parent class.

For instance, suppose that you create a class called car that has a function named Update(). In addition, suppose that you create a class called sports_car that also has a function named Update(). The sports_car class is derived from the car class. Whenever your program uses a variable of type sports_car to invoke the Update() function, the program invokes the Update() function in the sports_car class. It does not call the Update() function in the car class.

It's common to override functions in parent classes when you want the child class to add enhancements. Typically, the function in the child class calls the overridden function in the parent class. The car and sports_car classes are good examples. The Update() function in the sports_car class would call the Update() function in the car class. The Update() function in the sports_car class would also perform additional processing that the Update() function does not do in the car class.

Note that if you want to call the overridden function in the parent class using a child object, you can do so with the scope resolution operator.

Virtual Functions

A special type of function, called a virtual function, is used with pointers. The topic of pointers is beyond the scope of this overview. However, you should be aware that the functions in any class you want to use as a parent class should be virtual. Listing B.8 shows how to make functions virtual.

Listing B.8
A Class with Virtual Functions

```
1      class rigid_body : public point_mass
2      {
3      private:
4          // Rotational motion properties
5          angle_set_3d currentOrientation;
6          vector_3d angularVelocity;
7          vector_3d angularAcceleration;
8          vector_3d rotationalInertia;
9          vector_3d torque;
10
11     public:
12         rigid_body(void);
13
14         virtual void CurrentOrientation(
15             angle_set_3d newOrientation);
16         virtual angle_set_3d CurrentOrientation(void);
17
18         virtual void AngularVelocity(
19             vector_3d newAngularVelocity);
20         virtual vector_3d AngularVelocity(void);
21
22         virtual void AngularAcceleration(
23             vector_3d newAngularAcceleration);
24         virtual vector_3d AngularAcceleration(void);
25
26         virtual void RotationalInertia(
27             vector_3d inertiaValue);
28         virtual vector_3d RotationalInertia(void);
29
30         virtual void Torque(
31             vector_3d torqueValue);
32         virtual vector_3d Torque(void);
33
34         virtual bool Update(
35             scalar changeInTime);
36     };
```

The rigid_body class in Listing B.8 inherits from a class called point_mass. Other classes inherit from the rigid_body class. Because the rigid_body class serves as a parent class, its functions need to be virtual.

Exceptions

Advanced languages such as C++ provide a technique for handling errors called *exception handling*. If your software detects errors, it can throw exceptions. Exceptions should be used only in exceptional circumstances, such as when a fatal error occurs.

When your program throws an exception, the exception can be caught in the same function. It can also be caught by the function that called the current function. Alternatively, it can be caught by the function that called the function that called the current function, and so on.

Usually, your program creates an object that contains error information when it throws an exception. Listing B.9 shows the definition of such an object.

Listing B.9
An Exception Class

```
1      class pmlib_error
2      {
3      private:
4          std::string errorString;
5
6      public:
7          pmlib_error(std::string errorMessage);
8          std::string ErrorMessage(void);
9      };
```

The class in Listing B.9 has a private data member that holds an error string. Your program sets the error message when it creates an object of type pmlib_error. It can then throw an exception using that object. Listing B.10 demonstrates how.

Listing B.10
Throwing an Exception

```
1      inline matrix2x2 matrix2x2::Inverse()
2      {
3          scalar determinant=Determinant();
4          if (determinant==0.0)
5          {
6              pmlib_error theError(
7                  "Can't invert a matrix that has a determinant of 0.");
8              throw theError;
9          }
10
11         return(
12             matrix2x2(
```

```
13                    elements[1][1]/determinant, -elements[0][1]/determinant,
14                    -elements[1][0]/determinant, elements[0][0]/determinant));
15    }
```

It doesn't really matter in this discussion what the function in Listing B.10 does. What's important here is that it tests for an error on line 4. If it detects an error, it declares a variable of type pmlib_error on lines 6–7 and stores an error string in that variable. On line 8, it uses the throw statement to throw the exception. The exception is not caught in this function. The exception can be caught by any function that calls this one, as shown in Listing B.11.

Listing B.11
Handling Exceptions

```
1    matrix2x2 aMatrix;
2    try
3    {
4         aMatrix.Inverse();
5    }
6    catch (pmlib_error libError)
7    {
8         cout<<libError.ErrorMessage();
9    }
```

The block of code in Listing B.11 declares a variable of type matrix2x2. That's the class that the Inverse() function in Listing B.10 is a member of. On line 4, the code block uses the variable to call the Inverse() function. If the Inverse() function throws an exception, it is caught on line 6. The program then enters the catch block to handle the exception. In this case, the program simply outputs an error message.

Other Ways of Making Types

C++ provides other ways of making types in addition to classes. The three that I use most commonly in the source code for this book are structures, enumerated types, and typedef statements.

Structures

A structure is almost exactly the same thing as a class. The only real difference is that the default scope is private for classes and public for structures. Listing B.12 illustrates this difference.

Listing B.12
Structures Versus Classes

```
1    class point
2    {
3         int x,y;
4    };
5
6
7    struct point
8    {
9         int x,y;
10   };
```

Neither the structure nor the class shown in Listing B.12 has the C++ keywords public or private in them. By default, all members of the class are private. The default for structures is that all members are public. That's the only difference between structures and classes. Structures, like classes, can have data members, member functions, constructors, destructors, and so forth.

Enumerated Types

An *enumerated type* is a method of creating a type and associating specific values with it. Listing B.13 gives an example of an enumerated type.

Listing B.13
An Enumerated Type

```
1    enum cloth_constants
2    {
3         PARTICLES_PER_SQUARE=4,
4         TOP_LEFT_PARTICLE=0,
5         TOP_RIGHT_PARTICLE,
6         BOTTOM_LEFT_PARTICLE,
7         BOTTOM_RIGHT_PARTICLE,
8         TOP_SPRING = 0,
9         BOTTOM_SPRING,
10        RIGHT_SPRING,
11        LEFT_SPRING,
12        TOP_RIGHT_TO_BOTTOM_LEFT_SPRING,
13        TOP_LEFT_TO_BOTTOM_RIGHT_SPRING,
14        SPRINGS_PER_SQUARE=6,
15   };
```

The name of the type in Listing B.13 is `cloth_constants`. You can use the `cloth_constants` type name to declare variables. When you do, the variables can be assigned the values shown on lines 3–14. These values are actually integers. You can assign specific integer values to these constants, or you can let the compiler assign them. This example does both.

On lines 3 and 4, the values 4 and 0 are assigned to their respective constants. However, on lines 5–7, the constants are not explicitly assigned values. Instead, the compiler increments the value of the constant on line 4, which is 0, and assigns a 1 to the constant on line 5. The compiler continues to do the same for the constants on lines 6–7. So their values are 2 and 3, respectively.

typedef Statements

A `typedef` statement does not create a new type. It simply creates a new type name for an existing type. For example, the physics modeling framework uses the following `typedef` statement.

```
typedef point_mass_base invisible_point_mass;
```

This `typedef` statement creates the type name `invisible_point_mass` for the type `point_mass_base`. After this statement appears in a file, you can use either type name for the same thing. An `invisible_point_mass` is a `point_mass_base` in every respect. You're just creating an alias.

Using the `typedef` statement does not get rid of the original type name. You can use either name in your program.

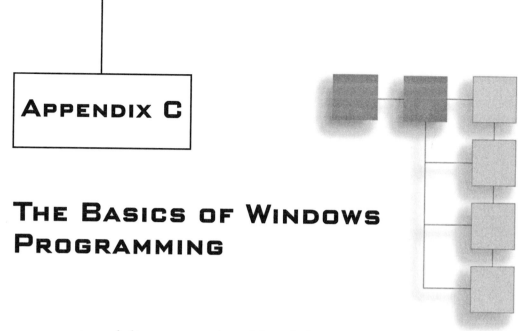

APPENDIX C

THE BASICS OF WINDOWS PROGRAMMING

M ost people have some version of the Windows operating system on their computers. To write games under the various Windows, you do not have to be an expert Windows programmer. You really just need to know a few basic concepts, such as the following:

- How to create a window with WinMain()
- How to define a Windows message handling procedure
- How to use Windows resources such as icons, cursors, and so forth

Welcome to WinMain()

Every Windows program must have a function called WinMain(). The WinMain() function is the program entry point. That is, program execution begins at WinMain(). It serves essentially the same purpose as the main() function in most other types of C or C++ programs.

The WinMain() function creates and displays the program's window. To do that, it must accomplish the following tasks:

1. Define a window class.
2. Register the window class.
3. Create a window based on the class.
4. Display the window.
5. Process messages with a message loop.

In addition to the WinMain() function, every Windows program requires a message handling procedure. This is a special function that handles the messages that are processed by the message loop in WinMain().

Writing a WinMain() Function

As mentioned previously, all Windows programs must have a WinMain() function. The file containing the WinMain() function must include the standard Windows header file Windows.h. This gives your game access to the definitions of types, functions, and so forth that it needs to establish itself as a Windows program.

The WinMain() function has a set of parameters specified by the Windows operating system. Listing C.1 shows an empty WinMain() function with its parameters.

Listing C.1
An Empty WinMain() Function

```
1     INT WINAPI WinMain(
2          HINSTANCE hInstance,
3          HINSTANCE hPrevInstance,
4          LPSTR lpCmdLine,
5          INT nCmdShow)
6     {
7          return (0);
8     }
```

The first two parameters to WinMain() are handles. A *handle* is a kind of generic identifier. The first of these two handles identifies the current instance of the program. It used to be the case that the second handle identified the previous instance of the game. You could use these handles to prevent the player from running more than one copy of your game at the same time. This is typically what you want. For most games, it doesn't make sense to run multiple copies of the program at once.

The second parameter to WinMain() is always NULL for Win32 applications. To detect whether multiple copies of your game are running, have the game create a Windows object called a *mutex*. To do so, call the CreateMutex() function, which is one of the Win32 API functions. Give the mutex a unique name when you create it. It needs to be something that no other program will use. After the CreateMutex() function returns, call GetLastError(), which is another Win32 API function. If GetLastError() returns the value ERROR_ALREADY_EXISTS, it means that another copy of your program is already running. Call the MessageBox() function to display an error message, and then exit.

Defining a Window Class

A window class is not the same as a C++ class. A window class tells Windows what type of window you want to create for your program. These days, programs use the WNDCLASSEX structure to define a window class. In the past, there was a WNDCLASS structure, but it is now obsolete according to Microsoft.

The WNDCLASSEX structure has a whole slew of members that describe the type of window you're creating. However, game programmers use only some of them. Listing C.2 gives a view of what is probably the simplest window class you can create.

Listing C.2
Defining a Simple Window Class

```
1     WNDCLASSEX myWindowClass =
2     {
3         sizeof(WNDCLASSEX),
4         CS_CLASSDC,
5         MsgProc,
6         0L,
7         0L,
8         GetModuleHandle(NULL),
9         NULL,
10        NULL,
11        NULL,
12        NULL,
13        "MyWindowClass",
14        NULL
15    };
```

In Listing C.2, the first member of the WNDCLASSEX structure is set to the size of the WNDCLASSEX structure. You *must* set this member to sizeof(WNDCLASSEX), or you will not be able to register the window class.

The second member of the WNDCLASSEX structure contains the window style. A typical window style for games is shown on line 4 of Listing C.2. The value shown here makes it easy for multiple threads in a program to share the same window. Other common values are CS_HREDRAW and CS_VREDRAW, which cause the window to be redrawn when it is resized. You can combine these values with a bitwise OR operator, like this:

CS_CLASSDC | CS_HREDRAW | CS_VREDRAW

The next member of the WNDCLASSEX structure must hold the address of the message handling procedure. This is the function in your program that reacts to all Windows messages. For more information on message handling procedures, see WindowProc in the Microsoft Win32 documentation.

You can allocate extra space for your data within the window class and in the window. This is an advanced technique that most programs don't use. As lines 6–7 show, programs typically initialize these two members to 0.

Line 8 demonstrates that the sixth member of the WNDCLASSEX structure contains the handle of the module in which the window class is defined. Your program calls the Win32 GetModuleHandle() function to obtain the module handle.

Line 9 sets the seventh member of the WNDCLASSEX structure, called hIcon, to NULL. This is usually not what you want. This member contains the resource ID of the icon that represents your program when the program gets minimized. I strongly recommend that you create an icon for your program and set hIcon to the icon's resource ID. You can create resources such as icons and mouse cursors with Visual Studio.

Although the next member of the WNDCLASSEX structure isn't used in Listing C.2, many games set it to a value other than NULL. This member, called hCursor, contains the resource handle of the mouse cursor to be used for your program. If your game is a first-person shooter or something similar, it will probably set this value to NULL, as shown on line 10. This tells Windows that your program uses no cursor. However, if your program needs a mouse cursor, it should set hCursor to a value.

To set a window's background to a particular color, your program must tell Windows to use an object called a *brush*. Games that use DirectX generally do not use brushes. Instead, they let DirectX paint the entire window. Therefore, DirectX-based games tend to set this value to NULL, as shown on line 11.

User interfaces for games are often extremely different from user interfaces for other types of Windows programs. As a result, they might or might not use the next member of the WNDCLASSEX structure, called lpszMenuName. As its name indicates, this structure contains the resource ID of the main menu for the window. It is not unusual for games to set this value to NULL, as line 12 indicates.

Your game must define a unique identifier for every window class that it registers with Windows. As line 13 of Listing C.2 demonstrates, this identifier is a string. It can be any string that you want, as long as it is unique. On line 13, I have used the string "MyWindowClass" to help describe what the structure member contains. However, you should use something more specific, like "*<my_game_name>*_WindowClass", where *<my_game_name>* represents the name of your game.

The final member of the WNDCLASSEX structure contains the resource handle of a smaller version of the icon identified in the hIcon member. Usually, games just set this to NULL.

Registering a Window Class

After you define the window class, you must register it with Windows. You do so with a call to the Win32 RegisterClassEx() function. Simply pass RegisterClassEx() the address of your WNDCLASSEX structure, like this:

```
RegisterClassEx(&myWindowClass);
```

Your game should test the return value of the RegisterClassEx() function to ensure that your window class was registered properly. If it wasn't, your game should display an error message and exit.

Creating a Window

After a window class is defined and registered, you can use it to create a window. Your program creates a window by invoking the Win32 CreateWindow() function.

Listing C.3
Calling the Win32 CreateWindow() Function

```
1      // Create the application's window.
2      hWnd = CreateWindow(
3          "MyWindowClass",
4          (LPCSTR)"Window Title",
5          WS_OVERLAPPEDWINDOW,
6          CW_USEDEFAULT,
7          CW_USEDEFAULT,
8          CW_USEDEFAULT,
9          CW_USEDEFAULT,
10         GetDesktopWindow(),
11         NULL,
12         myWindowClass.hInstance,
13         NULL);
```

The call to CreateWindow() in Listing C.3 assigns the function's return value to a variable called hWnd. This variable is of type HWND, which is a standard Windows type that's made available to your program when it includes the file Windows.h.

The first parameter to CreateWindow() is the name of the window class that your program registered. The second is the window's title. These two parameters are shown on lines 3–4 of Listing C.3.

Next, your program needs to specify a window style. If you do not want to run your program in full-screen mode, specify WS_OVERLAPPEDWINDOW, as shown on line 5. The Microsoft documentation on the CreateWindow() function gives you a wide variety of options. You can combine many of these using the bitwise OR operator. Table C.1 shows some common combinations.

Table C.1 Common Combinations of the Window Style Flags

Value	Description
WS_OVERLAPPEDWINDOW | WS_VISIBLE	The game is displayed in a standard Windows window that you can move, resize, and so forth. It is visible when the call to CreateWindow() completes. You do not have to call ShowWindow().
WS_POPUP | WS_VISIBLE	A common style for games that run in full-screen mode. The window has no border, is not resizable, and is initially visible.
WS_POPUP | WS_VISIBLE | WS_MAXIMIZE	A common style for games that run in full-screen mode. The window has no border, is not resizable, is initially visible, and is maximized.

The next two parameters assign the position of the upper-left corner of the window. If you want the window to run full screen, assign a 0 to both of these parameters. If you're running your game in windowed mode, use CW_USEDEFAULT. This enables Windows to decide where to position the window using its default values.

Lines 8–9 of Listing C.3 show that the CreateWindow() function requires your program to pass it the initial height and width of the game's window. If your game runs in windowed mode, you can set these two parameters to a variety of values. Most people have screens that are at least 800×600 pixels. Therefore, you can safely make your game's window 500×500 pixels. You can also let Windows decide how big to make the game's window by passing CW_USEDEFAULT for these parameters.

If, on the other hand, your game runs in full-screen mode, call the GetSystemMetrics() function twice. The first time, pass it the value SM_CXFULLSCREEN. The second call should pass the value SM_CYFULLSCREEN. These calls return the horizontal and vertical dimensions, respectively, of the screen. You can pass these two values to CreateWindow() to force your game's window to occupy the full screen area.

The parameter to CreateWindow() that is shown on line 10 of Listing C.3 is the handle of the parent window of the window your program is creating. When you're making a dialog box or a pop-up message window, pass the parent's handle in this parameter. For full-screen windows or the game's main window, pass the value returned by the Win32 function GetDesktopWindow().

If your window has a main menu, pass its resource handle as the value of the next parameter to CreateWindow(). If, like many games, your game doesn't have a main menu in its window, pass the value NULL, as shown on line 11 of Listing C.3.

If you're developing games under versions of Windows prior to Windows NT, you need to pass the handle to the current instance to CreateWindow(). The handle is in the structure your program passed to RegisterClassEx(). Line 12 demonstrates this. If your game is for Windows NT, Windows 2000, or Windows XP, set this parameter to NULL.

The last parameter to the CreateWindow() function is used as a way of passing information into the message handling procedure (discussed shortly) when it processes the WM_CREATE message. Most games just set this parameter to NULL.

Displaying the Window

If it's successful, the CreateWindow() function returns the handle of the window it created. Your game uses this handle to display the window, like this:

```
ShowWindow(hWnd,SW_SHOWDEFAULT);
UpdateWindow(hWnd);
```

By calling these two functions, your game tells Windows to display the window and send the window a message to update its contents.

Note that the second parameter to ShowWindow() in the previous example is SW_SHOWDEFAULT. This tells Windows to display the window in its default state. The default state can be minimized, normal, or maximized. Other common values that games use for this parameter are SW_SHOWNORMAL and SW_SHOWMAXIMIZED.

Processing Windows Messages

Windows reacts to events such as user input by sending messages to your program. Therefore, your program has to be able to handle those messages. It does this with a *message processing loop*, or message loop for short. Listing C.4 presents the message loop used in the physics modeling framework.

Listing C.4
The Physics Modeling Framework's Message Loop

```
1     MSG msg;
2     ZeroMemory(&msg,sizeof(msg));
3     while(msg.message!=WM_QUIT)
4     {
5         if(PeekMessage(&msg,NULL,OU,OU,PM_REMOVE))
6         {
7             TranslateMessage(&msg);
8             DispatchMessage(&msg);
9         }
10        else
11        {
```

```
12                  if (theApp.theGame->ProcessInput()==false)
13                  {
14                      pmlib_error fatalError(PMERROR_FATAL_INPUT_ERROR);
15                      throw fatalError;
16                  }
17
18                  if (theApp.theGame->UpdateFrame()==false)
19                  {
20                      pmlib_error fatalError(PMERROR_FATAL_FRAME_ERROR);
21                      throw fatalError;
22                  }
23                  theApp.Render();
24          }
25      }
```

Windows sends messages to your program in an MSG structure. This is a standard type defined when your program includes Windows.h. The identifier of each message is in the MSG structure's message member. The message loop should continue for as long as your program does not receive a WM_QUIT message.

Your program has a queue of messages that it pulls by calling the PeekMessage() function. Line 5 of Listing C.4 demonstrates this. If a message is on the queue, your program's message loop should call TranslateMessage() to make sure it is in a format that your program can process. Next, your program sends the message to a message handling procedure, which is presented in the next topic.

Handling Windows Messages

Standard Windows messages need to be handled by a message handling procedure. Programmers also call these special functions WindProcs or MessageProcs. Listing C.5 displays a minimal message handling procedure.

Listing C.5
A Minimal Message Handling Procedure

```
1       LRESULT WINAPI MsgProc(
2           HWND hWnd,
3           UINT msg,
4           WPARAM wParam,
5           LPARAM lParam)
6       {
7           switch(msg)
8           {
9               case WM_DESTROY:
10                  PostQuitMessage(0);
```

```
11              return 0;
12          break;
13      }
14      return DefWindowProc(hWnd,msg,wParam,lParam);
15  }
```

This message handling procedure responds only to the WM_DESTROY message. Programs get the WM_DESTROY message when the user has done something to indicate that it's time to quit. The message handling procedure passes all other message to Windows to be handled by calling DefWindowProc() on line 14.

Most games do not need a message handling procedure that is much more complex than this. That's because games process the majority of a user's input with DirectInput rather than the standard Windows messages.

INDEX

Symbols

Numbers

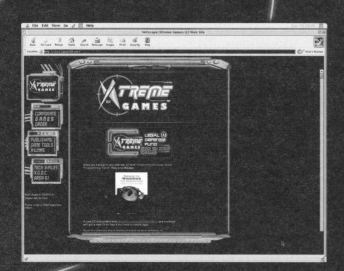

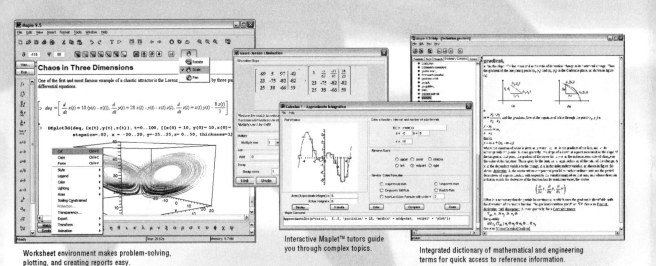

Gamedev.net

The most comprehensive game development resource

- The latest news in game development
- The most active forums and chatrooms anywhere, with insights and tips from experienced game developers
- Links to thousands of additional game development resources
- Thorough book and product reviews
- Over 1,000 game development articles!
  Game design
  Graphics
  DirectX
  OpenGL
  AI
  Art
  Music
  Physics
  Source Code
  Sound
  Assembly
  And More!

 **Gamedev.net**

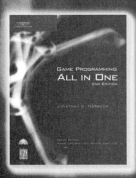

License Agreement/Notice of Limited Warranty